Cyberlaw: The Law of the Internet and Information Technology

First Edition

Cyberlaw: The Law of the Internet and Information Technology

Brian Craig

Globe University/Minnesota School of Business

Boston Columbus Indianapolis New York San Francisco Upper Saddle River
Amsterdam Cape Town Dubai London Madrid Milan Munich Paris Montreal Toronto
Delhi Mexico City São Paulo Sydney Hong Kong Seoul Singapore Taipei Tokyo

Editorial Director: Vernon Anthony
Executive Editor: Gary Bauer
Editorial Project Manager: Linda Cupp
Editorial Assistant: Tanika Henderson
Director of Marketing: David Gesell
Senior Marketing Manager: Stacey Martinez
Marketing Assistant: Les Roberts
Production Manager: Meghan DeMaio
Creative Director: Jayne Conte
Cover Designer: Bruce Kenselaar
Cover Art: Andreas Cuskos/iStockphoto
Full-Service Project Management & Composition: Anand Natarajan, Integra Software Services Pvt. Ltd.
Printer/Binder: LSC Communications
Cover Printer: LSC Communications
Text Font: 10/12, Palatino

Library of Congress Cataloging-in-Publication Data
Craig, Brian
Cyberlaw : the law of the internet and information technology/Brian Craig.—1st ed.
p. cm.
ISBN-13: 978-0-13-256087-0 (alk. paper)
ISBN-10: 0-13-256087-9 (alk. paper)
1. Internet—Law and legislation—United States. I. Title.
KF390.5.C6C73 2013
343.7309′944—dc23
2011035721

8 17

ISBN 10: 0-13-256087-9
ISBN 13: 978-0-13-256087-0

This book is dedicated to my beloved eternal companion, Valerie, and our sons, Everett and Eli.

BRIEF CONTENTS

CONTENTS

Appendixes

PREFACE

Cyberlaw: The Law of the Internet and Information Technology is written primarily for undergraduate students in paralegal, legal studies, criminal justice, business, and computer and information science programs to help them better understand the legal and policy issues associated with cyberlaw and the Internet. The text also includes compliance information that business managers, webmasters, and information technology professionals will find relevant and useful. The goal is to help readers better understand the legal and policy issues associated with the Internet. Cyberlaw is the field of law dealing with the Internet, encompassing cases, statutes, regulations, and disputes that affect people and businesses interacting through computers. With the ever-expanding role of the Internet and technology in people's lives, Internet law is at the heart of many legal and policy issues today, including jurisdictional questions, intellectual property rights, tort actions, privacy rights, e-commerce, cybercrimes, and online speech. Since the Internet is a fluid and dynamic medium, the need for a current text in the field written for a diverse audience exists.

TEXT FEATURES

Cases

Each chapter includes one or more leading case that relates to the chapter material. A background on each case is provided along with relevant portions of the court's actual opinion. Review and discussion questions are also available following each case.

Key Terms

As indicated above, each chapter contains a list of key legal terms that relate to the chapter material. These terms and their definitions can be found in the Glossary.

Internet Resources

Internet resources are provided with links to websites that include helpful information relating to the chapter material.

Review Questions

Each chapter contains questions for review based on the learning objectives to verify that readers comprehend the material in the chapter.

Discussion Questions

Each chapter contains discussion questions that can be used in classrooms discussions that may be used in both face-to-face and online classes.

Exercises

Each chapter includes exercises with simulated projects that a paralegal, manager, or other professional might perform. Many of these exercises include hypothetical situations based on actual cases.

End Notes

End notes are provided at the end of each chapter with references to primary and secondary sources. Readers may find these additional sources helpful.

Appendices contain the text of recent and relevant federal statutes governing the Internet. Appendix A contains the full text of the Digital Millennium Copyright Act (DMCA) Safe Harbor Provision, Appendix B contains the full text of the Trademark Dilution Revision Act of 2006, and Appendix C contains selections from the CAN-SPAM Act. Appendix D also contains the Federal Trade Commission Fair Information Practice Principles.

CHAPTER TOPICS AND ORGANIZATION

Chapter 1 provides a brief history on the development of the Internet and an introduction to the Internet. Chapter 1 then discusses jurisdictional issues in cyberspace, including the requirements for obtaining personal jurisdiction over defendants with online transactions. Chapters 2–4 focus on intellectual property issues. Chapter 2 provides an introduction to intellectual property in general and then focuses on copyright issues, including the fair use defense. Chapter 3 focuses on trademark issues and domain name disputes. Chapter 4 provides information on patents and trade secrets as they relate to the online environment. Chapter 5 explores concepts in e-commerce and online contracts. Chapter 6 provides information on tax-related issues relating to the Internet, including sales tax and income tax. Chapter 7 focuses on computer crimes with an emphasis on the key federal statutes. Chapter 8 focuses on torts relating to the Internet, especially the common law tort of invasion of privacy. Chapter 9 examines issues associated with online speech, including defamation actions and First Amendment issues. Chapter 10 provides information on privacy rights afforded under the U.S. Constitution, state constitutions, and key federal privacy statutes. Chapter 11 explores special topics in online privacy such as privacy issues associated with online social networking sites and workplace privacy policies.

RESOURCES FOR INSTRUCTORS

Supplemental teaching resources include:

Instructor's Manual

Includes content outlines for classroom discussion, teaching suggestions, and answers to end-of-chapter questions from the text.

Test Bank in MyTest Generator

The test bank is arranged by chapter, containing a variety of question formats such as true/false, multiple choice, completion, short answer, and essay.

PowerPoint Lecture Presentations

A PowerPoint presentation, organized by chapter, outlines and summarizes the major points covered, and corresponds with the organization of the text.

ABOUT THE AUTHOR

Brian Craig is the legal program chair with the Globe Education Network Online Division. The Globe Education Network includes Globe University, the Minnesota School of Business, and Broadview University (formerly Utah Career College). He predominantly teaches and develops online legal courses, including constitutional issues, intellectual property, legal research, and cyberlaw. Prior to joining the faculty of Globe University/Minnesota School of Business, Brian worked as an attorney at Thomson-Reuters from 2002 to 2008 where he dealt with a variety of intellectual property and privacy issues. He also previously worked as a legal editor for Wolters Kluwer, judicial law clerk for Idaho District Court Judge Carl Kerrick, and legislative aide for George Runner in the California State Legislature. Brian Craig earned his bachelor's degree in political science from Brigham Young University (UT) and Juris Doctor from the University of Idaho College of Law. Brian Craig previously taught legal writing as an adjunct instructor at the University of Minnesota Law School. In addition, he is an articles reviewer for the American Business Law Journal and a member of the Academy of Legal Studies in Business. His research interests focus on intellectual property, privacy, and constitutional issues with emerging technologies. He has written scholarly articles appearing in the *North Dakota Law Review*, *Real Estate Law Journal*, *Real Estate Review*, *Perspectives: Teaching Legal & Writing*, and *Raven: A Journal of Vexillology*. Brian lives in Providence, Utah, with his wife and two sons. Brian Craig can be reached via email at: bcraig@msbcollege.edu.

ACKNOWLEDGEMENTS

I wish to thank Gary Bauer, Linda Cupp, and Molly Schmidt at Pearson for their support and guidance. I also would like to recognize the contributions of my colleagues at Globe University, including Seth Tesdall, Kelly Schmidt, Kristen O'Connell, Meg Neubauer, Terri Lindfors, Cathy Kennedy, Kirstin Leighton-Lucas, Kim Maurer, and Charles Feige. I extend special thanks for those individuals involved with the original Advanced Research Projects Agency (ARPA) that established the groundwork for what became the ARPANET and later the Internet today. I also acknowledge of the role of James Madison as the principal architect of the Bill of Rights and other Founders in securing the blessings of liberty in the U.S. Constitution, which are needed now more than ever with the Internet. I also thank Professor James Macdonald from the University of Idaho and Professor Bill Daynes from Brigham Young University who inspired me to learn more about constitutional law. I am especially grateful for the support of my family, especially my loving wife, Valerie, and our boys, Everett and Eli, for their continued support and encouragement. I also appreciate the support and encouragement of other family members, including my parents, Keith Craig and Kathie Modugno, my brother, Kenneth Craig, Mary Morrison, Kent Morrison, and Ann Morrison. In addition, I wish to thank the following reviewers of the manuscript for their insights and comments.

Darlene Mallick
Anne Arundel Community College

Konnie Kustron
Eastern Michigan University

Todd H. Bailey
Miami University

Grant Alexander
Northeastern State University

Christine Russell
Eastern Carolina

Charlie Penrod
Northwestern State University

Susan Jaworowski
Kapiolani Community College

Russell R. Clark
George Washington University

Elizabeth Ivey McCowan
Pellissippi State Community College

Henry Sotelo
Truckee Meadows Community College

Jeffrey Pittman
Arkansas State University

Thomas Cary
City University of Seattle

Christy Powers
St. Petersburg College

Cyberlaw: The Law of the Internet and Information Technology

CHAPTER

1 Jurisdiction and Venue in Cyberspace

[T]he borders of cyberspace do not map onto the borders of real space, which poses a fundamental problem for courts whose jurisdiction is based on geography.

HON. MICHEL BASTARACHE[1]

LEARNING OBJECTIVES

After completing this chapter, you will be able to:

1. Explain the history of the Internet.
2. Describe the different types of jurisdiction, including subject matter jurisdiction, personal jurisdiction, and in rem jurisdiction.
3. Discuss how service of process plays a critical role in the commencement of litigation and how service of process can be effectuated via electronic means.
4. Explain what activities are considered minimum contacts for a website owner and the sliding scale used by courts for passive and active websites.
5. Describe the purpose of a choice-of-law provision and a forum selection clause in an online contract.

CHAPTER OVERVIEW

This chapter provides an introduction to cyberlaw and jurisdictional matters in cyberspace. In addition, this chapter addresses what contacts are sufficient to satisfy the Due Process Clause for personal jurisdiction, particularly in the context of Internet transactions and maintaining a website. Jurisdiction in criminal cases and cybercrimes is covered in Chapter 7.

HISTORY AND DEVELOPMENT OF THE INTERNET

The history of the Internet can be traced back to a military research network established in 1968 called the Arpanet, which was sponsored by the Advanced Research Projects Agency (ARPA) of the U.S. Department of Defense.[2] The original purpose of ARPA was to connect government computers across the country to exchange information during wartime without interruption.[3] In 1962, J.C.R. Licklider wrote about his Intergalactic Network concept, where everyone on the globe is interconnected and can access programs and data at any site from anywhere. Licklider became the first head of the computer research program at ARPA, which he called the Information Processing Techniques Office (IPTO).[4]

The Internet was later used by the private sector for exchanging research between universities. Now the Internet is a complex series of interconnected computer networks that communicate via telephone lines, fiber optics, copper wires, satellite transmissions, and other dedicated data connections. The Internet has grown exponentially to the ubiquitous and ever-present mass medium it is today. Over one billion people worldwide and 79 percent of adults in the United States now use the Internet.[5]

INTRODUCTION TO CYBERLAW

Cyberlaw
The field of law dealing with the Internet, encompassing cases, statutes, regulations, and disputes that affect people and businesses interacting through computers. Cyberlaw addresses issues of online speech and business that arise because of the nature of the medium, including intellectual property rights, free speech, privacy, e-commerce, and safety, as well as questions of jurisdiction.

Black's Law Dictionary defines "**cyberlaw**" as "the field of law dealing with the Internet, encompassing cases, statutes, regulations, and disputes that affect people and businesses interacting through computers."[6] With the ever-expanding role of the Internet and technology in people's lives, cyberlaw is at the heart of many legal and policy issues today, including jurisdictional questions, intellectual property rights, tort actions, privacy rights, e-commerce, cybercrimes, and online speech. Since the Internet is a fluid and dynamic medium, cyberlaw is a field of law that changes rapidly and it is important to stay current with recent trends.

Who controls the Internet? No single government or organization controls the Internet. The global nature of the Internet creates insurmountable challenges in having a general governmental regulatory body regulate it. This difficulty comes in part from the nature of the Internet itself. Unlike a television or radio broadcasts localized in a particular jurisdiction, the Internet has a global reach. Courts, government agencies, and other entities all have some function in governing the Internet. This book will focus on laws within the United States, but a number of international issues exist with governing the Internet. Without a central body in place to regulate a borderless medium like the Internet, the result is a complex system of laws governing a variety of different legal issues such as jurisdictional questions, intellectual property law, contract law, tort law, and numerous federal and state statutes.

Because so many laws govern the Internet, compliance can be a challenge for many companies. Heather Killen, former Yahoo! senior vice president of international operations, stated this challenge best when she said "It is very difficult to do business if you have to wake up every day and say 'Okay, whose laws do I follow?' . . . We have many countries and many laws and just one Internet."[7]

JURISDICTION IN CYBERSPACE

Jurisdiction
A court's power to decide a case or issue a decree.

One of the first questions in any case or controversy that involves the Internet is whether or not a particular court has **jurisdiction** to determine a certain case. Jurisdiction is a court's power to decide a particular case. There are several different types of jurisdiction, including subject matter jurisdiction, in rem jurisdiction, and personal jurisdiction. Many of the contested cases involving e-commerce and online transactions involve questions of personal jurisdiction.

Black's Law Dictionary defines **subject matter jurisdiction** as "jurisdiction over the nature of the case and the type of relief sought; the extent to which a court can rule on the conduct of persons or the status of things." In essence, subject matter jurisdiction is the authority of a particular court to hear a certain type of case. For example, the U.S. courts or federal courts have exclusive subject matter jurisdiction over patent infringement cases. If a plaintiff files a patent infringement case in state court, the case will likely be transferred to federal court or dismissed. Similarly, U.S. Bankruptcy Courts have exclusive jurisdiction over bankruptcy petitions. State courts have exclusive subject matter jurisdiction over other matters such as family law.

In rem jurisdiction involves jurisdiction over a particular thing or property. In rem jurisdiction claims are most often found in probate and land title cases.

Personal jurisdiction is a court's power to bring a person into its adjudicative process; jurisdiction over a defendant's personal rights, rather than merely over property interests. Personal jurisdiction is also called in personam jurisdiction, jurisdiction in personam, jurisdiction of the person, or jurisdiction over the person.

The rise of the Internet has led courts to examine personal jurisdiction doctrines. Courts faced with the application of new technologies, including the Internet, to personal jurisdiction issues have used traditional analysis of personal jurisdiction to these new communication tools.

In *International Shoe Co. v. Washington*, 326 U.S. 310 (1945), the U.S. Supreme Court established "minimum contacts" as the basic jurisdictional test in the United States for establishing personal jurisdiction. In *International Shoe*, the Supreme Court held that a state could exercise personal jurisdiction over a defendant if the defendant had minimum contacts with the state and it was fair for the defendant to defend the lawsuit there. In *Boschetto v. Hansing*, 539 F.3d 1011 (9th Cir. 2008) (Case 1.1), the U.S. Court

Subject Matter Jurisdiction
Jurisdiction over the nature of the case and the type of relief sought; the extent to which a court can rule on the conduct of persons or the status of things.

In Rem Jurisdiction
A court's power to adjudicate the rights to a given piece of property, including the power to seize and hold it.

Personal Jurisdiction
A court's power to bring a person into its adjudicative process; jurisdiction over a defendant's personal rights, rather than merely over property interests. Also called "in personam jurisdiction" or "jurisdiction over the person."

CASE 1.1

The Case of the Lemon 1964 Ford Galaxie Sold on eBay

Boschetto v. Hansing, ***539 F.3d 1011 (9th Cir. 2008)***

This appeal presents a question that remains surprisingly unanswered by the circuit courts: Does the sale of an item via the eBay Internet auction site provide sufficient "minimum contacts" to support personal jurisdiction over a nonresident defendant in the buyer's forum state? Plaintiff-Appellant Paul Boschetto ("Boschetto") was the winning bidder for a 1964 Ford Galaxie sold on eBay by the Defendant-Appellee, Jeffrey Hansing ("Hansing") for $34,106. Boschetto arranged for the car to be shipped from Wisconsin to California, but upon arrival it failed to meet his expectations or the advertised description. Boschetto sued in federal court; his complaint was dismissed for lack of personal jurisdiction. We now affirm.

All Defendants moved to dismiss based on lack of personal jurisdiction. On July 13, 2006, the district court granted the motion. The district court reasoned that the lone jurisdictionally relevant contact with California, an eBay sale consummated with a California purchaser, was insufficient to establish jurisdiction over any of the Defendants. Although Hansing used eBay to market the automobile, the district court observed that "eBay acted not as a 'distribution center' but rather as a virtual forum for the exchange of goods," and that in a standard eBay transaction—like the one at issue in this appeal—the item goes to whomever is the highest bidder, and so "the eBay seller does not purposefully avail himself of the privilege of doing business in a forum state absent some additional conduct directed at the forum state."

(Continued)

(Continued)

II. Personal Jurisdiction

When no federal statute governs personal jurisdiction, the district court applies the law of the forum state. California's long-arm statute is co-extensive with federal standards, so a federal court may exercise personal jurisdiction if doing so comports with federal constitutional due process. "For a court to exercise personal jurisdiction over a nonresident defendant, that defendant must have at least 'minimum contacts' with the relevant forum such that the exercise of jurisdiction 'does not offend traditional notions of fair play and substantial justice.'" *Schwarzenegger*, 374 F.3d at 801 (quoting *International Shoe Co. v. Washington*, 326 U.S. 310, 316, 66 S.Ct. 154, 90 L.Ed. 95 (1945)). There are two forms of personal jurisdiction that a forum state may exercise over a nonresident defendant-general jurisdiction and specific jurisdiction. We deal here only with the latter.

A. The district court correctly dismissed Boschetto's complaint for lack of personal jurisdiction.

We apply a three-part test to determine whether the exercise of specific jurisdiction over a nonresident defendant is appropriate:

1. The non-resident defendant must purposefully direct his activities or consummate some transaction with the forum or resident thereof; or perform some act by which he purposefully avails himself of the privilege of conducting activities in the forum, thereby invoking the benefits and protections of its laws;
2. the claim must be one which arises out of or relates to the defendant's forum-related activities; and
3. the exercise of jurisdiction must comport with fair play and substantial justice, i.e. it must be reasonable.

For part one of this three-part test, we have typically analyzed cases that sound primarily in contract-as Boschetto's case does-under a "purposeful availment" standard. To have purposefully availed itself of the privilege of doing business in the forum, a defendant must have "performed some type of affirmative conduct which allows or promotes the transaction of business within the forum state." *Sher*, 911 F.2d at 1362 (internal quotation marks and citation omitted).

Here, Boschetto fails at step one of the test for specific jurisdiction, as the lone transaction for the sale of one item does not establish that the Defendants purposefully availed themselves of the privilege of doing business in California. The arrangement between Boschetto and Hansing which is, at bottom, a contract for the sale of a good, is insufficient to have created a substantial connection with California. Hansing did not create any ongoing obligations with Boschetto in California; once the car was sold the parties were to go their separate ways.

In *Cybersell, Inc. v. Cybersell, Inc.*, 130 F.3d 414, 419 (9th Cir.1997), we discussed with approval a sliding scale analysis that looks to how interactive an Internet website is for purposes of determining its jurisdictional effect. ("In sum, the common thread, well stated by the district court in *Zippo*, is that the 'likelihood that personal jurisdiction can be constitutionally exercised is directly proportionate to the nature and quality of the commercial activity that an entity conducts over the Internet.'") (quoting *Zippo Mfg. Co. v. Zippo Dot Com,* 952 F.Supp. 1119, 1124 (W.D.Pa.1997)). The plaintiff in Cybersell relied on the fact that the defendant operated a website, accessible in the forum state, that contained allegedly infringing trademarks. 130 F.3d at 416. The defendant's website advertised its services but did not allow parties to transact business via the site. Id. at 419. Noting the lack of interactivity on the defendant's website, the court concluded that the defendant had "done no act and [ ] consummated no transaction, nor has it performed any act by which it purposefully availed itself of the privilege of conducting activities, in Arizona, thereby invoking the benefits and protections of Arizona law." Id.

This was a one-time contract for the sale of a good that involved the forum state only because that is where the purchaser happened to reside, but otherwise created no "substantial connection" or ongoing obligations there. Where eBay is used as a means for establishing regular business with a remote forum such that a finding of personal jurisdiction comports with "traditional notions of fair play and substantial justice," International Shoe Co., 326 U.S. at 316, 66 S.Ct. 154, then a defendant's use of eBay may be properly taken into account for purposes of establishing personal jurisdiction. But on the facts of this case—a one-time transaction—the use of eBay as the conduit for that transaction does not have any dispositive effect on jurisdiction.

Case Questions

1. In opposition to a defendant's motion to dismiss for lack of personal jurisdiction, which party bears the burden of establishing that jurisdiction is proper?
2. According to the holding of the U.S. Supreme Court in *International Shoe Co. v. Washington* cited in *Boschetto v. Hansing*, what level of contacts are needed to exercise personal jurisdiction over a nonresident defendant?
3. What is the three-part test used by the U.S. Court of Appeals for the Ninth Circuit (a federal appeals court) in *Boschetto v. Hansing* to determine whether the exercise of specific jurisdiction over a nonresident defendant is appropriate?
4. Do you agree with the court's holding that the seller was not subject to specific personal jurisdiction? Why or why not?

of Appeals for the Ninth Circuit, a federal appeals court, applied the minimum contacts test set forth in *International Shoe* and dismissed a California lawsuit brought by a California-based plaintiff who purchased an automobile on eBay from a private Wisconsin-based seller because the Wisconsin seller defendant did not have sufficient minimum contacts with the State of California based on the eBay sale to a California purchaser.

LONG-ARM STATUTES AND DUE PROCESS

Each state has a **long-arm statute** that allows a state court to exercise jurisdiction over a particular defendant. For example, the Minnesota long-arm statute permits Minnesota courts to assert personal jurisdiction over defendants to the extent permitted by the federal constitution.[8] To determine whether a court may exercise jurisdiction over a nonresident defendant, a court determines whether jurisdiction in the forum state satisfies the federal requirements of due process. (See Figure 1.1.)

Long-arm Statute
Statute that provides for jurisdiction over a nonresident defendant who has had some contact with the jurisdiction in which the petition is filed.

Finding the Long-Arm Statute in a Particular State

A paralegal, legal assistant, or other professional may need to locate the long-arm statute in a particular state. Usually the text of the long-arm statute will not expressly include the phrase "long-arm" but rather use the language similar to the Minnesota statute in Figure 1.1 that states "exercise personal jurisdiction over any foreign corporation or any nonresident individual." To find the long-arm statute in a particular state, one option is to run a search in state cases for "long-arm" and find the relevant statute cited in the judicial opinion. Another option is to search for the phrase "jurisdiction over nonresident" in either a natural language search or a terms and connectors search. On Westlaw, searching with the West Key Number 106k12(2), which relates to long-arm jurisdiction, can be helpful. Westlaw (whose main competitor is Lexis-Nexis) is a popular fee-based online legal research service used by many judges, lawyers, and paralegals. West's Key Number System is a comprehensive and widely used indexing system for caselaw materials to assist in legal research. (See Figure 1.2.)

Constitutional Protections of Due Process

The due process clauses found in the Fifth and Fourteenth Amendments to the U.S. Constitution provide that a court is limited in exercising its powers over a nonresident defendant. The Due Process Clause of the Fifth Amendment states that "no person shall be deprived of life, liberty, or property without the due process

Subdivision 1. Personal jurisdiction. As to a cause of action arising from any acts enumerated in this subdivision, a court of this state with jurisdiction of the subject matter may exercise personal jurisdiction over any foreign corporation or any nonresident individual, or the individual's personal representative, in the same manner as if it were a domestic corporation or the individual were a resident of this state. This section applies if, in person or through an agent, the foreign corporation or nonresident individual:

(1) owns, uses, or possesses any real or personal property situated in this state; or
(2) transacts any business within the state; or
(3) commits any act in Minnesota causing injury or property damage; or
(4) commits any act outside Minnesota causing injury or property damage in Minnesota, subject to the following exceptions when no jurisdiction shall be found:
    (i) Minnesota has no substantial interest in providing a forum; or
    (ii) the burden placed on the defendant by being brought under the state's jurisdiction would violate fairness and substantial justice.

Subd. 2. Service of process. The service of process on any person who is subject to the jurisdiction of the courts of this state, as provided in this section, may be made by personally serving the summons upon the defendant outside this state with the same effect as though the summons had been personally served within this state.

Subd. 3. Acts enumerated. Only causes of action arising from acts enumerated in subdivision 1 may be asserted against a defendant in an action in which jurisdiction over the defendant is based upon this section.

Subd. 4. No limit right to serve process. Nothing contained in this section shall limit or affect the right to serve any process in any other manner now or hereafter provided by law or the Minnesota Rules of Civil Procedure.

Subd. 5. Definition. "Nonresident individual," as used in this section, means any individual, or the individual's personal representative, who is not domiciled or residing in the state when suit is commenced.

FIGURE 1.1 Minnesota's Long-Arm Statute, M.S.A. § 543.19

of law."[9] The Fourteenth Amendment to the U.S. Constitution adopted after the U.S. Civil War, which extended to the principle of due process to state and local governments, states that "no state shall . . . deprive any person of life, liberty, or property without the due process of law."[10]

In *International Shoe Co. v. Washington*, 326 U.S. 310 (1945), the U.S. Supreme Court held that a court's exercise of personal jurisdiction must be consistent with the Due Process Clause, which imposes a general fairness test requiring that certain minimum contacts exist between the nonresident defendant and the forum such that maintenance of the suit does not offend traditional notions of fair play and substantial justice.

The Fourteenth Amendment's Due Process Clause allows a court to exercise personal jurisdiction over any defendant that has sufficient "minimum contacts" with the forum so that the suit does not offend traditional notions of fair play and substantial justice.

If browsing the West Key Number Digest, find the West Key Number 106k12(2), which relates to long-arm jurisdiction, under the following topic and key numbers:

106 Courts
106I Nature, Extent, and Exercise of Jurisdiction in General
106k10 Jurisdiction of the Person
106k12 Domicile or Residence of Party
106k12(2) Actions by or Against Nonresidents; "Long-Arm" Jurisdiction in General

FIGURE 1.2 West's Key Number System for Finding the Long-Arm Statute

Federal Rule of Civil Procedure 4(e)
Serving an Individual Within a Judicial District of the United States.
Unless federal law provides otherwise, an individual—other than a minor, an incompetent person, or a person whose waiver has been filed—may be served in a judicial district of the United States by:

(1) following state law for serving a summons in an action brought in courts of general jurisdiction in the state where the district court is located or where service is made; or
(2) doing any of the following:
   (A) delivering a copy of the summons and of the complaint to the individual personally;
   (B) leaving a copy of each at the individual's dwelling or usual place of abode with someone of suitable age and discretion who resides there; or
   (C) delivering a copy of each to an agent authorized by appointment or by law to receive service of process.

FIGURE 1.3 Service of Process Under the Federal Rules of Civil Procedure

A related term involving personal jurisdiction is **service of process**. Service of process is defined as the formal delivery of a writ, summons, or other legal process. (See Figure 1.3.) The most common method for service of process is through personal service. Rule 4 of the Federal Rules of Civil Procedure governs service of process in the federal courts. Other forms of service of process might include delivery via certified mail or publication in a newspaper.[11]

Service of Process
The formal delivery of a writ, summons, or other legal process. Also called "service."

Although hand-delivered service of process is the preferred method for service of process, sometimes personal service is not possible. The widespread use of the Internet, including online social networking sites like Facebook, raises questions whether electronic publication for service of process can be accomplished. In 2008, an Australian judge recognized services of process via Facebook (see Case 1.2). Shortly thereafter, in 2009, New Zealand followed suit, citing the Australian case and allowing service of process via Facebook in an intra-familial business dispute.[12] A number of jurisdictions outside the United States now allow parties to be served via social networking sites like Facebook. The question remains, however, whether a court in the United States would allow services of processional through a social network site like Facebook or Twitter.

When a nonresident defendant has been properly served with notice, the court then asks whether the exercise of personal jurisdiction over defendant violates due process. There are two recognized bases for exercising personal jurisdiction over nonresident defendants: (1) "general jurisdiction," which arises when the defendant's activities in the forum are sufficiently "substantial" or "continuous and systematic" to justify the exercise of jurisdiction over it in all matters; and (2) "specific jurisdiction," which arises when a defendant's specific contacts with the forum give rise to the claim in question.

Courts often use a sliding scale to determine whether a website has minimum contacts with a forum state to recognize personal jurisdiction. Courts have held that passive or informational websites that are used only for purposes, such as advertising, are not sufficient to establish minimum contacts to support exercise of personal jurisdiction over a nonresident defendant.[13] Courts are more likely to recognize personal jurisdiction when the defendant maintains an interactive website. Interactive websites have repeated contacts and transmissions, and may also allow participants to enter into contracts. In *Grimaldi v. Guinn*, 72 A.D.3d 37, 895 N.Y.S.2d 156 (2d Dep't 2010), a New York state court held that when analyzing whether a defendant's business transactions are sufficient to justify exercise of long-arm jurisdiction, it is the quality of the defendants' contacts that is the primary consideration. The court in *Grimaldi* held that a nonresident defendant's passive website, when combined with other business

CASE 1.2

Service of Process Via Facebook

On December 12, 2008, Master David Harper of the Supreme Court of the Australian Capital Territory authorized service of a default judgment via the social networking site Facebook. The defendant couple had defaulted on a $150,000 home refinancing loan. After the couple failed to appear in court, lawyers for the lending company applied to the court for a judgment for the loan amount and for possession of the defendants' home. The court granted default judgment on October 31, 2008. Australian law required that the lending company locate the defendants and serve the defendants with notice of the judgment. Lawyers for the plaintiff lending company published notice in the Canberra Times and hired private investigators to serve the judgment. After a number of failed attempts to serve the couple with notice, the lawyers for the lending company applied to the Supreme Court of the Australian Capital Territory to serve notice of the judgment via Facebook. The Facebook profiles of the defendants showed the defendants' names, dates of birth, and e-mail addresses. The court held that the lawyers showed that the Facebook profiles were those of the defendants.

Case Questions

1. Do you think a U.S. court would accept service of process via Facebook?
2. Would a U.S. court accept service of process via Twitter if the recipient responded to the "Tweet" or message?
3. Is a person more likely to be notified of a legal action via a Facebook account than a legal notice in a newspaper? Does this make a difference for substituted service?

Andriana L. Shultz, *Superpoked and Served: Service of Process via Social Networking Sites,* 43 U. Rich. L. Rev. 1497, note 1 (2009), citing Noel Towell, *Lawyers to Serve Notices on Facebook,* SYDNEY MORNING HERALD, Dec. 16, 2008, *available at* http://www.smh.com.au/articles/2008/12/16/1229189579001.html.

activity, provided a reasonable basis for exercising personal jurisdiction over the defendant under New York's long-arm statute. Courts go back to the minimum contacts test set forth in *International Shoe* and often decide matters on a case-by-case basis.

CHOICE-OF-LAW PROVISION

Choice-of-Law Provision
A contractual provision by which the parties designate the jurisdiction whose law will govern any disputes that may arise between the parties. Also called choice-of-law clause.

After jurisdiction has been established, the next question in a case or controversy is which law governs. Many online contracts contain a choice-of-law provision. A **choice-of-law provision** is a contractual provision by which the parties designate the jurisdiction whose law will govern any disputes that may arise between the parties. A choice-of-law clause or provision in a contract names a particular state and provides that the substantial laws of that jurisdiction will be used to determine the validity and construction (or interpretation) of the contract.

Contracts that contain choice-of-law clauses ordinarily are honored, so long as the result is not contrary to public policy and as long as there is a reasonable relationship between the parties or the transaction to the state whose law is chosen. The parties to a contract may select the law by which they intend to be bound if the jurisdiction is the domicile of at least one of the contracting parties and is that in which the contract is intended to be performed. For example, the online retailer giant Amazon.com, whose corporate headquarters are located in Seattle, Washington, has a choice-of-law provision in its conditions of use agreement that all disputes will be governed according to the laws o the state of Washington. The Amazon.com choice-of-law provision states: "APPLICABLE LAW: By visiting Amazon.com, you agree that the laws of the state of Washington, without regard to principles of conflict of laws, will govern these Conditions of Use and any dispute of any sort that might arise between you and Amazon."

Sometimes courts will not enforce a choice-of-law provision in a contract because the contract violates public policy. In *Fiser v. Dell Computer Corporation*, 144 N.M. 464, 188 P.3d 1215 (N.M. 2008), the New Mexico Supreme Court examined as a threshold question whether New Mexico state law or Texas state law would govern a consumer class action lawsuit against Dell, a computer manufacturer, where the complaint alleged that the website misrepresented the amount of memory in computers purchased online. Even though the contract contained a choice-of-law clause directing that Texas law be applied, the New Mexico Supreme Court held that the choice-of-law clause was unenforceable and New Mexico courts will not give effect to another state's laws where those laws would "violate some fundamental principle of justice."

VENUE

Along with a choice-of-law provision, many online contracts contain a forum selection clause. A **forum selection clause** is a contractual provision in which the parties establish the place (such as the country, state, or type of court) for specified litigation between them.[14] A forum selection clause is also called a choice-of-exclusive-forum clause. The purpose of a forum selection clause is to provide a specific **venue** if a conflict arises. *Venue* refers to the specific court where the case will be decided or the county or other territory over which a trial court has jurisdiction. For example, a breach of contract action based on a violation of a terms of use agreement could be decided in the venue of Los Angeles County, California, rather than another county in California. Meanwhile, *jurisdiction* refers to the power of a particular court to hear a particular case.

Forum Selection Clause
A contractual provision in which the parties establish the place (such as the country, state, or type of court) for specified litigation between them. Also called "choice-of-exclusive-forum clause."

Venue
The proper or a possible place for a lawsuit to proceed, usually because the place has some connection either with the events that gave rise to the lawsuit or with the plaintiff or defendant. The county or other territory over which a trial court has jurisdiction.

The test of whether the courts will enforce a forum selection provision is reasonableness under all the circumstances. Courts also scrutinize forum selection clauses for fundamental fairness. A forum selection clause is unenforceable for a plaintiff who did not have sufficient notice of the forum selection clause prior to entering the contract.

In *Monsanto Co. v. McFarling*, 302 F.3d 1291 (Fed. Cir. 2002), the U.S. Court of Appeals for the Federal Circuit held that under either Missouri or Mississippi law, a forum selection clause in a technology agreement entered by a farmer and by the owner of patents on herbicide-resistant plants, seeds, and related inventions was valid and enforceable, even though the farmer claimed that he failed to read clause, which was on reverse side of signature page, and that the selected forum was unfair. The farmer voluntarily failed to read what he signed, and the choice of forum in which patent owner's principal place of business was located was reasonable.

The eBay User Agreement contains a forum selection clause that all disputes will brought in Santa Clara County, California, has been the subject of litigation. See *Tricome v. Ebay, Inc.*, 2009 WL 3365873 (E.D. Pa. Oct. 19, 2009); *Universal Grading Service v. eBay, Inc.*, 2009 WL 2029796 (E.D.N.Y. Jun. 10, 2009). The eBay User Agreement states in part states in part, "You agree that any claim or dispute you may have against eBay must be resolved exclusively by a state or federal court located in

Santa Clara County, California. . . . You agree to submit to the personal jurisdiction of the courts located within Santa Clara County, California for the purpose of litigating all such claims or disputes." In both *Tricome v. Ebay, Inc.* and *Universal Grading Service v. eBay, Inc.* federal courts enforced the forum selection clause found in the eBay User Agreement.

In *CoStar Realty Information, Inc. v. Field*, 612 F. Supp. 2d 660 (D. Md. 2009) (Case 1.3), the court held that a forum selection clause in the online terms of use agreement was enforceable. Jurisdiction was proper over defendants who used the plaintiff's

CASE 1.3

The Case of Consenting to Jurisdiction through an Online Agreement

CoStar Realty Information, Inc. v. Field, *612 F. Supp. 2d 660 (D. Md. 2009)*

Alliance entered into two 11-user written license agreements with CoStar. The first one in June 2002 and the other in November 2004. The contract provided that Alliance would not provide third parties access to or use of CoStar's database, sub-license the use of the database, and, also, specifically provided that Alliance could not share its user ID or passcode without the express written consent of CoStar. CoStar alleges that Alliance shared its user ID and passcode with Lawson and Gressett in violation of their contract; and as a result Lawson and Gressett continuously used CoStar's services, receiving Alliance's contractual benefit with CoStar, without CoStar's express authorization.

II. Motions to Dismiss

A. Personal Jurisdiction The Defendants first challenge this Court's authority to assert personal jurisdiction on the basis that they lack sufficient connections with Maryland to satisfy the State's long-arm statute, or Due Process. CoStar asserts that jurisdiction is proper over the Defendants based on both the forum selection clause located within the Terms of Use on its website and under the Maryland long-arm statute, consistent with Due Process. Specifically, CoStar argues that Lawson and Gressett have consented to jurisdiction in Maryland by accepting the Terms of Use on its website, and due to their continuous tortious conduct in Maryland for their private business purposes. Lawson and Gressett argue that presence and consent is lacking because neither of the Defendants have ever been to Maryland or done any business in Maryland, their actions in Maryland lack sufficient effects in Maryland, and the complaint fails to allege sufficient facts to support formation of a contract in Maryland.

2. Forum Selection Clause Users of CoStar's website who do not enter into a written licensing agreement, but pay to use CoStar's database on an à la carte basis, agree to a Terms of Use provision which has a forum selection clause that provides, in relevant part:

> You irrevocably consent to the jurisdiction of the federal and state courts located in the State of Maryland, and to the jurisdiction of the federal and state courts located in any State where you are located, for any action brought against you in connection with these Terms of Use or use of the Product.

CoStar argues that the forum selection clauses are binding, and by accepting the Terms of Use, within the forum selection clause, Lawson and Gressett consented to personal jurisdiction in Maryland. In addition CoStar posits, and the Court agrees, that Lawson and Gressett availed themselves of the contractual benefits provided by CoStar and Alliance and should be subject to the same jurisdictional requirements as Alliance. Lawson and Gressett dispute the validity of the forum selection clause and argue that they in no way formed a contract with CoStar or consented to personal jurisdiction in this Court. CoStar maintains that in order to access its database an authorized user must have a valid user ID and passcode. CoStar maintains, and the Defendants do not dispute, that Alliance provided its user name and passcode to Lawson and Gressett who then illegally accessed CoStar's database, in violation of Alliance's written contractual agreement with CoStar. CoStar alleges that Lawson and Gressett accessed its website on several occasions over a four year period and agreed to the Terms of Use.

Courts have aptly addressed the issue whether parties are bound by user agreements, containing forum selection clauses, in the internet context. *Burcham v. Expedia, Inc.* [2009 WL 586513 (E.D. Mo. Mar. 6, 2009)] involved a lawsuit brought by an attorney, Burcham, against Expedia, where Burcham used Expedia's website service to book a hotel reservation. The website contained a user agreement with a forum selection clause. The court, in determining that Burcham was bound to bring a lawsuit in a different jurisdiction pursuant to the forum selection clause located within the online agreement, noted, "the legal effect of online agreements is an emerging area of the law that has been addressed by a number of courts. Courts presented with the issue apply traditional principles of contract law and focus on whether the plaintiff had reasonable notice of and manifested assent to the online agreement."

In this case, the forum selection clause is mandatory and valid and Defendants fail to show its unreasonableness. The forum selection clause states that a user "irrevocably consents" to the jurisdiction of a federal or state court located in Maryland. Defendants fail to make any argument referencing the validity of the forum selection clause other than to state that there is no contract based on the Terms of Use which contains the forum selection clause. As noted above, several courts have found that an online user agreement, in this case referred to as the Terms of Use, may constitute a valid contract, and this Court agrees.

Case Questions

1. Should failure to read an enforceable online agreement excuse compliance with the terms of an online contract?
2. Although the court enforced the forum selection clause in *CoStar Realty Information, Inc. v. Field*, under what circumstances might a court find a forum selection clause unenforceable and unreasonable?

online databases without authorization, because the defendants likely would have seen the terms of service, and the choice of forum clause contained in the terms of service agreement. There was no showing of unreasonableness or that the formation of the contract was made by fraud or duress so the court enforced the forum selection clause.

The choice-of-law provision determines which state law governs the contract. The forum selection clause determines the particular place where the dispute will be decided. Sometimes these two clauses will appear together and sometimes the clauses will be in separate sections of the contract. The choice-of-law provision might have the heading "Applicable Law" or "Controlling Law" in the contract. See Chapter 5 for more discussion of online contracts.

FULL FAITH AND CREDIT CLAUSE

Once a court obtains jurisdiction over a particular defendant, a judgment may be entered. Sometimes a plaintiff will try to enforce a judgment that was originally entered in a different state. Article IV of the U.S. Constitution contains the **Full Faith and Credit Clause**. The Full Faith and Credit Clause states that "Full faith and credit shall be given in each state to the public acts, records, and judicial proceedings of every other state. And the Congress may by general laws prescribe the manner in which such acts, records, and proceedings shall be proved, and the effect thereof."[15]

Full Faith and Credit Clause Clause in Article VI § 1 of the U.S. Constitution, which requires states to give effect to the acts, public records, and judicial decisions of other states.

The Full Faith and Credit Clause requires that each state give effect to the official acts of another state. A judgment entered in one state must be respected in another, provided that the first state had jurisdiction over the parties and the subject matter.

For example, a Wisconsin state court is required to recognize a judgment in an Illinois state court. The Full Faith and Credit Clause mandates each state to enforce the rights and duties validly created under the laws of other states. However, the Full Faith and Credit Clause requires that states only give the same force to judgments as would be given by the courts of the state in which the judgment was rendered.

For a court to recognize a violation of the Full Faith and Credit Clause, it is not enough that a state court misconstrue the law of another state. Instead, the misconstruction must contradict the law of the other state that is clearly established and that has been brought to the court's attention. *Sun Oil Co. v. Wortman*, 486 U.S. 717, 108 S. Ct. 2117, 100 L. Ed. 2d 743 (1988).

Courts apply the general rules of construction under the Full Faith and Credit Clause in cases that involve technology and software. In *Patriot Commercial Leasing Co. v. Jerry Enis Motors, Inc.*, 928 So. 2d 856 (Miss. 2006), a judgment creditor sought to enforce a foreign judgment from Pennsylvania in Mississippi state court against the seller of an automobile dealership involving a software lease executed by dealership buyer. The Mississippi Supreme Court held that the lack of jurisdiction over the parties is the primary limitation that tempers application of full faith and credit of foreign judgments. The Mississippi Supreme Court cited the U.S. Supreme Court case *Fauntleroy v. Lum*, 210 U.S. 230, 237 (1908), which held that lack of jurisdiction over the person or the subject matter might be shown to deny full faith and credit. The Full Faith and Credit Clause applies only where the judgment of a foreign state is founded upon adequate jurisdiction of the parties and subject matter. Since the service of process on seller was defective, under Pennsylvania law, the Mississippi court could not enforce the judgment. In *Fine v. Am. Online, Inc.*, 139 Ohio App. 3d 133, 743 N.E.2d 416 (Ohio Ct. App. 2000), customers brought a class action against AOL, an Internet service provider (ISP), to recover for poor service in the wake of unlimited access for a flat fee. The Ohio Court of Appeals held that settlement of a class action in another state did not violate the due process rights of absent class members and, therefore, was entitled to full faith and credit.

In online transactions and e-commerce, courts will generally enforce a judgment entered in another state provided the court where the judgment was originally entered had proper jurisdiction.

Summary

The history of the Internet can be traced back to a military research network established by the Advanced Research Projects Agency (ARPA) of the U.S. Department of Defense to connect government computers across the country to exchange information during wartime without interruption. Cyberlaw is the field of law dealing with the Internet, encompassing cases, statutes, regulations, and disputes that affect people and businesses interacting through computers. One of the first issues in any case involving the Internet is jurisdiction. *Jurisdiction* is defined as the power of a court to hear a particular case. Jurisdiction includes subject matter jurisdiction, in rem jurisdiction, and personal jurisdiction. To exercise personal jurisdiction over nonresident defendants, courts utilize the state long-arm statute. If the defendant has sufficient minimum contacts in the forum state, a court will likely find that there is no violation of the Due Process Clause for the court to exercise jurisdiction. Courts apply a sliding scale for website owners and operators, and generally hold that a passive website for advertising along does meet the requirements for minimum contacts. Online contracts will often contain a choice-of-law provision and a forum selection clause. A choice-of-law provision is a contractual provision by which the parties designate the jurisdiction whose law will govern any disputes that may arise between the parties. A forum selection clause is a contractual provision in which the parties establish the place (such as the country, state, or type of court) for specified litigation between them. The choice-of-law provision determines which state law governs the contract. The forum selection clause determines the particular place where the dispute will be decided. The Full Faith and Credit Clause requires that each state give effect to the official acts of another state. In online transactions and e-commerce, courts will generally enforce a judgment entered in another state provided the court where the judgment was originally entered had sufficient jurisdiction.

Key Terms

choice-of-law provision *8*
cyberlaw *2*
forum selection clause *9*
Full Faith and Credit Clause *11*
jurisdiction *2*
in rem jurisdiction *3*
long-arm statute *5*
personal jurisdiction *3*
service of process *7*
subject matter jurisdiction *3*
venue *9*

Review Questions

1. Explain the history of the Internet.
2. Explain the difference between subject matter jurisdiction, personal jurisdiction, and in rem jurisdiction.
3. What is required to maintain personal jurisdiction over a nonresident defendant who operates a website?
4. Explain the difference between a choice-of-law clause and a forum selection clause. Why would a company include these provisions in an online agreement?

Discussion Questions

1. Who do think should have a greater role in regulating activities on the Internet: the federal government, state governments, or nongovernmental organizations? Why?
2. Do you think a court should approve service of process via e-mail or other electronic means as a substitute for personal delivery? Why or why not?
3. Many companies that conduct transactions via the Internet will include a forum selection clause in their online agreements. Is this fair for the consumer? Should courts enforce this type of forum selection clause and choice-of-law provision? Why or why not? What types of accommodations should be made for parties (e.g., telephonic or video appearances; scheduling of depositions near the plaintiff's home)?

Exercises

1. Locate the long-arm statutes for California and Texas. Conduct legal research using Westlaw, LexisNexis, a law library, or Internet resources, and write a brief memorandum where you provide the citation and text of the long-arm statutes. Then discuss the similarities and differences between the two long-arm statutes.
2. You are the contracts specialist for Acme Online, Inc. (a fictitious online retailer), and your supervisor at Acme Online, Inc. wants to include a terms of use agreement on its website where all disputes will be exclusively resolved by a state or federal court located in Hennepin County, Minnesota, and governed by the law of the state of Minnesota (or your own county and state). Conduct research online and find the conditions of use agreement for Amazon.com, another online retailer. Visit the website for Amazon.com and click on "Conditions of use" at the bottom of the main page and look for the sections entitled "Applicable Law" and "Disputes." Using the Amazon.com agreement as a model, draft the text of a choice-of-law provision and forum selection clause for Acme Online, Inc. Then discuss why Acme Online would want to include a choice-of-law provision and a forum selection clause in its online terms of use agreement.

3. Locate the forum selection clauses for three different companies such as eBay, Amazon.com, and Google. Then evaluate the strengths and weaknesses of each forum selection clause from the consumer's perspective.
4. Mark, a resident of New York, visits a travel company's website that advertises a resort in Puerto Rico that claims to have "white sandy beaches, crystal clear water, fresh fish and a superb international cuisine." Based on the advertisement, Mark made reservations for the resort through the defendant's agent. When Mark arrives at the resort location, the waters were murky, the beach was swarming with insects, the hotel rooms were infested with bed bugs, and the restaurant's food made him ill with intestinal poisoning. The travel company maintains an active website and allows customers to research, select, and book vacation packages and recommended travel agencies located in specific New York areas who were qualified to book vacations for the company. Mark files a lawsuit against the travel company alleging fraud, negligence, breach of contract, unjust enrichment, deceptive business practices, and violation of the Truth in Travel Act. Discuss whether a New York state court would maintain personal jurisdiction of the defendant travel company. See *Kaloyeva v. Apple Vacations*, 21 Misc. 3d 840, 866 N.Y.S.2d 488 (N.Y. City Civ. Ct. 2008).

Related Internet Sites

http://www.digestiblelaw.com/
Internet Case Law Digest provided by the law firm Perkins Coie

http://www.megalaw.com/top/conflictoflaws.php
Conflict of Law and Choice-of-law Cases and Resources

http://www.lexisnexis.com/lawschool/study/understanding/pdf/ConflictsCh1.pdf
Tutorial on Understanding the Conflict of Laws

http://www.hcch.net
Website for the Hague Conference on Private International Law

http://www.findlaw.com/01topics/10cyberspace/index.html
FindLaw Cyberspace Law Resources

http://www.law.berkeley.edu/bclt.htm
Berkeley Center for Law and Technology

http://cyberspacelaw.org/
Learning Cyberlaw in Cyberspace Training Modules

End Notes

1. Hon. Michel Bastarache, *The Challenge of the Law in the New Millennium*, 25 MAN. L.J. 411–19 (1997–1998).
2. Computer History Museum, Internet History, available at http://www.computerhistory.org/internet_history/.
3. Michelle Z. Hall, Comment, *Internet Privacy or Information Piracy: Spinning Lies on the World Wide Web*, 18 N.Y.L. SCH. J. HUM. RTS. 609, 611–13 (2002).
4. Mindy P. Fox, *Does It Really Suck?: The Impact of Cutting-Edge Marketing Tactics on Internet Trademark Law and Gripe Site Domain Name Disputes*, 20 FORDHAM INTELL. PROP. MEDIA & ENT. L.J. 225, 229 (2009).
5. Jack Goldsmith and Tim Wu, Who Controls the Internet? Illusions of a Borderless World 2 (2006).
6. Black's Law Dictionary (9th ed. 2009).
7. Jessica E. Bauml, *It's a Mad, Mad Internet: Globalization and the Challenges Presented by Internet Censorship*, 63 FED. COMM. L.J. 697 (2011) citing Jack Goldsmith & Tim Wu, *Who Controls the Internet? Illusions of a Borderless World* 2 (2006).
8. *Domtar Inc. v. Niagara Fire Ins. Co.*, 533 N.W.2d 25, 29 (Minn.1995).
9. U.S. Const. amend. V.
10. U.S. Const. amend. XIV.
11. Fed. R. Civ. P. 4.
12. Ronald J. Hedges, Kenneth N. Rashbaum, and Adam C. Losey, *Electronic Service of Process at Home and Abroad: Allowing Domestic Electronic Service of Process in the Federal Courts*, 4 FED. CTS. L. REV. 55, 68 (2010).
13. See *Swoboda v. Hero Decks*, 36 So. 3d 994 (La. Ct. App. 2010).
14. Black's Law Dictionary (9th ed. 2009).
15. U.S. Const. Art. IV.

CHAPTER

2 Copyright Law in the Digital Age

The Congress shall have power . . . To promote the Progress of Science and useful Arts, by securing for limited Times to Authors and Inventors the exclusive Right to their respective Writings and Discoveries.

U.S. Constitution Article I, Section 8

LEARNING OBJECTIVES

After completing this chapter, you will be able to:

1. Compare and contrast copyright law with other areas of intellectual property law.
2. Explain the scope of copyright protection for websites and software.
3. Describe the benefits of copyright notice and copyright registration.
4. Discuss the four fair use defense factors and how courts apply these factors in a copyright infringement action.
5. Explain the major provisions of the Digital Millennium Copyright Act.

CHAPTER OVERVIEW

The law of intellectual property, and particularly copyright law, stands at the forefront of legal issues related to the Internet. Intellectual property law encompasses the law governing copyrights, trademarks, patents, and trade secrets. This chapter provides an introduction to intellectual property law and focuses on copyright issues as they relate to technology and online content. Chapter 3 will cover trademark law and Chapter 4 will cover patents and trade secrets. This chapter also focuses on the scope of copyright protection, copyright notice, copyright registration, copyright duration, and the fair use defense with respect to computers and new technology.

INTRODUCTION TO INTELLECTUAL PROPERTY

Black's Law Dictionary defines *property* as simply as the right to possess, use, and enjoy a certain thing.[1] Several different types of property exist. Personal property includes any movable or intangible thing that is subject to ownership and not classified as real property. Examples of personal property include a laptop computer or a cell phone. Real property encompasses land and anything growing on, attached to, or erected on it, excluding anything that may be severed without injury to the land. Real property can consist of a single-family home, a commercial building, or land used for farming. For example, the buildings and land for the Google corporate headquarters, fondly nicknamed the Googleplex, in Mountain View, California, fall under the realm of real property. But the copyrights, trademarks, patents, and trade secrets owned by Google are categorized as intellectual property.

Property rights can also be classified into the categories of tangible property and intangible property. Tangible property has a physical existence and includes personal property that can be seen, weighed, measured, felt, or touched, or is in any other way perceptible to the senses, such as furniture, cooking utensils, and books. Intangible property lacks a physical existence. Examples of intangible property include stock options and business goodwill. Intellectual property rights also fall under the umbrella of intangible property. Intellectual property covers a category of intangible rights protecting commercially valuable products of the human intellect. Intellectual property is sometimes abbreviated as "IP" and intellectual property law is often shortened to "IP law." The acronym "IP" may also refer to "Internet Protocol" so spelling out "intellectual property" in full will help avoid any confusion.

Intellectual Property
A category of intangible rights protecting commercially valuable products of the human intellect that comprises primarily copyright, trademark, patent, and trade secret rights.

Intellectual property law protects the results of human creative endeavor. The general types of intellectual property are (1) copyrights; (2) trademarks; (3) patents; and (4) trade secrets. These general categories may often overlap. Article I, Section 8 of the U.S. Constitution grants power to Congress to pass laws dealing with intellectual property. (See Figure 2.1.) This section also known as the "Copyright Clause" states that "The Congress shall have power . . . To promote the Progress of Science and useful Arts, by securing for limited Times to Authors and Inventors the exclusive Right to their respective Writings and Discoveries."[2]

A trademark can be a word, name, symbol, or logo used in the ownership of a product or service. Trademark law protects the rights of businesses who use distinctive names, designs, logos, slogans, or other signifiers to identify and distinguish their products and services. Trademarks last perpetually as long as they are in use and do not become generic. A patent is a grant from the government that permits the owner the right to prevent others from making, using, importing, or selling an invention. Patents are only available for novel, useful, and non-obvious inventions. A trade secret is valuable business information that if known by a competitor would afford the competitor some advantage. Examples of trade secrets include customer lists, marketing plans, and secret formulas such as the secret formula for Coca-Cola. The owner must make reasonable attempts to maintain secrecy of the trade secret. For more information relating to trademarks, patents, and trade secrets, see Chapters 3–4.

Intellectual Property Law Chart

	Copyrights	Trademarks	Patents	Trade Secrets
Definition	Protection granted to authors of original works of authorship, fixed in a tangible form	A word, name, symbol, or device used to indicate origin, quality, and ownership of a product or service	Grant of right to exclude another from making, using, selling, or importing a patented invention or discovery	Any valuable business information that if known by a competitor would afford the competitor some advantage
What Is Protected	Motion pictures, sound recordings, photographs, books, articles	Trademark or service mark used in the source, qualify, and ownership of a product or service	Utility patents protect any new and useful process, machine. Design patents protect new, original designs for articles of manufacture	Any information as long as it has commercial value, not in the public domain, and owner has made reasonable attempts to maintain secrecy
Examples	Gone with the wind book and motion picture. Sound recording for NBC chime	Tradenames and logos. Nike's "Swoosh," Target's "Bullseye"	New manufacturing process, pharmaceutical drugs	Coca-Cola formula, customer lists, marketing plans
Duration of Protection	Generally, life of the author plus 70 years. For works made for hire, 95 years from publication or 120 years from creation	Generally perpetually as long as they are in use and do not become generic. Registration lasts 10 years and is renewable	Generally, 20 years from date of filing an application for utility and design patents. For plant patents, 14 years from date of grant	Perpetually as long as they are properly protected
Infringement Test	Have any of the exclusive rights been violated by impermissible copying or unauthorized use?	Likelihood of confusion between the marks	Does the accused invention fall within the claims language of the patent or is it substantially similar?	Has the trade secret been misappropriated?
Notice Requirements	Not required but recommended. Notice: © (copyright symbol), years of first publication, owner's name	Not required but recommended. Registered marks displayed with ® symbol. Unregistered trademarks and unregistered servicemarks used TM and SM symbols in superscript	Not required by recommended. Notice includes word *patent* (or abbreviation) and patent number	Not required but recommended. Documents should be marked "Confidential" or other notices
Governing Law	15 U.S.C. 1501 et. seq. (Landham Act)	17 U.S.C. 101 et. seq. (Copyright Act)	35 U.S.C. 100 et. seq. (Patent Act)	Various state statutes, cases, and private contracts
Governing Agency	U.S. Patent and Trademark Office	U.S. Copyright Office	U.S. Patent and Trademark Office	None

FIGURE 2.1 Intellectual Property Overview

SCOPE OF COPYRIGHT LAW

What Copyright Law Protects

Copyright
The right to copy a property right in an original work of authorship fixed in any tangible medium of expression, giving the holder the exclusive right to reproduce, adapt, distribute, perform, and display the work. Copyright includes literary, musical, dramatic, choreographic, pictorial, graphic, sculptural, and architectural works; motion pictures and other audiovisual works; and sound recordings.

Copyright Act of 1976
A major revision of U.S. copyright law, extending the term of protection to the life of the author plus 50 years, measured from the date of creation; greatly expanding the types of works that qualify for protection; dropping the requirement that the work be published before it can be protected; making fair use a statutory defense to a claim in infringement; and preempting state common-law copyright. Also called 1976 Copyright Act. 17 U.S.C. §§ 101 et seq.

Copyright is a form of protection provided by the laws of the United States to the authors of "original works of authorship," including literary, dramatic, musical, artistic, and certain other intellectual works. This protection is available to both published and unpublished works. Section 106 of the **1976 Copyright Act** (17 U.S.C. § 106) generally gives the owner of a copyright the exclusive right to do and to authorize others to do the following:

- To reproduce the work in copies or phonorecords;
- To prepare derivative works based upon the work;
- To distribute copies or phonorecords of the work to the public by sale or other transfer of ownership, or by rental, lease, or lending;
- To perform the work publicly, in the case of literary, musical, dramatic, and choreographic works, pantomimes, and motion pictures and other audiovisual works;
- To display the work publicly, in the case of literary, musical, dramatic, and choreographic works, pantomimes, and pictorial, graphic, or sculptural works, including the individual images of a motion picture or other audiovisual work; and
- In the case of sound recordings, to perform the work publicly by means of a digital audio transmission.[3]

Websites

As a general rule, original content for a website is considered an "original work of authorship" under the Copyright Act and can receive copyright protection. Copyright law protects web design, text, images, photographs, midi files, clipart, and audio associated with websites provided the work is original.[4]

Computer Programs and Software

The copyrightability of computer programs is firmly established, and a computer program is a "work of authorship" entitled to protection under the Copyright Act. Open source software, such as Open Office, in contrast, is not protected by copyright protection.

Video Games

Video games can receive protection under copyright law as audiovisual works, since a video game consists of visual and aural features of an audiovisual display containing original variations sufficient to render the display copyrightable as an audiovisual work. The copyright on the audiovisual display of a video game is valid even though the computer program producing the display is not copyrighted. In *Midway Mfg. Co. v. Artic Int'l, Inc.*, 704 F.2d 1009, 1012 (7th Cir. 1983), a federal appeals court held video game output was sufficiently fixed in the circuit board to permit copyright protection. But copyrighted video game programs containing unprotected aspects that may not be examined without copying are afforded a lower degree of protection than more traditional literary works. With the U.S. computer and video game software industry contributing $4.9 billion to the U.S. economy in 2009, according to the Entertainment Software Association (ESA), copyright protection for video games is significant. See Video Games in the 21st Century, 2010 Report, Entertainment Software Association.

Derivative Works

Copyright ownership also includes the right to derivative works. A **derivative work** is a work based on a pre-existing work that entitles only the holder of the copyright on the original form to produce or permit someone else to produce a derivative work. For example, the motion picture *Twilight* is a derivative of the vampire-romance novel *Twilight* written by Stephanie Meyer. Bookmarks, posters, calendars, and other merchandise based on the original novel and motion picture are also considered derivate works.

Derivative Work
A work that is based on a preexisting work. Only the holder of the copyright on the original form can produce or permit someone else to produce a derivative work.

What Copyright Law Does Not Protect

Although copyright law protects a wide variety of material, several categories of material do not receive copyright protection. These categories include:

- Works that have not been fixed in a tangible form of expression.
- Titles, names, short phrases, and slogans; familiar symbols or designs; mere variations of typographic ornamentation, lettering, or coloring; mere listings of ingredients or contents.
- Ideas, procedures, methods, systems, processes, concepts, principles, discoveries, or devices, as distinguished from a description, explanation, or illustration.
- Works consisting entirely of information that is common property and containing no original authorship (for example: standard calendars, height and weight charts, tape measures and rulers, and lists or tables taken from public documents or other common sources).

Copyright protection does not cover works created by the federal government, including work prepared by an officer or employee of the federal government as part of that person's official duties. For example, no one can claim copyright protection with reports written by government agencies. State governments and agencies are not barred from being copyright owners under statutory provisions.

The U.S. Court of Appeals for the Eight Circuit held in *C.B.C. Distribution & Marketing, Inc. v. Major League Baseball Advanced Media, L.P.*, 505 F.3d 818 (8th Cir. 2007), that an online fantasy baseball providers' use of baseball statistics were facts in the **public domain**. The statistics were readily available in newspapers and online and did not belong to Major League Baseball. Therefore, copyright protects only works of original authorship. The key is that the work must be original.

Public Domain
Works that are not protected by intellectual-property rights and are therefore available for anyone to use without liability for infringement. When copyright, trademark, patent, or trade-secret rights are lost or expire, the intellectual property they had protected becomes part of the public domain.

COPYRIGHT NOTICE

While copyright law previously required notice of a copyright, U.S. law now no longer requires the use of a copyright notice. Effective March 1, 1989, U.S. copyright law was amended by the Berne Convention Implementation Act, which made copyright notice permissible (or voluntary) rather than mandatory.[5] Although copyright law no longer requires copyright notice, notice is still encouraged. Copyright notice can help defeat defenses based on innocent infringement in a copyright infringement action. Also, notice requirement remains in effect for works that were created before the **Berne Convention**.

According to the U.S. Copyright Office, copyright notice should be placed "in such a way that it gives reasonable notice of the claim of copyright. The notice should be permanently legible to an ordinary user of the work under normal conditions of use and should not be not be concealed from view upon reasonable examination."

Berne Convention
An international copyright treaty providing that works created by citizens of one signatory nation will be fully protected in other signatory nations, without the need for local formalities. Also called the Berne Convention for the Protection of Literary and Artistic Property.

Copyright © 1995-2011 eBay Inc. All Rights Reserved.
Facebook © 2011
© 2011 YouTube, LLC
© 2011 CBS Interactive. All rights reserved.
© 1997–2011 Netflix, Inc. All rights reserved.

FIGURE 2.2 Examples of Copyright Notices for Popular Websites

Copyright notice consists of three elements:

1. The symbol © (letter C in a circle); the word "Copyright"; or the abbreviation "Copr."
2. The year of first publication; and
3. The name of the copyright owner, an abbreviation by which the name can be recognized, or a generally known alternative designation of owner.

For websites, the copyright notice is usually placed at the bottom of the webpage. This notice usually consists of (1) the copyright symbol "©" or the word "copyright"; (2) the year of first publication or years of operation for the website; and (3) and the name of the copyright owner, which is usually the company name. Figure 2.2 provides examples of copyright notices for some popular websites. Some works might include the phrase "All rights reserved," but the phrase "all rights reserved" is no longer required for copyright notice. The phrase "all rights reserved" resulted from international practice before the United States joined the Berne Convention, an international treaty that includes protection for copyright owners. Since software can also receive copyright protection, copyright notice should also be included or affixed with software. In *United States v. Manzer*, 69 F.3d 222 (8th Cir. 1995), a federal appeals court held that copyright notice on a plastic module containing copyrighted software was sufficient to put the defendant on notice for purpose of willfulness of copyright infringement. A federal regulation, 37 C.F.R. 201.20(g)(4), permits copyright notice to be affixed to containers that are permanent receptacles for software copies. Website designers, software developers, and others working in technology should ensure that copyright notice appears affixed to any works that may be protected by copyright law.

COPYRIGHT REGISTRATION

Like copyright notice, copyright registration is also voluntary. Even though the law does not require copyright registration, registration has several advantages. One of the benefits of copyright registration is that registration is a prerequisite to a copyright infringement lawsuit. Entitlement to statutory damages, legal costs, and attorneys' fees in an infringement suit are also advantages to copyright registration. Another benefit is that registration establishes a public record of the work and provides notice that the work is owned by the registrant. The certificate of registration is prima facie evidence that the work is original and owned by the registrant. With registration, naming an employer as the owner of a work can eliminate future confusion and possible litigation as to who owns the work.

There are three different methods for registering a copyright with the U.S. Copyright Office. Regulations governing copyright registration with the U.S. Copyright Office are contained in Title 37 of the Code of Federal Regulations (CFR). The primary registration method with the U.S. Copyright Office is the Copyright Office online system and registration with the Electronic Copyright Office (eCO). One advantage of the online registration is a lower filing fee for a basic claim. The next best option for registering basic claims is to complete the fill-in Form CO. A third option is to complete the registration with a paper form. Paper versions of Form TX (literary works); Form VA (visual arts works); Form PA (performing arts works, including motion pictures); Form SR (sound recordings); and Form SE (single serials) are available. For more information and tutorials for registration of a copyright, visit the U.S. Copyright Office website at http://www.copyright.gov/forms/.

While the time to process an application with U.S. Copyright Office varies, those who file the online application will have the fastest processing time. The application time also varies depending on the number of applications the U.S. Copyright Office is currently receiving and the extent of questions associated with the application. Many online filers should receive a certificate within six months, and many will receive their certificates earlier.

The U.S. Copyright Office will not always accept the application. In *Darden v. Peters*, 488 F.3d 277 (4th Cir. 2007), a website designer challenged a rejected application with the U.S. Copyright Office. Plaintiff William Darden created a website called "appraisers.com," an online referral service for consumers to locate real estate appraisers throughout the United States. The website features a series of maps that enable visitors to find an appraiser in a desired location by pointing to and clicking on the appropriate map. The homepage of appraisers.com features a stylized map of the United States that serves as a link to a separate page displaying a detailed map of any state selected by the user. The state maps, in turn, are divided into counties; the consumer can retrieve a list of local appraisers by selecting the appropriate county. The Examining Division of the Copyright Office rejected the application for copyright, concluding that the work lacked the authorship necessary to support a copyright claim. The federal appeals court upheld the examiner's decision and concluded that the webpage designer's additions to preexisting, standard census maps, such as color, shading, and labels using standard fonts and shapes, fell within the narrow category of works that lacked even a minimum level of creativity and, thus, did not meet the minimum standard of originality required for a copyrightable claim under 17 U.S.C. § 102(a)(5).

If the application meets the requirements under the Copyright Act, the Register of Copyrights will issue a certificate of registration to the applicant. But if the application does not meet the requirements for copyrightable material, the Register will reject the registration. A party can challenge the decision of the Register, but courts will only reverse and set aside the decision if it was arbitrary or capricious and there has been an abuse of discretion.

Plaintiffs in a copyright infringement action must register the work as a prerequisite to filing a copyright infringement action. In 2010, the U.S. Supreme Court held in *Reed Elsevier, Inc. v. Muchnick*, 130 S. Ct. 1237 (2010), that the Copyright Act's registration requirement in 17 U.S.C. § 411(a) is merely a precondition to suing for copyright infringement, and does not deprive a federal court of subject matter jurisdiction to decide a class action lawsuit for infringement claims involving both registered and unregistered works. In *Reed Elsevier, Inc. v. Muchnick*, freelance authors who contracted with publishers to author works for publication in print media, and who retained the copyrights in those works, brought a class action lawsuit against the publishers, such as the *New York Times*, alleging electronic reproduction of the works by the publishers infringed their copyrights. The trial court dismissed the action based on lack of subject matter jurisdiction, and the U.S. Court of Appeals affirmed that decision, but the U.S. Supreme Court reversed and held that courts cannot dismiss an action based on lack of subject matter jurisdiction to approve a class action settlement agreement encompassing the alleged infringement of both registered and unregistered works. While copyright registration is not required, there are many reasons why owners should register a copyright.

COPYRIGHT DURATION

As a general rule, for works created after January 1, 1978, copyright protection lasts for the life of the author plus an additional 70 years. For works made for hire and anonymous and pseudonymous works created after 1978, the duration of copyright is 95 years from first publication or 120 years from creation, whichever is shorter (unless the author's identity is later revealed in Copyright Office records, in which case the term becomes the author's life plus 70 years).[6] A "work made for hire" is either (1) a work prepared by an employee within the scope of his or her employment; or (2) a work specially ordered or commissioned and created by an independent contractor. For example, works created by employees of DreamWorks Animation for the movie *Shrek* and sequels would be considered works made for hire since the work was prepared by employees within the scope of their employment.

Copyright Term Extension Act (CTEA) Act passed by Congress in 1998 that extended the duration of copyright protection by 20 years for works copyrighted after January 1, 1923. 17 U.S.C. §§ 302–304.

In 1998, Congress extended the duration of copyright protection for certain works with the Sonny Bono **Copyright Term Extension Act (CTEA)**.[7] Walt Disney Company's copyright on Mickey Mouse, who first debuted in the 1928 cartoon short "Steamboat Willie," was set to expire in 2003. Disney's rights to Pluto, Goofy, and Donald Duck were also set to expire a few years later. Congress passed the Sonny Bono Copyright Term Extension Act (CTEA) in 1998. The CTEA extended the duration of copyright protection by 20 years for works copyrighted after January 1, 1923.

Once the duration for copyright protection expires, the work falls into the public domain. Works that are not protected by intellectual-property rights and are therefore available for anyone to use without liability for infringement are considered part of the public domain. Amazon's Kindle, a device for reading e-books, has a vast library of older, out-of-copyright, pre-1923 books in its free book collection. With nearly 2 million titles in Amazon's free book collection, including classics such as *Uncle Tom's Cabin* by Harriet Beecher Stowe and *Sense and Sensibility* by Jane Austen, the public domain covers a vast array of original works where copyright protection has expired. It will be many years before the *Harry Potter* fantasy book series, written by J.K. Rowling, will fall into the public domain. Since the *Harry Potter* books were created after 1978 and Rowling is still alive, the Harry Potter books will not fall into the public domain until Rowling dies and then another 70 years pass.

DIGITAL MILLENIUM COPYRIGHT ACT

In 1998, Congress passed the Digital Millennium Copyright Act (DMCA) to protect copyright owners and respond to the increase in popularity and usage of digital content.[8] The DMCA limits copyright liability for Internet service providers and expands the ability of software owners to copy programs. The DMCA also extends copyright protection to computer programs, movies, and other audiovisual works worldwide. The statute also attempts to regulate cyberspace and forbids devices whose purpose is to evade digital antipiracy tools. The DMCA also bars the production or distribution of falsified copyright-management information.

The DMCA includes a "safe harbor" provision that allows websites and Internet service providers to avoid liability for copyright infringement if they follow certain procedural safeguards. The DMCA "safe harbor" provision in 17 U.S.C. § 512(c), (m) and (n) is designed to relieve websites from the burden of checking user-generated material before the content is posted. In *Viacom Intern. Inc. v. YouTube, Inc.*, 718 F. Supp. 2d 514

(S.D.N.Y. 2010), U.S. District Court Judge Louis Stanton said that the popular video website YouTube, purchased by Google in 2006, could not be held responsible when people post clips from productions such as Viacom's *The Daily Show* with Jon Stewart without Viacom's consent. Judge Stanton found that since Google "identifies an agent to receive complaints of infringement, and removes identified material when he learns it infringes" the DMCA safe harbor provision applies. YouTube received the DMCA takedown notices and removed the material. YouTube has also implemented a policy of terminating a user after warnings from YouTube (stimulated by its receipt of DMCA notices) that the user has uploaded infringing matter (a "three strikes" repeat-infringer policy). Other websites that seek to take advantage of the DMCA safe harbor provision should follow YouTube's lead and quickly remove content after receiving a DMCA takedown notice and should also delete user accounts that repeatedly upload infringing matter.

The DMCA safe harbor provision also requires that any person filing a complaint for a takedown notice must declare, under penalty of perjury, that they are authorized to represent the copyright holder, and that they have a good-faith belief that the use is infringing. The notification must do more than identify infringing files. The holding in *Perfect 10, Inc. v. CCBill LLC*, 488 F.3d 1102 (9th Cir. 2007), now more fully protects fair use content under the DMCA's notice-and-takedown system. A DMCA compliant takedown notice must include the copyright owner's good faith statement that the user's content is unauthorized by law and that the copyright owner must consider fair use to make this good faith statement.

Under the DMCA safe harbor provision in 17 U.S.C. § 512(c), notification of claimed infringement must be a written communication provided to the designated agent of a service provider that includes substantially the following:

i. A physical or electronic signature of a person authorized to act on behalf of the owner of an exclusive right that is allegedly infringed.

ii. Identification of the copyrighted work claimed to have been infringed, or, if multiple copyrighted works at a single online site are covered by a single notification, a representative list of such works at that site.

iii. Identification of the material that is claimed to be infringing or to be the subject of infringing activity and that is to be removed or access to which is to be disabled, and information reasonably sufficient to permit the service provider to locate the material.

iv. Information reasonably sufficient to permit the service provider to contact the complaining party, such as an address, telephone number, and, if available, an electronic mail address at which the complaining party may be contacted.

v. A statement that the complaining party has a good faith belief that use of the material in the manner complained of is not authorized by the copyright owner, its agent, or the law.

vi. A statement that the information in the notification is accurate, and under penalty of perjury, that the complaining party is authorized to act on behalf of the owner of an exclusive right that is allegedly infringed.

For the full text of the safe harbor provision in the 17 U.S.C. § 512 Safe Harbor Provision, see Appendix A at the end of the book. The DMCA also provides for criminal penalties for copyright infringement. Chapter 7 provides additional discussion of the criminal aspects with the DMCA.

COPYRIGHT INFRINGEMENT

Copyright Infringement The act of violating any of a copyright owner's exclusive rights granted by the Copyright Act.

If a person or entity has used a copyrighted work without permission, the copyright owners may file an action for **copyright infringement**. A plaintiff in a copyright infringement lawsuit has a number of remedies available against the defendant:

1. *Monetary damages.* The plaintiff may recover actual damages and lost profits from unauthorized use of the copyrighted material.
2. *Statutory damages.* Copyright owners who register the work with the U.S. Copyright Office prior to the infringement can recover statutory damages in lieu of actual damages. A copyright owner may elect, at any time before final judgment is rendered, to recover statutory damages instead of actual damages and profits. The award of statutory damages must be no less than $750 nor more than $30,000 for all infringements involved in the action, with respect to any one work. Where the copyright infringement was committed willfully, the court in its discretion may increase the award of statutory damages to a sum of not more than $150,000.[9]
3. *Attorneys' fees.* A prevailing plaintiff in a copyright infringement action may recover reasonable attorneys' fees.
4. *Preliminary Injunction or Temporary Restraining Order (TRO).* In addition to monetary damages, statutory damages, and attorneys' fees, plaintiffs can also seek a preliminary injunction or temporary restraining order. The court can order a website operator to remove certain content.

A court can also issue an injunction that prevents the sale of certain software, print publications, and online content. For example, in the Napster and Grokster cases, courts issued injunctions to remove infringing content. The website at www.grokster.com now reads, "The United States Supreme Court unanimously confirmed that using this service to trade copyrighted material is illegal. Copying copyrighted motion picture and music files using unauthorized peer-to-peer services is illegal and is prosecuted by copyright owners."

Peer-to-Peer File Sharing

In a landmark copyright infringement case involving a peer-to-peer file sharing service for motion pictures, the U.S. Supreme Court held in *Metro-Goldwyn-Mayer Studios Inc. v. Grokster, Ltd.*, 545 U.S. 913 (2005), that "information content providers may be liable for contributory infringement if their system is designed to help people steal music or other material in copyright." The court also held that one who distributes a device with the object of promoting its use to infringe copyright, as shown by clear expression or other affirmative steps taken to foster infringement, is liable for the resulting acts of infringement by third parties. Under *Grokster*, *contributory infringement* refers to the concept of inducement that one infringes contributorily by intentionally inducing or encouraging direct infringement.[10] The syllabus of the decision in *Grokster* is provided below in Case 2.1.

Under the holding in *Grokster*, providers of peer-to-peer (P2P) file sharing services can now be found liable for the copyright infringement of their users despite never actually infringing on any copyrights. Despite high-profile legal victories against P2P network operators like Grokster, P2P piracy still continues. Attempts to shut down decentralized P2P have been somewhat less successful, and new services such as BitTorrent and LimiWire have emerged. Copyright issues with "peer-to-peer" file-sharing services still continue.

CASE 2.1

The Case of the Peer-to-Peer Movies

Metro-Goldwyn-Mayer Studios Inc. v. Grokster, Ltd., *545 U.S. 913 (2005)*

Syllabus

Respondent companies [Grokster] distribute free software that allows computer users to share electronic files through peer-to-peer networks, so called because the computers communicate directly with each other, not through central servers. Seeking damages and an injunction, a group of movie studios and other copyright holders (hereinafter MGM) sued respondents for their users' copyright infringements, alleging that respondents knowingly and intentionally distributed their software to enable users to infringe copyrighted works in violation of the Copyright Act.

Discovery revealed that billions of files are shared across peer-to-peer networks each month. After the notorious file-sharing service, Napster, was sued by copyright holders for facilitating copyright infringement, both respondents promoted and marketed themselves as Napster alternatives. They receive no revenue from users, but, instead, generate income by selling advertising space, then streaming the advertising to their users. As the number of users increases, advertising opportunities are worth more. There is no evidence that either respondent made an effort to filter copyrighted material from users' downloads or otherwise to impede the sharing of copyrighted files.

While acknowledging that respondents' users had directly infringed MGM's copyrights, the District Court nonetheless granted respondents summary judgment as to liability arising from distribution of their software. The Ninth Circuit affirmed. It read *Sony Corp. of America v. Universal City Studios, Inc.*, 464 U.S. 417 (1984), as holding that the distribution of a commercial product capable of substantial noninfringing uses could not give rise to contributory liability for infringement unless the distributor had actual knowledge of specific instances of infringement and failed to act on that knowledge. Because the appeals court found respondents' software to be capable of substantial noninfringing uses and because respondents had no actual knowledge of infringement owing to the software's decentralized architecture, the court held that they were not liable. It also held that they did not materially contribute to their users' infringement because the users themselves searched for, retrieved, and stored the infringing files, with no involvement by respondents beyond providing the software in the first place. Finally, the court held that respondents could not be held liable under a vicarious infringement theory because they did not monitor or control the software's use, had no agreed-upon right or current ability to supervise its use, and had no independent duty to police infringement.

Held: One who distributes a device with the object of promoting its use to infringe copyright, as shown by clear expression or other affirmative steps taken to foster infringement, going beyond mere distribution with knowledge of third-party action, is liable for the resulting acts of infringement by third parties using the device, regardless of the device's lawful uses.

a. The tension between the competing values of supporting creativity through copyright protection and promoting technological innovation by limiting infringement liability is the subject of this case. Despite offsetting considerations, the argument for imposing indirect liability here is powerful, given the number of infringing downloads that occur daily using respondents' software. When a widely shared product is used to commit infringement, it may be impossible to enforce rights in the protected work effectively against all direct infringers, so that the only practical alternative is to go against the device's distributor for secondary liability on a theory of contributory or vicarious infringement. One infringes contributorily by intentionally inducing or encouraging direct infringement, and infringes vicariously by profiting from direct infringement while declining to exercise the right to stop or limit it. Although "[t]he Copyright Act does not expressly render anyone liable for [another's] infringement," Sony, 464 U.S., at 434, these secondary liability

(*Continued*)

(Continued)

doctrines emerged from common law principles and are well established in the law, e.g., id., at 486. Pp. 10–13.

b. *Sony* addressed a claim that secondary liability for infringement can arise from the very distribution of a commercial product. There, copyright holders sued Sony, the manufacturer of videocassette recorders, claiming that it was contributorily liable for the infringement that occurred when VCR owners taped copyrighted programs. Because the VCR was "capable of commercially significant noninfringing uses," the Court held that Sony was not liable. In this case, the Ninth Circuit misread *Sony* to mean that when a product is capable of substantial lawful use, the producer cannot be held contributorily liable for third parties' infringing use of it, even when an actual purpose to cause infringing use is shown, unless the distributors had specific knowledge of infringement at a time when they contributed to the infringement and failed to act upon that information. *Sony* did not displace other secondary liability theories.

c. Nothing in *Sony* requires courts to ignore evidence of intent to promote infringement if such evidence exists. It was never meant to foreclose rules of fault-based liability derived from the common law. Where evidence goes beyond a product's characteristics or the knowledge that it may be put to infringing uses, and shows statements or actions directed to promoting infringement, Sony's staple-article rule will not preclude liability. At common law a copyright or patent defendant who "not only expected but invoked [infringing use] by advertisement" was liable for infringement. *Kalem Co. v. Harper Brothers*, 222 U.S. 55, 62–63. The rule on inducement of infringement as developed in the early cases is no different today. Evidence of active steps taken to encourage direct infringement, such as advertising an infringing use or instructing how to engage in an infringing use, shows an affirmative intent that the product be used to infringe, and overcomes the law's reluctance to find liability when a defendant merely sells a commercial product suitable for some lawful use. A rule that premises liability on purposeful, culpable expression and conduct does nothing to compromise legitimate commerce or discourage innovation having a lawful promise.

d. On the record presented, respondents' unlawful objective is unmistakable. The classic instance of inducement is by advertisement or solicitation that broadcasts a message designed to stimulate others to commit violations. MGM argues persuasively that such a message is shown here. Three features of the evidence of intent are particularly notable. First, each of the respondents showed itself to be aiming to satisfy a known source of demand for copyright infringement, the market comprising former Napster users. Respondents' efforts to supply services to former Napster users indicate a principal, if not exclusive, intent to bring about infringement. Second, neither respondent attempted to develop filtering tools or other mechanisms to diminish the infringing activity using their software. While the Ninth Circuit treated that failure as irrelevant because respondents lacked an independent duty to monitor their users' activity, this evidence underscores their intentional facilitation of their users' infringement. Third, respondents make money by selling advertising space, then by directing ads to the screens of computers employing their software. The more their software is used, the more ads are sent out and the greater the advertising revenue. Since the extent of the software's use determines the gain to the distributors, the commercial sense of their enterprise turns on high-volume use, which the record shows is infringing. This evidence alone would not justify an inference of unlawful intent, but its import is clear in the entire record's context. Pp. 20–23.

e. In addition to intent to bring about infringement and distribution of a device suitable for infringing use, the inducement theory requires evidence of actual infringement by recipients of the device, the software in this case. There is evidence of such infringement on a gigantic scale. Because substantial evidence supports MGM on all elements, summary judgment for respondents was error.

Case Questions

1. What are the two competing values that were the subject of the *Grokster* case?
2. What attempt, if any, did Grokster make to filter copyrighted works?
3. What is the rule on inducement of infringement?
4. How does the rule in *Sony v. Universal* cited by the court in *Grokster* apply to videos uploaded to YouTube?

Contributory Infringement

A defendant may be held liable for contributory infringement. To make a prima facie case for contributory copyright infringement, there must actually be direct infringement.[11] A prerequisite to contributory liability for copyright infringement is that the defendant must have aided or encouraged someone who actually engaged in copyright infringement. Liability for copyright infringement can be imposed for vicarious or contributory infringement, even without regard to a defendant's intent to infringe, or a defendant's knowledge of the infringement. In *U-Haul Intern., Inc. v. WhenU.com, Inc.*, 279 F. Supp. 2d 723 (E.D. Va. 2003), the federal trial court judge held that a pop-up advertising scheme, which caused an ad to appear when the copyright holder's web page was accessed, did not interfere with holder's right to display its copyrighted works.

Deep-Linking

Some courts have considered whether deep-linking constitutes copyright infringement. Black's Law Dictionary defines a "deep link" as "a webpage hyperlink that, when clicked, opens a page on another website other than that site's home page." In *Live Nation Motor Sports, Inc. v. Davis*, No. 3:06-CV-276-L, 2007 WL 79311, at *2 (N.D. Tex. Jan. 9, 2007), the defendant operated a website and directly linked to an audio webcast from the plaintiff's site. The court held that although the same audio webcast link was freely distributed by ClearChannel, the defendant "violated SFX's copyrights by providing a link of its webcasts without authorization. . . ." Deep-linking is a classic example of the tension that exists between intellectual property laws and the generally accepted operating policies of the Internet. The areas of deep-linking, pop-up advertisements, and embedded content in websites will continue to be topics of debate for years to come in copyright infringement actions.

COPYRIGHT INFRINGEMENT DEFENSES

A defendant in a copyright infringement lawsuit may assert a variety of defenses, including public domain use, the DMCA safe harbor provision, the first sale doctrine, and the fair use defense. Public domain use and the DMCA safe harbor provision are discussed earlier in this chapter. The defendants in a copyright infringement action may also claim that they lawfully obtained a license to use to the work.

First Sale Doctrine

Defendants in a copyright infringement action may assert the **first sale doctrine** as an affirmative defense. The first sale doctrine limits the owner of a copyright to the exclusive right to distribute a copy of the work when the original work is purchased by another. Under the Copyright Act, "the owner of a . . . copy . . . is entitled, without the authority of the copyright owner, to sell . . . that copy." Under the first sale doctrine, a purchaser of a physical copy of a copyrighted work, such as a book or CD, may give or sell that copy to someone else without infringing the copyright owner's exclusive distribution rights. For example, authors generally receive royalties for new books sold on Amazon.com and by other online and retail book sellers, but authors do not normally receive royalties for the sale of used copies. Similarly, artists do not generally receive royalties for sales on used compact discs. Under the first sale doctrine, once a copyright owner consents to release a copy of a work to an individual (by sale or gift), the copyright owner surrenders or relinquishes all rights to that particular copy.[12]

First Sale Doctrine The rule that the purchaser of a physical copy of a copyrighted work, such as a book or CD, may give or sell that copy to someone else without infringing the copyright owner's exclusive distribution rights.

Fair Use Doctrine

Fair Use
A reasonable and limited use of a copyrighted work without the author's permission, such as quoting from a book in a book review or using parts of it in a parody. Fair use is a defense to an infringement claim, depending on the following statutory factors: (1) the purpose and character of the use, (2) the nature of the copyrighted work, (3) the amount of the work used, and (4) the economic impact of the use. 17 U.S.C. § 107.

Most copyright infringement cases that end up in the courts involve a question of the **fair use** defense. (See Figure 2.3.) The fair use doctrine is a statutory limitation on the exclusive rights of a copyright owner. Fair use is defined as a reasonable and limited use of a copyrighted work without the author's permission, such as quoting from a book in a book review or using parts of it in a parody. Congress set forth four non-exclusive factors in the Copyright Act in determining whether the fair defense doctrine applies.

1. The purpose and character of the use;
2. The nature of the copyrighted work;
3. The amount of the work used; and
4. The economic impact of the use.

The U.S. Supreme Court has described fair use as "a privilege in others than the owner of the copyright to use the copyrighted material in a reasonable manner without his consent." *Harper & Row Publishers, Inc. v. Nation Enters.*, 471 U.S. 539, 549 (1985). Section 107 of the Copyright Act specifically permits the unauthorized use of copyrighted work "for purposes such as criticism, comment, news reporting, teaching (including multiple copies for classroom use), scholarship, or research." 17 U.S.C. § 107.

The fair-use doctrine balances the need for individual incentive to create public works with the public's interest in dissemination of information. The party that claims fair use of copyrighted material, usually the defendant, carries the burden of proof. The case *A.V. v. iParadigms, LLC*, 562 F.3d 630 (4th Cir. 2009) (Case 2.2), involving a plagiarism detection service, is typical of how courts apply the four fair use defense factors. In *A.V. v. iParadigms, LLC*, high school students who submitted written assignments to the online plagiarism detective service, Turnitin.com, brought a copyright infringement action against iParadigms, the operators of the service. The court outlined the statutory basis of copyright law and the doctrine of fair use through the four-factor test in section 107 of the Copyright Act. The Fourth Circuit concluded that iParadigms' use of the student's copyrighted work constituted "fair use" and the district court properly issued summary judgment on the copyright infringement claim.

The 2001 case involving Napster, a popular website for downloading unauthorized copies of music files, demonstrates how courts will reject the fair use defense if the use has a significant impact on the market. See *A&M Recs., Inc. v. Napster, Inc.*, 239 F.3d 1004 (9th Cir. 2001). A federal appeals court found Napster liable for contributory

Section 107 of the 1976 Copyright Act (codified in 17 U.S.C. § 107):

Fair use of a copyrighted work, including such use by reproduction in copies or phonorecords or by any other means specified by that section, for purposes such as criticism, comment, news reporting, teaching (including multiple copies for classroom use), scholarship, or research, is not an infringement of copyright. In determining whether the use made of a work in any particular case is a fair use the factors to be considered shall include—

(1) the purpose and character of the use, including whether such use is of a commercial nature or is for nonprofit educational purposes;
(2) the nature of the copyrighted work;
(3) the amount and substantiality of the portion used in relation to the copyrighted work as a whole; and
(4) the effect of the use upon the potential market for or value of the copyrighted work.

The fact that a work is unpublished shall not itself bar a finding of fair use if such finding is made upon consideration of all the above factors.

FIGURE 2.3 Text of the Fair Use Statute

CASE 2.2

The Case of the Plagiarism Detection Service

AV. Ex. Rel. Vanderhye v. iParadims, LLC, ***562 F.3d 630 (4th Cir. 2009)***

Plaintiffs brought this copyright infringement action against defendant iParadigms, LLC, based on its use of essays and other papers written by plaintiffs for submission to their high school teachers through an online plagiarism detection service operated by iParadigms.

Congress provided four nonexclusive factors for courts to consider in making a "fair use" determination:

1. the purpose and character of the use, including whether such use is of a commercial nature or is for nonprofit educational purposes;
2. the nature of the copyrighted work;
3. the amount and substantiality of the portion used in relation to the copyrighted work as a whole; and
4. the effect of the use upon the potential market for or value of the copyrighted work.

Section 107 [17 U.S.C. § 107] contemplates that the question of whether a given use of copyrighted material is "fair" requires a case-by-case analysis in which the statutory factors are not "treated in isolation" but are "weighed together, in light of the purposes of copyright."

With these general principles in mind, we consider each of the statutory factors.

First Factor [Purpose and Character of the Use]

The first fair use factor requires us to consider "the purpose and character of the use, including whether such use is of a commercial nature or is for nonprofit educational purposes." 17 U.S.C. § 107(1). A use of the copyrighted material that has a commercial purpose "tends to weigh against a finding of fair use."

In considering the character and purpose of iParadigms' use of the student works, the district court focused on the question of whether the use was transformative in nature. The court concluded that "iParadigms, through Turnitin, uses the papers for an entirely different purpose, namely, to prevent plagiarism and protect the students' written works from plagiarism . . . by archiving the students' works as digital code." Accordingly, the court concluded that the first factor weighed in favor of a finding of fair use.

The district court, in our view, correctly determined that the archiving of plaintiffs' papers was transformative and favored a finding of "fair use." iParadigms' use of these works was completely unrelated to expressive content and was instead aimed at detecting and discouraging plagiarism.

Second Factor [Nature of the Copyrighted Work]

In considering the nature of the copyrighted work, the Supreme Court has instructed that "fair use is more likely to be found in factual works than in fictional works," whereas "a use is less likely to be deemed fair when the copyrighted work is a creative product." *Stewart v. Abend,* 495 U.S. 207, 237, 110 S.Ct. 1750, 109 L.Ed.2d 184 (1990).

Plaintiffs contend that the district court's application of this factor was flawed in two respects. First, they argue that the court failed to account for the fact that their works were unpublished. Because an author enjoys the "right to control the first public appearance of his undisseminated expression," the fair use of an unpublished work is narrower in scope. We disagree that the lack of an express reference to the unpublished status of plaintiffs' works undermines the court's analysis under § 107(2).

Moreover, it is clear that iParadigms' use of plaintiffs' works did not have the "*intended purpose*" or "incidental effect" of supplanting plaintiffs' rights to first publication. iParadigms did not publicly disseminate or display plaintiffs' works and did not send them to any third party

(Continued)

(Continued)

"other than the instructor to whom plaintiffs submitted their own papers." [N]o employee of iParadigms read or reviewed the works submitted by plaintiffs. We find no basis whatsoever for concluding that iParadigms' use of the plaintiffs' papers undermined their right to first publication.

Plaintiffs contend that the district court's consideration . . . was flawed [because] the district court ignored the fact that the works in question were works of fiction and poetry, which are considered "highly creative" in nature and deserving of the strongest protection. This argument is unpersuasive. iParadigms' use of the works in the case—as part of a digitized database from which to compare the similarity of typewritten characters used in other student works—is likewise unrelated to any creative component. Thus, we find no fault in the district court's application of the second fair use factor.

Third Factor [Amount and Substantiality]

The third fair use factor requires us to consider "the amount and substantiality of the portion used in relation to the copyrighted work as a whole." 17 U.S.C. § 107(3). Generally speaking, "as the amount of the copyrighted material that is used increases, the likelihood that the use will constitute a 'fair use' decreases." But this statutory factor also requires courts to consider, in addition to quantity, the "quality and importance" of the copyrighted materials uses . . . whether the portion of the copyrighted material was "the heart of the copyrighted work."

The district court found that this factor, like the second factor, did not favor either party. Having already concluded that such use of plaintiffs' works was transformative, the district court concluded that iParadigms' use of the entirety of plaintiffs' works did not preclude a finding of fair use.

Fourth Factor [Effect on the Market]

Finally, § 107 directs us to examine the market of the copyrighted work to determine "the effect of the use upon the potential market for or value of the copyrighted work." 17 U.S.C. § 107(4). The Supreme Court described this factor as the "single most important element of fair use," considering that a primary goal of copyright is to ensure that "authors [have] the opportunity to realize rewards in order to encourage them to create."

The district court concluded that iParadigms' Turnitin system did not serve as a market substitute or even harm the market value of the works, highlighting the deposition testimony of the plaintiffs—each of whom denied that iParadigms' "impinged on the marketability of their works or interfered with their use of the works."

On appeal, plaintiffs' primary contention is that the district court focused on whether there was evidence of actual damages, failing to consider the effect of iParadigms' use on the "potential market" for plaintiffs' works. Clearly, this assertion is incorrect. The district court considered the potential market effects suggested by plaintiffs but concluded that plaintiffs' arguments were theoretical and speculative.

In sum, we conclude, viewing the evidence in the light most favorable to the plaintiffs, that iParadigms' use of the student works was "fair use" under the Copyright Act and that iParadigms was therefore entitled to summary judgment on the copyright infringement claim.

Case Questions

1. What is the primary goal of copyright?
2. What is the single most important element of fair use?
3. The more transformative the new work (which means adds something new), to what extent are the other factors considered?
4. Why is impact on the market an important factor in the fair use defense?
5. Fair use cases often involve subjective judgments and are often affected by factors such as a judge or jury's personal sense of right or wrong. Despite the fact that the U.S. Supreme Court has indicated that offensiveness is not a fair use factor, a judge or jury may rationalize a decision against fair use if the judge or jury is morally offended by the defendant's conduct. To what extent, if any, should courts apply a "fifth" fair use factor on offensiveness if the defendant is "good" or "bad"?

infringement because its services were designed to enable users to locate and download music files. The court reasoned that Napster materially contributed to its users' infringement since evidence showed Napster had actual knowledge of infringing activity on the network but failed to purge the system. Additionally, the court found Napster vicariously liable for its users' infringing activities because the central index provided Napster with the right and ability to supervise its users. Although Napster's service was free to users, the unauthorized materials increased traffic and advertising revenue. The court concluded that Napster harmed the market in at least two ways: it reduced audio CD sales among college students, and it raised barriers to entry into the market for the digital downloading of music. With the popularity of iTunes and other licensed digital download websites, the aftermath of Napster shows that the digital download market for music and other content is significant.

No bright-line rules exist in a fair use defense case. One common myth is that using only a certain percentage of the work, such as copying one page out of a 300-page book, falls under fair use. Courts apply all four statutory fair use defense factors as a whole and decide the outcome on a case-by-case basis. No magic mathematical formula exists with the fair use defense. As a result, the outcome in fair use defense cases may be difficult to predict. The U.S. Supreme Court held that the fair use defense "calls for case-by-case analysis. . . . Nor may the four statutory factors be treated in isolation, one from another. All are to be explored, and the results weighed together, in light of the purposes of copyright." *Campbell*, 510 U.S. at 577–578.

Judicial opinions that analyze the fair use defense case often discuss **transformative use**. Transformative use was first applied by the U.S. Supreme Court in *Campbell v. Acuff–Rose Music, Inc.*, where the court held that a parody of the rap group 2 Live Crew's song, "Pretty Woman," did not infringe on Acuff Rose's copyright in Roy Orbison's "Oh Pretty Woman." In *Campbell*, transformative use involves use of copyrighted material in a manner, or for a purpose, that differs from the original use in such a way that the expression, meaning, or message is essentially new. Essentially, transformative use is creating something new.

Transformative Use Use of copyrighted material in a manner, or for a purpose, that differs from the original use in such a way that the expression, meaning, or message is essentially new.

INTERNATIONAL ENFORCEMENT OF COPYRIGHTS

While no single treaty governs copyrights throughout the world among all nations, the United States has entered in various international agreements and treaties to protect the interests of U.S. copyright owners. The main agreements to protect these interests are the Berne Convention, the Universal Copyright Convention, and the Trade Related Aspects of International Property Rights Agreement (TRIPS Agreement).

Berne Convention

The Berne Convention, also called the Berne Convention for the Protection of Literary and Artistic Property, is an international copyright treaty providing that works created by citizens of one signatory nation will be fully protected in other signatory nations, without the need for local formalities. The treaty was drafted in Berne, Switzerland in 1886 and revised in Berlin, Germany, in 1908. The Berne Convention, now administered by the World Intellectual Property Organization (WIP), prescribes minimum levels and terms of copyright protection. The U.S. ratified (or adopted) the Berne Convention in 1989 with the passage of the Berne Convention Implementation Act and changed several aspects of U.S. copyright law to comply with the terms of the treaty.

Universal Copyright Convention

The Universal Copyright Convention is a 1952 treaty that binds signatories (countries that have signed the treaty) to give citizens of other member nations the same copyright protection that their own citizens receive. The central provision of the Universal Copyright Convention is that each member county is required to accord to the published works of nationals of any other member country the same protection as that accorded to works of its own citizens. Protection is also accorded to unpublished works. The author of a work protected under the Universal Copyright Convention has the exclusive right to publish or to authorize publication of translations of that work.

WIPO Copyright Treaty

The WIPO Copyright Treaty (WCT) is a 1996 treaty that made changes in the Berne Convention in light of the TRIPs Agreement and dealt with new copyright issues raised by the emergence of the Internet and other digital technology. The WIPO Treaty expressly protects computer software and databases and expressly excludes from protection ideas, procedures, methods of operation or mathematical concepts as such.

TRIPS Agreement

The U.S. entered into the Trade Related Aspects of International Property Rights Agreement (TRIPS Agreement) in 1999. 1869 U.N.T.S. 299, 33 I.L.M. 1197 (1994). The TRIPS Agreement, signed in 1994, came into force on January 1, 1995. As a result of the emergence of TRIPS, the main forum for rulemaking shifted from the World Intellectual Property Organization (WIPO) to the World Trade Organization (WTO), and the agreement transformed the substantive rules of previous international IP standards. Unable to resolve the issue of piracy of DVDs found in China, the United States initiated a WTO dispute against China in 2007 charging China with violating its obligations under the TRIPS Agreement. The United States brought three claims concerning copyright, customs, and criminal law. In January of 2009, the WTO panel found a number of shortcomings in the protection of IPRs in China that were incompatible with TRIPS obligations.[13] According to the WTO panel, it is a violation of TRIPS for China to refuse copyright protection of works that do not meet China's legal standards, but there was insufficient evidence to conclude that China's threshold for prosecution in its criminal law was a violation of TRIPS. China and the U.S. accepted the panel's findings, and China negotiated with the United States to implement the recommendations by March of 2010.

Prioritizing Resources and Organization for Intellectual Property Act

To help enforce copyright laws through the world, President George W. Bush signed into law the Prioritizing Resources and Organization for Intellectual Property Act of 2008 (PRO-IP Act), PL. 110-403, 122 Stat. 4256.[14] The PRO-IP Act strengthens border enforcement programs around the world, increases damages in criminal infringement cases, and creates a "copyright czar" within the Executive Office of the President who oversees the country's efforts to curb piracy and counterfeiting. The copyright czar or "IP Enforcement Representative" (also called "IP Enforcement Coordinator") is appointed by the president and approved by the Senate. On September 24, 2009, President Barack Obama appointed Victoria A. Espinel as the first U.S. Intellectual Property Enforcement Coordinator.

Summary

A copyright is a right protecting original works of authorship fixed in any tangible medium of expression, giving the holder the exclusive right to reproduce, adapt, distribute, perform, and display the work. Copyright law protects original content in the field of cyberspace, including websites, software, video games, music, and motion pictures. While not required, there are significant advantages for notice and registration of copyrights. For works created after 1978, copyright protection lasts for the life of the author plus seventy years and even longer for works made for hire. Defenses in a copyright infringement action include public domain use, the first sale doctrine, and the fair use doctrine. The four statutory factors in the fair use defense are (1) the purpose and character of the use, (2) the nature of the copyrighted work, (3) the amount of the work used, and (4) the economic impact of the use. The main purposes of the Digital Millennium Copyright Act (DMCA) are to protect copyright owners and respond to the increase in popularity and usage of digital content. The DMCA includes a safe harbor provision that allows websites and Internet service providers to avoid liability for copyright infringement after receiving a DMCA complaint. The Berne Convention, the Universal Copyright Convention, and the Trade Related Aspects of International Property Rights Agreement (TRIPS Agreement) are international treaties to protect the rights of U.S. copyright owners abroad.

Key Terms

Berne Convention *19*
copyright *18*
copyright infringement *24*
Copyright Term Extension Act (CTEA) *22*
derivative work *19*
fair use *28*
first sale doctrine *27*
intellectual property *16*
public domain *19*
transformative use *31*

Review Questions

1. What types of works are exempt from copyright protection? Give specific examples of websites that have content that is not protected by copyright law.
2. What is the duration of a copyright for a work made for hire?
3. What types of works are considered works for hire?
4. What are the benefits of copyright registration with the U.S. Copyright Office?
5. What are the four fair use defense factors? Provide examples of each factor.
6. What is the meaning in transformative use?
7. What is the safe harbor provision under the Digital Millennium Copyright Act?

Discussion Questions

1. The duration of rights for patents and copyrights are fixed by Congress and expire after a certain number of years. As a general rule, the duration of a copyright is the life of the author plus 70 years, and the duration of a design patent is 20 years from the date of application. Rights in trademarks and trade secrets, in contrast, can be perpetual. Why do you think that intellectual property rights in copyrights and patents expire, while intellectual property rights in trademarks and trade secrets can last indefinitely? Do you think that the duration of intellectual property rights should be extended or reduced? Why or why not? Does your position change if you are consumer rather than an author or inventor?
2. Works produced by the U.S. Government (including works produced by federal government employees within the scope of their employment) are not subject to copyright protection, while works produced by some state and local governments may receive copyright protection. Should works produced by employees of state and local governments receive copyright protection? Why or why not? Would you support or oppose proposed legislation in your state that would give copyright protection for works produced by state employee?

Exercises

1. You are working for the corporate legal department of XYZ Corporation. The associate general counsel for XYZ Corporation asks you to find out how to obtain copyright permission for a book published by Random House. Write a memorandum to your supervisor where you discuss the following: (1) where to locate the online copyright permissions form for Random House; (2) the address where the completed form should be mailed; and (3) how long it takes to receive a written response from Random House.
2. Go to the U.S. Copyright Office website and find the online Copyright Catalog for works created after 1978. The Copyright Office Catalog contains approximately 20 million records for works registered and documents recorded with the Copyright Office since 1978. Run a search for the novel *The Da Vinci Code* by Dan Brown first published by Doubleday in 2004. Then find derivative works for the novel, including the 2006 film directed by Ron Howard and the 2007 wall calendar by Columbia Pictures. Find the name of the work, author of the work, and copyright registration number from the U.S. Copyright Office for these works.
3. Go to the U.S. Copyright Office website and locate the paper form for copyright registration of sound recordings. What is the name of the form? What is the current filing fee? Can this completed form be filed electronically? How can authors submit the audio file to the Copyright Office?
4. You are the website owner and operator for www.acme.com (a fictitious website). The website includes tutorials for home improvement projects. After using a tool that searches the Internet for unauthorized use of copyrighted materials, you find that another website located at www.acme.net/page2.html that has copied the material you created. Acme.net also includes Google AdSense code on its webpage. Google AdSense is a program for web publishers who want to display advertising on webpages they control. Run a search on the Internet and find the Google AdSense DMCA complaint form and then draft a letter for a DMCA complaint to Google. The letter should include all of the information requested in the online form.
5. Run a search on the Internet and visit the website for the Google Book Search Copyright Class Action Settlement. Read the frequently asked questions (FAQs) about the lawsuit. What is the lawsuit about? What are the main terms and conditions of the settlement agreement? What are the rights of authors included in the class? Discuss any changes you would advise.
6. A publisher plans to release a new book written by a prominent politician. The publisher maintains strict control over the release of excerpts or other material from the book. For example, releases of advance copies to the media for review have been allowed only on the condition that no material from, or review of, the book be published until the book's release and all recipients of such copies have been required to sign nondisclosure agreements. The publisher finds that significant portions of the book are posted to a blog owned by an online media company. The online media company did not use the material to create anything new, but rather copied material in order to attract visitors to its blog. If more people visit the blog, the more compensation the online media company could seek from advertisers. The publisher moves for a temporary restraining, and the online media company argues that the fair use defense should apply. How would a court rule on the motion for a temporary restraining order and petition for a preliminary injunction? Discuss and apply each of the four fair use defense factors in your analysis. See *HarperCollins Publishers L.L.C. v. Gawker Media LLC*, 721 F. Supp. 2d 303 (S.D.N.Y. 2010).

Related Internet Sites

http://copyright.gov/
Official website of the U.S. Copyright Office

http://www.copyright.gov/circs/circ1.pdf/
Copyright Basic, Circular 1, U.S. Copyright Office

http://www.law.cornell.edu/uscode/
Full text of the United States Code (U.S.C.) maintained by the Legal Information Institute at the Cornell University Law School. The full text of The Copyright Act is codified in Title 17 of the United States Code.

http://fairuse.stanford.edu/
Stanford Copyright & Fair Use site that provides updates on newly filed copyright lawsuits, pending legislation, regulations, copyright office news, scholarly articles, and blog and twitter feeds from practicing attorneys and law professors. The site also includes court documents of district court cases that The Center for Internet and Society Fair Use Project is involved with as well as other cases of high interest.

http://topics.law.cornell.edu/wex/Copyright
Overview of Copyright Law provided by the Legal Information Institute (LII) at Cornell University Law School.

http://www.csusa.org/
The Copyright Society of the U.S.A. is a center of the U.S. copyright community for business people, lawyers in private practice and in-house, and law professors and law students who share a common interest in copyright and related intellectual property rights.

http://www.copyright.com/
The Copyright Clearance Center provides a service where individuals and organizations can request copyright permission to publishers for a fee.

http://www.bitlaw.com/copyright/
BitLaw website on copyright law and IP law maintained by lawyer Dan Tysver of the Minneapolis law firm of Beck & Tysver.

http://www.chicagoiplitigation.com/
Blog maintained by R. David Donoghue, partner with the law firm Holland & Knight in Chicago, that focuses on new developments in intellectual property law with an emphasis on IP law developments in the Northern District of Illinois.

http://www.denison.edu/library/copyright/podcasts.html
Podcasts by Denison University, Copyright in 90 Seconds, that provides information on copyright law. The podcasts are also available for free on iTunes.

http://www.copyscape.com/
Copyscape is a tool that searches the Internet for unauthorized use of copyrighted materials. Copyscape has professional solutions used by webmasters and content owners worldwide to check the originality of new content, prevent duplicate content, and track down copies of content on the web.

Endnotes

1. Black's Law Dictionary (9th ed. 2009).
2. U.S. Constitution, Article I, Section 8.
3. 17 U.S.C. § 106.
4. *Syntek Semiconductor Co., Ltd. v. Microchip Technology Inc.*, 307 F.3d 775 (9th Cir. 2002); *Sony Computer Entertainment, Inc. v. Connectix Corp.*, 203 F.3d 596, 180 A.L.R. Fed. 655 (9th Cir. 2000).
5. U.S. Copyright Office, Circular 3: Copyright Notice.
6. 17 U.S.C. § 101.
7. Sonny Bono Copyright Term Extension Act (CTEA), Pub. L. 105-298, 112 Stat. 2827 (1998).
8. Digital Millennium Copyright Act (DMCA), Pub. L. No. 105-304, 112 Stat. 2860.
9. 17 U.S.C. § 504.
10. Daniel Gervais, *The Regulation of Inchoate Technologies*, 47 Hous. L. Rev. 665, 689 (2010).
11. *Lifetime Homes, Inc. v. Residential Development Corp.*, 510 F. Supp. 2d 794, 807 (M.D. Fla. 2007).
12. See *Brilliance Audio, Inc. v. Haights Cross Communications, Inc.*, 474 F.3d 365, 372 (6th Cir. 2007).
13. Jung Yun (Jennifer) Yang, *Bringing the Question of Chinese IPR Enforcement to the WTO under TRIPS: An Effective Strategy or a Meaningless and Overused Tactic by the U.S.?*, 10 U. Pitt. J. Tech. L. & Pol'y 2 (2010).
14. Prioritizing Resources and Organization for Intellectual Property Act of 2008 (PRO-IP Act), Pub. L. No. 110-403, 122 Stat. 4256.

CHAPTER

3 Trademarks in E-Commerce

The essential purpose of trademark law is to prevent confusion [among consumers], not to bar new entrants into the market.

Spraying Systems Co. v. Delavan, Inc., 762 F. Supp. 772, 780 (N.D. Ill. 1991)

LEARNING OBJECTIVES

After completing this chapter, you will be able to:

1. Explain and define a trademark under the Lanham Act.
2. Explain the scope of trademark protection for Internet content, software, and other technology-related products and services.
3. Describe the marking requirements for trademarks, particularly for online content.
4. Explain the likelihood-of-confusion test for trademark infringement actions.
5. Explain the purpose of the Anticybersquatting Consumer Protection Act of 1999 and the Trademark Dilution Revision Act of 2006 (TDRA).

TRADEMARKS GENERALLY

In short, a **trademark** is a brand name. A trademark includes any word, name, symbol, device, or any combination, used, or intended to be used, in commerce to identify and distinguish the goods of one manufacturer or seller from goods manufactured or sold by others, and to indicate the source of the goods. The purpose of trademark law is to protect the public from confusion regarding the sources of goods or services and to protect businesses from the diversion of trade through the misrepresentation or appropriation of another's goodwill.[1]

The **Lanham Act** which governs trademarks, also called the federal Trademark Act or the United States Trademark Act, defines a *trademark* as any word, name, symbol, or device, or any combination thereof used to identify and distinguish one's goods from those manufactured or sold by others and to indicate the source of the goods.[2] Under the Uniform Deceptive Trade Practices Act (UDTPA), a *trademark* is a mark used by a person to identify goods and to distinguish them from the goods of others. The UDTPA defines a *mark* as a word, name, symbol, device, or any combination thereof in any form or arrangement.

Lanham Act
The federal statute, found in Title 15 United States Code, that governs the law of trademarks. Also called the United States Trademark Act.

A *trade name* is a distinctive word, name, symbol, or other designation that identifies and distinguishes a business from the businesses of others. Under the Lanham Act, the terms *trade name* and *commercial name* mean any name used by a person to identify his business or vocation.[3]

The term **service mark** under the Lanham Act, includes any word, name, symbol, or device, or any combination thereof (1) used by a person, or (2) which a person has a bona fide intention to use in commerce to identify and distinguish the services of one person, including a unique service, from the services of others and to indicate the source of the services, even if that source is unknown.[4] A service mark is a word, logo, phrase, or device used to indicate the source, quality, and ownership of a service. The term *service* does not apply to services that are solely for benefit of the performer, but, rather, the services must be rendered to others. Service marks are intended to identify and afford protection to things of an intangible nature, such as services, as distinguished from the protection already provided for marks affixed to things of a tangible nature, such as goods and products. Service marks are common in the online environment and may be the subject of litigation. For example, the service mark Buddy List became the subject of a dispute involving American Online, Inc. (AOL) and AT&T Corporation (AT&T).[5]

Service Mark
A word, logo, phrase, or device used to indicate the source, quality, and ownership of a service.

There are countless trade names and service marks used in e-commerce today. (See Figure 3.1.) Owners and operators of websites, online content, and software can use and market a variety of marks. For example, the trade name "you've got mail" is a registered trademark owned by AOL. Many companies have successfully registered and protected ownership interests in a ".com" trade name. Technology giants such as Cisco, Google, Microsoft, and Yahoo! each have ownership interest in numerous trademarks used in e-commerce.

Trademark	Status	Generic Descriptor(s)
AIM	®	Messaging service; software
American Online	®	Service; software
America Online Logo	®	Service; software
America Takes It Off	®	Service
AOL	®	Service; software
AOL Music Now	™	Service
AOL Music Now Logo	™	Service
AOLBuddy	®	Feature
Buddy List	®	Feature; service; window
Customers List This	™	Service
DigitalCity	®	Service
EnjoySavings	®	Service
FinAIM	®	Service

(Continued)

(*Continued*)

Trademark	Status	Generic Descriptor(s)
ICQ	®	Program; software; service
Lightningcast	®	Software; hardware
Mapquest	®	Software; publication; service
Mapquest.com	®	Software; publication; service
Mapquest Logo	®	Software; publication; service
Moviefone	®	Service
Netscape	®	Software; publication; service
Safety Clicks	™	Software; service
Superbuddy	®	Icons
TripQuest	®	Service
Vplex	®	Service
You've Got AOL	®	Computer program; service
You've Got Mail	®	Computer program; service
You've Got Pictures	®	Publication; service
You've Got Prizes	™	Service

FIGURE 3.1 Below is a list of selected trademarked owned by AOL. For a complete list, visit http://about.aol.com/aolnetwork/trademarks.

ACQUISITION OF A TRADEMARK

To establish the right to trademark protection under the Lanham Act, a plaintiff must show that it has actually used the designation at issue as a trademark. The mere adoption of a mark without bona fide use, in an attempt to reserve it for the future, does not create trademark rights.[6] Trademark or service mark ownership is not acquired by federal or state registration. Rather, ownership rights flow only from the prior appropriation and actual use in the market.[7] For websites, the standard rule applies that a word buried in the middle of text in an advertisement or order form is not a trademark use. For example, there is no trademark use of a word buried in the text of a website from which a product could be ordered.

In 2007, a federal district court in New York considered a case brought by the owner of the trademark "FragranceNet.com" against a competitor that used the name "FragranceX.com" for alleged misuse of a trademark.[8] The court held that defendant who operated the FrangenceX.com website did not "use" the trademark "FragranceNet.com," for Lanham Act purposes, by using the trademark as a keyword to prompt competitor's appearance as a sponsored link in Google's search engine or by including the trademark as a metatag on the competitor's website. The defendant competitor did not place the trademark on any product, good, or service, and the trademark was not used in any way that would indicate source or origin. Therefore, to prevail in a trademark infringement action, the plaintiff must show that the defendant actually placed and used the trademark in commerce.

United States Patent and Trademark Office (USPTO or PTO) Federal agency within the U.S. Department of Commerce charged with registering trademarks and granting patents.

REGISTRATION OF TRADEMARKS

The **United States Patent and Trademark Office (USPTO or PTO)** is the federal agency for granting U.S. patents and registering trademarks. The USPTO registers trademarks based on the Commerce Clause of the Constitution (Article 1, Section 8, Clause 3). Each registration remains in force for 10 years and each registration may be renewed for another 10 years. Provided the trademark continues to be used in commerce, trademark protection may last indefinitely. Some trademarks are more than 100 years old, such as Nabisco's Cream of Wheat logo with a chef holding a bowl of hot cereal and Pabst Milwaukee Blue Ribbon Beer.[9] Nearly 1 million registered trademarks are in use today, including the oldest U.S. trademark still in use, SAMSON, with the design of a man and a lion, registered on May 27, 1884, for use on cords, line and rope.

The owner of a trademark used in commerce may register the trademark under the Lanham Act in the Principal Register.[10] The **Principal Register**, maintained by the USPTO, is the list of distinctive marks approved for federal trademark registration. Applicants for trademark registration file an electronic application through the **Trademark Electronic Application System (TEAS)**. Only one mark is permissible per application, although a mark may consist of several elements that are joined to form a composite whole (e.g., words plus a design). During the registration process, marks appear in the Official Gazette. **The Official Gazette for Trademarks (OG)** is published each Tuesday by the USPTO, and contains bibliographic information and a representative drawing for each mark published, along with a list of cancelled and renewed registrations. The OG is available in electronic form (.pdf format) for the most recent fifty-two (52) issues on the USPTO website. Information about each mark may also be found in the comprehensive, searchable trademark database, which is updated daily and accessible directly from the home page of the USPTO website. The USPTO also publishes the Official Gazette for Patents. All marks capable of distinguishing goods or services and not able to be registered on the Principal Register may be registered in the Supplemental Register if they have been in lawful use in commerce for at least one year preceding the application.

While registration is not required, federal registration has several advantages, including a notice to the public of the registrant's claim of ownership of the mark, a legal presumption of ownership nationwide, and the exclusive right to use the mark on or in connection with the goods or services set forth in the registration.[11] Registration of a mark on the Principal Register is constructive notice of the claim of ownership thereof, and a strong presumption of validity is created by registration of a mark under the federal trademark laws. Registration creates a rebuttable presumption of the mark's validity.

The USPTO has created the **Trademark Electronic Search System (TESS)**, an online search engine that allows visitors to search the USPTO's database of registered trademarks and prior pending applications, to find marks that may prevent registration due to a likelihood-of-confusion refusal. Before filing an application for registration, applicants will need to search the Trademark Electronic Search System (TESS) to verify that similar marks are not already in existence.

If the USPTO examiner denies an application for registration, the applicant can appeal the decision before the **USPTO Trademark Trial and Appeal Board (TTAB)**. The TTAB, an administrative board within the USPTO, hears and decides adversary proceedings. The TTAB also handles appeals of final refusals issued by USPTO examining attorneys within the course of the prosecution of applications. An applicant that seeks to appeal the decision of the TTAB can also seek judicial review in the court system. The U.S. Court of Appeals for the Federal Circuit has appellate jurisdiction over applications for the registration of marks and other related proceedings. The U.S. Court of Appeals for the Federal Circuit will usually have final say since the U.S. Supreme Court rarely considers cases involving registration of trademarks.

The U.S. Court of Appeals for the Federal Circuit considered the rejected trademark registration for a website in the case *In re Sones*, 590 F.3d 1282 (Fed. Cir. 2009). The applicant appealed a decision of the TTAB denying registration application for the mark "ONE NATION UNDER GOD" for charity bracelets sold on a website. The federal appeals court reversed the decision of the TTAB and held that a picture is not a mandatory requirement for a website-based specimen of use under trademark law. The court held that the test for an acceptable website-based specimen, just as any other

Principal Register
Publication maintained by the USPTO, that lists distinctive marks approved for federal trademark registration.

Trademark Electronic Application System (TEAS)
The USPTO's system for electronic filing of trademark documents, including applications for trademarks.

Official Gazette for Trademarks (OG)
The weekly publication of the USPTO of trademarks for purposes of opposition that contains bibliographic information and a representative drawing for each mark published, along with a list of cancelled and renewed registrations.

Trademark Electronic Search System (TESS)
The USPTO's online search engine allows visitors to search the USPTO's database of registered trademarks and prior pending applications.

Trademark Trial and Appeal Board (TTAB)
An administrative board within the USPTO that hears and decides adversary proceedings between two parties, namely, oppositions (party opposes a mark after publication in the Official Gazette) and cancellations (party seeks to cancel an existing registration). The TTAB also handles interference and concurrent use proceedings, as well as appeals of final refusals issued by USPTO examining attorneys within the course of the prosecution of applications.

specimen, is simply that it must in some way evince that the mark is "associated" with the goods and serves as an indicator of source.

Trade Name
A name used to identify a company or business.

To trademark the name of a website, the **trade name** must not be generic. The U.S. Court of Appeals for the Federal Circuit rejected the application to trademark the name "Hotels.com" in the case of *In re Hotels.com, L.P.*, 573 F.3d 1300 (Fed. Cir. 2009) (Case 3.1) finding the name too generic and therefore a name that cannot be a trademark or service mark.

CASE 3.1

The Case of the Generic Tradename

In re Hotels.com, L.P., ***573 F.3d 1300 (Fed. Cir. 2009)***

On application for registration on the Principal Register, the examiner denied registration on the ground that HOTELS.COM is merely descriptive of hotel reservation services, and that the applicant's evidence was insufficient to show acquired distinctiveness under Section 2(f) of the Lanham Trademark Act. The examiner also stated that the proposed mark appeared to be generic. The TTAB affirmed the rejection, but on the ground that HOTELS.COM is a generic term for hotel information and reservations, and that the "dot-com" shows internet commerce and does not convert the generic term "hotels" into a brand name.

The TTAB explained that the word "hotels" "identifies the central focus of the information and reservation services provided on applicant's website," and concluded that "the term HOTELS.COM, consisting of nothing more than a term that names that central focus of the services, is generic for the services themselves." The TTAB stated that addition of the dot-com domain designation does not impart registrability to a generic term.

Standards of Proof and Review

Whether a particular term is generic, and therefore cannot be a trademark or service mark, is a question of fact. The Patent and Trademark Office (PTO) bears the burden of establishing that a proposed mark is generic, and must demonstrate generic status by clear evidence.

Discussion

A generic term cannot be registered as a trademark, for generic terms by definition are incapable of indicating source. However, a term that is descriptive, but not generic, may acquire distinctiveness and serve as a trademark. "Whether a term is entitled to trademark status turns on how the mark is understood by the purchasing public." *In re Montrachet S.A.,* 878 F.2d 375, 376 (Fed. Cir. 1989). In the generic-descriptive-suggestive-arbitrary-fanciful continuum of words and their usage as marks of trade, there is no fixed boundary separating the categories; each word must be considered according to its circumstances.

The applicant argues that the Board's approach was fundamentally flawed, because the proposed mark is not "hotels," but HOTELS.COM. The applicant states that the dot-com component of HOTELS.COM negates any generic nature of the word "hotels," and that the mark, viewed in its entirety, is not a generic name but an indicator of the applicant's services. The applicant further argues that HOTELS.COM is not a generic term for a hotel, but is used to indicate an information source and travel agency. Citing *Merrill Lynch*, 828 F.2d at 1571, the applicant argues that HOTELS.COM does not "immediately and unequivocally describe [ ] the purpose and function of appellant's goods" and therefore is not the generic name for those goods. The applicant points out that the context in which a term is used is evidence of how the term is perceived by prospective customers, and that the dot-com domain name is a significant aspect of the context of HOTELS.COM, negating the genericness finding. The applicant points to its survey evidence, and states that on the entirety of the record there was not clear evidence that the mark is generic.

The TTAB relied on definitions, websites, and similar "hotel" domain names, and criticized the proffered rebuttal evidence. The TTAB cited various definitions of "hotel," and various search printouts showing "hotels" as the equivalent of or included within "temporary lodging."

The TTAB started its analysis with dictionary, encyclopedia, and thesaurus definitions of "hotel," "temporary lodging," and ".com." For example, the American Heritage Dictionary of the English Language defines "hotel" as: "An establishment that provides lodging and usually meals and other services for travelers and other paying guests," and defines ".com" as: "ABBREVIATION: commercial organization (in Internet addresses)." The TTAB included these definitions in its evidence that "hotels" and ".com" name the services provided.

The TTAB also discussed printouts from various websites providing information about hotels and reservations, as showing that such sites are referred to as "hotel information sites" and "hotel reservation sites." The TTAB listed several sites that combine "hotels" and ".com," including www.all-hotels.com ("Hotels, travel, discount hotels-reservations and lodgings"); www.web-hotels.com ("hotel reservations and bookings"); www.dealsonhotels.com ("Low Internet Hotel Rates Guaranteed").

The TTAB found that hotels are the "focus" of the applicant's services, citing the applicant's advertisements. The TTAB found that the word "hotels" "names a key aspect of applicant's services, i.e., that aspect of applicant's information services and reservation services that deal with hotels," and concluded that HOTELS.COM is properly viewed in the same way and having the same meaning as the word "hotels" by itself. The TTAB found that the composite term HOTELS.COM communicates no more than the common meanings of the individual components, that is, that the applicant operates a commercial website via the internet, that provides information about hotels, but adds nothing as an indication of source. The TTAB concluded that the combination of HOTELS and .COM does not produce a new meaning in combination.

We agree with the TTAB that for the mark here at issue, the generic term "hotels" did not lose its generic character by placement in the domain name HOTELS.COM. See *Reed Elsevier,* 482 F.3d at 1377 (holding that LAWYERS.COM is generic for services provided by lawyers for "providing an online interactive database featuring information exchange in the fields of law, legal news, and legal services" encompasses the generic services provided by lawyers).

We conclude that the Board satisfied its evidentiary burden, by demonstrating that the separate terms "hotel" and ".com" in combination have a meaning identical to the common meaning of the separate components. The Board's finding that HOTELS.COM is generic was supported by substantial evidence. The refusal of the registration is AFFIRMED.

Case Questions

1. Why did the court agree with the decision of the Trademark Trial and Appeals Board (TTAB) that the name HOTELS.COM is too generic term to be registered as a trademark?
2. What evidence did the Trademark Trial and Appeals Board (TTAB) consider in the case? Why did the TTAB and court reject this rebuttal evidence?
3. Why is distinctiveness under Section 2(f) of the Lanham Trademark Act required for trademark registration?

Website owners and operators that hope to trademark .com, .net, .org, or .info **domain names** should ensure that the name is not too generic. To receive trademark protection, a company may need to come up with a new trade name and market the mark to customers. For example, in May 2009, Microsoft released Bing as a new trade name for its new Internet search engine. In October 2010, Microsoft filed an application with the USPTO to register "BING" as a word mark for computer services in the nature of providing search engines for obtaining data over computer networks, the Internet, and wireless networks.

Domain Name
The words and characters that website owners designate for their registered Internet addresses.

Along with federal registration of trademarks, many states allow for registration of trademarks. As with federal registration, registration of a trademark at the state level does not create or confer any additional substantive rights. Rather, the effect of registration merely recognizes rights that have already been acquired. The purpose of state registration

Registered Marks
Acceptable notice that a mark is registered with the USPTO:
"®"
"Registered, U.S. Patent and Trademark Office" or
"Reg. U.S. Pat. & Tm. Off."
Unregistered Marks
Acceptable notice for unregistered marks:
"TM" (unregistered trademark)
"SM" (unregistered service mark)

FIGURE 3.2 Trademark Notice

of trademarks is to give additional protection to the owner of the mark, and also to prevent duplication and confusion in the adoption and use of trademarks.

MARKING REQUIREMENTS

The federal registration symbol consists of the letter R enclosed within a circle—®—with the mark. The registration symbol may be used once the mark is actually registered in the USPTO. Even though an application is pending, the registration symbol may not be used before the mark has actually become registered. The federal registration symbol should only be used on goods or services that are the subject of the federal trademark registration.

Use of the symbols "TM" for trademarks and "SM" for service marks are not governed by federal regulations but may be governed by local, state, or foreign laws. These designations usually indicate that a party claims rights in the mark and are often used before a federal registration is issued. Merely adding the symbol "TM" or "SM" onto a word, absent other indicia of proper usage, will not transform a non-trademark use into a trademark or service mark use. (See Figure 3.2.) Courts have held that improper use of the ® symbol, when used with the intent to mislead the public into believing that the trademark is registered, is grounds for denying the registration of an otherwise registrable trademark. Additionally, use of the ® symbol with unregistered trademarks may constitute false advertising.

TRADEMARK INFRINGEMENT

A trademark owner may file a lawsuit if a person, company, or entity infringes on a trademark.[12] This is also called a trademark infringement action. A party may be liable for trademark infringement under the Lanham Act if the plaintiff establishes that (1) the plaintiff has a valid mark that is entitled to protection under the Lanham Act; and that (2) the defendant used the mark, (3) in commerce, (4) in connection with the sale . . . or advertising of goods or services, . . . without the plaintiff's consent."

Likelihood-of-Confusion Test
A test for trademark infringement, based on the probability that a substantial number of ordinarily prudent buyers will be misled or confused about the source of a product.

In deciding whether a defendant has infringed on a trademark, courts apply the **likelihood-of-confusion test** between the two marks. Courts generally consider the following factors in the likelihood of confusion test: (1) the degree of similarity between the marks; (2) the intent of the alleged infringer in using the mark; (3) evidence of actual confusion; (4) similarity of products and manner of marketing; (5) the degree of care likely to be exercised by purchasers; and (6) the strength or weakness of the marks. As in any ordinary civil litigation, the plaintiff bears the burden of proving by a preponderance of the evidence that a likelihood of confusion exists.[13] Surveys of customers are routinely admitted in trademark cases to show confusion and establish that certain associations have been drawn in the public mind.[14] Actual consumer confusion may be shown by direct evidence, diversion of sales or direct testimony from public, or by circumstantial evidence such as consumer surveys.[15]

Contributory Trademark Infringement

Contributory trademark infringement is a judicially created doctrine that derives from the common law of torts. The seminal or leading U.S. Supreme Court dealing with the topic of contributory trademark infringement is *Inwood Laboratories, Inc. v. Ives Laboratories, Inc.*, 456 U.S. 844 (1982). In *Tiffany (NJ) Inc. v. eBay Inc.*, 600 F.3d 93 (2nd Cir. 2010) (Case 3.2), the U.S. Court of Appeals for the Second Circuit applied the holding in *Inwood* and considered

CASE 3.2

The Case of the Counterfeit Merchandise Sold on eBay

Tiffany (NJ) Inc. v. eBay Inc., *600 F.3d 93 (2nd Cir. 2010)*

Facts

Sometime before 2004, Tiffany became aware that counterfeit Tiffany merchandise was being sold on eBay's site. Prior to and during the course of this litigation, Tiffany conducted two surveys known as "Buying Programs," one in 2004 and another in 2005, in an attempt to assess the extent of this practice. Under those programs, Tiffany bought various items on eBay and then inspected and evaluated them to determine how many were counterfeit. Tiffany found that 73.1% of the purported Tiffany goods purchased in the 2004 Buying Program and 75.5% of those purchased in the 2005 Buying Program were counterfeit.

Contributory Trademark Infringement

The more difficult issue, and the one that the parties have properly focused our attention on, is whether eBay is liable for contributory trademark infringement—i.e., for culpably facilitating the infringing conduct of the counterfeiting vendors. Acknowledging the paucity of case law to guide us, we conclude that the district court correctly granted judgment on this issue in favor of eBay.

Contributory trademark infringement is a judicially created doctrine that derives from the common law of torts. The Supreme Court most recently dealt with the subject in *Inwood Laboratories, Inc. v. Ives Laboratories, Inc.*, 456 U.S. 844, 102 S.Ct. 2182, 72 L.Ed.2d 606 (1982). There, the plaintiff, Ives, asserted that several drug manufacturers had induced pharmacists to mislabel a drug the defendants produced to pass it off as Ives'. According to the Court, "if a manufacturer or distributor intentionally induces another to infringe a trademark, or if it continues to supply its product to one whom it knows or has reason to know is engaging in trademark infringement, the manufacturer or distributor is contributorially responsible for any harm done as a result of the deceit."

For contributory trademark infringement liability to lie, a service provider must have more than a general knowledge or reason to know that its service is being used to sell counterfeit goods. Some contemporary knowledge of which particular listings are infringing or will infringe in the future is necessary.

[W]e agree with the district court that "Tiffany's general allegations of counterfeiting failed to provide eBay with the knowledge required under *Inwood*." *Tiffany*, 576 F.Supp.2d at 511. Tiffany's demand letters and Buying Programs did not identify particular sellers who Tiffany thought were then offering or would offer counterfeit goods. And although the NOCIs and buyer complaints gave eBay reason to know that certain sellers had been selling counterfeits, those sellers' listings were removed and repeat offenders were suspended from the eBay site. Thus Tiffany failed to demonstrate that eBay was supplying its service to individuals who it knew or had reason to know were selling counterfeit Tiffany goods. Accordingly, we affirm the judgment of the district court insofar as it holds that eBay is not contributorially liable for trademark infringement.

(Continued)

(Continued)

Case Questions

1. What are the requirements to prove contributory trademark infringement liability for a website or service provider?
2. Following the policies established by eBay, what can other website owners and operators do when they find out a user has sold counterfeit products?
3. Discuss whether Tiffany could and should create its own online auction website to sell Tiffany products to compete with eBay.

whether eBay, the online auction website, engaged in contributory trademark infringement of Tiffany-branded jewelry. The court held that eBay's use of Tiffany's jewelry mark on its website and in sponsored links did not constitute direct trademark infringement. The Second Circuit also held that eBay's generalized knowledge of infringement of Tiffany's trademark on its website was not sufficient to impose upon eBay an affirmative duty to remedy the problem. Thus, eBay was not found not liable for contributory trademark infringement for facilitating the infringing conduct of counterfeiting vendors.

Banner-Advertising, Linking, and Pop-Up Advertising

The common practice among search engines, such as Google and Yahoo!, in selling the use of trademarks as key words and banner advertising raises questions under trademark law. Internet search engines, such as Google, sell "keywords" to companies. The result is that when a user enters such a keyword in Google's search engine, the search displays the usual list of results along with "sponsored links" to the companies that bought the right to have their link appear.

In April 2009, in the case of *Rescuecom Corp. v. Google Inc.*, 562 F.3d 123 (2nd Cir. 2009), the U.S. Court of Appeals for Second Circuit considered whether Google's sale of trademarks as AdWords constituted a violation of the Lanham Act for infringement, false designation of origin, and dilution of Rescuecom's trademark. The court held that Google's practice of recommending and selling to advertisers computer services franchising company's trademark as a search term to trigger advertisers' sponsored links each time Internet users searched company's trademark was a "use in commerce" under the Lanham Act. If Internet users entered the Rescuecom trademark into their Google search, they were exposed to advertisements by Rescuecom's competitors and links to their websites. When Rescuecom Corp. brought suit against Google, the district court dismissed the Lanham Act claims but the Second Circuit held that the sale of Rescuecom's trademark and its use as an AdWord indeed satisfied the requirement for use of commerce. The court in *Rescuecom* was careful to note that it was only dealing with a threshold question of whether the trademark was in "use." The plaintiff in a keyword case must also show likelihood of confusion. The *Rescuecom* case has resulted in numerous other lawsuits against Google in the United States and abroad.[16]

The practice of linking to other websites, deep-linking to other websites, and using pop-up advertisements raises questions under trademark law. In *Wyatt Technology Corp. v. Smithson*, 345 Fed.Appx. 236 (9th Cir. 2009), a federal appeals court held that the fact that a website with a trademarked domain name contained a link to a commercial business was sufficient to show a use of the mark in connection with the sale of goods for purposes of establishing trademark infringement claim.[17] Therefore, website owners and operators should take preventive measures and use caution with linking to other websites with trademarked domain names.

The use of trademarks in pop-up advertisements on the web has also been the subject of litigation. In *1-800 Contacts, Inc. v. WhenU.Com, Inc.*, 414 F.3d 400, 406–407 (2nd Cir. 2005), the defendant's software used the plaintiff's trademark to generate pop-up ads. When users visited the website for 1-800 Contacts, competitors' ads would pop up on the user's screen. The district court awarded 1-800 a preliminary injunction, but the Second Circuit reversed, finding that "WhenU does not 'use' 1-800's trademarks within the meaning of the Lanham Act."[18] Of key importance was the fact that the pop-up ads never showed 1-800's trademark and the ads were always in new windows, making customer confusion unlikely. The use of metatags, banner advertising, linking, and pop-up advertising will likely be the subject of trademark infringement cases for years to come and courts will continue to examine these issues and apply traditional trademark law to these applications.

Trademark Dilution

Trademark **dilution** is the impairment of a famous trademark's strength, effectiveness, or distinctiveness through the use of the mark on an unrelated product, usually blurring the trademark's distinctive character or tarnishing it with an unsavory association.[19] The elements of trademark dilution are (1) ownership of a famous mark and (2) actual dilution. Trademark dilution may occur even when the use is not competitive and when it creates no likelihood of confusion.

Dilution
Unauthorized acts that tend to blur the distinctiveness of a famous mark or to tarnish it.

Marks are adjectives, and should be used only as such. Trademark owners should avoid using marks as nouns or verbs. Over time, using a mark as a noun or verb can result in genericness, or a finding of unintentional abandonment. For example, owners of marks such as *Coke*®, *Kleenex*®, *Xerox*®, and *FedEx*®, expend considerable efforts to educate the public concerning the proper use of marks.

Trademark Dilution Revision Act of 2006

Congress enacted the **Trademark Dilution Revision Act of 2006 (TDRA)** to clarify the scope of trademark dilution, and to overturn the holding of the U.S. Supreme Court in *Mosley v. V Secret Catalogue, Inc.*, 537 U.S. 418 (2003), which required plaintiffs to establish proof of "actual dilution."[20] Now, a plaintiff needs to only establish a "likelihood of dilution." The TDRA identifies a number of statutory factors to consider when determining whether plaintiff's mark is famous: (1) the duration, extent and geographic reach of advertising and publicity of the mark, whether advertised or publicized by the owner or third parties; (2) the amount, volume, and geographic extent of sales of goods or services offered under the mark; (3) the extent of actual recognition of the mark, and (4) whether the mark was registered on the principal register with the USPTO.[21] In order for a mark to be considered "famous," the mark must be widely recognized by the general consuming public as a designation of source of the goods and services of the mark's owner. For the text of the Trademark Dilution Revision Act of 2006, Pub. L. No. 109-312, 120 Stat 1730, see Appendix B at the end of the book.

Trademark Dilution Revision Act (TDRA)
Law passed by Congress in 2006 to overturn the holding of the U.S. Supreme Court in *Mosley v. V Secret Catalogue, Inc.*, 537 U.S. 418 (2003), which required plaintiffs to establish proof of "actual dilution." Now, a plaintiff needs to only establish a "likelihood of dilution." The TDRA identifies a number of statutory factors to consider when determining whether plaintiff's mark is famous.

Remedies for Trademark Infringement

An injunction is the usual and standard remedy once trademark infringement has been found. Courts have the power to issue a temporary restraining order (TRO), temporary injunction, or a permanent injunction. A preliminary or temporary injunction may be issued where necessary to prevent substantial and irreparable injury to the plaintiff. For a permanent injunction in a trademark infringement action, the plaintiff must demonstrate under 15 U.S.C. § 1116 the following: (1) that the plaintiff has suffered an irreparable injury; (2) that remedies available at law, such as monetary damages, are inadequate to compensate for that injury; (3) that, considering the balance of hardships between the

Legal researchers can use the West Key Number Digest to find Internet related trademark infringement cases by the using West Key Number 382Tk1435. Run a search on Westlaw in cases for "382Tk1435" or browse the West Key Number Digest under the heading for:

382T Trademarks
382TVIII Violations of Rights
382TVIII(A) In General
382Tk1435 k. Internet use.

FIGURE 3.3 Researching Internet Related Trademark Infringement Cases

plaintiff and defendant, a remedy in equity is warranted; and (4) that the public interest would not be disserved by a permanent injunction.

In *Internet Specialties West, Inc. v. Milon-DiGiorgio Enterprises, Inc.*, 559 F.3d 985 (9th Cir. 2009), a federal appeals court affirmed a permanent injunction sought by an Internet service provider, that used the domain name "ISWest.com" action against a competitor that used the domain name "ISPWest.com." The appeals court held that the injunction issued by the trial court was not overbroad and the injunction was properly fashioned to prevent likelihood of confusion among consumers.

In addition to injunctive relief, the Lanham Act also permits courts to award monetary damages to trademark owners. The Lanham Act allows the plaintiff to recover (1) the defendant's profits, (2) any damages sustained by the plaintiff, and (3) the costs of the action, including attorney's fees. The Lanham Act also allows for enhanced statutory damages for willful infringement. In *Gucci America, Inc. v. Tyrrell-Miller*, 678 F.Supp.2d 117 (S.D.N.Y. 2008), an Internet vendor's sale of counterfeit Gucci handbags was willful, and the court warranted an imposition of $3 million in enhanced statutory damages in a trademark infringement action. The vendor persisted in selling counterfeit Gucci handbags for months after being informed of her infringement, and fifteen trademarks were involved in the case. This persistence in selling the counterfeit handbags was a factor in awarding the enhanced statutory damages.

DEFENSES TO INFRINGEMENT OF TRADEMARKS

Defendants in trademark infringement lawsuits may claim a variety of defenses, including the First Amendment and parody, laches, unclean hands, and fraud in obtaining trademark registration.

First Amendment and Parody

Parody is a recognized form of free speech protected by the First Amendment.[22] A parody is a use of a well-known work for purposes of satirizing, ridiculing, critiquing, or commenting on the original work, as opposed to merely alluding to the original to draw attention to the later work. A parody of a trademark is not an affirmative defense to an infringement charge. Rather, parody is a way of arguing that there will be no trademark infringement because there will be no likelihood of confusion.

Many websites that use trademarks may claim parody as a defense. In *Smith v. Wal-Mart Stores, Inc.*, 537 F.Supp.2d 1302 (N.D.Ga. 2008), a federal judge sided with a Georgia man whose satirical websites, now available at www.walocaust.com, likens retail giant Wal-Mart to the Holocaust. Smith arranged for some of his designs to be printed on T-shirts and other items like mugs, underwear, camisoles, teddy bears, bumper stickers, and bibs. The court held that Smith's designs were parodies that did not create any likelihood of confusion or dilution of Wal-Mart's trademarks. Similarly, in *Mattel, Inc. v. Walking Mountain Productions*, 353 F.3d 792 (9th Cir. 2003), the court recognized that a commercial artist's parody and use of the toy "Barbie" mark in titles of photographs on his website was noncommercial speech protected by First Amendment.

Laches

The defendant in a trademark infringement action may also assert the defense of **laches**. Black's Law Dictionary (9th ed. 2009) defines laches as "the unreasonable delay in pursuing a right or claim in a way that prejudices the party against whom relief is sought." The mere passage of time is not sufficient to constitute laches. In determining whether the laches defense applies in a trademark infringement case under the Lanham Act, the court determines whether (1) the plaintiff's delay in bringing suit was unreasonable, and (2) whether the defendant was prejudiced or harmed by the delay.

Laches
An unreasonable delay in asserting one's rights that causes prejudice or harm to another; a common defense asserted in intellectual property infringement actions.

The U.S. Court of Appeals for the Ninth Circuit considered whether the defense of laches applied in a case brought by an Internet service provider in *Internet Specialties West, Inc. v. Milon-DiGiorgio Enterprises, Inc.*[23] The plaintiff that used the domain name "ISWest.com" and became aware that a competitor used the domain name "ISPWest.com" offered Internet access, e-mail, and web hosting in same geographic area under remarkably similar names. The defendant asserted the defense of laches but the court rejected this defense and held that the defendant competitor with the domain name "ISPWest.com" was not prejudiced by the ISWest's delay in bringing the action alleging infringement of the "ISWest.com" trademark. The defense of laches is related to the statute of limitations but is considered a separate doctrine. The laches doctrine holds that even if the delay is for a shorter period of time than that of the statute, it may still bar equitable relief if it is unreasonable and prejudicial to the defendant. One federal judge wrote in an opinion that a trademark owner should not be held responsible for delay and laches if it does not immediately find an infringement on the Internet as soon as it is posted to a website.

Unclean Hands

The doctrine of **unclean hands** is a possible affirmative defense in a trademark infringement suit under the Lanham Act if the trademark owner has acted with "bad intent." The affirmative defense of unclean hands is frequently invoked, but rarely succeeds in light of the strict requirements. To show that a trademark plaintiff's conduct is inequitable and for the unclean hands doctrine to apply, the defendant must show that the plaintiff used the trademark to deceive consumers. In *Perfumebay.com Inc. v. EBAY, Inc.*, 506 F.3d 1165, 1178 (9th Cir. 2007), the court held that the plaintiff's various forms of the mark "Perfumebay" did not infringe on the defendant's mark for "eBay." The court held that there was no evidence of "bad intent" necessary to for the unclean hands defense to apply.

Unclean Hands
A defense often raised in infringement actions; an assertion that the plaintiff's own wrongful conduct precludes recovery and relief.

Fraud in Obtaining Trademark Registration

Fraud and misrepresentation by the plaintiff in obtaining registration is another possible defense in a trademark infringement action. Even if the defendant succeeds in proving that the plaintiff's registration was fraudulently obtained, the plaintiff's common law rights in the mark continue and may warrant an injunction against an infringing defendant.[24] Fraud on the USPTO in connection with trademark registration requires the following:

1. The challenged statement was a false representation regarding a material fact.
2. The person making the representation knew that the representation was false.
3. An intent to deceive the USPTO.

4. Reasonable reliance on the misrepresentation.
5. Damage proximately resulting from such reliance.[25]

DOMAIN NAME DISPUTES

Domain name disputes and cybersquatting remain at the heart of many trademark disputes in cyberspace. A domain name consists of the words and characters that website owners designate for their registered Internet addresses.[26] Cybersquatting is the act of reserving a domain name on the Internet, especially a name that would be associated with a company's trademark, and then seeking to profit by selling or licensing the name to the company that has an interest in being identified with it.[27] The two most important regulatory frameworks for resolving domain name disputes are the ICANN Uniform Domain Name Dispute Resolution Policy (UDRP) and the Anticybersquatting Consumer Protection Act (ACPA), 15 U.S.C. § 1125.

ICANN (Internet Corporation for Assigned Names and Numbers) Nonprofit corporation that oversees domain names.

Uniform Domain Name Dispute Resolution Policy (UDRP) The dispute resolution policy adopted by ICANN.

Anticybersquatting Consumer Protection Act (ACPA) A 1999 federal law authorizing a trademark owner to obtain a federal-court order transferring ownership of a domain name from a cybersquatter to the trademark owner. Also called Trademark Cyberpiracy Prevention Act. 15 U.S.C. § 1125.

On November 25, 1998, the U.S. Department of Commerce officially recognized **ICANN (Internet Corporation for Assigned Names and Numbers)**, a nonprofit corporation that oversees domain names, as the global, nonprofit consensus organization designated to carry on administration of the Internet name and address system, also known as the DNS (Domain Name System). As of January 2000, all global top level registrars had adopted the ICANN **Uniform Domain Name Dispute Resolution Policy (UDRP)**.[28] The UDRP applies to all accredited registrars in the .biz, .com, .info, .name, .net, and .org top-level domains. All those who reserve a domain name in one of those top level domains must agree to abide by the dispute resolution policy.

In 1999, Congress adopted the **Anticybersquatting Consumer Protection Act (ACPA)**, also called the Trademark Cyberpiracy Prevention Act, to prohibit cybersquatting.[29] The Act authorizes trademark owners to obtain a federal-court order transferring ownership of a domain name from a cybersquatter to the trademark owner. A mark's owner must show that (1) the mark and the domain name are identical or confusingly similar; (2) the mark was distinctive when the domain name was first registered; (3) the trademark's owner used the mark commercially before the domain name was registered; and (4) the domain registrant acted in bad faith and intended to profit from the trademark's use.[30] Registering a domain name with the intent to sell it to the trademark owner is presumptively an act of bad faith. If the defendant can prove a legitimate reason for the domain-name registration, the defendant may be allowed to keep the name.

While the ACPA and the UDRP have been effective in the context of traditional cybersquatting on trademarks, other questions involving domain name disputes exist. For example, the current domain name system currently suffers from a lack of cohesive and coherent underlying theory for dealing with deliberate misspellings of trademarks, deliberate misspellings of personal names, generic words and phrases, and "sucks"-type domain names such as nikesucks.com.

INTERNATIONAL ENFORCEMENT OF TRADEMARKS

The global reach of the Internet raises questions of whether U.S. trademark owners can enforcement trademarks abroad and also whether foreigners can enforce trademarks in the United States. The Paris Convention, Madrid Protocol, and Trademark Law Treaty (TLT) are the leading international treaties dealing with trademarks. The rule of territoriality of marks is basic to U.S. trademark law. Under the territoriality doctrine, a trademark is recognized as having a separate existence in each country in which it is registered or legally recognized as a mark. Because a trademark has a separate legal existence under each country's laws, ownership of a mark in one country does not automatically confer upon the owner the exclusive right to use that mark in another country. Trademark owners must take the appropriate steps to ensure that their rights to that mark are recognized in any country where they seek to assert them.

Paris Convention

The Paris Convention for the Protection of Industrial Property, also called the **Paris Convention**, is the principal international treaty governing patents, trademarks and unfair competition. Members form the "Paris Union," which has more counties (with 173 countries, including the United States) than any other treaty dealing with intellectual property rights.[31] The World Intellectual Property Organization (WIPO) serves as the administering agency for the activities of the Paris Union.[32] The Paris Convention is essentially a compact or agreement between the various member nations. The underlying principle is that foreign nationals should be given the same treatment in each of the member countries as that country makes available to its own citizens.

Paris Convention
An international agreement providing that foreign trademark and patent owners may obtain in a member country the same protection for their trademarks and patents as can citizens of the member country. Also called the Paris Convention for the Protection of Industrial Property.

Madrid Protocol

The Protocol Relating to the Madrid Agreement Concerning the International Registration of Marks—the **Madrid Protocol**—is one of two treaties comprising the Madrid System for international registration of trademarks. The Madrid protocol is a filing treaty and not a substantive harmonization treaty.[33] It provides a cost-effective and efficient way for trademark holders—individuals and businesses—to ensure protection for their marks in multiple countries through the filing of one application with a single office, in one language, with one set of fees, in one currency. The International Bureau of the World Intellectual Property Organization (WIPO), in Geneva, Switzerland administers the international registration system. The Madrid Protocol also simplifies the subsequent management of the mark, since a simple, single procedural step serves to record subsequent changes in ownership or in the name or address of the holder with World Intellectual Property Organization's International Bureau. Since the Madrid Protocol went into effect in the United States in 2000, U.S. trademark owners can submit an international application to the USPTO to forward to the International Bureau in Geneva, Switzerland. Similarly, foreign trademark owners can seek extension of protection of an international registration of a mark to the United States.

Madrid Protocol
An international agreement that provides for an international trademark registration system.

Trademark Law Treaty

The Trademark Law Treaty (TLT) is a multilateral treaty that harmonizes and unifies among its member nations many of the administrative requirements for trademark registration.[34] The goal of the treaty is to reduce the costs of obtaining trademark registration in various nations around the world by eliminating certain formalistic administrative requirements. Over 30 nations, including the United States, are now parties to the Treaty. The Trademark Law Treaty Act, ratified by the United States in 1998 and implemented by the United States in 1999, amended several sections of the Lanham Act to conform the application and renewal procedure to the requirements of the Treaty, which was designed to simplify and harmonize worldwide registration formalities.

Summary

A trademark is any word, name, symbol, or device used in commerce. The growth of the Internet has led to disputes involving the registration and use of trademarks. The Lanham Act governs federal registration of trademarks, and the USPTO is the federal agency responsible for registration of trademarks. In a trademark infringement action, courts apply the likelihood-of-confusion test. The defenses commonly invoked in a trademark infringement action are the First Amendment and parody, laches, unclean hands, and fraud in obtaining trademark registration. Plaintiffs in a trademark infringement action may be entitled to both injunctive relief and monetary damages. The Anticybersquatting Consumer Protection Act (ACPA) and Uniform Domain Name Dispute Resolution Policy (UDRP) address cybersquatting of trademarks. The Paris Convention, Madrid Protocol, and Trademark Law Treaty are the leading international treaties governing trademarks.

Key Terms

Anticybersquatting Consumer Protection Act (ACPA) *48*
dilution *45*
domain name *41*
ICANN (Internet Corporation for Assigned Names and Numbers) *48*
laches *47*
Lanham Act *37*
likelihood-of-confusion test *42*
Madrid Protocol *49*
Official Gazette for Trademarks (OG) *39*
Paris Convention *49*
principal register *39*
service mark *37*
trademark *36*
Trademark Dilution Revision Act (TDRA) *45*
Trademark Electronic Application System (TEAS) *39*
Trademark Electronic Search System (TESS) *39*
Trademark Trial and Appeal Board (TTAB) *39*
trade name *40*
unclean hands *47*
Uniform Domain Name Dispute Resolution Policy (UDRP) *48*
United States Patent and Trademark office (USPTO or PTO) *38*

Review Questions

1. What is the definition of a trademark? Give three examples of trademarks for website owners.
2. What are some of the reasons that the USPTO may give in denying an application for trademark registration of a website?
3. How can an applicant for registration on the Principal Register appeal the decision of the examiner?
4. What is the likelihood-of-confusion test?
5. What are the common defenses asserted in a trademark infringement action?
6. What are the different remedies available for trademark infringement?
7. What are the international treaties governing trademarks?
8. What is the purpose of the Anticybersquatting Consumer Protection Act of 1999?
9. What is the purpose of the Trademark Dilution Revision Act of 2006 (TDRA)?

Discussion Questions

1. While an applicant is not required to hire an attorney to assist with trademark filings, what are the advantages of hiring an attorney with a trademark registration? What are the potential advantages and disadvantages for a business owner of using an online legal document preparation service, such as LegalZoom, for trademark registration applications?
2. What precautions can companies take to prevent marks from becoming too generic? Why is it important for a trademark owner to take affirmative steps to prevent dilution?
3. Which governing body should decide domain disputes? Should federal courts have exclusive jurisdiction to decide domain disputes between U.S. citizens and

businesses, or should disputes be decided by ICANN? Explain your position.

4. What are the factors considered when selecting a new URL or domain name?
5. Typosquatting is a form of Internet cybersquatting, based on the probability that a certain number of Internet users will type in the wrong name of a website. For example, in 2011, RepairClinic.com was awarded ownership of the domain name "repairclinc.com" by the World Intellectual Property Organization in a legal case against Spoofy, Inc. RepairClinic.com customers and potential customers who mistakenly omitted the last "i" when searching for "repairclinic.com" would be redirected to a website that listed sponsored links to competitors of RepairClinic.com. To what extent, if any, should typosquatting be prohibited?

Exercises

1. Run a search on the Internet and find a law firm in your area that specializes in trademark law. Provide the name of the law firm along with the firm's mailing address, phone number, and firm website. Consider using a law firm directory at www.findlaw.com or www.martindale.com.
2. Access ICANN's website and locate the Uniform Domain Name Dispute Resolution Policy. What does Section 4(d) provide?
3. Your supervisor asks you to write a brief memorandum on how to record an assignment of a trademark. Visit the USPTO website and find out how to record an assignment or name change for an existing trademark. In the memorandum, describe how to record the assignment, the fee associated with the assignment, and how to pay the filing fee.
4. Run a search on the USPTO website on the Trademark Electronic Search System (TESS) for the mark "YOU CAN GET IT ON EBAY" and provide the description for the mark, date that the mark was first used in commerce, registration date, owner of the mark, and attorney of record.
5. You are the manager for a company that wants to develop a new trade name for a new mobile application (mobile app). Come up with a new trade name for the mobile app and search for possible conflicts on the USPTO website on the Trademark Electronic Search System (TESS). You should search not only for your proposed mark but also for other marks that are logically close, such as synonyms and variant spellings.
6. *Hypothetical:* Apple Inc. sells accessories over the Internet for the iPad, iPad2, and other Apple products. Plaintiff is the owner of certain service marks and contends that the defendant has used the service marks in commerce without its consent. Specifically, the plaintiff contends that the defendant and its affiliates bid on the service marks as keywords to generate a sponsored link for the defendant on Google and other search engines. Moreover, because the defendant's sponsored links were generated when a consumer entered "iPad accessories" as the search term, the sponsored links were likely to cause confusion as to source, affiliation, or sponsorship. How would a court rule in the action? See *1-800 Contacts, Inc. v. Lens.com*, Inc., 755 F.Supp.2d 1151 (D. Utah 2010) based on similar facts involving 1-800 Contacts v. Lens.com.
7. Run a search on the Internet, such as Google News, or through your library's database of newspapers and magazines and find an article involving a recent domain name dispute. Summarize the article and present your findings in a PowerPoint presentation.

Related Internet Sites

http://www.uspto.gov/
Official website for the U.S. Patent and Trademark Office (USPTO)

http://www.uspto.gov/trademarks/process/appeal/index.jsp
Official website for the Trademark Trial and Appeal Board (TTAB) within the U.S. Patent and Trademark Office (USPTO).

http://www.law.cornell.edu/uscode/
Full text of the United States Code (U.S.C.) maintained by the Legal Information Institute at the Cornell University Law School. The full text of Lanham Act is codified in Title 15, Chapter 22 of the U.S. Code.

http://cyber.law.harvard.edu/
Website for the Berkman Center for Internet & Society at Harvard University.

http://law.lexisnexis.com/practiceareas/Top-Cases/Trademark-Law/Trademark-Law—Top-Cases/
Recent Trademark Law Cases provided by LexisNexis.

http://www.inta.org/
Website for the International Trademark Association (INTA). The INTA, founded in 1878, is a not-for-profit membership association of 5,900 trademark owners, professionals-and academics, from more than 190 countries, dedicated to the support and advancement of trademarks and related intellectual property as

elements of fair and effective national and international commerce.

http://www.icann.org/
ICANN (Internet Corporation for Assigned Names and Numbers) official website.

http://topics.law.cornell.edu/wex/Trademark
Overview of Trademark Law provided by the Legal Information Institute (LII) at Cornell University Law School.

http://www.bu.edu/lawlibrary/research/ip/trademark.html#stat
Trademark law research guide maintained Boston University Law Library.

http://www.theiplawblog.com/
Intellectual Property law blog maintained by the law firm Weintraub Genshlea Chediak that includes updates on trademark law.

http://www.abanet.org/intelprop/
Website for the intellectual property section of the American Bar Association (ABA).

http://www.stopfakes.gov/
The International Trade Administration (ITA), U.S. Department of Commerce, manages this global trade site to protect intellectual property rights.

Endnotes

1. Lanham Trade-Mark Act (15 U.S.C. §§ 1051-1127, as amended).
2. *HBP, Inc. v. American Marine Holdings, Inc.*, 290 F. Supp. 2d 1320 (M.D. Fla. 2003).
3. 15 U.S.C. § 1127.
4. Id.
5. *America Online, Inc. v. AT & T Corp.*, 243 F.3d 812 (4th Cir. 2001).
6. 74 Am. Jur. 2d Trademarks and Tradenames § 8.
7. 1 McCarthy on Trademarks and Unfair Competition § 3:3 (4th ed.).
8. *FragranceNet.com, Inc. v. FragranceX.com, Inc.*, 493 F. Supp. 2d 545 (E.D.N.Y. 2007).
9. U.S. Patent and Trademark Office, Some Well-Known U.S. Trademarks Celebrate One Hundred Years, Jun. 15, 2000, available at http://www.uspto.gov/news/pr/2000/00-38.jsp.
10. 15 U.S.C. § 1072.
11. 74 Am. Jur. 2d Trademarks and Tradenames § 68.
12. 74 Am. Jur. 2d Trademarks and Tradenames § 81.
13. *Sally Beauty Co., Inc. v. Beautyco, Inc.*, 304 F.3d 964 (10th Cir. 2002).
14. *Schering Corp. v. Pfizer Inc.*, 189 F.3d 218 (2nd Cir. 1999).
15. *Brunswick Corp. v. Spinit Reel Co.*, 832 F.2d 513 (10th Cir. 1983).
16. Richard J. Pinto, Elliott J. Stein and Christine B. Savoca, *Recent Developments in Trademark and Copyright Law*, ASPATORE, May, 2010.
17. *Wyatt Technology Corp. v. Smithson*, 345 Fed.Appx. 236 (9th Cir. 2009).
18. *1-800 Contacts, Inc. v. WhenU.Com, Inc.*, 414 F.3d 400 (2d Cir. 2005).
19. Black's Law Dictionary (9th ed. 2009).
20. Trademark Dilution Revision Act of 2006, Pub. L. No. 109–312, 120 Stat. 1730.
21. 15 U.S.C. § 1117.
22. *Cliffs Notes, Inc. v. Bantam Doubleday Dell Pub. Group, Inc.*, 886 F.2d 490, 493 (2nd Cir. 1989).
23. *Internet Specialties West, Inc. v. Milon-DiGiorgio Enterprises, Inc.*, 559 F.3d 985 (9th Cir. 2009).
24. *First Jewellery Co. of Canada, Inc. v. Internet Shopping Network LLC*, 53 U.S.P.Q.2d 1838, 2000 WL 122175 (S.D.N.Y. 2000).
25. 6 McCarthy on Trademarks and Unfair Competition § 31:61 (4th ed.).
26. 4 McCarthy on Trademarks and Unfair Competition § 25:73 (4th ed.).
27. 15 U.S.C. § 1125(d).
28. Jacqueline D. Lipton, *Bad Faith In Cyberspace: Grounding Domain Name Theory In Trademark, Property, And Restitution*, 23 HARV. J.L. & TECH. 447, 448 (2010).
29. Anticybersquatting Consumer Protection Act (ACPA), Pub. L. No. 106-113, 113 Stat. 1536.
30. *ITC Ltd. v. Punchgini, Inc.*, 482 F.3d 135, 155 (2nd Cir. 2007).
31. World Intellectual Property Organization (WIPO), Contracting Parties > Paris Convention (Total Contracting Parties: 173) (2010), available at http://www.wipo.int/treaties/en/ShowResults.jsp?lang=en&treaty_id=2/'/.
32. 5 McCarthy on Trademarks and Unfair Competition § 29:25 (4th ed.).
33. USPTO, Madrid Protocol (2010), available at: http://www.uspto.gov/trademarks/law/madrid/index.jsp/.
34. 5 McCarthy on Trademarks and Unfair Competition § 29:34 (4th ed.).

CHAPTER

4 Patents and Trade Secrets in the Information Age

An inventor is a man who looks around upon the world, and is not content with things as they are. He wants to improve whatever he sees; he wants to benefit the world; he is haunted by an idea. The spirit of invention possesses him, seeing materialization.

ALEXANDER GRAHAM BELL[1]

LEARNING OBJECTIVES

After completing this chapter, you will be able to:

1. Explain the scope of patent protection for Internet patents and what is meant by obviousness.
2. Describe the requirements for patentability.
3. Explain the patent application and appeals process.
4. Describe the process for protecting assets as trade secrets.

PATENTS GENERALLY

A **patent** is an intellectual property right granted by the U.S. government to an inventor to exclude others from making, using, offering for sale, or selling the invention throughout the United States or importing the invention into the United States for a limited time in exchange for public disclosure of the invention when the patent is granted.[2] Generally, the term of a new patent is 20 years from the date on which the application for the patent was filed in the United States.

In Article I, Section 8 of U.S. Constitution, the Founders recognized the importance of strong patent rights by granting Congress the power "To promote the Progress of Science and useful Arts, by securing for limited Times to Authors and Inventors the exclusive Right to their respective Writings and Discoveries."

The primary purpose of the patent system is not the reward of the individual, but advancement of the arts and sciences.[3] The fundamental policy of the patent system is to encourage the creation and disclosure of new, useful, and nonobvious advances in technology and design, by granting the reward of the exclusive right to practice the invention for a period of years to the inventor.

There are three basic types of patents: (1) utility patents; (2) design patents; and (3) plant patents.[4]

Utility patents may be granted to anyone who invents or discovers any new and useful process, machine, article of manufacture, or composition of matter, or any new and useful improvement. Utility patents are the most commonly issued patents.

Design patents may be granted to anyone who invents a new, original, and ornamental design for an article of manufacture. A design patent protects a product's appearance or nonfunctional aspects.[5]

Plant patents may be granted to anyone who invents or discovers and asexually reproduces any distinct and new variety of plant.

Patent
A patent is an intellectual property right granted by the U.S. government to an inventor to exclude others from making, using, offering for sale, or selling the invention throughout the United States or importing the invention into the United States for a limited time in exchange for public disclosure of the invention when the patent is granted. Generally, the term of a new patent is 20 years from the date on which the application for the patent was filed in the United States.

Utility Patent
A patent granted for one of the following types of inventions: a process, a machine, a manufacture, or a composition of matter (such as a new chemical). Utility patents are the most commonly issued patents.

Design Patent
A patent granted for a new, original, and ornamental design for an article of manufacture; a patent that protects a product's appearance or nonfunctional aspects. Design patents have a term of only 14 years from the date the patent is granted.

Business Method Patent
A U.S. patent that describes and claims a series of process steps that, as a whole, constitutes a method of doing business. Also called cyberpatent.

Patentability of Software and Business Method Patents

A U.S. patent describes and claims a series of process steps that, as a whole, constitutes a method of doing business. Until 1998, methods for doing business were not expressly recognized as being patentable. In that year, the Federal Circuit in *State Street Bank & Trust Co. v. Signature Fin. Group, Inc.*, 149 F.3d 1368 (Fed. Cir. 1998), held that **business method patents** are subject to the same legal requirements for patentability as any other process or method. A related term for a business method patent is an Internet patent or cyberpatent. A cyberpatent or Internet patent is a type of utility patent granted on an invention that combines business methods and software programs for Internet applications.

The U.S. Supreme Court settled the question that business methods are patentable subject matter in *Bilski v. Kappos*, 130 S.Ct. 3218 (2010) in a narrow 5-4 decision decided in 2010. The Court rejected the Federal Circuit of Court of Appeals' "machine-or-transformation" test for determining the patentability of a process. The Court also declined to adopt a rule that business methods are not patentable. In the aftermath of *Bilski*, business methods are patentable subject matter until Congress decides otherwise. The decision in *Bilski* is a narrow one and leaves open the question concerning the scope of business methods patents to other courts.

This chart shows some of the patents owned by Google, Inc. In total, Google owns over 500 patents.

Patent Number	Title
7,814,486	Multi-thread runtime system
7,814,159	Time line display of chat conversations
7,814,155	Email conversation management system
7,814,103	Systems and methods for using anchor text as parallel corpora for cross-language information retrieval
7,814,085	System and method for determining a composite score for categorized search results
7,813,582	Method and apparatus for enhancing object boundary precision in an image
7,810,030	Fault-tolerant romanized input method for non-roman characters
7,809,785	System using router in a web browser for inter-domain communication
7,809,769	Database partitioning by virtual partitions
7,809,725	Acquiring web page experiment schema

FIGURE 4.1 Selected Google Patents

Role of the USPTO

Congress established the United States Patent and Trademark Office (USPTO) to administer and manage patents within the United States. The USPTO is an agency within the U.S. Department of Commerce. The Patent Office, as a distinct bureau, dates from the year 1802. The Patent Office remained in the Department of State until 1849, when it was transferred to the Department of Interior. In 1925 it was transferred to the Department of Commerce, where it is today. The name of the Patent Office was changed to the Patent and Trademark Office (PTO) in 1975, and changed to the United States Patent and Trademark Office (commonly abbreviated as the USPTO) in 2000. The acronym PTO is also still frequently used.

Requirements for Patentability

To receive a patent, the inventor must invent a new or useful process. Section 101 of the 1952 Patent Act provides "Whoever invents or discovers any new and useful process, machine, manufacture, or composition of matter, or any new and useful improvement thereof, may obtain a patent therefor, subject to the conditions and requirements of this title."[6] In the Patent Act of 1952, the requirements for acquiring a patent include novelty, utility, and nonobviousness. Figure 4.2 is the federal statute that sets forth the conditions for patentability.

The Patent Act, 35 U.S.C. § 102, sets forth the conditions for patentability.
A person shall be entitled to a patent unless—

a. the invention was known or used by others in this country, or patented or described in a printed publication in this or a foreign country, before the invention thereof by the applicant for patent, or
b. the invention was patented or described in a printed publication in this or a foreign country or in public use or on sale in this country, more than one year prior to the date of the application for patent in the United States, or
c. he has abandoned the invention, or
d. the invention was first patented or caused to be patented, or was the subject of an inventor's certificate, by the applicant or his legal representatives or assigns in a foreign country prior to the date of the application for patent in this country on an application for patent or inventor's certificate filed more than twelve months before the filing of the application in the United States, or
e. the invention was described in (1) an application for patent, published under section 122(b), by another filed in the United States before the invention by the applicant for patent or (2) a patent granted on an application for patent by another filed in the United States before the invention by the applicant for patent, except that an international application filed under the treaty defined in section 351(a) shall have the effects for the purposes of this subsection of an application filed in the United States only if the international application designated the United States and was published under Article 21(2) of such treaty in the English language; or
f. he did not himself invent the subject matter sought to be patented, or
g. (1) during the course of an interference conducted under section 135 or section 291, another inventor involved therein establishes, to the extent permitted in section 104, that before such person's invention thereof the invention was made by such other inventor and not abandoned, suppressed, or concealed, or (2) before such person's invention thereof, the invention was made in this country by another inventor who had not abandoned, suppressed, or concealed it. In determining priority of invention under this subsection, there shall be considered not only the respective dates of conception and reduction to practice of the invention, but also the reasonable diligence of one who was first to conceive and last to reduce to practice, from a time prior to conception by the other.

FIGURE 4.2 Conditions for Patentability

"First to Invent" Doctrine

In the United States, patent ownership is based on who is the "first to invent" rather than who was the "first to file" a patent application. This concept is often called the "first to invent" doctrine.[7] Patent applications filed by two competing inventors at or around the same time can give rise to a priority contest which is called an "interference." **Interference** is an administrative proceeding in the USPTO to determine who is entitled to the patent when two or more applicants claim the same invention, or when an application interferes with an existing patent.[8] This proceeding occurs when the same invention is claimed (1) in two pending applications, or (2) in one pending application and a patent issued within a year of the pending application's filing date. Priority contests are both time consuming and expensive. The average pendency of an interference before the USPTO is 30.5 months and some have continued for decades.[9]

Interference
An administrative proceeding in the USPTO to determine who is entitled to the patent when two or more applicants claim the same invention, or when an application interferes with an existing patent. This proceeding occurs when the same invention is claimed (1) in two pending applications, or (2) in one pending application and a patent issued within a year of the pending application's filing date.

The U.S. Court of Appeals for the Federal Circuit reaffirmed the fundamental rule that the patentee must be the first inventor in the case *In re Giacomini*, 612 F.3d 1380 (Fed. Cir. 2010). Giacomini's application for a patent entitled "Method and Apparatus for Economical Cache Population" claimed a technique for selectively storing electronic data in a readily accessible memory called a "cache." When a system retrieves requested data from a source, it stores the data in its cache so that it can retrieve the data more quickly next time. The Board of Patent Appeals and Interferences, and later the U.S. Court of Appeals for the Federal Circuit, determined that Giacomoni's full patent application came after a provisional application and under first to invent doctrine and denied Giacomoni's application for a patent. Patent law protects the first to invent.

PATENT APPLICATIONS AND PROCEEDINGS

Where an application for a patent is properly made, the Director of the USPTO is required to cause a thorough examination of the alleged new invention or discovery. The USPTO examiner is a patent officer responsible for determining the patentability of an invention submitted to the patent office. The purpose of the examination is to determine whether the claimant is entitled to a patent under the law and whether the invention is sufficiently useful and important to warrant the grant of a patent.

Patent Agent
A specialized legal professional—not necessarily a licensed lawyer—who prepares and prosecutes patent applications before the Patent and Trademark Office. Patent agents must be licensed by the Patent and Trademark Office.

Inventors can prepare and file their own applications with the USPTO, but most inventors will utilize the services of a registered patent attorney or patent agent.

Patent agents are non-attorneys that represent inventors before the patent office. Patent agents and patent attorneys have equal privileges to practice before the Patent Office. Patent agents can conduct patent novelty searches; advise clients whether an invention may be eligible for patenting; may prepare, file, and prosecute United States and international patent applications with the Patent Office; and may pursue foreign patent protection through foreign associates. Patent attorneys and patent agents assist clients in the process of applying for a patent through the U.S. Patent and Trademark Office and negotiating with the patent examiner, which is also commonly called "**patent prosecution**."

Patent Prosecution
The process of applying for a patent through the U.S. Patent and Trademark Office and negotiating with the patent examiner.

The standards of patentability are defined by statute under 35 U.S.C. § 101. Patents may issue for "any new and useful process, machine, manufacture, or composition of matter" that is not "obvious at the time the invention was made to a person having ordinary skill in the art."[10]

Many cases focus on whether a patent is "obvious." If a patent is obvious, then a court will not recognize the validity of a patent. Obviousness can arise in the context of a patent application or in the context of a patent infringement action. The test of nonobviousness is whether the differences between the subject matter sought to be patented and the prior art are such that the subject matter as a whole would have been obvious at the time the invention was made to a person having ordinary skill in the art to which said subject matter pertains.

On February 21, 2006, the USPTO issued patent number 7 million to DuPont senior researcher John P. O'Brien for "polysaccharide fibers" and a process for their production. The fibers have cotton-like properties, are biodegradable, and are useful in textile applications. It took 75 years to get from the first patent to 1 million. It has taken less than one tenth of that time to go from 6 million to 7 million. Patent number 6,000,000 was issued on December 7, 1999. Patent No. 1 was issued in 1836. Earlier patents were not numbered, although the first U.S. patent was issued in 1790.

FIGURE 4.3 USPTO Issues 7 Millionth Patent
Source: USPTO, United States Patent & Trademark Office Issues 7 Millionth Patent, Press Release, Feb. 14, 2006, available at http://www.uspto.gov/news/pr/2006/ 06-09.jsp/.

The U.S. Court of Appeals for the Federal Circuit considered whether a "public online, pay-as-you-use communications terminal" or online kiosk was "obvious" in the case of *In re Mettke*, 570 F.3d 1356 (Fed. Cir. 2009) (Case 4.1). The court affirmed the decision of the Board of Patent Appeals and Interferences and denied the patent claim based on obviousness.

CASE 4.1

The Case of the Rejected Patent for Obviousness

In re Mettke, *570 F.3d 1356 (Fed. Cir. 2009)*

Richard P. Mettke appeals the decision of the Board of Patent Appeals and Interferences [Board] affirming the examiner's rejection of the sole remaining claim (claim 6) in his application for reissue of U.S. Patent No. 5,602,905. The Board concluded that claim 6 would have been obvious in light of any of several different combinations of references, and was therefore properly rejected under 35 U.S.C. § 103(a). We *affirm*.

Background

On January 23, 1995, Mr. Mettke applied for a patent directed to an "On-Line Communication Terminal/Apparatus." This application matured into the '905 patent, which issued on February 11, 1997 with five claims, four of which were for a "public online, pay-as-you-use communications terminal," and one for a method of using such a terminal. The Summary of the Invention lists several components that are combined to produce the communications terminal, and states that the invention allows users to "conveniently access commercial on-line services and the Internet at other locations other than from their fixed terminal at an office or home."

On August 17, 1998, Mr. Mettke applied for reissue of the '905 patent pursuant to 35 U.S.C. § 251.

Three parties, including TouchNet Information Systems, Inc., filed protests to the reissue under 37 C.F.R. § 1.291(a), and provided several references not previously considered during prosecution of the '905 patent. The examiner then rejected the new claims, and the Board affirmed the examiner's rejections and also entered a new ground of rejection for obviousness.

The examiner maintained the rejection of claim 6, and the Board again affirmed. In a lengthy opinion, the Board concluded that claim 6 would have been obvious in light of five different combinations of references. Mr. Mettke appeals.

Discussion

The question is whether the Board correctly concluded that, at the time Mr. Mettke filed his original application, the subject matter of claim 6 would have been obvious to a person of ordinary

(*Continued*)

(Continued)

skill in the field of the invention. Obviousness is a legal conclusion based on underlying findings of fact. *In re Thrift,* 298 F.3d 1357, 1363 (Fed. Cir. 2002). The factual inquiries relevant to obviousness are set forth in *Graham v. John Deere Co.,* 383 U.S. 1, 17-18, 86 S.Ct. 684, 15 L.Ed.2d 545 (1966), and include (1) the scope and content of the prior art, (2) the differences between the prior art and the claims, (3) the level of ordinary skill in the relevant art, and (4) any objective indicia of non-obviousness such as commercial success, long felt need, and failure of others. We review the Board's factual findings for support by substantial evidence, and the Board's ultimate conclusion of obviousness without deference. *In re Gartside,* 203 F.3d 1305, 1316 (Fed.Cir.2000).

Mr. Mettke criticizes the Board's finding that the field of endeavor is "pay-for-use public communication terminals," arguing that this field was too broad and led the Board to consider non-analogous art. Mr. Mettke argues that the term "communication" broadly sweeps in such fields as facsimile machines, telephones, televisions, cellular phones, and global positioning systems. He contends that the field of his reissue application is limited in claim 6 to an "Internet terminal." However, the specification describes various communication media, including facsimile machines and email, as related to the invention. The Board recognized that the specific aspect to which claim 6 is directed is "providing access to the Internet," but found that the asserted prior art references are within the field of the invention or are analogous art. This finding is supported by substantial evidence.

The Board found that reference Exhibit E describes a "free-standing pay-for-use Touch Fax . . . public communications terminal (kiosk) for locations such as airports, hotels, truck stops, and supermarkets," that provides services including "phone, fax, computer, word processing, copying, and information services."

The Board found that Exhibit F describes a "Public Communications Terminal from Touch Fax, in a stand-alone housing including a telephone, speaker, touch-screen monitor, a credit card reader for payment of services, a full-size keyboard for computer database access or word processing, an option panel, a flatbed scanner, a 386 CPU, and a laser printer," which provides services including "telephone, send or receive a fax, photocopying, word processing and laser printing, and access to a growing number of information databases from Wall Street news to international sports scores."

The Board found that Exhibits E and F disclose every element of claim 6 except the "means for accessing the Internet" and the "software . . . to allow interface with the internet and credit card service centers." However, the Board found that the communications software discussed in Exhibit F would have suggested the use of such software to communicate between the credit card reader device that is shown in Exhibit E, and a remote credit card service center.

The Board concluded that the subject matter of claim 6 would have been obvious in view of the combination of Exhibit E, Exhibit F, and Shah. Mr. Mettke argues that the references do not contain any motivation to combine the "means for accessing the Internet" with the other elements of claim 6. Mr. Mettke contends the Board engaged in hindsight analysis, using his patent as a blueprint for the combination of elements from various sources. Mr. Mettke is correct that the selective hindsight combination of references that show various elements of the claim generally does not suffice to establish obviousness. *See KSR Int'l Co. v. Teleflex Inc.,* 550 U.S. 398, 418, 127 S.Ct. 1727, 167 L.Ed.2d 705 (2007) ("[A] patent composed of several elements is not proved obvious merely by demonstrating that each of its elements was, independently, known in the prior art.").

But the Board's analysis included more than a combination of disparate references disclosing different elements, for the Board explained why *Shah* teaches the very combination of elements that Mr. Mettke sought to claim. The Board found that *Shah* does not merely disclose "accessing the Internet" as a general matter; *Shah* expressly teaches Internet access in connection with information and communication kiosks—the kinds of public communication terminals described in Exhibits E and F. Shah provides explicit support for the Board's finding that a person of ordinary skill would have been motivated to modify existing information kiosks or terminals to provide access to the Internet. We affirm that the Board established a prima facie case of obviousness.

Mr. Mettke also states that "over 50% of all [now-existing] kiosks have all of the elements" of claim 6, suggesting commercial success. The Board found that Mr. Mettke failed to establish a "nexus" between this asserted wide use and his invention. *See In re Paulsen,* 30 F.3d 1475, 1482 (Fed.Cir.1994) ("When a patentee offers objective evidence of nonobviousness, there must be a sufficient relationship between that evidence and the patented invention."). We note that when the commercially successful device is the claimed invention itself, there is a presumption of nexus. *See Demaco Corp. v. F. Von Langsdorff Licensing Ltd.,* 851 F.2d 1387, 1392 (Fed.Cir.1988). However, the Board found that Mr. Mettke failed to meet his burden because he has not shown that the alleged commercial success is due to the claimed invention. We conclude that the evidence of obviousness was not, in this case, rebutted by the asserted commercial success.

Taking all of the evidence in its entirety, *see In re Rinehart,* 531 F.2d 1048, 1052 (CCPA 1976), the Board's conclusion of obviousness based on the combination of Exhibit E, Exhibit F, and *Shah* was correct, in that it was based on findings supported by substantial evidence and not rebutted by objective evidence. The decision of the Board, denying patentability of reissue application claim 6, is affirmed.

Case Questions

1. What are the four factual inquiries relevant to obviousness for a patent as set forth by the U.S. Supreme Court in *Graham v. John Deere Co.* discussed in *In re Mettke*?
2. Why did the Federal Circuit reject the application for reissue of the patent?
3. What was the effect of Mettke failing to establish a "nexus" or sufficient relationship between asserted wide use and his patented invention?

Prior Art and Anticipation

To meet the novelty requirement for the validity of a patent, an invention must have occurred before anticipation by prior art or reference.[11] **Prior art** is the knowledge, usage, patents, and descriptions relating to an invention in existence before the invention. If the invention was known or used by others in this country, or patented or described in a printed publication in this or a foreign country, it has been "anticipated" by the prior art.[12] If an invention is anticipated, it does not meet the novelty requirement.

In *Storage Technology Corp. v. Quantum Corp.,* 370 F. Supp. 2d 1116 (D. Colo. 2005), a patent involving magnetic computer data storage tape with an optical servo pattern located on the back surface was not anticipated by prior art patents, although the USPTO had taken contradictory positions about whether the claimed tape was novel in light of prior art.[13] For patentability, the patent must pass the novelty requirement.

Appeals

If the patent examiner and the administrative patent judge reject the application for a patent, an applicant can appeal the decision to the **Board of Patent Appeals and Interferences (BPAI)**. An applicant is required to exhaust administrative remedies by appealing to the BPAI (sometimes simply called the Board).[14] The federal statute provides: "The Board of Patent Appeals and Interferences shall, on written appeal of an applicant, review adverse decisions of examiners upon applications for patents and shall determine priority and patentability of invention in interferences."[15] The Manual of Patent Examining Procedure sets forth the procedures for appellants, respondents, and patent examiners to follow in appeals in the reexamination proceeding.

If an applicant elects to appeal the decision of the BPAI, the applicant can seek judicial review. The **United States Court of Appeals for the Federal Circuit (also called**

Prior Art
In patent cases, knowledge that is publicly known, used by others, or available on the date of invention to a person of ordinary skill in an art, including what would be obvious from that knowledge.

Board of Patent Appeals and Interferences (BPAI)
The quasi-judicial body in the U.S. Patent and Trademark Office that hears (1) appeals from patent applicants whose claims have been rejected by a patent examiner, and (2) interference contests between two or more applicants trying to patent the same invention. The U.S. Court of Appeals for the Federal Circuit hears appeals from this tribunal.

U.S. Court of Appeals for the Federal Circuit
An intermediate-level appellate court with jurisdiction to hear appeals in patent cases and some administrative agencies. Among the purposes of its creation were ending forum-shopping in patent suits, settling differences in patent-law doctrines among the circuits, and allowing a single forum to develop the expertise needed to rule on complex technological questions that arise in patent suits. Also called Federal Circuit or CAFC.

the "Federal Circuit" or "CFAC") has exclusive jurisdiction over appeals from the decisions of the Board of Patent Appeals and Interferences of the United States Patent and Trademark Office with respect to patent applications.[16] Applicants can then appeal the decision of the Federal Circuit to the U.S. Supreme Court, but the U.S. Supreme Court rarely grants review. In most circumstances, the Federal Circuit has the final word in approving or denying patent applications.

PATENT INFRINGEMENT

Like infringement of copyrights and trademarks, patent holders may also sue for infringement of their intellectual property rights. Analysis of patent infringement requires two steps. First, the district court construes the claims of the patent, determining their scope and meaning. Second, the claims, as construed by the court in step one, are compared limitation by limitation to the features of the allegedly infringing device.[17] Because an invalid patent gives rise to no rights, there can be no infringement of an invalid patent.

Jurisdiction

The U.S. District Courts, also called federal District Courts, have original jurisdiction of any civil action arising under any act of Congress relating to patents.[18] If a patent infringement case is filed in state court, the case will either be dismissed or removed to federal court. The United States Court of Appeals for the Federal Circuit (also called the Federal Circuit) has exclusive jurisdiction over appeals from the decisions of the Board of Patent Appeals and Interferences of the United States Patent and Trademark Office as well as exclusive appellate jurisdiction of U.S. District Court decisions in patent infringement cases. The Federal Circuit was created in 1982 to resolve inconsistent application of patent law, forum shopping, and inter-circuit conflicts.[19]

Types of Infringement

There are several different types of infringement, including direct infringement, contributory infringement, induced infringement, literal infringement, and the doctrine of equivalents.

Patentee
A patent gives to the patentee or holder of the patent the right to exclude others from making, using, offering for sale, or selling the patented invention.

DIRECT INFRINGEMENT A patent gives to the **patentee** or holder of the patent the right to exclude others from making, using, offering for sale, or selling the patented invention.[20] If the invention is a process, the right to exclude others from using, offering for sale, or selling throughout the United States, products made by that process, referring to the specifications for the particulars. Direct infringement occurs when a person, company, or entity makes, uses, offers to sell, or sells any patented invention within the United States during the patent's term, or imports into the United States any patented invention during the term of the patent.

CONTRIBUTORY INFRINGEMENT Contributory infringement is the intentional aiding of one person by another in the unlawful making or selling or using of a patented invention. A claim of contributory infringement requires that plaintiff establish that defendants sold material to be used in patented process; that said material constituted a material part of patented process; that defendants knew material to be especially adapted for use in infringement of such patent; and that material did not constitute staple article suitable for substantial noninfringing use. There can be no contributory infringement unless there is direct infringement. There must also be a showing that the alleged contributory infringer had knowledge and intent.

INDUCED INFRINGEMENT Whoever actively induces infringement of a patent is liable as an infringer.[21] Active inducement is limited to those situations where the defendant has induced another party to infringe the plaintiff's patent, but has not personally infringed the patent by making, using, or selling the invention. There must be direct infringement before there can be active inducement of infringement.[22]

In 2011, the U.S. Supreme Court held in *Global-Tech Appliances, Inc. v. SEB S.A.*, 131 S. Ct. 2060 (2011), that while inducement of infringement of infringement requires knowledge that the induced conduct itself infringes, that knowledge element can be met by a showing of "willful blindness." The U.S. Supreme Court rejected the Federal Circuit's adoption of a "deliberate indifference" standard and endorsed the "willful blindness" approach to knowledge. Like contributory infringement, inducement of infringement requires that the defendant knew that the third party's conduct constitutes an infringement. The same knowledge of "willful blindness" applies to both contributory infringement and induced infringement.

LITERAL INFRINGEMENT Literal infringement occurs only if each limitation of the claim is present in the accused device. In determining whether there has been literal infringement of a patent, courts apply a two-step analysis: once claims have been correctly construed to determine their scope, the claims must be compared to the accused device, and to find literal infringement, each limitation of the claim must be present in the accused device, as any deviation from the claim precludes such a finding. In *Telemac Cellular Corp. v. Topp Telecom, Inc.*, 247 F.3d 1316 (Fed. Cir. 2001), the Federal Circuit rejected a literal infringement claim involving a mobile cellular telephone system having a host processor and internal accounting capabilities for performing real-time call debiting.[23]

Doctrine of Equivalents

Infringement under the doctrine of equivalents requires the patentee to prove that the accused device contains an equivalent for each limitation not literally satisfied. The doctrine evolved to prevent parties from evading liability for patent infringement by making trivial changes to avoid the literal language of the patent claims. In determining whether infringement exists under the doctrine of equivalents, the U.S. Supreme Court ruled that a court must first determine whether the accused product or process contains an element identical or equivalent to each claimed element of the patented invention.[24] The doctrine of equivalents is a judicially created theory for finding patent infringement when the accused process or product falls outside the literal scope of the patent claims.[25]

Patent Infringement with Google's AdWords

Google's AdWords have been the subject of patent infringement litigation. AdWords ads are displayed along with search results when someone searches Google using certain keywords. Ads appear under "Sponsored links" in the side column of a search page, and may also appear in additional positions above the free search results. AdWords is Google's main advertising product and main source of revenue. Bid for Position, which owns rights to U.S. Patent #7,225,151, titled "Online Auction Bid Management System and Method," filed a patent infringement lawsuit against AOL and Google alleging that the companies infringed on the Bid for Position patent because they use auction bids to determine pricing for ads on search results.

U.S. District Court Judge Jerome Friedman ruled in 2008 in favor of Google and AOL in a summary judgment that neither company's system infringed the '151 patent and Bid for Position appealed the decision. In *Bid for Position, LLC v. AOL, LLC*, 601 F.3d 1311 (Fed. Cir. 2010), the U.S. Court of Appeals affirmed the decision of Judge Friedman that Google did not infringe on Bid for Position's patent.

CASE 4.2

The Patent Infringement Case Involving Google's AdWords

Bid for Position, LLC v. AOL, LLC, *601 F.3d 1311 (Fed. Cir. 2010)*

Plaintiff Bid for Position, LLC, appeals from a final judgment of noninfringement entered in its patent infringement suit against defendants Google, Inc., and AOL, LLC. The patent-in-suit, U.S. Patent No. 7,225,151, describes a method for conducting a continuous auction, such as a consumers' auction on the internet for goods or services, or a vendors' auction for positions in an internet advertising display. The claimed method allows a bidder to select a position of priority in the auction and automatically adjusts the bidder's bid so as to maintain that chosen priority status. The accused system is Google's internet advertising system, AdWords, which runs continuous auctions to determine the placement of advertisements on Google's search results pages. AOL's system, AOL Search Marketplace, is a rebranded version of Google's AdWords that does not contain the Position Preference feature. Google's AdSense for Content is also a rebranded version that places advertisements on Google's partner sites.

In the accused AdWords system, advertisers choose keywords to trigger the display of their advertisements. When a keyword is used in a search performed on Google.com, AdWords runs an auction to determine the order in which the advertisements will be placed next to the search results. Each advertiser submits a bid in the form of a Maximum Cost-Per-Click ("CPC"), i.e., the maximum price the advertiser is willing to pay each time its advertisement is "clicked" by a user of the search engine. AdWords then multiplies each bid by a "Quality Score," also known as the estimated Click Through Rate ("eCTR"), which predicts the likelihood that a user searching for the designated keyword will click on the subject advertisement, based on a confidential algorithm that considers various historical factors.

The two claims at issue in this appeal are a method claim and a corresponding system claim.

Markman Hearing
In patent cases, a hearing at which the court receives evidence and arguments concerning the construction to be given to terms in a patent claim at issue. Based on *Markman v. Westview Instruments, Inc.*, 52 F.3d 967, 984–85 (Fed. Cir. 1995).

Following a ***Markman* hearing**, the district court issued a claim construction order on July 11, 2008. Only three clauses in the claims are relevant to this appeal: (1) "information for selecting one of the two or more positions of priority that the first bidder wishes to maintain in the auction" (claim 1) and "selected one of the two or more positions of priority that the first bidder wishes to maintain in the auction" (claim 11); (2) "wherein the relative position of priority for providing the service for the first bidder is dependent upon whether the value of the first bid exceeds the value of the second bid"; and (3) "the auction for determining continuing priority for providing an ongoing service."

On October 15, 2008, the district court granted summary judgment in favor of the defendants. With respect to AdWords without Position Preference, the court found non-infringement as to each of the three contested limitations.

We affirm the district court's ruling that AdWords without Position Preference does not infringe, because we agree with the court that the '151 patent does not read on a system that simply selects the highest ranking position of priority that is available for the offered bid, which is what AdWords does when the Position Preference feature is not activated. Bid for Position's argument to the contrary is barred by the claim language, particularly when read in light of the prosecution history.

The claims recite that the bidder must submit information for selecting a priority position that the bidder wishes to maintain in the auction. That language suggests that the bidder must select a particular position, not simply accept whatever position its bid will support. The prosecution history confirms that the patent does not cover a system in which the bidder simply bids for the "best available" position. During prosecution, the patent examiner issued a rejection stating that the prior art already taught "selecting a bidding position, specifically the highest ranking bid position," and then "automatically reducing the first bid to a minimum which allows the bidder to keep the selected position of priority."

We reach the same conclusion with respect to AdWords with the Position Preference feature activated, but for a different reason. While AdWords with Position Preference allows a bidder to select a specific position of priority, it does not satisfy the limitation of the '151 patent that states: "the relative position of priority for providing the service for the first bidder is dependent on whether the value of the first bid exceeds the value of the second bid."

The district court interpreted the "value" of a bid, as used in the patent, to mean the monetary "amount" of the bid, i.e., the price offered by the bidder. Bid for Position contends that the term "value" includes equivalents of the monetary amount of the bid. Bid for Position further argues that the Quality Score in the AdWords system is obtained simply through a mechanical conversion of the bid amount (i.e., the Maximum CPC), akin to a currency exchange conversion. Therefore, according to Bid for Position, the "value" of the bid, as that term is used in the '151 patent, includes the Ad Rank that results from adjusting the bid by the Quality Score.

The flaw in Bid for Position's argument is that the order of the bidders' bid amounts, arranged according to Maximum CPC, can be entirely different from the order of the bidders' Ad Ranks. If the conversion of bids to Ad Ranks were simply substitutions of equivalent values, the same order of positions would obtain after the conversions. Instead, the application of the Quality Score creates rankings that have no consistent mapping to the original bids.

The specification supplies further evidence that the terms "bid" and "value of the bid" mean the same thing in the '151 patent. In the detailed description of the first preferred embodiment, for example, the patent provides that a bidder may enter maximum bids into the system and that the system will increase the bidder's lower bids "until they reach desired bidding positions entered by the bidders as long as the bids do not exceed maximum values entered by the respective bidders." The system will ensure relative priority for the bidder "as long as the maximum bid is not exceeded." '151 patent, col. 3, ll. 40–52. As applied to AdWords, the "maximum values entered by the respective bidders" cannot refer to the Ad Ranks, since the bidders do not know what Quality Score the system might assign to their advertisements. Instead, "value," as used in that passage, can only refer to the bid amount, a quantity that the bidders do control.

The consistent use of the term "value" throughout the patent thus confirms that the '151 patent does not read on AdWords with Position Preference, which bases the award of priority on something other than a comparison of the bid amounts. The district court therefore correctly entered summary judgment of no literal infringement with respect to AdWords with Position Preference.

Apart from literal infringement, Bid for Position also argues briefly that the AdWords system infringes the "position of priority" limitation under the doctrine of equivalents. The district court held that a reasonable fact-finder could not conclude that the "ranking of advertisements based upon their Ad Rank is substantially similar to the ranking of advertisements based upon their bid amounts." *Bid for Position,* slip op. at 17. The court explained that the advertiser controls the ranking of its advertisements when the ranking is based on the bid amount, but not when it is based on Ad Rank. An Ad Rank "is not the monetary amount of the bid, and the conversion of a bid to an Ad Rank changes the nature or status of the bid from a monetary amount into a nonmonetary quantity." Id. at 18.

We agree that the method recited in the '151 patent, in which the amount of the bidder's bid determines the placement of the advertisement, is substantially different from AdWords, with or without Position Preference. In the method of the '151 patent, the ultimate placement of an advertisement is purely a function of the relative amounts of the competing advertisers' bids, whereas in AdWords the ultimate placement of an advertisement is dictated by the product of the

(Continued)

(Continued)

bid amount and the Quality Score that AdWords assigns. Thus, AdWords is not a pure bidding system, such as the system recited in the '151 patent, but instead operates in a quite different manner that enables the bid recipient, i.e., Google, to exercise substantial control over the outcome of the auction. That difference is sufficiently fundamental that we conclude, as did the district court, that a trier of fact could not properly find the AdWords system to be equivalent to the system recited in the '151 patent.

Case Questions

1. Following the *Markman* hearing, what were the three clauses in the claims that were relevant to the appeal in *Bid for Position, LLC v. AOL, LLC*?
2. What were the main reasons given by the court in finding that there was not literal infringement by the patent for AdWords with Position Preference?
3. Why did the Federal Circuit reject the doctrine of equivalents argument?
4. Bid for Position argued that the Google AdWords system infringes the "position of priority" under which doctrine?

Markman Hearings

In patent infringement cases, the court will often conduct a Markman hearing. A Markman hearing is a hearing where the court receives evidence and arguments concerning the construction to be given to terms in a patent claim.[26] The name "Markman" originates from the landmark decision *Markman v. Westview Instruments, Inc.*, 52 F.3d 967 (Fed. Cir. 1995), where the Federal Circuit held that the construction of patent claims, and therefore the scope of the patentee's rights, is a question of law. In a Markman hearing, the court interprets the claims before the question of infringement is submitted to the fact-finder.

Remedies in Patent Infringement Cases

If the patentee prevails in a patent infringement case, the patentee may be entitled to money damages and injunctive relief. The typical remedies in a patent infringement include a permanent injunction to prevent future infringement and damages designed to compensate the patent owner for past infringement.[27] The court may order a preliminary and/or a permanent injunction in a patent infringement action.

An injunction can prohibit the sale or use of an infringing device or method. In 2008, the Federal Circuit in *Broadcom Corp. v. Qualcomm Inc.*, 543 F.3d 683 (Fed. Cir. 2008), affirmed a permanent injunction that enjoined Qualcomm from importing chipsets used in mobile radio devices such as cell phone handsets. The technology at issue involved wireless voice and data communications on cellular telephone networks in so-called third-generation ("3G") baseband processor.[28]

A patent owner who establishes infringement can also recover reasonable royalties. A reasonable royalty is the royalty which a licensee would be willing to pay and still make a reasonable profit from use of the patented invention.[29] Where damages are calculated on a reasonable royalty basis, no other compensatory damages may be awarded. For design patents, patent owners may recover lost profits. The federal statute provides that the infringer of a design patent "shall be liable to the owner to the extent of his total profit."[30]

The court, in a patent infringement suit, may also increase the damages, up to three times the amount found, for willful, deliberate, and intentional infringement.[31] "Willfulness" requires the fact finder (either the judge or jury) to find that "clear and convincing" evidence shows that infringer acted in disregard of the patent and had no reasonable basis for believing it had right to do the acts.[32] To obtain enhanced damages requires, at least, a showing of "objective recklessness."[33] The court, in exceptional cases, may also award reasonable attorney's fees to the prevailing party in a patent infringement suit.[34]

Utilization of Alternative Dispute Resolution in Patent Cases

Because patent cases often involve complicated technical matters that require the consultation of experts, patent litigation can be very expensive and may last for many years. To save time and money, many parties in patent cases will often utilize alternative dispute resolution (ADR). Federal courts are now requiring the use of ADR whenever possible. Settlement negotiation, mediation, and arbitration are common forms of alternative dispute resolution in patent cases. The threat of injunctive relief can be a strong incentive for using ADR.

In 2001, NTP sued RIM (owner of BlackBerry handheld devices) for infringing its wireless technology patents.[35] After the jury found NTP's patent to be valid and RIM to have willfully infringed the patent, approximately $33 million in compensatory damages was awarded to NTP along with a permanent injunction to enjoin RIM from further manufacture, use, importation, or sale of all alleged BlackBerry systems, software, and handhelds. The Federal Circuit affirmed the infringement claim in 2005, which meant that an injunction may ensue for the BlackBerry devices. Under the threat of injunctive relief, RIM agreed to settle the dispute for $612.5 million.

TRADE SECRETS

Along with copyrights, trademarks, and patents, business owners may also secure intellectual property rights in trade secrets. Trade secret law only protects secret information. A trade secret is a formula, process, device, or other business information that is kept confidential to maintain an advantage over competitors.[36] A party may protect information as a trade secret as long as it is not generally known in the industry or readily ascertainable through independent investigation.

Unlike patent law, which is governed by federal law, the law of trade secrets is governed by state law. The Uniform Trade Secrets Act (UTSA) is a 1979 model statute that codifies the basic principles of common-law trade-secret protection. It protects information, regardless of the manner, mode, or form in which it is stored, whether on paper, in a computer, in one's memory, or in any other medium. For liability to exist under the UTSA, a trade secret must exist, and either a person's acquisition of the trade secret, their disclosure of the trade secret to others, or their use of the trade secret must be improper. As of 2010, the UTSA has been adopted in some form or another in 45 states, the District of Columbia, and the U.S. Virgin Islands. Legislation has also been introduced in Massachusetts, New Jersey, and New York.

A plaintiff claiming misappropriation of a trade secret must prove that (1) the plaintiff possessed a trade secret; (2) the defendant is using that trade secret in breach of an agreement, confidence, or duty, or as a result of discovery by improper means; and (3) the defendant's use of the trade secret is to the plaintiff's detriment.[37] Customer lists, prices, costs, processes, novel software, and specific implementations of manufacturing concepts are common examples of trade secrets.

The Internet, widespread use of cell phones, and the other technological tools pose problems for companies that want to secure trade secrets. Many courts assume that a trade secret posted on the Internet is generally known and consequently has lost its trade secret status. Even when a party posting trade secret information may not have intended to cause harm to the trade secret owner, the nature of the Internet is such that the secret could nonetheless be destroyed.[38] In *Religious Technology Center v. Lerma*, 908 F. Supp. 1362 (E.D. Va. 1995), a disgruntled former member of the Church of Scientology published documents taken from a court record on the Internet. The court refused to issue an injunction sought by the Church because the documents no longer qualified as trade secrets.[39] The court explicitly stated that "[o]nce a trade secret is posted on the Internet, it is effectively part of the public domain, impossible to retrieve."

A trade secret requires that the owner take reasonable precautions to protect the secret. The most common situation involving a trade secret misappropriation involves an employer bringing an action against a former employee. Companies should adopt policies regarding remote access to company computer networks and systems, telecommuting, e-mail, and Internet usage, and access rights to sensitive information. Companies can also utilize technological tools such as firewalls, user monitoring, and encryption to protect data to protect trade secrets. Unlike patents and copyrights, trade secrets may be protected for an indefinite period, so long as the information remains valuable and secret.

An owner of a trade secret may enter into a confidentiality agreement to prevent disclosure of protected trade secrets. A trade secret owner must establish that it took reasonable measures to protect its purported trade secrets. Based on one study, confidentiality agreements with employees and business partners are the most important factors when courts decide reasonable measures.[40] In order to protect companies' trade secrets, such as software or databases, companies often use non-disclosure and confidentiality agreements with their prospective and current clients in software licenses to protect their interests while rendering critical information about the operation of their software available to their clients.

The owner of a trade secret may file a motion for a preliminary injunction to enforce a confidentiality agreement and prevent disclosure of trade secrets. In deciding whether to grant a motion for a preliminary injunction, courts often weigh four factors: (1) whether the plaintiff can show a likelihood of success on the merits, (2) whether the plaintiff can show that it would suffer irreparable harm if the injunction was denied, (3) the balance of the relevant hardships, and (4) any impact that the court's ruling may have on the public interest. In *ANSYS, Inc. v. Computational Dynamics North America, Ltd.*, 595 F.3d 75 (1st Cir. 2010), the U.S. Court of Appeals denied a software manufacturer's motion for preliminary injunction filed against a former employee who took a job with a competitor. The software manufacturer failed to show that it suffered irreparable harm. Even if the former employee had access to confidential proprietary information, the software manufacturer failed to show that the employee was likely to use that confidential information during the course of his employment with the competitor. Therefore, for an owner of a trade secret to succeed in a motion for a preliminary injunction to enforce a confidentiality agreement, the plaintiff must show "irreparable harm" or that it would face injury from the disclosure.

Summary

A patent is an intellectual property right granted by the U.S. government to an inventor to exclude others from making, using, offering for sale, or selling the invention throughout the United States. Generally, the term of a new patent is 20 years. There are three basic types of patents: (1) utility patents; (2) design patents; and (3) plant patents. Business methods are patentable subject matter. A cyberpatent or Internet patent is a type of utility patent granted on an invention that combines business methods and software programs for Internet applications. To be patentable, a patent must be nonobvious. Patent prosecution involves the process of applying for a patent through the USPTO and negotiating with the patent examiner. Applicants for a patent may appeal the decision of the patent examiner to the Board of Patent Appeals and Inferences (BPAI) and the U.S. Court of Appeals for the Federal Circuit (Federal Circuit). There are several different types of patent infringement, including direct infringement, contributory infringement, induced infringement, literal infringement, and the doctrine of equivalents. Prevailing plaintiffs may recover both money damages and injunctive relief in a patent infringement action. Triple damages may be awarded for willful, deliberate, and intentional infringement. Because of the expense and time associated with patent infringement litigation, many parties will use alternative dispute resolution, including settlement negotiation, mediation, and arbitration. The Uniform Trade Secrets Act (UTSA) is a 1979 model statute that codifies the basic principles of common-law trade-secret protection. A trade secret requires that the owner take reasonable precautions to protect the secret. Unlike patents and copyrights, trade secrets may be protected for an indefinite period, so long as the information remains valuable and secret.

Key Terms

Board of Patent Appeals and Interferences (BPAI) *59*
business method patent *54*
design patent *54*
interference *56*
Markman hearing *62*
patent *53*
patentee *60*
patent agent *56*
patent prosecution *56*
prior art *59*
U.S. Court of Appeals for the Federal Circuit ("Federal Circuit" or "CAFC") *59*
utility patent *54*

Review Questions

1. Describe the requirements for patentability and what is considered nonobvious.
2. What are the requirements for obtaining a business method patent? Provide an example of a business method patent.
3. What is patent prosecution?
4. What is the procedure for an applicant to appeal the decision of the USPTO in denying a patent application?
5. What is a Markman hearing?
6. What are the remedies available in a patent infringement action if the infringement is willful?
7. How can a company protect trade secrets?

Discussion Questions

1. In 1982, Congress created the U.S. Court of Appeals for the Federal Circuit that has exclusive jurisdiction over patent appeals. What are the advantages of having one specialized appellate court to hear patent cases? What are the potential disadvantages?
2. In patent prosecution, applicants for a patent are required to exhaust administrative remedies by appealing the decision of the patent examiner with the Board of Patent Appeals and Interferences before filing an action for judicial review in federal court. Why should an applicant for a patent be required to exhaust administrative remedies before seeking judicial review?
3. The USPTO, like other federal agencies, has a limited budget despite the growth in the number of patent applications awaiting first action and the number of applications still pending. Visit the USPTO website and find the Patents Data Visualization Center (Patent Dashboard) that visually displays patent statistics, including the time to process applications and the current backlog. What effect does a backlog in the time for processing patent applications have on innovation and the rights of inventors? Some individuals have proposed that the budget of the USPTO should be increased and others have called for increased filing fees to help offset the cost of patent examiners. What do you think is the best solution for dealing with the lag time in processing patent applications? Explain.

Exercises

1. Run a search on the Internet, such as Google News, or through your library's database of newspapers and magazines and find a recent patent infringement case involving a technology company. You might consider a search for "patent infringement" or something similar. Then write a summary of the patent infringement case and explain how you would decide the case if you were a juror or judge in the case. The news article can involve a recently filed complaint, judicial opinion, verdict, or appeal. In addition, retrieve the full text of the patent in question on the USPTO website and any corresponding images.
2. You are working for a law firm or company where you frequently need to research U.S., European, and Japanese patents. The leading fee-based patent research systems are Micropatent.com, Lexis, Westlaw, Dialog, and Delphion. After researching these different fee-based patent research services on the Internet, write a memorandum to your supervisor where you compare and contrast the different fee-based systems for researching patents. In your memorandum, you should also make a recommendation on which service to use and justify the expense. You might start your research by looking under foreign patents at Zimmerman's Research Guide at http://law.lexisnexis.com/infopro/zimmermans/ to explore different fee-based patent research systems.
3. In October 2010, Microsoft Corp. filed a patent infringement action against Motorola, Inc. for infringement of nine Microsoft patents by Motorola's Android-based smartphones (also called "Droid" phones). The patents at issue relate to a range of functionality embodied in Motorola's Android smartphone devices that are essential to the smartphone user experience, including synchronizing e-mail, calendars and contacts, scheduling meetings, and notifying applications of changes in signal strength and battery power. Retrieve "U.S. Patent No. 5,579,517 Common name space for long and short filenames" from the USPTO website or Google Scholar. Then provide the following information for U.S. Patent No. 5,579,517 which is one of the patents at issue in the case involving the Android phones: (1) Names of inventors; (2) Name of assignee; (3) Date of filing; (4) Date of patent; (5) Name of the Primary Examiner; (6) Name of the Attorney, Agent or Firm.
4. You are working for the corporate legal department for Google. Oracle has filed a lawsuit against Google claiming that Google's popular Android operating system infringed Java patents that it acquired when it bought Sun Microsystems. Conduct research online to learn more about the actual Oracle vs. Google lawsuit. Then write a memorandum to the senior general counsel at Google where you discuss the advantages and advantages of settling the lawsuit against Oracle rather than litigating the claims. In the memorandum, you should also make a recommendation on whether should Google should defend the lawsuit or settle with Oracle.

Related Internet Sites

http://www.uspto.gov/
U.S. Patent and Trademark Office official website

http://patft.uspto.gov/netahtml/PTO/search-adv.htm
USPTO Patent Full-Text and Image Search

http://www.uspto.gov/web/offices/pac/doc/general/
USPTO General Information Concerning Patents

http://www.uspto.gov/web/offices/pac/mpep/index.htm
Manual of Patent Examining Procedure

http://www.cafc.uscourts.gov/
U.S. Court of Appeals for the Federal Circuit Official Website

http://www.patentlyo.com/
Patent Law Blog maintained by Dennis Crouch, Associate Professor at the University of Missouri School of Law

http://www.theiplawblog.com/
Intellectual property blog maintained by the law firm Weintraub Genshlea Chediak

http://ipwatchdog.com/
IPWatchdog is a blog maintained by patent attorney Gene Quinn.

http://www.chicagoiplitigation.com/
Chicago IP Litigation Blog

http://patentlawcenter.pli.edu/
PLI Patent Practice Center

http://www.law.berkeley.edu/bclt.htm
Berkeley Center for Law & Technology

http://www.oyez.org/cases/2000-2009/2009/2009_08_964
Oral arguments from the U.S. Supreme Court in *Bilski v. Kappos*, 130 S.Ct. 3218 (2010)

End Notes

1. University of New Hampshire School of Law's Franklin Pierce Law Center for Intellectual Property, Quotes on Patent Lawyers—Compiled by Homer Blair, available at: http://www.ipmall.info/hosted_resources/blair_quotes.asp.
2. 35 U.S.C. § 154.
3. *Sinclair & Carroll Co. v. Interchemical Corp.*, 325 U.S. 327, 330-331 (1945).
4. USPTO, General Information Concerning Patents, Rev. January 2005, available at: http://www.uspto.gov/web/offices/pac/doc/general/#patent/.
5. 35 U.S.C. § 101.
6. Pub. L. No. 593, §§ 1-3, 66 Stat. 792 (codified at 35 U.S.C.).
7. Peter A. Jackman, *Adoption of a First-to-File Patent System: A Proposal*, 26 U. BALT. L. REV. 67, 67 (1997).
8. Black's Law Dictionary (9th ed. 2009).
9. Hillary Greene, *Patent Pooling Behind The Veil of Uncertainty: Antitrust, Competition Policy, and the Vaccine Industry*, 90 B.U. L. REV. 1397, 1405 (2010) .
10. 35 U.S.C. § 103.
11. 60 Am. Jur. 2d Patents § 93.
12. Black's Law Dictionary (9th ed. 2009).
13. *Storage Technology Corp. v. Quantum Corp.*, 370 F. Supp. 2d 1116 (D. Colo. 2005).
14. 60 Am. Jur. 2d Patents § 646.
15. 35 U.S.C. § 6.
16. 28 U.S.C. § 1295(a)(4)(A).
17. *Searfoss v. Pioneer Consol. Corp.*, 374 F.3d 1142, 1148 (Fed. Cir. 2004).
18. 28 U.S.C. § 1338.
19. Jack Q. Lever, Jr., *The New Court of Appeals for the Federal Circuit (Part I)*, 64 J. PAT. OFF. SOC'Y 178, 188 (1982).
20. 60 Am. Jur. 2d Patents § 782.
21. *Sing v. Culture Products, Inc.*, 469 F.Supp. 1249, 1254 (E.D.Mo. 1979).
22. 60 Am. Jur. 2d Patents § 783.
23. *Telemac Cellular Corp. v. Topp Telecom, Inc.*, 247 F.3d 1316 (Fed. Cir. 2001).
24. *Festo Corp. v. Shoketsu Kinzoku Kogyo Kabushiki Co.*, 535 U.S. 722, 731-32 (2002).
25. *Lee v. Dayton-Hudson Corp.*, 838 F.2d 1186, 1190 (Fed. Cir. 1988).
26. Black's Law Dictionary (9th ed. 2009).
27. Mark A. Lemley & Ragesh K. Tangri, Ending Patent Law's Willfulness Game, 18 BERKELEY TECH. L.J. 1085, 1110 (2003).
28. *Broadcom Corp. v. Qualcomm Inc.*, 543 F.3d 683 (Fed. Cir. 2008).
29. 60 Am. Jur. 2d Patents § 956.
30. 35 U.S.C. § 289.
31. 35 U.S.C. § 284.
32. *American Medical Systems, Inc. v. Medical Engineering Corp.*, 6 F.3d 1523, 1530 (Fed. Cir. 1993).
33. *In re Seagate Technology, LLC*, 497 F.3d 1360 (Fed. Cir. 2007).
34. 60 Am. Jur. 2d Patents § 966.
35. *NTP, Inc. v. Research in Motion, Ltd.* (BlackBerry), 418 F.3d 1282 (Fed. Cir. 2005).
36. Uniform Law Commissioners, A Few Facts About the Uniform Trade Secrets Act, available at: http://www.nccusl.org/update/uniformact_factsheets/uniformacts-fs-utsa.asp/.
37. *Bear, Stearns Funding, Inc. v. Interface Group-Nevada, Inc.*, 361 F. Supp. 2d 283, 304 (S.D.N.Y. 2005).
38. Elizabeth A. Rowe, *Introducing a Takedown for Trade Secrets on the Internet*, 2007 WIS. L. REV. 1041, 1047 (2007).
39. *Religious Tech. Ctr. v. Lerma*, 908 F. Supp. 1362 (E.D. Va. 1995).
40. David S. Almeling, et. al., *A Statistical Analysis of Trade Secret Litigation in State Courts*, 46 Gonz. L. Rev. 57, 61 (2010–2011).

CHAPTER

5 E-Commerce and Online Contracts

A contract is no less a contract simply because it is entered into via a computer.

JUDGE JOHN M. STEADMAN *in Forrest v. Verizon Communications, Inc., 805 A.2d 1007, 1010 (D.C. 2002)*

LEARNING OBJECTIVES

After completing this chapter, you will be able to:

1. Explain the sources of contract law relating to e-contracts, including the Uniform Electronic Transactions Act (UETA), E-SIGN Act, and the Principles of the Law of Software Contracts.
2. Describe the basic requirements for a valid contract, including mutual assent and consideration.
3. Explain fundamental principles of contract law, including capacity, legal purpose, and the statute of frauds.
4. Compare and contrast clickwrap agreements and browsewrap agreements.
5. Explain the enforceability of e-contracts.
6. Explain and identify the common clauses contained in an end user license agreement (EULA).

CHAPTER OVERVIEW

The rise and growth of the Internet has also led to the increased use of e-contracts. This chapter discusses the validity and enforcement of contracts entered by means of a computer or technology. This chapter will discuss the main sources of contract law, including the Uniform Electronic Transactions Act (UETA), E-SIGN Act, and the Principles of the Law of Software Contracts. This chapter will also discuss the basic requirements for forming a valid contract and the enforceability of contracts. An analysis of common provisions in an end user license agreement (EULA) will also be given.

SOURCES OF CONTRACT LAW

In the United States, the principal sources of contract law are the common law, Restatement (Second) of Contracts, the Uniform Commercial Code (UCC), and the United Nations Convention on Contracts for the International Sale of Goods (CISG).

Software licensing agreements and commercial transactions conducted via the Internet are also governed by the Uniform Electronic Transactions Act (UETA), the Electronic Signatures in Global and National Commerce Act (E-Sign Act), the Uniform Computer Information Transactions Act (UCITA), the Principles of the Law of Software Contracts, and federal intellectual property laws.

Common Law

In most jurisdictions, contract law is principally governed by the **common law** which is often called caselaw. The common law is the body of law derived from judicial decisions, rather than from statutes or constitutions.[1] The common law is based on statements of principles found in the decisions of the courts created by judges.[2] The common law in the United States traces its origins in part to the common law of England.

Restatement (Second) of Contracts

The **Restatement** (Second) of Contracts, adopted by the American Law Institute (ALI) has no legal force but still provides highly persuasive legal authority with respect to contracts. The Restatement uses a distinctive format of black-letter rules, official comments, illustrations, and reporter's notes. Although the Restatements are frequently cited in cases and commentary, a Restatement provision is not binding on a court, unless it has been officially adopted as the law by that jurisdiction's highest court.[3]

Uniform Commercial Code

The **Uniform Commercial Code (UCC)** is a uniform law that governs commercial transactions, including sales of goods, secured transactions, and negotiable instruments. The UCC (or sometimes simply called the "Code") has been adopted in some form by every state as well as the District of Columbia. Article 2 of the UCC governs the sale of goods.

United Nations Convention on Contracts for the International Sale of Goods

The **United Nations Convention on Contracts for the International Sale of Goods (CISG)** (pronounced "sis-gee") governs many transactions for the sale of goods between parties with places of business in different nations. The Convention has been ratified by many of the leading trading nations including the United States, China, Canada, Mexico, Germany, Denmark, and Australia.[4] The Convention also went into effect for Japan on August 1, 2009.[5] All European Union members are signatories to the CISG with the notable exceptions of the United Kingdom, Ireland, and Portugal.

Uniform Electronic Transactions Act

The **Uniform Electronic Transactions Act (UETA)** legitimized the ability of parties to form contracts electronically. EUTA applies to "transactions" defined as "the conduct of business, commercial or governmental affairs." The UETA, which has been adopted in 47 states (all except Illinois and New York, which have their own broad laws on

Common Law
The body of law derived from judicial decisions, rather than from statutes or constitutions. Also called caselaw.

Restatement
One of several influential treatises published by the American Law Institute describing the law in a given area and guiding its development such as the Restatement (Second) of Contracts and the Restatement (Second) of Torts.

Uniform Commercial Code (UCC)
A uniform law that governs commercial transactions, including sales of goods, secured transactions, and negotiable instruments. The UCC has been adopted in some form by every state and the District of Columbia.

United Nations Convention on Contracts for the International Sale of Goods (CISG)
An international treaty that establishes uniform rules to govern international commercial contracts in order to remove "legal barriers in . . . and promote the development of international trade." In 1986, the United States became a party to the CISG, which went into force in 1988. U.S. courts are required to apply the treaty, where appropriate, to settle international contract disputes rather than using the previously applicable Uniform Commercial Code (UCC) rules of the various states.

electronic transactions, and Washington, which has a somewhat narrower law), plus the District of Columbia, Puerto Rico, and the U.S. Virgin Islands, establishes that electronic and non-electronic records are equal.[6]

Uniform Electronic Transactions Act (UETA) A 1999 model law designed to support electronic commerce by providing means for legally recognizing and retaining electronic records, establishing how parties can bind themselves in an electronic transaction, and providing for the use of electronic records by governmental agencies.

Electronic Signatures in Global and National Commerce Act

In 2000, Congress passed the Federal **Electronic Signatures in Global and National Commerce Act (E-SIGN Act)** which is a federal counterpart to the UETA.[7] The E-SIGN Act makes electronic and paper-and-ink transactions equally enforceable for interstate and foreign contracts. This federal law allows states to preempt it by enacting the UETA. The UETA and E-SIGN Act have now legitimized the ability of parties to form contracts electronically both at the federal and state levels. Unlike the E-SIGN Act, however, under UETA parties must first agree to contract electronically. (See Figure 5.1.) When the parties are silent on the issue, an agreement via e-mail can be implied. An **electronic signature**, also called a **digital signature**, is an electronic symbol, sound, or process that is either attached to or logically associated with a document (such as a contract or other record) and executed or adopted by a person with the intent to sign the document. Types of electronic signatures include a typed name at the end of an email, a digital image of a handwritten signature, and the click of an "I Accept" button on an e-commerce site.

Electronic Signatures in Global and National Commerce Act (E-SIGN Act) A federal law that establishes the legal equivalency of electronic contracts, electronic signatures, and other electronic records with their paper counterparts. 15 U.S.C. §§ 7001–7031.

Electronic Signature An electronic symbol, sound, or process that is either attached to or logically associated with a document (such as a contract or other record) and executed or adopted by a person with the intent to sign the document. Types of electronic signatures include a typed name at the end of an e-mail, a digital image of a handwritten signature, and the click of an "I Accept" button on an e-commerce site.

Digital Signature A secure, digital code attached to an electronically transmitted message that uniquely identifies and authenticates the sender. Consists of a "hashed" number combined with a number assigned to a document (a private-encryption key).

Uniform Computer Information Transactions Act

The **Uniform Computer Information Transactions Act (UCITA)** was approved by the National Conference of Commissioners on Uniform State Laws (NCCUSL) in 2000 and amended in 2002, succeeding the Uniform Computer Information Transactions Act promulgated in 1999. The UCITA is called it a "commercial contract code for computer information transactions."[8]

To date, only Virginia and Maryland have adopted the UCITA. Several states have enacted anti-UCITA provisions, including Iowa, North Carolina, West Virginia, and Vermont.[9] While UCITA was originally submitted as a proposed Uniform Act and modification to the Uniform Commercial Code (UCC) by the National Conference of

The text of the Electronic Signatures in Global and National Commerce Act (E-SIGN Act), 15 U.S.C. § 7001, states in part:

a. In general

Notwithstanding any statute, regulation, or other rule of law (other than this subchapter and subchapter II of this chapter), with respect to any transaction in or affecting interstate or foreign commerce—

(1) a signature, contract, or other record relating to such transaction may not be denied legal effect, validity, or enforceability solely because it is in electronic form; and
(2) a contract relating to such transaction may not be denied legal effect, validity, or enforceability solely because an electronic signature or electronic record was used in its formation.

b. Preservation of rights and obligations

This subchapter does not—

(1) limit, alter, or otherwise affect any requirement imposed by a statute, regulation, or rule of law relating to the rights and obligations of persons under such statute, regulation, or rule of law other than a requirement that contracts or other records be written, signed, or in nonelectronic form;

FIGURE 5.1 E-SIGN Act

The American Law Institute is the leading independent organization in the United States producing scholarly work to clarify, modernize, and otherwise improve the law. The Institute (made up of 4,000 lawyers, judges, and law professors of the highest qualifications) drafts, discusses, revises, and publishes Restatements of the Law, model statutes, and principles of law that are enormously influential in the courts and legislatures, as well as in legal scholarship and education. The ALI adopted the Principles of the Law of Software Contracts and the Restatement Second of Contracts. The ALI is a 501(c)(3) nonprofit organization incorporated in the District of Columbia with headquarters in Philadelphia. The Restatements, adopted by the American Law Institute (ALI) are not binding on the courts, but are generally very persuasive. To learn more about the ALI, visit www.ali.org.

FIGURE 5.2 The American Law Institute (ALI)

Uniform Computer Information Transactions Act (UCITA)
A model law that regulates software licensing and computer-information transactions. UCITA applies to contracts for the licensing or purchase of software, contracts for software development, and contracts for access to databases through the Internet.

Commissioners on Uniform State Laws (NCCUSL) and the American Law Institute (ALI), it was withdrawn in 2002 after the ALI did not grant its assent.

Principles of the Law of Software Contracts

The Principles of the Law of Software Contracts (Principles) was approved by the American Law Institute (ALI) membership in May 2009. (See Figure 5.2.) The goal of the project is to "clarify and unify the law of software transactions."[10] However, the Principles will not become law in any jurisdiction unless and until a court adopts them. Only time will tell whether the project will accomplish this goal.

The current law of software transactions, comprised of common law, Article 2 of the Uniform Commercial Code (UCC), and federal intellectual property law, among other things, lacks uniformity among the different states. The Principles of the Law of Software Contracts hopes to clarify and uniform the law.

FUNDAMENTAL PRINCIPLES OF CONTRACT LAW

The basic requirements for an agreement are mutual agreement and consideration. Black's Law Dictionary (9th ed. 2009) defines a contract as "an agreement between two or more parties creating obligations that are enforceable or otherwise recognizable at law." Parties to a contract must also have capacity to enter into the contract, and the contract must have a legal purpose. Some contracts, such as a contract for the sale of real estate, must be in writing to satisfy the statute of frauds.

Mutual Assent

One of the requirements for a valid contract is mutual assent or mutual agreement. The Restatement (Second) of Contracts states that mutual assent is usually reached after one party has made an offer and the offer is "followed by an acceptance by the other party."

Acceptance occurs when a party communicates a willingness to be bound by the proposed agreement. The parties must have a "meeting of the minds" as to all essential and material terms of the agreement. A purported acceptance that changes or qualifies an offer's material terms is considered a rejection of the offer and a counter-offer rather than an acceptance. The term *agreement*, although frequently used as synonymous with the word *contract*, is really an expression of greater breadth of meaning and less technicality.[11] Every contract is an agreement; but not every agreement is a contract. In its colloquial sense, the term *agreement* would include any arrangement between two or more persons intended to affect their relations (whether legal or otherwise) to each other.

When dealing with online contracts and end user license agreements (EULAs), acceptance often takes place when a user clicks "I agree" to the terms and conditions of the contract. If an offer is made electronically, it can clearly be accepted by electronic means. Similarly, as long as electronic communication is customary in the particular business involved, electronic acceptance is sufficient. Through a series of e-mails, alone or combined with other forms of communication such as telephone, the parties can come to an understanding sufficient to form the basis of a contract.

Consideration

To be enforceable, a contract must be supported by consideration, which is defined as something of legal value given in exchange for a promise. Consideration can be a promise to pay money, property, providing services, a promise not to do something, or anything else of value. For example, in a contract where Jane promises to develop a new website for Acme Corp. in exchange for $2,500, Jane's consideration is the promise to develop the website, and Acme Corp.'s consideration is the promise to pay money.

A gift promise, also called a gratuitous promise, is an unenforceable promise because it lacks consideration. For example, suppose Walter promises to give his grandson a new Camaro sports car and then rescinds the promise. The grandson would have no recourse because it was a gift promise that lacked consideration. But suppose Walter promised his grandson a new Camaro sports car for getting a 4.0 GPA during his first year in college, and the grandson performed as required under the contract, then the contract would be enforceable.

As a general rule, past consideration is not sufficient consideration for an enforceable contract. Past consideration is a prior act or performance that will not support a new contract. New consideration must be given.

A promise also lacks consideration if a person promises to perform an act where they already have an obligation to do so. A pre-existing duty is a promise that lacks consideration if a person promises to perform an act or do something they already have an obligation to do. A pre-existing duty sometimes arises where one of the parties to an existing contract seeks to modify the terms of the contract. To modify an existing contract, there must be new consideration agreed to by both parties. In *Karvaly v. eBay, Inc.*, 245 F.R.D. 71, 87 (E.D. N.Y. 2007), a federal court in New York affirmed the pre-existing duty rule in a case involving a settlement agreement involving PayPal (owned by eBay). The court held that PayPal is "already under an obligation to make the changes to its website that are contemplated by the . . . [a]greement, its performance of that pre-existing duty cannot constitute consideration for the . . . [new] release."

Capacity

In order to form a valid and legal contract, the contracting parties must have the legal capacity to do so. A court will not uphold a contract if one of the parties lacks the capacity to enter into a contract, such as minors or people who are mentally incapacitated. Contract law defines an infant as a person under the age of eighteen. Infancy may be used as a defense in a court action to enforce a contract.[12]

There is an important distinction between "void" and "voidable" contracts. A void contract is no contract at all. It binds no one and is a mere nullity.[13] For example, a contract for the sale of illegal drugs is void since it is an illegal contract. If a contract is voidable, the transaction is not wholly void. The parties may later ratify the contract by either express or implied conduct. If a person wants to rely upon the invalidity of a voidable contract, the person must disclaim it and refuse to permit anything to be done under the contract. Most courts hold that an infant is required to disaffirm a contract within a reasonable time after attaining majority or age eighteen.

In *A.V. ex rel. Vanderhye v. iParadigms, LLC*, 562 F.3d 630 (4th Cir. 2009), which was also discussed in Chapter 2 on copyrights, four high school students filed a copyright infringement action against iParadigms, LLC, the company that owns the plagiarism detection software Turnitin found on www.turnitin.com. The students argued that the clickwrap agreement was unenforceable based on the doctrine of infancy. The court held that the contract with an infant is not void, only voidable by the infant upon attaining the age of majority. Plaintiffs cannot use the doctrine of infancy as a "sword" to void a contract while retaining the benefits of the contract. The court in *iParadigms* quoted the contracts law treatise Williston on Contracts § 9.14 (4th ed.) that "[w]hen the infant has received consideration which he still possesses, . . . he cannot, upon reaching majority, keep it and refuse to pay."

Legal Purpose

An illegal contract is not enforceable. A contract that is illegal or in violation of the law is void as is a contract that aids or assists any party in violating the law.[14] Thus, an illegal contract confers no right upon the wrongdoer. A court will not enforce a contract with an inherent purpose to violate the law.

Where the performance of a contract would make the parties guilty of a crime, the contracts should not be enforced. Similarly, where the consideration involves an illegal act or violates public policy, the agreement is void. For example, online transactions for the sale of illegal narcotics or firearms are unenforceable in a court of law.

In *Smith v. Saulsbury*, 649 S.E.2d 344 (Ga. App. 2007), a Georgia Court of Appeals court held that a contract between an Internet advertiser and a software producer to advertise and sell software for copying DVDs was not void as illegal for purposes of the advertiser's action seeking unpaid commissions. The court decided that even if the purchasers of the software may have violated federal copyright law by using it to copy commercial DVDs containing anticopying encryption, the illegal use was not required for performance under the contract.

Statute of Frauds

Under the **statute of frauds**, certain types of contracts, such as contracts for the sale of real estate, are unenforceable unless the contract is in writing and signed. (See Figure 5.3.) According to the Restatement (Second) of Contracts § 110, the following classes of contracts are subject to some form of the statute of frauds and are unenforceable unless there is a written memorandum or an exception:

Statute of Frauds A statute (based on the English Statute of Frauds) designed to prevent fraud and perjury by requiring certain contracts to be in writing and signed by the party to be charged.

1. a contract of an executor or administrator to answer for a duty of his or her decedent (the executor-administrator provision);
2. a contract to answer for the duty of another (the suretyship provision);
3. a contract made upon consideration of marriage (the marriage provision);
4. a contract for the sale of an interest in land (the land contract provision); and
5. a contract that is not to be performed within one year from the making thereof (the one-year provision).

Some courts have held that e-mails are insufficient to meet the statute of frauds, in part, because they were "unsigned" by the party to be charged.[15] In some cases, courts have held that e-mail messages bearing the typed name of the sender, rather than a handwritten signature or an electronic copy of such a signature, were signed writings. In *Sigg v. Coltrane*, 45 Kan. App. 2d 65, 253 P.3d 781 (Kan. Ct. App. 2010), the Kansas Court of Appeals held that an e-mail exchange to purchase certain land was not sufficient to satisfy the requirements of the statute of frauds. The court stated that

The California Civil Code Section 1624 codifies the general statute of frauds

a. The following contracts are invalid, unless they, or some note or memorandum thereof, are in writing and subscribed by the party to be charged or by the party's agent:
   (1) An agreement that by its terms is not to be performed within a year from the making thereof.
   (2) A special promise to answer for the debt, default, or miscarriage of another, except in the cases provided for in Section 2794.
   (3) An agreement for the leasing for a longer period than one year, or for the sale of real property, or of an interest therein; such an agreement, if made by an agent of the party sought to be charged, is invalid, unless the authority of the agent is in writing, subscribed by the party sought to be charged.
   (4) An agreement authorizing or employing an agent, broker, or any other person to purchase or sell real estate, or to lease real estate for a longer period than one year, or to procure, introduce, or find a purchaser or seller of real estate or a lessee or lessor of real estate where the lease is for a longer period than one year, for compensation or a commission.
   (5) An agreement that by its terms is not to be performed during the lifetime of the promisor.
   (6) An agreement by a purchaser of real property to pay an indebtedness secured by a mortgage or deed of trust upon the property purchased, unless assumption of the indebtedness by the purchaser is specifically provided for in the conveyance of the property.
   (7) A contract, promise, undertaking, or commitment to loan money or to grant or extend credit, in an amount greater than one hundred thousand dollars ($100,000), not primarily for personal, family, or household purposes, made by a person engaged in the business of lending or arranging for the lending of money or extending credit. For purposes of this section, a contract, promise, undertaking or commitment to loan money secured solely by residential property consisting of one to four dwelling units shall be deemed to be for personal, family, or household purposes.

FIGURE 5.3 California Civil Code section 1624

the agreement clearly falls within the ambit of the statute of frauds since there no instrument in writing signed by the defendant that would take the agreement out of the statute of frauds. In *Leist v. Tugendhaft*, 64 A.D.3d 687, 882 N.Y.S.2d 521 (N.Y.A.D. 2009) (Case 5.1), a New York state court determined that an e-mail exchange to buy a beachfront house failed to satisfy the writing requirement under the statute of frauds since the "party to be charged" did not authorize the transaction owner. If a contract falls under the statute of frauds, the contract must be signed the "party to be charged" against whom enforcement of the contract is sought.

CASE 5.1

The Case of an E-Mail Exchange to Buy a Beachfront House

Leist v. Tugendhaft, *64 A.D.3d 687, 882 N.Y.S.2d 521 (N.Y.A.D. 2009)*

The plaintiff commenced this action, inter alia, for specific performance of a purported contract for the sale of real property and filed a notice of pendency against the defendants' beachfront property located in Westhampton, New York. The purported contract consisted of a "Memo of Sale," subscribed by no one, sent as an attachment to an e-mail from the defendants' "listing agent" to the plaintiff's attorney. The plaintiff wrote on the memo of sale that he unconditionally accepted the terms set forth therein, signed it, and asserted that this constituted an enforceable contract.

General Obligations Law § 5-703(2) [New York's statute of fraud provision] states that a contract for the sale of real property "is void unless the contract or some note or memorandum thereof, expressing the consideration, is in writing, subscribed by the party to be charged, or by his lawful agent thereunto authorized by writing." Assuming, arguendo, that an e-mail is sufficient to comply with the statute of frauds with respect to contracts for the conveyance of real property, the document in issue here nevertheless is clearly inadequate, since it was not subscribed, even electronically, by the defendants who are the parties to be charged, or by anyone purporting to act in their behalf.

The fact that the listing agent was identified as the sender in the e-mail to which the attachment was made does not satisfy the subscription requirement. At best, the e-mail was the equivalent of a cover letter to a proposed contract, the signing of which is insufficient to satisfy the subscription requirement.

In any event, an agent may only bind a party to a real estate contract if authorized to do so in writing (*see* General Obligations Law 5-703[2]; *Bowling v. Pedzik,* 302 A.D.2d 343, 754 N.Y.S.2d 653). The unwritten apparent authority of an agent is insufficient to satisfy the statute of frauds . . . and in the instant case, there is no evidence that the listing agent even had apparent authority (see *Friedman v. New York Tel. Co.*, 256 N.Y. 392, 176 N.E. 543).

Case Questions

1. Who is the party to be charged in the transaction?
2. Why did the court decide that the "Memo of Sale" did not satisfy the statute of frauds?
3. What was the agent's conduct insufficient to satisfy the statute of frauds?

E-COMMERCE LAW

One of the most significant changes in society over the last decade has been the pervasive use of the Internet in e-commerce and people's lives. *Time* magazine even named "You" as its Person of the Year for 2006, acknowledging the prolific growth and undeniable importance of Internet users worldwide.[16]

The growth of **e-commerce** has also led to the increased use of e-contracts. An e-contract is simply any type of contract formed in the course of e-commerce by (1) the interaction of two or more individuals using electronic means, such as e-mail, (2) the interaction of an individual with an electronic agent, such as a computer program, or (3) the interaction of at least two electronic agents that are programmed to recognize the existence of a contract.[17] The term *e-contract* can also be a verb defined as "to form a binding agreement by means of a computer or other electronic or automated technology."

One of the most common types of e-contracts in use today is the **clickwrap agreement**. The term *clickwrap agreement* is borrowed from the idea of shrinkwrap agreements, which are generally license agreements placed inside the cellophane shrinkwrap of consumer software boxes that, by their terms, become effective once the shrinkwrap is opened.[18] A clickwrap agreement is an electronic version of a shrink-wrap license in which a computer user agrees to the terms of an electronically displayed agreement by pointing the cursor to a particular location on the screen and then clicking. Clickwrap agreements usually require express acceptance only once but may include a clause providing for a user's ongoing-acceptance of any changes to the agreement's terms, whether or not the user is notified of the changes. A clickwrap agreement can be used in software downloaded from the Internet or for software installed on a CD-ROM.

Another type of contract on the Internet is the **browsewrap agreement**. With a browsewrap agreement, the website terms and conditions of use are posted on the

e-Commerce
The practice of buying and selling goods and services through online consumer services on the Internet.

Clickwrap Agreement
An electronic version of a shrink-wrap license in which a computer user agrees to the terms of an electronically displayed agreement by pointing the cursor to a particular location on the screen and then clicking. Usually requires express acceptance only once but may include a clause providing for a user's ongoing-acceptance of any changes to the agreement's terms, whether or not the user is notified of the changes. Also called point-and-click agreement. See also Browsewrap Agreement.

Browsewrap Agreement
Terms and conditions of use posted on a website typically as a hyperlink at the bottom of the screen. Unlike a clickwrap agreement, a browsewrap agreement allows the user to view the terms of the agreement, but does not require the user to take any affirmative action before the website performs its end of the contract.

End User License Agreement (EULA) A clipwrap agreement or a browsewrap agreement.

Terms of Use Agreement (TOA) A clipwrap agreement or a browsewrap agreement.

website typically as a hyperlink at the bottom of the screen. Unlike a clickwrap agreement, a browsewrap agreement, a browsewrap agreement allows the user to view the terms of the agreement, but does not require the user to take any affirmative action before the website performs its end of the contract. With a browsewrap agreement, users do not need to "click" to accept the website terms. Instead, browsewraps indicate in some fashion that use of the site constitutes acceptance of its terms of service. A clipwrap agreement or a browsewrap agreement may be also called an **end user license agreement (EULA)** or a **terms of use agreement (TOA)**.

Many courts have recognized the validity of clickwrap agreements. Judge John M. Steadman wrote in *Forrest v. Verizon Communications, Inc.*, 805 A.2d 1007, 1010 (D.C. 2002) that "[a] contract is no less a contract simply because it is entered into via a computer." Some courts, however, have refused to enforce shrinkwrap or clickwrap agreements, considering them to be counteroffers or proposals for additional terms.[19] Courts are more likely to uphold a browsewrap agreement or EULA when the terms are prominently displayed and provide easy access to the full EULA terms. In *Major v. McCallister*, 302 S.W.3d 227 (Mo. Ct.App. 2009), a 2009 Missouri court upheld a browsewrap agreement where each web page contained "immediately visible notice of existence of license terms" and a hyperlink to those terms. But in *Specht v. Netscape Comms. Corp.*, 306 F.3d 17, 22 (2nd Cir. 2002), the court refused to enforce a browsewrap agreement where users of the web page would not see any notice of agreement unless they scrolled down to another screen. Managers should ensure that terms of use agreements and EULAs are prominently displayed and immediately visible to users.

In analyzing the validity of a browsewrap agreement, courts consider primarily whether the visitor to the website had actual or constructive knowledge of a site's terms and conditions prior to using the site. Constructive knowledge or constructive notice refers to knowledge that one using reasonable care or diligence should have discovery. In *Hines v. Overstock.com, Inc.*, 668 F. Supp. 2d 362 (E.D.N.Y. 2009) (Case 5.2), a federal court held that the restocking fee with Overstock.com's Terms and Conditions of Use agreement could not be enforced because users to the website did not have either actual or constructive notice. For a browsewrap agreement to be enforceable, the agreement must be prominently displayed so that users have actual notice. Online retailers should provide notice to customers of any restocking fee, or other terms and conditions, by prominently displaying the notice to customers. For example, a restocking fee could be displayed to customers during the checkout process when a customer enters payment information.

CASE 5.2

The Case of the Hidden Restocking Fee for an Online Retailer

Hines v. Overstock.com, Inc., ***668 F. Supp. 2d 362 (E.D.N.Y. 2009)***

Plaintiff Cynthia Hines ("Plaintiff" or "Hines") initiated this purported class action pursuant to the Court's diversity jurisdiction, alleging that defendant Overstock.com, Inc.'s ("Defendant" or "Overstock") decision to impose a "restocking fee" amounted to a breach of contract. Overstock is an online, "closeout" retailer. On or about January 8, 2009, Plaintiff purchased an Electrolux Oxygen 3 Ultra Canister vacuum from Overstock's website. After receiving the vacuum, Plaintiff returned it to Defendant and was reimbursed the full amount she had paid for it, minus a $30.00 restocking fee. Plaintiff claims that she had been advised that she could return the vacuum without incurring any costs and that Defendant never disclosed that a restocking fee would be charged.

In support of the Motion, Defendant avers that: "All retail purchases from Overstock are conducted through Overstock's Internet website. When an individual accesses the website, he or she accepts Overstock's terms, conditions and policies, which govern all of Overstock's customer purchases." Overstock's "Terms and Conditions" state that "Entering this Site will constitute your acceptance of these Terms and Conditions" and include a provision that requires that "any dispute relating in any way to your visit to the Site . . . be submitted to confidential arbitration in Salt Lake City, Utah."

Plaintiff affirms, however, that she "never had any notice that disputes with Overstock.com require mandatory arbitration in Salt Lake City, Utah." Plaintiff affirms that when she accessed Overstock's website to purchase the vacuum, she was never made aware of the Terms and Conditions.

Discussion

It is a basic tenet of contract law that in order to be binding, a contract requires a "meeting of the minds" and "a manifestation of mutual assent" [citations omitted]. The making of contracts over the internet "has not fundamentally changed the principles of contract." *Register.com, Inc. v. Verio, Inc.*, 356 F.3d 393, 403 (2nd Cir. 2004). On the internet, the primary means of forming a contract are the so-called "clickwrap" (or "click-through") agreements, in which website users typically click an "I agree" box after being presented with a list of terms and conditions of use, and the "browsewrap" agreements, where website terms and conditions of use are posted on the website typically as a hyperlink at the bottom of the screen. Unlike a clickwrap agreement, a browsewrap agreement "does not require the user to manifest assent to the terms and conditions expressly . . . [a] party instead gives his assent simply by using the website" [citation omitted].

In ruling upon the validity of a browsewrap agreement, courts consider primarily "whether a website user has actual or constructive knowledge of a site's terms and conditions prior to using the site."

In *Specht*, the plaintiffs had downloaded free software from the defendant's website; because they did not scroll down the page, they did not see the notice advising site-users to review and agree to the software license agreement's terms prior to downloading. The Second Circuit held that the plaintiffs were not bound by the license agreement's terms because they "were responding to an offer that did not carry an immediately visible notice of the existence of license terms or require unambiguous manifestation of assent to those terms" [citations omitted]. *Motise v. America Online, Inc.*, 346 F. Supp. 2d 563, 564–65 (S.D.N.Y.2004) (finding no notice where terms of use were available on website, but not presented to plaintiff).

In the instant case, it is clear that Plaintiff had no actual notice of the Terms and Conditions of Use. Defendant has also failed to show that Plaintiff had constructive notice. The Hawkins Affidavit, upon which Defendant relies, conclusory states that by accessing Overstock's website, an individual accepts Overstock's Terms and Conditions-but, crucially, does not explain how a site-user such as Plaintiff is made aware of the Terms and Conditions. Despite Defendant's assertion that "all customers to Overstock's website are advised of the company's terms and conditions prior to their entry onto the site," . . . Notably, unlike in other cases where courts have upheld browsewrap agreements, the notice that "Entering this Site will constitute your acceptance of these Terms and Conditions," was only available within the Terms and Conditions . . . Hines therefore lacked notice of the Terms and Conditions because the website did not prompt her to review the Terms and Conditions and because the link to the Terms and Conditions was not prominently displayed so as to provide reasonable notice of the Terms and Conditions. Very little is required to form a contract nowadays—but this alone does not suffice.

Case Questions

1. What is the most basic tenet or doctrine under contract law for a binding contract?
2. What is the primary means of forming a contract via the Internet?
3. In ruling upon the validity of a browsewrap agreement, what do courts primarily consider?
4. How could Overstock.com have provided actual notice of the restocking fee?

The Guinness Book of Records credits Mark Cuban, dot-com billionaire and owner of the NBA's Dallas Mavericks, with the "largest single e-commerce transaction," after paying $40 million for his Gulfstream V jet in October 1999 through Gulfstream's website.

FIGURE 5.4 Largest e-Commerce Transaction In History[20]

COMMON CLAUSES IN ONLINE AND SOFTWARE CONTRACTS

Although variations exist, common clauses or categories found in online and software contracts involve warranties, limitation of liability, arbitration, indemnity, severability, merger, forum selection, and **choice of law**. A clause or provision is a distinct section or provision of a legal document or instrument such as a contract. Contracts will often include a heading or label for different clauses such as "Warranty" or "Arbitration" to provide users with notice of the terms and conditions. Where applicable, this section will reference these specific clauses in the eBay User Agreement.

Warranties

Virtually all of the best-selling software products include express warranties and disclaimers of the warranties in the EULAs. In fact, a 2009 study published in the *Yale Journal of Law & Technology* found that of fifty-four software titles from the top one hundred best-selling software products in which the licensor made its End User License Agreement (EULA) available on its website without a purchase, fifty-three or 98 percent contained express warranties on the website and e-disclaimers in the EULAs. Software titles in the study included several Apple, Microsoft, and Adobe products.[21]

Article 2 of the UCC applies only to the sales of goods. Whether software is a good or a service was hotly debated in the 1980s in the context of Article 2 of the UCC. Today, courts consider most contracts involving bundled software, either off-the-shelf or custom, within Article 2 as a sale of goods.[22] There is still a split of opinion on whether unbundled (standalone) software qualifies as a good because of its dominant service aspect, although the majority of cases have held that the transaction is one for goods, governed by the UCC.

Article 2 of UCC allows software vendors the opportunity to limit the risks they assume in marketing with warranty disclaimers. No reported decision has unequivocally held that a software vendor has breached an express warranty.[23] Courts generally uphold implied warranty disclaimers unless they are found to be unconscionable.[24]

In *Moore v. Microsoft Corp.*, 741 N.Y.S.2d 91 (N.Y.A.D. 2002), a software user brought a claim against Microsoft alleging statutory violations and deceptive trade practices. The court rejected the claims and held that the cause of action was barred by the terms of the EULA since Microsoft gave no warranty that the software product was error-free. In addition, Microsoft disclaimed all warranties, either express or implied in the agreement.

Warranty disclaimers often appear in all capital letters since courts have recognized that a warranty disclaimer is conspicuous to the buyer if it appears in large capital letters. For example, the software EULA for Microsoft Office Home and Student 2007 includes the following warranty disclaimer: "NO OTHER WARRANTIES. THE LIMITED WARRANTY IS THE ONLY DIRECT WARRANTY FROM MICROSOFT. MICROSOFT GIVES NO OTHER EXPRESS WARRANTIES, GUARANTEES OR CONDITIONS."

The eBay User Agreement provides:

> We do not transfer legal ownership of items from the seller to the buyer. California Commercial Code § 2401(2) and Uniform Commercial Code § 2-401(2) applies to the transfer of ownership between the buyer and the seller, unless the buyer and the seller agree otherwise. Further, we cannot guarantee continuous or secure access to our sites, services or tools, and operation of our sites, services or tools may be interfered with by numerous factors outside of our control. Accordingly, to the extent legally permitted, we exclude all implied warranties, terms and conditions. We are not liable for any loss of money, goodwill or reputation, or any special, indirect or consequential damages arising, directly or indirectly, out of your use of or your inability to use our sites, services and tools. Some jurisdictions do not allow the disclaimer of warranties or exclusion of damages, so such disclaimers and exclusions may not apply to you.[25]

The ALI adopted the Principles of the Law of Software Contracts in 2009 to clarify and unify the law of software transactions. Principles of the Law of Software Contracts § 3.03 dealing with the implied warranty of merchantability states:

- **a.** Unless excluded or modified, a transferor that deals in software of the kind transferred or that holds itself out by occupation as having knowledge or skill peculiar to the software warrants to the transferee that the software is merchantable.
- **b.** Merchantable software at minimum must
  1. pass without objection in the trade under the contract description; and
  2. be fit for the ordinary purposes for which such software is used; and
  3. be adequately packaged and labeled.

Only time will tell whether courts adopt the Principles of the Law of Software Contracts and replace the UCC for warranties relating to software. In the meantime, software vendors will continue to include disclaimers of warranty in EULAs to limit their liability.

Limitation of Liability

Software vendors and website owners can limit their liability and the remedies available to a plaintiff under the UCC by contract. One common method of limitation is through the use of a liquidated damages provision. Another method is to include within the contract a clause that: (1) provides a specific, exclusive, limited remedy, such as repair or replacement of defective parts; (2) limits the total liability of the vendor to a specific dollar amount, such as the total price paid on the contract or the total amount paid during a specified time period; or (3) limits the buyer to only direct damages by excluding all special, incidental, or consequential damages.

By way of illustration, the eBay User Agreement states in part "if we are found to be liable, our liability to you or to any third party is limited to the greater of (a) any amounts due under the eBay Buyer Protection Policy up to the full cost of the item (including any applicable sales tax) and its original shipping costs, (b) the total fees (under eBay Fees and Services) you paid to us in the 12 months prior to the action giving rise to the liability, and (c) $100."[26]

Although limitations of liability are not generally favored by courts because of public policy concerns, the UCC allows parties to disclaim liability for consequential damages, subject to the overriding principle of good faith. UCC Section 2-719 allows disclaimers for consequential damages, unless they are unconscionable or unless the limitation of liability causes the remedy to fail of its essential purpose.

Arbitration

Arbitration
is an alternative dispute resolution (ADR) method involving one or more neutral third parties who are usually agreed to by the disputing parties and whose decision is binding.

Arbitration is an alternative dispute resolution (ADR) method involving one or more neutral third parties who are usually agreed to by the disputing parties and whose decision is binding. Companies choose arbitration over litigation because it can save time and money. The contract may contain a provision that any disputes under the contract will be decided by an arbitration provider, such as the American Arbitration Association (AAA) or the National Arbitration Forum (NAF).

Although online terms of use agreements and EULAs often contain arbitration provisions, several recent judicial opinions have found arbitration provisions unenforceable.

In *Harris v. Blockbuster, Inc.*, 622 F. Supp. 2d 396 (N.D. Tex. 2009), a 2009 federal court for the Northern District of Texas held that the terms of use agreement for Blockbuster Online, which allows customers to rent movies through the Internet, was "illusory and unenforceable." The court denied Blockbuster's motion to compel arbitration as stipulated in the terms of use agreement. The court held that the terms of use agreement written by Blockbuster and agreed to by the plaintiff was unenforceable because of a lack of adequate consideration and unconscionable terms. In *Specht v. Netscape Commc'ns Corp.*, 306 F.3d 17, 21–25 (2nd Cir. 2002), a federal appeals court held that an arbitration provision in an e-contract was unenforceable. Then Judge Sonia Sotomayor (now a U.S. Supreme Court Justice) wrote the opinion of the court in *Specht*, which held that the user "did not unambiguously manifest assent to the arbitration provision contained in the license terms." The arbitration provision was presented below the "I Accept" button and therefore a reasonably prudent Internet user would not notice the terms. Similarly, in *Bragg v. Linden Research, Inc.*, 487 F. Supp. 2d 593 (E.D. Pa. 2007), a court found the Terms of Service of Second Life or "TOS" to be an adhesion contract and found the arbitration clause unenforceable due to procedural and substantive unconscionability. In *Trujillo v. Apple Computer, Inc.*, 578 F. Supp. 2d 979, 995 (N.D. Ill. 2008), a court found the EULA with a service provider of Apple's iPhone compelling arbitration unconscionable on the grounds that the terms came too late and the buyer had reason to believe that returning the phone would reduce his refund to cover a 10 percent restocking fee. The court found that the arbitration requirement was procedurally unconscionable.

The arbitration option in the Ebay User Agreement states:

> For any claim (excluding claims for injunctive or other equitable relief) where the total amount of the award sought is less than $10,000, the party requesting relief may elect to resolve the dispute in a cost effective manner through binding non-appearance-based arbitration. In the event a party elects arbitration, they shall initiate such arbitration through an established alternative dispute resolution ("ADR") provider mutually agreed upon by the parties. The ADR provider and the parties must comply with the following rules: (a) the arbitration shall be conducted by telephone, online and/or be solely based on written submissions, the specific manner shall be chosen by the party initiating the arbitration; (b) the arbitration shall not involve any personal appearance by the parties or witnesses unless otherwise mutually agreed by the parties; and (c) any judgment on the award rendered by the arbitrator may be entered in any court of competent jurisdiction.

Some online agreements include an arbitration agreement that prohibits parties from bringing class actions in arbitration or in court. Courts have been inconsistent in their interpretation of arbitration agreements that prohibit parties from bringing class actions. In a class action lawsuit against Dell based on allegations that Dell sold defective laptops, the U.S. Court of Appeals of Appeals for the Ninth Circuit considered the validity of Dell's arbitration clause in *Omstead v. Dell, Inc.*, 594 F.3d 1081 (9th Cir. 2010) (Case 5.3). The court held that Dell's class waiver of arbitration in the contract was unconscionable under California law. The court held that arbitration provisions with class action waivers are unconscionable under California law if: (1) waiver is found in a consumer contract of adhesion, (2) the contractual setting is one in which disputes between the contracting parties predictably involve small amounts of damages, and (3) it is alleged that the party with the superior bargaining power has carried out a scheme to deliberately cheat large numbers of consumers out of individually small sums of money. An adhesion contract is a standard-form contract prepared by one party, to be signed by another party in a weaker position, usually a consumer, who adheres to the contract with little choice about the terms. The case against Dell will have a significant impact because Dell is the second-largest consumer personal computer (PC) vendor in the United States.[27] Hewlett-Packard has a market share of 26 percent of PC sales in the U.S. followed by Dell with 22 percent.

CASE 5.3

The Case of Dell's Binding Arbitration Agreement

Omstead v. Dell, Inc., *594 F.3d 1081 (9th Cir. 2010)*

Plaintiffs-appellants, Michael Omstead, Melissa Malloy, and Lisa Smith (collectively, "plaintiffs"), brought a proposed class action against Dell, Inc. ("Dell"), asserting various claims under California state law predicated on the allegation that Dell designed, manufactured, and sold defective notebook computers. The district court granted Dell's motion to stay proceedings and compel arbitration. Plaintiffs refused to comply with the arbitration order, and the district court dismissed the action for failure to prosecute. Plaintiffs appeal the dismissal and the underlying arbitration order. We REVERSE.

Background

Between July 2004 and January 2005 plaintiffs purchased notebook computers for $1200 to $1500 through Dell's website. At the time of purchase, plaintiffs were required to accept a written agreement titled "U.S. Terms and Conditions of Sale" (the "Agreement"). The Agreement contained the following provisions relevant to this appeal:

> **11 Governing Law**
>
> THIS AGREEMENT AND ANY SALES THERE UNDER SHALL BE GOVERNED BY THE LAWS OF THE STATE OF TEXAS, WITHOUT REGARD TO CONFLICTS OF LAWS RULES.
>
> **13 Binding Arbitration**
>
> ANY CLAIM, DISPUTE, OR CONTROVERSY . . . BETWEEN CUSTOMER AND DELL . . . SHALL BE RESOLVED EXCLUSIVELY AND FINALLY BY BINDING ARBITRATION ADMINISTERED BY THE NATIONAL ARBITRATION FORUM (NAF). . . . NEITHER CUSTOMER NOR DELL SHALL BE ENTITLED TO JOIN OR CONSOLIDATE CLAIMS BY OR AGAINST OTHER CUSTOMERS, OR ARBITRATE ANY CLAIM AS A REPRESENTATIVE OR CLASS ACTION. . . .

(Continued)

(Continued)

Dell moved to stay proceedings and compel individual arbitration pursuant to the Agreement, and the district court granted the motion. Plaintiffs moved for reconsideration of the arbitration order; the district court denied reconsideration and directed the parties to file a joint status statement describing the status of their arbitration proceedings.

In the joint status statement, plaintiffs stipulated that they would not arbitrate their claims individually because it was not economically feasible for them to do so, and because the arbitration forum mandated by the Agreement was "blatantly biased" against consumers.

Discussion

The District Court Erred When It Granted Dell's Motion to Stay Proceedings and Compel Arbitration.

Under the Federal Arbitration Act, 9 U.S.C. §§ 1-16, a written arbitration provision is valid and enforceable "save upon such grounds as exist at law or in equity for the revocation of any contract." 9 U.S.C. § 2. Generally applicable contract defenses, such as unconscionability, may render an arbitration provision unenforceable. *Shroyer v. New Cingular Wireless Servs., Inc.*, 498 F.3d 976, 981 (9th Cir. 2007). Whether an arbitration provision is unconscionable is governed by state contract law.

The Agreement in this case contains a choice-of-law provision that states the Agreement is governed by Texas law. Plaintiffs argue the choice-of-law provision is unenforceable, and California law applies. This Court agreed that the choice-of-law provision was not enforceable and that under California choice-of-law rules, California law applied.

In Oestreicher I, plaintiff Harry Oestreicher brought a proposed class action against Alienware Corporation ("Alienware"), asserting various violations of California state law arising out of Alienware's alleged sale of defective notebook computers. Oestreicher purchased his computer through Alienware's website and was required to accept a sales agreement at the time of purchase, which contained an arbitration provision with a class action waiver and a choice-of-law provision designating Florida law as the governing law. Alienware moved to compel arbitration pursuant to the terms of the sales agreement. The district court denied the motion . . . and this Court affirmed on appeal.

The district court first concluded that application of Florida law would be contrary to a fundamental policy of California because the sales agreement's class action waiver was unconscionable under California law. Specifically, the district court found the class action waiver satisfied all three prongs of the Discover Bank test: (1) the sales agreement was an adhesion contract, (2) $4000, which was the approximate purchase price of Oestreicher's computer, was a small enough amount to prevent consumers from pursuing their individual claims, and (3) Oestreicher alleged a deliberate practice to deprive consumers of money because he alleged "Alienware was aware of material defects in its products, concealed these defects from consumers, and chose to sell defective products." The district court next found that California had a materially greater interest in applying its law because the proposed class consisted solely of California residents asserting violations of California consumer protection laws for goods shipped into California. California's interest therefore outweighed Florida's interest as the place of contracting and place of performance.

Here, the Agreement's choice-of-law provision is unenforceable for the same reasons identified in Oestreicher I. The class action waiver is unconscionable under California law because it satisfies the Discover Bank test, and California has a materially greater interest than Texas in applying its own law. Accordingly, the validity of the arbitration provision is governed by California law. Having found the class action waiver unconscionable under California law, the only remaining question is whether the class action waiver can be severed from the remainder of the arbitration provision. See Cal. Civ.Code § 1670.5(a) (making discretionary a court's decision to sever an unconscionable contract clause). We find it cannot be severed because the class action waiver is "central" to the arbitration provision. Because we decline "to assume the role of contract author rather than interpreter," (quoting *Ingle v. Circuit City Stores, Inc.*, 328 F.3d 1165, 1180 (9th Cir. 2003)), the class action waiver renders the entire arbitration provision unenforceable. The district court erred when it found to the contrary and granted Dell's motion to stay proceedings and compel arbitration.

Conclusion

We . . . reverse the district court's order granting Dell's motion to stay proceedings and compel arbitration. We remand for further proceedings consistent with this opinion.

Case Questions

1. Why did the plaintiffs not want to arbitrate the dispute?
2. Why did the court find the Dell arbitration provision unconscionable?
3. Why was the class action waiver not severable from the remainder of the arbitration provision?

In *AT&T Mobility v. Concepcion*, 131 S. Ct. 1740 (2011), the U.S. Supreme Court addressed whether the Federal Arbitration Act (FAA) precludes states from forbidding class-arbitration waivers as unconscionable components of arbitration agreements. When the dispute involves numerous similarly situated individuals, a few individuals may conduct the arbitration on behalf of the larger groups (similar to a class action lawsuit). The U.S. Supreme Court held that the FAA preempts California's judicial rule regarding the unconscionability of class arbitration waivers in consumer contracts.

Indemnity

Many contracts, including e-contracts, will include an indemnity clause. Contractual indemnity is where two parties agree that one party will reimburse the other party for liability resulting from the former's work.[28] A contract with an indemnity clause where one party agrees to indemnify the other is also called a hold-harmless agreement. Indemnity means the right of an injured party to claim reimbursement for its loss, damage, or liability from a person who has such a duty.

The eBay User Agreement includes a contractual indemnity clause that states "You will indemnify and hold us (and our officers, directors, agents, subsidiaries, joint ventures and employees) harmless from any claim or demand, including reasonable attorneys' fees, made by any third party due to or arising out of your breach of this Agreement, or your violation of any law or the rights of a third party."[29]

Severability

Some online contracts will also include a severability clause. A **severability clause** is a provision that keeps the remaining provisions of a contract in force if any portion of that contract is judicially declared void, unenforceable, or unconstitutional. A severability clause is also called a saving clause or separability clause. A severability clause may state, "Should any provision of this agreement be declared or be determined by any court of competent jurisdiction to be illegal, invalid, or unenforceable, the legality, validity and enforceability of the remaining parts, terms or provisions shall not be affected by such declaration or determination, and the illegal, unenforceable or invalid part, term or provisions shall be deemed not to be a part of this Agreement."[30] Some e-contracts may include a severability clause for just certain sections in the contract. For example the eBay User Agreement severability clause states, "The following Sections survive any termination of this Agreement: Fees and Services (with respect to fees owed for our services), Release, Content, Liability, Indemnity and Legal Disputes."[31]

Severability Clause
Provision that keeps the remaining provisions of a contract or statute in force if any portion of that contract or statute is judicially declared void, unenforceable, or unconstitutional.

Merger

A merger clause is a contractual provision stating that the contract represents the parties' complete and final agreement and supersedes all informal understandings and oral agreements relating to the subject matter of the contract.[32] A merger clause may also be called an **integration clause** or an entire-agreement clause. A merger clause is often used in contracts to merge prior discussions, negotiations, and representations into the written document and avoid litigation over the question of whether there were oral representations made outside the written agreement. An integration clause prevents a contracting party from arguing that an oral promise was made as part of the bargain.

Integration Clause
A contractual provision stating that the contract represents the parties' complete and final agreement and supersedes all informal understandings and oral agreements relating to the subject matter of the contract. Also called merger clause or entire-agreement clause.

A merger clause is often included in a contract to prevent a party from introducing "parol evidence" or extrinsic evidence of negotiations that occurred before or while the agreement was being reduced to its final written form. The parol evidence rule is a common-law principle under contract law that a writing intended by the parties to be a final embodiment of their agreement cannot be modified by evidence of earlier or contemporaneous agreements that might add to, vary, or contradict the writing. Note that proper spelling is "parol evidence" and not "parole evidence" in this context. The eBay User Agreement merger clause states, "This Agreement sets forth the entire understanding and agreement between us with respect to the subject matter hereof."[33]

Forum Selection/Choice-of-law

Many EULAs contain choice-of-law and forum selection clauses. In a 2008 study of EULAs, 75 percent had choice-of-law clauses, and 28 percent had choice of forum clauses.[34]

Forum Selection Clause
A contractual provision in which the parties establish the place (such as the country, state, or type of court) for specified litigation between them. Also called "choice-of-exclusive-forum clause."

The heading for a **forum selection clause** or choice-of-law provision is sometimes entitled "Applicable Law."

A choice-of-law provision is a contractual provision by which the parties designate the jurisdiction whose law will govern any disputes that may arise between the parties. A choice-of-law provision is also sometimes called a choice-of-law clause. A "choice-of-law" provision in a contract names a particular state and provides that the substantial laws of that jurisdiction will be used to determine the validity and construction (or interpretation) of the contract. A forum selection clause is a contractual provision in which the parties establish the place (such as the country, state, or type of court) for specified litigation between them. A forum selection clause is also called a choice-of-exclusive-forum clause. The purpose of a forum selection clause is to provide a specific venue if a conflict arises.

While courts will generally enforce a forum selection or choice-of-law provision and courts have held that forum selection clauses are presumptively valid, some courts have found choice-of-law and forum selection provisions unenforceable if they violate public policy. In *Janson v. LegalZoom.com, Inc.*, 727 F. Supp. 2d 782 (W.D. Mo. 2010), a Missouri federal court held that a forum selection clause and choice-of-law provision for the legal forms website LegalZoom.com violated public policy. The forum selection clause which stated that "California law shall govern any disputes," and California courts shall "have exclusive jurisdiction," violated strong Missouri public policy against the unauthorized practice of law in the state, and thus clause was invalid. The court determined that the legality of documents produced by the website would likely need to be addressed by Missouri courts under Missouri law for the benefit of Missouri citizens, and transferring litigation from Missouri to California forum under these circumstances would run contrary to Missouri's interest in resolving matters tied closely to the unauthorized practice of law within its borders. In *Bragg v. Linden Research, Inc.*, 487 F. Supp. 2d 593 (E.D. Penn. 2007), involving the virtual world of Second Life, the court invalidated the forum selection clause along with the arbitration provision in the Terms of Service of Second Life or "TOS" agreement.

The eBay User Agreement choice-of-law clause states that disputes shall be governed by California state law, and the forum selection clause states that disputes shall be decided in a court located in Santa Clara County, California. Businesses will usually select the county and state where the company headquarters are located in a forum selection and choice-of-law clause. For eBay Inc., the headquarters are located in San Jose, California, located in Santa Clara. The eBay User Agreement provides:

> This Agreement shall be governed in all respects by the laws of the State of California as they apply to agreements entered into and to be performed entirely within California between California residents, without regard to conflict of law provisions. You agree that any claim or dispute you may have against eBay must be resolved exclusively by a state or federal court located in Santa Clara County, California, except as otherwise agreed by the parties or as described in the Arbitration Option paragraph below. You agree to submit to the personal jurisdiction of the courts located within Santa Clara County, California for the purpose of litigating all such claims or disputes.

In two separate cases, *Tricome v. Ebay, Inc.* and *Universal Grading Service v. eBay, Inc.*, federal courts enforced the forum selection clause found in the eBay User Agreement. For more discussion of forum selection and choice of law, see Chapter 1.

Forum selection and choice-of-law clauses allow a party to litigate in their own backyard while simultaneously forcing opponents to travel to an inconvenient forum. Since forum selection clauses have tremendous advantages for online businesses, Internet vendors should utilize forum selection and choice-of-law clauses.

Summary

In the United States, the principal sources of contract law are the common law, Restatement Second of Contracts, the Uniform Commercial Code (UCC), and the United Nations Convention on Contracts for the International Sale of Goods (CISG). Software licensing agreements and commercial transactions conducted via the Internet are also governed by the Uniform Electronic Transactions Act (UETA), the Electronic Signatures in Global and National Commerce Act (E-SIGN Act), the Uniform Computer Information Transactions Act (UCITA), the Principles of the Law of Software Contracts, and federal intellectual property laws. The basic requirements for a valid contract are mutual assent (often manifested through an offer and acceptance) and consideration. Contracting parties must have capacity to enter into a contract, and a valid contract must not have an illegal purpose. Some contracts, such as contracts for the sale of real estate, must be in writing and are governed by the statute of frauds. The rise in the Internet has led to increased use of clickwrap agreements and browsewrap agreements. A clickwrap agreement is an electronic version of a shrink-wrap license in which a computer user agrees to the terms of an electronically displayed agreement by pointing the cursor to a particular location on the screen and then clicking. With a browsewrap agreement, the website terms and conditions of use are posted on the website typically as a hyperlink at the bottom of the screen. Both clickwrap agreements and browsewrap agreements can also be called terms of use agreements or end user license agreements (EULAs). Common clauses found in online and software contracts involve warranties, limitation of liability, arbitration, indemnity, severability, merger, forum selection, and choice of law. Earlier decisions upheld forum selection and arbitration clauses as valid and enforceable; however, recent decisions indicate that the tide may be turning with EULAs in favor of consumers.

Key Terms

arbitration *82*
browsewrap agreement *77*
choice of law *80*
clickwrap agreement *77*
common law *71*
digital signature *72*
e-commerce *77*
electronic signature *72*
Electronic Signatures in Global and National Commerce Act (E-SIGN Act) *72*
end user license agreement (EULA) *78*
forum selection *86*
integration clause *86*
restatement *71*
severability clause *85*
statute of frauds *75*
terms of use agreement (TOA) *78*
Uniform Commercial Code (UCC) *71*
Uniform Computer Information Transactions Act (UCITA) *72*
Uniform Electronic Transactions Act (UETA) *71*
United Nations Convention on Contracts for the International Sale of Goods (CISG) *71*

Review Questions

1. What are the principal sources of contract law for software contracts?
2. What types of contracts are covered by the statute of frauds?
3. What are the basic requirements for a valid contract entered into via the Internet?
4. What are the differences between a clickwrap agreement and a browsewrap agreement?
5. What are the common provisions found in an end user license agreement?
6. Why would an online business want to include a forum selection clause?
7. How can a contracting party disclaim warranties for online transactions?

Discussion Questions

1. What are some examples of software that you have personally downloaded from the Internet where you agreed to a license agreement by clicking "I agree"? Have you ever read the entire agreement? Should you be bound to the terms in the contract? Why or why not?
2. What can be done to prevent fraudulent online purchases with a stolen credit card?
3. A virtual world, such as Second Life, is an online environment in which thousands of people can interact with one another on a persistent basis through their online personae known as avatars. How should disputes over virtual world items, such as virtual money or Second Life islands, be decided?

Exercises

1. If you have a cell phone or wireless agreement, locate and read the full text of the agreement. Then identify whether any of the following clauses are included in the contract: (1) warranties; (2) arbitration; (3) limitation of liability; (4) indemnity; and (5) early termination fee. Write a memorandum where you identify these clauses in the agreement. If you do not have a cell phone agreement or are unable to find the agreement, run a search on an Internet search engine such as Google for "Verizon wireless customer agreement" to locate the Verizon Wireless Customer Agreement.
2. You are the manager for a new software company that will make software available for users to download from the Internet. What clauses would you want to include in the end user license agreement (EULA) or clipwrap agreement? Would any of these clauses cause potential customers to look for competing software? Explain your answer.
3. At age seventeen, John Renslow, sells his baseball card collection on eBay to buy a new video game system. Two years later, Mark Renslow, John's father, finds out that John has sold the baseball cards and sues eBay and the winning eBay bidder for money damages and specific performance for return of the baseball card collection. How would a court decide the case?
4. Conduct legal research online, and locate the specific statute of frauds statute for your state. Provide the

Bluebook citation format for the specific statute, and describe in your own words which types of contracts must be in writing and signed by the party to be charged. Conduct additional research in cases and find any recognized exceptions to the statute of frauds.

5. *Hypothetical:* Julia, a website user who lives in Missouri, files a lawsuit against Acme Corp., an Internet referral website based in Denver, Colorado, after she become dissatisfied with services of contractors obtained through the website. The website offers free referrals to prescreened construction contractors. Jane then hires a contractor to remodel her home in Missouri based on a referral. The website process involved a series of computer screens or web pages. Each page was hyperlinked to Acme's terms and conditions, which included a choice-of-law provision and a forum selection clause limited to Denver County, Colorado. How would a court rule on enforceability of the terms and conditions found in the online agreement? See *Major v. McCallister*, 302 S.W.3d 227 (Mo. Ct. App. 2009).

Related Internet Sites

http://law.scu.edu/FacWebPage/Neustadter/contractsebook/main/Restatement/index.html#1
Restatement of the Law, Second, Contracts, The American Law Institute. Reproduced with permission for educational purposes only.

http://www.law.cornell.edu/ucc/ucc.table.html
Text of the Uniform Commercial Code (U.C.C.), reproduced, published and distributed with the permission for the limited purposes of study, teaching, and academic research.

http://papers.ssrn.com/sol3/papers.cfm?abstract_id=1554546
Robert A. Hillman and Maureen A., O'Rourke, *Principles of the Law of Software Contracts: Some Highlights*, TULANE LAW REVIEW, Forthcoming; Cornell Legal Studies Research Paper No. 010-003. (February 17, 2010).

http://pages.ebay.com/help/policies/user-agreement.html
Text of the eBay User Agreement

http://www.adobe.com/misc/terms.html
Text of the Adobe Terms of Use Agreement

http://ecommercelaw.typepad.com/
E-Commerce Law Blog maintained by Jonathan Frieden, a principal in with the Virginia law firm Odin, Feldman & Pittleman, P.C.

http://pblog.bna.com/techlaw/
E-Commerce and Tech Law Blog maintained by legal publisher BNA

http://www.adr.org/si.asp?id=4125
Drafting Dispute Resolution Clauses—A Practical Guide produced by the American Arbitration Association

http://www.internetlibrary.com/
The Internet Law Library, authored by Martin H. Samson, a partner in the New York law firm of Davidoff Malito & Hutcher LLP, features summaries of cases involving the Internet, including browse-wrap agreements.

http://www.lexisnexis.com/lawschool/study/outlines/html/contracts/index.asp
LexisNexis Law School Student Outline for Contracts

End Notes

1. Black's Law Dictionary (9th ed. 2009).
2. 15A Am. Jur. 2d Common Law § 1.
3. Black's Law Dictionary (9th ed. 2009).
4. Pace Law School Institute of International Commercial Law, CISG Database, CISG: Table of Contracting States, available at http://www.cisg.law.pace.edu/cisg/countries/cntries.html/.
5. Ronald A. Brand, *The European Magnet and the U.S. Centrifuge: Ten Selected Private International Law Developments of 2008*, 15 ILSA J. INT'L & COMP. L. 367, 379–80 (2009).
6. Peter W. Schroth, *Financial Leasing of Equipment in the Law of the United States*, 58 AM. J. COMP. L. 323, note 38 (2010).
7. Electronic Signatures in Global and National Commerce Act, Pub. L. No. 106–229, 114 Stat. 464 (2000) (codified as amended at 15 U.S.C. §§ 7001–7031).
8. Frederick E. Schuchman, III, *A Law for Contracting in the 21st Century*, 80-SEP MICH. B.J. 60, 61 (2011).
9. Michael Traynor, *The First Restatements and the Vision of the American Law Institute, Then and Now*, 32 S. ILL. U.L.J. 145, note 29 (2007).
10. Robert A. Hillman and Maureen A. O'Rourke, *Principles of the Law of Software Contracts: Some Highlights*, 84 TULANE L. REV. 1519 (2010).
11. Black's Law Dictionary (9th ed. 2009), citing 2 *Stephen's Commentaries on the Laws of England* 5 (L. Crispin Warmington ed., 21st ed. 1950).
12. *A.V. v. iParadigms*, 544 F. Supp. 2d 473, 480–81 (E.D. Va. 2008).
13. 17A Am. Jur. 2d Contracts § 10.
14. 17A Am. Jur. 2d Contracts § 223.
15. NTS Am. Jur. 2d Computers and the Internet § 29.
16. Lev Grossman, *Time Person of the Future: You*, Time, Dec. 25, 2006, at 38.
17. Black's Law Dictionary (9th ed. 2009).
18. *Stomp, Inc. v. NeatO, LLC*, 61 F. Supp. 2d 1074, 1080 n.11 (C.D. Cal. 1999).

19. *Forrest v. Verizon Communications, Inc.*, 805 A.2d 1007, 1010 (D.C.2002). See also *DeJohn v. The TV Corp. Int'l.*, 245 F. Supp. 2d 913, 921 (N.D. Ill. 2003); *Koresko v. RealNetworks, Inc.*, 291 F. Supp. 2d 1157, 1162–63 (E.D. Cal. 2003); *i.Lan Systems, Inc. v. Netscout Serv. Level Corp.*, 183 F. Supp. 2d 328, 338 (D. Mass. 2002); Enforceability of "Clickwrap" or "Shrinkwrap" Agreements Common in Computer Software, Hardware, and Internet Transactions, 106 A.L.R.5th 309 (2003).
20. *The Life of a Maverick: A Chat with Billionaire Mark Cuban*, Trader Daily, July 17, 2010, available at http://www.traderdaily.com/2010/07/the-life-of-a-maverick-an-interview-with-billionaire-mark-cuban/.
21. A. Hillman and Ibrahim Barakat, *Warranties and Disclaimers in the Electronic Age*, 11 YALE J.L. & TECH. 1 (2009).
22. Michael D. Scott, *Tort Liability for the Vendors of Insecure Software: Has the Time Finally Come?*, 67 Md. L. Rev. 425, 434 (2008).
23. Hillman, *supra* note 21.
24. Scott, *supra* note 22, at 439–40.
25. eBay User Agreement, available at http://pages.ebay.com/help/policies/user-agreement.html.
26. Id.
27. *Gartner Says Worldwide PC Shipments in First Quarter of 2011 Suffer First Year-Over-Year Decline in Six Quarters*, Bus. Wire, April 13, 2011, available at Westlaw, 4/13/11 Bus. Wire 22:59:00/.
28. Black's Law Dictionary (9th ed. 2009).
29. eBay User Agreement, *supra* note 25.
30. 1 Am. Jur. Legal Forms 2d § 4:13.
31. eBay User Agreement, *supra* note 25.
32. Black's Law Dictionary (9th ed. 2009).
33. eBay User Agreement, *supra* note 25.
34. Amy J. Schmitz, *Legislating In The Light: Considering Empirical Data in Crafting Arbitration Reforms*, 15 HARV. NEGOT. L. REV. 115, 137 (2010) citing Florencia Marotta-Wurgler, *Competition and the Quality of Standard Form Contracts: The Case of Software License Agreements*, 5 J. EMPIRICAL LEGAL STUD. 447 (2008).

CHAPTER

6 Online Tax-Related Issues

The Internet has exceeded our collective expectations as a revolutionary spring of information, news, and ideas. It is essential that we keep that spring flowing. We must not thwart the Internet's availability by taxing access to it.

CHRIS CANNON, *former member of the U.S. House of Representatives (R-Utah)*[1]

LEARNING OBJECTIVES

After completing this chapter, you will be able to:

1. Describe the role of the Internal Revenue Service (IRS) in tax collection and tax law enforcement.
2. Explain when state sales tax is imposed for online transactions.
3. Describe the scope and application of the Internet Tax Freedom Act.
4. Describe the income tax responsibility for online sellers.
5. Describe the current issues relating to taxing winnings from online gambling.
6. Explain the state income tax issues for telecommuters.

CHAPTER OVERVIEW

The growth of the Internet and e-commerce raises a number of questions and issues involving taxation. This chapter provides an introduction to tax law and describes the role of the Internal Revenue Service. This chapter also discusses sales tax, use tax, and income tax issues with online transactions. Tax-related public policy with regards to online gambling and income taxes for telecommuters will also be addressed in this chapter.

Internal Revenue Service (IRS)
A unit in the U.S. Department of the Treasury responsible for enforcing and administering the internal-revenue laws and other tax laws except those relating to alcohol, tobacco, firearms, and explosives.

Internal Revenue Code (IRC)
Title 26 of the U.S. Code, containing all current federal tax laws.

Treasury Regulations
Regulations promulgated by the U.S. Department of the Treasury to explain or interpret a section of the Internal Revenue Code.

Income Tax
A tax on an individual's or entity's net income. The federal income tax in the Internal Revenue Code is the federal government's primary source of revenue, and most states also have income taxes.

United States Tax Court
A federal court that hears appeals by taxpayers from adverse IRS decisions about tax deficiencies.

INTRODUCTION TO TAX LAW

In the movie *The Day After Tomorrow*, several characters threw library books into the fireplace to keep warm when one of the characters states, "Uh . . . 'scuse me? You guys? Yeah . . . there's a whole section on tax law down here that we can burn."[2]

While tax law is often considered one of the more mundane and often ridiculed areas of the law, tax law is an important facet of our lives and tax-related issues remain important considerations for e-commerce businesses.

At the federal level, the **Internal Revenue Service (IRS)** is a bureau of the U.S. Department of the Treasury that is responsible for tax collection and tax law enforcement.[3] The IRS is responsible for interpretation and enforcement of the **Internal Revenue Code (IRC)**. The Internal Revenue Code contains the federal tax laws enacted by Congress. The IRC is found (or codified) in Title 26 of the United States Code (26 U.S.C.). For example, I.R.C. § 1, dealing with taxable income, may also be cited as 26 U.S.C. § 1.

Treasury regulations, commonly referred to as federal tax regulations, pick up where the Internal Revenue Code (IRC) leaves off, by providing the official interpretation of the IRC by the U.S. Department of the Treasury.[4] **Treasury regulations** are contained in Title 26 of the Code of Federal Regulations (26 C.F.R.).

Federal **income tax** litigation begins in one of three forums: the **U.S. Tax Court**, the U.S. District Court, or the U.S. Court of Federal Claims (see Figure 6.1).

If the taxpayer has not paid the tax, then the appropriate forum is the **U.S. Tax Court**. In this forum, there is no right to a jury trial. The judges have more tax expertise and sophistication due to the specialized nature of the court. When the IRS and the Commissioner of Internal Revenue determine that a taxpayer owes money or has a tax deficiency, the taxpayer may dispute the deficiency in the U.S. Tax Court before paying any disputed amount.

If the taxpayer has paid the disputed tax and is then refused a refund, the forum is either the U.S. District Court (where the taxpayer is entitled to a jury trial) or the U.S. Court of Federal Claims.

Appeals from U.S. Tax Court and U.S. District Court decisions are to the U.S. Circuit Court of Appeals covering the taxpayer's state of residence. Appeals from the U.S. Court of Federal Claims are to the U.S. Court of Appeals for the Federal Circuit.

The U.S. Department of Justice Tax Division is responsible for representing the U.S. government in tax cases where the federal government is a party. A taxpayer challenging a decision by the U.S. Court of Appeal or the U.S. Court of Federal Claims

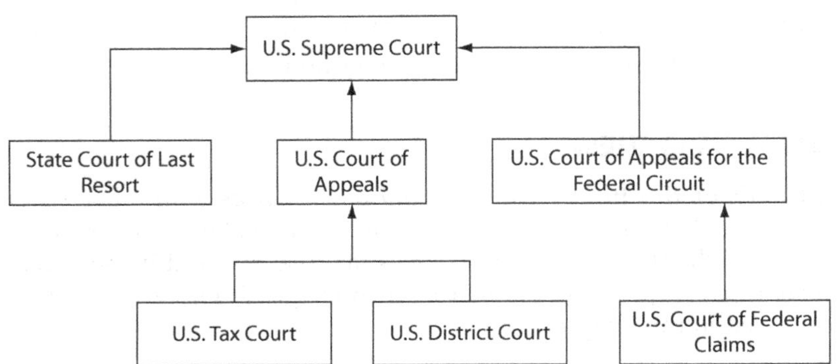

FIGURE 6.1 Tax Litigation Chart

can appeal to the U.S. Supreme Court, but the U.S. Supreme Court will rarely grant review in tax cases. Congress can also override a decision by the courts or an agency regulation adopted by the IRS and the U.S. Department of the Treasury.

The federal government obtains revenue mainly from individual income taxes and payroll taxes. In fiscal year 2009, individual income taxes accounted for 43.5 percent of all federal revenues and payroll taxes (such as Medicare and Social Security) accounted for 42.3 percent of federal revenues.[5] Corporate income taxes, excise taxes, estate and gift taxes, customs duties, and miscellaneous receipts make up the balance.

Each state has its own tax laws. States have administrative agencies, similar to the IRS, responsible for interpretation and enforcement of state tax laws. For example, the New York State Department of Taxation and Finance interprets and enforces tax laws in New York State. At the state level, state governments receive revenue from personal income tax, corporate income tax, sales tax, and real property tax. All states except Alaska, Delaware, Montana, New Hampshire, and Oregon, collect sales taxes.[6] Forty-one states also impose a personal income tax. New Hampshire and Tennessee apply state income tax only to income from interest and dividends. Seven states (Alaska, Florida, Nevada, South Dakota, Texas, Washington, and Wyoming) do not tax personal income.

Tax litigation at the state level varies by state. As a general rule, a taxpayer is required to exhaust administrative appeals with the state agency responsible for enforcement of tax laws before seeking judicial review. A taxpayer can then appeal a final agency decision in the court system and eventually appeal the case before the highest court in the state, which is usually called the state Supreme Court or state court of last resort. In New York State, the court of last resort is called the New York Court of Appeals. In California, the court of last resort is the California Supreme Court. If the case involves a question under the U.S. Constitution, the U.S. Supreme Court may review a case decided by the state court of last resort.

Benjamin Franklin, in a letter to Jean-Baptiste Le Roy in 1789, is credited with saying that "in this world nothing can be said to be certain, except death and taxes."[7] While taxes certainly exist, many questions remain unanswered with respect to the tax liability of business and individuals who engage in transactions via the Internet. While a variety of tax-related questions exist, this chapter will focus on sales tax and income tax issues.

SALES TAX FOR ONLINE TRANSACTIONS

A **sales tax** is a tax imposed on the sale of goods ad services, usually measured as a percentage of their price. The question of whether or not states can collect sales tax for purchases made online is one of the biggest issues surrounding the Internet, which involves millions of dollars in potential revenue for states. All states except Alaska, Delaware, Montana, New Hampshire, and Oregon, collect sales taxes. Some states have a single rate throughout the state though most states permit local city and county additions to the base tax rate.

Sales Tax
A tax imposed on the sale of goods and services, usually measured as a percentage of their price.

Internet Tax Freedom Act (ITFA)
A federal law that mainly prevents states from imposing a sales tax on Internet connection fees. Despite its name, ITFA does not prevent state and local governments from imposing sales tax collection requirements on companies selling over the Internet.

Internet Tax Freedom Act

Despite its name, the **Internet Tax Freedom Act (ITFA)** does not prevent state and local governments from imposing sales tax collection requirements on companies selling over the Internet. The ITFA was primarily intended to prevent state and local governments from imposing new or discriminatory taxes on Internet transactions and on the Internet on the amount of monthly Internet access fees that exceeds $25.00.[8] Texas is permitted to tax

Internet access even in light of the prohibition of the ITFA, because Texas was already taxing such access before the enactment of the ITFA.[9] The ITFA, first passed in 1998, has been renewed through November 1, 2014. The ITFA mainly prevents states from imposing a sales tax on Internet connection fees. It also stops states from imposing a sales tax on items sold via the Internet that aren't taxed in brick-and-mortar stores. In addition, the ITFA prevents states from collecting higher taxes for e-commerce purchases than for brick-and-mortar and mail-order purchases. The ITFA also prevents duplicative taxes on the same purchase, so that a state cannot levy both a sales and use tax on the same purchase.

Substantial Nexus Test

In *Quill v. North Dakota*, 504 U.S. 298 (1992), the U.S. Supreme Court ruled that retailers are exempt from collecting sales taxes in states where they have no "nexus" or physical presence, such as a store, office, or warehouse. Although the case dealt with a catalog mail-order company, the ruling has subsequently been applied to online retailers. The Court said that requiring companies to comply with the varied sales tax rules and regulations would burden interstate commerce. The bright-line test in *Quill v. North Dakot*a established the rule that if an online retailer has a physical presence in a particular state, such as a store, business office, or warehouse, the online retailer must collect sales tax from customers in that state. If a business does not have a physical presence in a state, the business is not required to collect sales tax for sales into that state. Advertising alone does not trigger the nexus.

The *Quill* Court applied both the Due Process "minimum connection" test and the Commerce Clause **"substantial nexus" test**, concluding that for a state tax to be constitutional, it must satisfy both standards. The U.S. Supreme Court adopted the bright-line physical presence test to encourage predictability and foster growth in interstate commerce.

Substantial Nexus Test
Test set forth in *Quill v. North Dakota*, 504 U.S. 298 (1992) that retailers are exempt from collecting sales taxes in states where they have no "nexus" or physical presence, such as a store, office, or warehouse.

Some of the key cases dealing with the validity of state sales tax from online purchases have involved Internet booksellers such as Borders, Barnes & Noble, and Amazon.

In the 2005 case of *Borders Online, LLC v. State Bd. of Equalization*, 129 Cal. App. 4th 1179, 29 Cal. Rptr. 3d 176 (2005), a California court required Borders Online to collect state sales tax because Borders Online had an effective presence in California. Borders Group, Inc. owned both Borders Online, LLC and Borders, Inc. Borders stores accepted returns from online orders, Borders Online advertised that the products could be returned to the physical stores, and store employees were encouraged to refer customers to the website.[10]

The court determined that because the Borders Books and Music stores accepted returns, they were acting as Borders Online's agents and had a nexus with California. The practical consequence of the Borders decision is that companies with online divisions that do not wish to collect sales taxes for online orders must create a corporate structure where the online division is completely distinct from the brick-and-mortar division.

Two years after the Borders Online decision, a federal court in Louisiana faced with similar facts found that bookseller Barnesandnoble.com, LLC was not responsible for collecting state and local taxes. In *St. Tammany Parish Tax Collector v. Barnesandnoble.com*, LLC, 481 F. Supp. 2d 575 (E.D. La. 2007) (Case 6.1), the court determined that Barnesandnoble.com did not have a sufficient nexus to pass the test set forth by the U.S. Supreme Court in *Quill v. North Dakota* because (1) Barnes & Noble stores only gave Barnesandnoble.com customers store credit, not cash, for merchandise purchased online and returned to the stores; and (2) stores would give similar credit to purchasers from competitive stores. For some online stores, the presence of a brick-and-mortar store in the state, where the site and the store are affiliated and interconnected, may lead to a nexus.

CASE 6.1

The Case of Taxing the Online Bookseller

St. Tammany Parish Tax Collector v. Barnesandnoble.com, LLC, *481 F. Supp. 2d 575 (E.D. La. 2007)*

This is an action for collection of sales and use taxes under Louisiana law.

Background

Defendant barnesandnoble.com, LLC ("Online") is an internet retailer of books, movies, and music at the internet address www.barnesandnoble.com. The company accepts orders from customers across the country, including in St. Tammany Parish, and fills these orders through a national distribution system that has no physical presence in Louisiana except for the use of common carriers to deliver merchandise from out-of-state that was ordered online. During the period in question in this case, January 2001 through December 31, 2005, the company did not maintain a mailing address or telephone number in the State of Louisiana. It had no employees in Louisiana and owned no tangible property in the State.

From January 2001 through October 2003, Barnes & Noble, Inc. owned 40% of Online. Between October 2003 and May 2004, Barnes & Noble, Inc. owned 80% of Online through a wholly-owned subsidiary. Between May 2004 and December 31, 2005, Barnes & Noble, Inc. owned 100% of Online through a wholly-owned subsidiary, B & N Holding Corp.

During the period at issue, Barnes & Noble, Inc. also wholly owned Barnes & Noble Booksellers, Inc. ("Booksellers"). Booksellers owned and operated retail stores throughout the country, including one in St. Tammany Parish, under the brand name "Barnes and Noble." The Booksellers retail outlet in St. Tammany Parish was located in the City of Mandeville. Although the two companies were both owned, in whole or in part, by the same parent corporation, Booksellers and Online did not share management, employees, offices, and other important elements of their businesses.

On October 31, 2005, the St. Tammany Parish Tax Collector sued defendants in Louisiana state court on behalf of various taxing jurisdictions within the Parish for sales and use taxes that Online allegedly failed to collect during the tax period. On November 16, 2005, defendants removed the case to this Court. The parties cross-moved for summary judgment, and on January 17, 2007, the Court held oral argument on the issues raised in the cross-motions. At the hearing, the parties agreed to submit the issue for trial on the briefs and the stipulated record.

Discussion

A. Substantial Nexus

Before it may impose a tax on an out-of-state entity, a state or local jurisdiction must establish that the imposition of the tax is consistent with the Commerce Clause of the Constitution. See *Quill Corp. v. North Dakota*. The state must show that the "tax [1] is applied to an activity with a substantial nexus with the taxing state, [2] is fairly apportioned, [3] does not discriminate against interstate commerce, and [4] is fairly related to the services provided by the State." This case involves only the first of these requirements.

Specifically, the Parish cites five aspects of the business relationship between Online and Booksellers as evidence that a substantial nexus existed during the relevant period:

1. The companies offered a membership program in which customers paid an annual fee and received discounts on merchandise purchased from either company, and Online derived revenue from the annual fees.
2. Booksellers sold gift cards that were redeemable with Online and included Online's web address.

(Continued)

(Continued)

3. Online received commissions on merchandise ordered at Booksellers retail stores but shipped directly to the customer.
4. The two companies engaged in advertising on behalf of each other.
5. Booksellers stores gave preferential treatment to returns of merchandise purchased from Online.

According to plaintiff, these five characteristics of the companies' relationship establish a substantial nexus between Booksellers and Online. The Court describes each of these factors separately.

1. The Membership Program During the period in question, Online, Booksellers, and several other retailers participated in a customer loyalty program run by Barnes & Noble, Inc., the companies' parent corporation. Under the program, customers purchased $25 memberships that entitled them to discounts and other special offers from participating retailers. The proceeds from the membership fees were distributed by Barnes & Noble, Inc. among the participating companies on a pro rata basis according to the percentage of overall discounts under the program awarded by each company. Thus, Online did not receive revenue from sales made by Booksellers, and Booksellers did not receive revenue from sales made by Online. Further, neither company made sales or took orders for the other.

Both Booksellers and Online advertised and marketed the membership program within their respective arenas. This included advertising the availability of discounts from the other participants in the program. In addition, the participants in the program shared all member names and e-mail addresses, which were used for direct marketing.

2. Gift Cards Online participated in a multi-retailer gift card program with several other retailers, including Booksellers. In most relevant respects, the gift card program mirrored that of the membership program. Gift cards were available and redeemable at Booksellers stores and at Online's website, as well as at other participating retailers. The promotional materials used by program participants, including Booksellers' Mandeville store, advertised that gift cards were redeemable at Online's website.

Thus, a participating retailer would interact only with MSMC and the customer in fulfilling its obligations under the program. The retailer would receive revenue only upon sending the proceeds from the sale of a card to MSMC or upon use of the card to purchase merchandise from that retailer. As with the membership program, a participating retailer derived revenue only from selling gift cards directly to customers or from accepting gift cards as payment for items purchased from that retailer. Participants therefore did not derive revenue from sales made by other participating retailers.

3. Commissions on In-Store Sales During the tax period, when a Booksellers store did not carry an item requested by a customer, the customer could place an order with a clerk and have the item shipped to the store for pickup or directly to the customer. The store would "source" the item through a computer system that found the item among various wholesalers and distribution centers, including Booksellers' own warehouses and those of third-parties. Booksellers' stores were not able to choose a particular source through the system, but the computer would determine the source in accordance with predetermined criteria such as price and proximity. In some cases, the system sourced the order to Online's distribution centers, which shipped the item directly to the customer or to the Booksellers store. Online charged Booksellers a wholesale price plus a commission for the purchase, and Booksellers would resell the item to the customer. In filling these orders, Booksellers would collect any applicable state and local sales taxes.

4. Cross-Promotional Advertising The taxing authority relies on certain activity by Online that promoted Booksellers' stores. Online's website provided a "store locator" to identify nearby locations. The website also provided information about events taking place at Booksellers retail stores, including the Mandeville store. The only evidence that Booksellers promoted Online during the tax period was in connection with their activities in advertising the multi-retailer gift and membership programs discussed, supra. As the manager of the Mandeville store testified, store employees would provide information about the website only if asked by a customer.

5. Returns During the tax period, Booksellers stores accepted returns of merchandise carried by Booksellers stores regardless of where the merchandise was purchased. Customers who had purchased items from Online could return an item and, upon showing a receipt, receive store credit from Booksellers for the amount paid to Online for the item.

B. Nexus Analysis

Considering the relationship between Booksellers and Online, the Court concludes that Online did not have a substantial nexus with the Parish. The activities of Booksellers in St. Tammany Parish on behalf of Online were not of the order of magnitude necessary to establish that Booksellers marketed Online's products on Online's behalf in the Parish. The existence of a close corporate relationship between companies and a common corporate name does not mean that the physical presence of one is imputed to the other. Booksellers and Online were formally separate corporate entities that were wholly owned by the same parent company for only part of the period in issue. The two companies clearly shared a common name and brand identity under the "Barnes & Noble" banner, but there was no overlap between the companies' management or directors. There is no allegation that the companies intermingled assets or that they were under financed. And to the extent the companies may have shared financial or market data, that fact is not of independent significance. The companies did not hold themselves out as the same entity. Thus, the Court finds that attributional nexus does not apply merely by virtue of the affiliation between the companies.

Further, the nature and extent of the activities performed by Booksellers on behalf of Online within St. Tammany Parish were insufficient to treat Booksellers as acting as a marketing presence for Online in the Parish. In *Tyler Pipe and Scripto*, the Supreme Court was concerned that companies could avoid tax obligations merely by reclassifying employees, such as salespeople, as independent contractors. In both cases, the out-of-state concerns had in-state sales representatives acting continuously on their behalf to solicit orders for sales to customers. Further, *Quill* established that the Court has not adopted a "slightest presence" standard so that a *de minimis* amount of property in the taxing jurisdiction does not suffice to establish the requisite nexus. Booksellers' activities were not tantamount to acting as a sales presence for Online. Booksellers has never taken or solicited orders on behalf of Online and did not provide facilities to place orders with Online. The absence of such activity by the in-state affiliate was significant in cases finding no nexus. There is no evidence that Booksellers treats Online any differently from other third-party wholesalers in its system. Further, the evidence shows that Booksellers treats this type of sale as its own sale and collects any applicable taxes. In fact, Booksellers stores cannot even choose the source of these items, but instead relies on a computer system.

The final factor cited by the Parish is Booksellers' return policy. Booksellers' return policy was preferential to Online in that Booksellers accepted Online's merchandise as if it were its own, whereas with other retailers, Booksellers' policy was to give store credit in the amount of the price of the item in Booksellers' store at that time, although the local manager had discretion to give full refunds if customers presented receipts from other retailers. Online advertised this benefit on its website. Both the *SFA Folio Collections v. Tracy* and *Bloomingdale's By Mail v. Pennsylvania* courts rejected the argument that a preferential return policy established substantial nexus.

Accordingly . . . the Court finds that a substantial nexus does not exist upon which to base tax liability.

Case Questions

1. Which clause of the U.S. Constitution requires a substantial nexus to base tax liability?
2. What were the five aspects of the business relationship between Online and Booksellers offered by the Parish to create a substantial nexus?
3. Why did the court in *St. Tammany Parish Tax Collector v. Barnesandnoble.com, LLC* not find a substantial nexus?

New York adopted its so-called Amazon law in 2008 requiring sales tax collections by out-of-state vendors that use in-state marketing affiliates. A number of other states have also adopted similar "Amazon" laws. Both Amazon.com and Overstock.com have challenged the constitutionality of the New York law. One reason why Amazon does not want to pay sales tax is that Amazon wants their prices to appear smaller, since the tax is paid by the consumer.

In November 2010, a New York state appellate court ruled that New York's law does not violate either the Commerce Clause or the **Due Process Clause** of the U.S. Constitution.[11] The court rejected the argument brought by Amazon.com that the state did not have the authority to require online retailers to collect sales tax based on the nexus provided their in-state sales affiliates. Amazon will likely appeal the decision. The constitutional questions raised by the New York law could cause the U.S. Supreme Court to examine issue in the future.

Due Process Clause
The constitutional provision that prohibits the government from unfairly or arbitrarily depriving a person of life, liberty, or property. There are two Due Process Clauses in the U.S. Constitution, one in the Fifth Amendment applying to the federal government, and one in the Fourteenth Amendment applying to the states (although the Fifth Amendment's Due Process Clause also applies to the states under the incorporation doctrine).

Amazon, and others, could decide to end the affiliate program to avoid state sales tax. Mere advertising does not trigger the New York statute. Amazon has previously eliminated its affiliate program in North Carolina and Rhode Island. Amazon also severed ties with all Colorado-based affiliate accounts after a new law, passed by the state's legislature, would have forced them to collect and pay state sales taxes.[12] When similar legislation was introduced in California, Amazon wrote a letter to Governor Schwarzenegger informing him that "[i]f . . . enacted, Amazon would have little choice but to end its advertising relationships with California-based participants in the Amazon 'Associates Program,' " and " '[t]hus, [the legislation] would provide no new tax revenue collected by Amazon or others who sever their relationships with California-based advertisers.'"

Other large Internet retailers, such as Overstock.com, have followed Amazon's lead and also cut affiliate ties with states that have passed similar legislation. Advertising alone does not trigger sales tax so ending the affiliate program may be a practical business decision for some online sellers to avoid collection of state sales tax.

Consumer Obligation to Pay Use Tax

Consumers who live in a state that collects sales tax are technically required to pay the tax to the state, even when the Internet retailer does not charge state sales tax. When consumers pay tax directly to the state, it is referred to as a "use" tax rather than a sales tax. Stated another way, a "sales tax" is a tax on a purchase whereas a "**use tax**" is a levy upon the privilege of storing, using, or consuming tangible personal property purchased at retail.[13]

Use Tax
A tax imposed on the use of certain goods that are bought outside the taxing authority's jurisdiction. Designed to discourage the purchase of products that are not subject to the sales tax.

One common misconception is that unless a state has no sales tax, some tax is legally required to be paid on every sale, whether it be a sales tax or use tax (but not both). The Internet is not tax-free.

The use tax is a substitute for the state sales tax for products where sales tax isn't collected. For example, if a person buys a $15 CD from Amazon.com, Amazon won't collect sales tax in California because it does not have a nexus in California.[14] A consumer is technically supposed to pay sales tax to the state, but most individuals don't pay the use tax.

The use tax applies to purchases of goods to be consumed in-state, even though the goods were bought out-of-state or online. States have failed miserably in collecting use taxes on online purchases of common consumer goods such as books, DVDs, and CDs.[15] On the other hand, states have been fairly successful in collecting use taxes from automobile purchases via the Internet, since the purchase is reported to the state when the buyer registers the vehicle and/or a lender perfects a security interest or lien on the vehicle. With shortfalls in revenue for state budgets, states will likely increase their efforts to collect use taxes in the coming years.

Streamlined Sales Tax Project

Because every state has its own system and rules for state sales tax, online vendors face various challenges in complying with state sales tax laws. The **Streamlined Sales Tax Project (SSTP)** is a multi-state initiative to make sales tax laws, rules, and systems more uniform across states and, thus, make it easier for vendors to collect states' sales taxes.[16] The SSTP's main objective is to simplify and modernize sales and use tax collection and administration in the United States by creating a set of universal rules called the **Streamlined Sales and Use Tax Agreement (SSUTA)** by the participating states. Started in November of 2002, as of October 2009, twenty states had fully conformed their sales taxes to SSUTA and become full members of its Governing Board, with an additional three associate member states. These states comprise roughly one-third of the population of the states with sales taxes (roughly equal to the combined populations of California, New York, and Texas).

Streamlined Sales Tax Project (SSTP)
A multi-state initiative to make sales tax laws, rules, and systems more uniform across states and, thus, make it easier for vendors to collect states' sales taxes.

Streamlined Sales and Use Tax Agreement (SSUTA)
A set of universal rules aimed to simplify and modernize sales and use tax collection and administration in the United States.

The SSUTA contains a wide range of administrative simplifications and uniformity measures that have been approved by the member states. Key provisions of the SSUTA include:

- All local sales and use taxes must be administered and collected by the state.
- The tax base for local sales and use taxes must be the same as the state tax base.
- A state must have only one state sales tax rate, except that a second rate (which rate may be zero) may be imposed on food, prescription drugs, and electricity.
- A local jurisdiction that imposes a sales and use tax may have only a single tax rate. In some states, multiple layers of local governments may impose tax a single transaction.
- States must establish a centralized registration system that allows a seller to register in all member states.
- States must use uniform definitions for a number of common features of sales taxes (e.g., sales price, lease, rental) as well as various products such as food and food ingredients (including various subcategories), clothing, telecommunications services (including various subcategories), various categories and types of software, certain digital products, and the like.
- Each state must maintain a taxability matrix that defines the manner in which that state treats all defined items (e.g., whether it taxes or exempts them).
- States are prohibited from limiting the amount of tax on a transaction (cap) or providing that only a portion of the purchase price of a product is exempt (threshold).
- Those states that allow local governments to impose sales and use taxes must provide a data base of local government boundaries as well as a data base that provides the correct tax rate for any physical address in the state.
- States must offer all sellers the option to file a simplified electronic tax return, and they must adopt uniform rules governing the process of making electronic tax remittances.

The SSTP is developing computer software that would automatically calculate taxes for any given jurisdiction, thereby eliminating much of the burden on retailers' crossing multiple states' boundaries. While the SSTP has standardized definitions across member states, a number of economically important states are not parties to the standardization, including California, Texas, New York, Florida, Illinois, Georgia, and Pennsylvania.[17]

INCOME TAX ISSUES

With the rise of e-commerce in today's marketplace, a host of income tax issues exist along with the sales tax issues. This section will focus on tax-related issues for online sellers, online gambling winnings, income from virtual world transactions, and telecommuters.

Tax-Related Issues for Online Sellers

While the Internet Tax Freedom Act prohibits the taxing of access to the Internet, the Act does not apply to tax on income from online sales or sales or use tax on purchases made online. Some individuals mistakenly think that the law exempts income from Internet sales and online auctions from income tax. Online sellers who engage in e-commerce on websites such as eBay, Amazon, and Google Checkout may face income tax liability at both the federal and state levels.[18]

In *Orellana v. Commissioner*, T.C. Summ. Op. 2010-51, U.S. Tax Court (Apr. 20, 2010) (Case 6.2), an IRS officer was found liable for back taxes and penalties for not reporting income on nearly 2,000 transactions on eBay. Andrea Fabiana Orellana failed to report $41,842 in income in 2004 and 2005 from sales of designer clothing, shoes, and other items, according to the U.S. Tax Court opinion. Orellana, who worked as an IRS revenue officer, testified that she never kept receipts. "That would be ridiculous, unheard of. Unless there was some really bizarre reason why I kept a receipt, there were no receipts," she said according to the court documents. Orellana claimed her eBay sales were not a business, and characterized it as an online garage sale. She said she liked to shop for designer clothes and that this was a way to clean out her closets. The court rejected Orellana's arguments and ordered the taxpayer to pay income taxes on eBay sales along with penalties. In a Bloomberg News article, eBay declined to comment on the specific case but sent an e-mailed statement that stated, "Sellers are responsible for paying all required state and federal taxes."[19]

CASE 6.2

The Case of the IRS Officer and eBay Seller

Orellana v. Commissioner, *T.C. Summ. Op. 2010-51, U.S. Tax Court (Apr. 20, 2010)*

Background

Petitioner [Orellana-the taxpayer] has been employed by the Internal Revenue Service (IRS) since 2001. During the years at issue and at the time of trial petitioner was employed as a revenue officer.

Between 2000 and 2005 petitioner was involved in over 7,000 eBay transactions. During all or part of the tax years at issue petitioner sold items under several eBay user IDs, including, "ambassgwf", "andreafo", "askme12go", and "BlackTheRipper". Petitioner reported no income or expenses from her eBay transactions on her Federal income tax returns for the years at issue.

In an effort to verify petitioner's income for [2004 and 2005, the IRS] performed a bank deposits analysis (BDA) using bank records she had obtained through summonses issued to Washington Mutual Bank, brokerage account records with ShareBuilder Securities Corporation, and some PayPal records. The BDA indicated that petitioner had unreported gross receipts for both years. Using the bank deposits method, TCO Brooks determined that petitioner had unreported income of $15,320.67 in 2004 and $21,062 in 2005.

After reviewing the files in petitioner's case, the Appeals Office . . . issued the statutory notice of deficiency determining unreported income of $14,163.01 for 2004 and $18,595.25 for 2005.

Because petitioner did not maintain any records of her purchases and sales of items on eBay, respondent [the Internal Revenue Service] subpoenaed records pertaining to petitioner from eBay/PayPal. The company complied with respondent's subpoena by producing voluminous "duplicates of reports and records maintained by eBay/PayPal" pertaining to petitioner under the names "Andrea Fabiana Orellana", "Andrea Orellana Nadres" and "Andrea Nadres". The [Revenue Agent's] examination of the PayPal records resulted in a determination that petitioner had approximately 1,200 eBay sales in 2004 and 600 in 2005.

Discussion

I. Reconstruction of Gross Income

Section 6001 requires a taxpayer to maintain sufficient records to allow for the determination of the taxpayer's correct tax liability. If a taxpayer fails to maintain or does not produce adequate books and records, the Commissioner is authorized to reconstruct the taxpayer's income. Indirect methods may be used for this purpose.

A. Bank Deposits Petitioner argues that she did not consider herself to be in "business" and therefore did not think she was required to maintain records to account for the gross receipts from her online sales. The Court therefore finds that it was reasonable for respondent to use an indirect method, the bank deposits method, to aid in reconstructing petitioner's income for 2004 and 2005.

Bank deposits constitute prima facie evidence of income. The bank deposits method of determining income assumes that all the money deposited into a taxpayer's bank accounts during a specific period constitutes gross income.

As part of her BDA for each year at issue, the RA [IRS Revenue Agent] created summaries of nontaxable deposits as identified by petitioner and allowed by respondent and nontaxable deposits as identified by petitioner and not allowed by respondent.

B. Specific Items of Income In addition to unexplained deposits to her bank accounts, respondent has determined from eBay/PayPal records that petitioner had substantial gross receipts from sales of items on the Internet. Respondent was able to identify and eliminate from petitioner's bank deposits transfers of funds from her PayPal account to her bank accounts.

II. Petitioner's Arguments

With respect to respondent's determinations petitioner makes the following observations . . . because she did not believe she was conducting a business she kept neither receipts nor records of her eBay sales activity; and respondent has not properly allowed the deductions to which she is entitled.

Petitioner Not in "Business"

As to her . . . observation, petitioner's subjective belief that she was not engaged in a "business" does not relieve her of the responsibility to report gains from property sales. See sec. 61(a)(3); sec. 1.61-6, Income Tax Regs. In order to determine whether she had gains from property sales, petitioner would have had to keep track of her cost or other basis in the property sold and the amount realized upon sale. Secs. 1001, 1012, 1014, 1015.

Petitioner argues that she was just taking things in her home and her garage and selling them online; she characterized it as an "online garage sale". Petitioner explained that she liked to shop for and buy designer clothes, some of which "were sitting in her closet". She testified that while the clothes were "used most of them; some are new," so she "would put them on eBay". She might sell a $350 pair of shoes for $50 but that was better than having them sitting in her closet "wasting space", she testified.

On the other hand, petitioner admitted that she "occasionally" purchased items for sale in the ordinary course of her eBay sales activity that would still "have tags on them". When she was reminded that most of the items she sold were "advertised" as new, petitioner responded: "I always advertise as new only because you can get a better price for that." And she added, "So basically when you're asking these questions about why things are new, I document them as new if it appears new. Is that wrong?" Petitioner explained that she sold clothing and shoes of various sizes because she contracted plantar fasciitis and was unable to keep up her exercise routine.

(Continued)

(Continued)

Petitioner's Bases in Items and Expenses

Petitioner's documentary evidence consisted of a disorganized hodgepodge of eBay records for one screen name; PayPal records [most of which cannot be identified as connected with petitioner]; various checks, summaries, and statements without explanatory information.

Where a taxpayer has established that he has incurred an expense, failure to prove the exact amount of the otherwise deductible item may not always be fatal. Petitioner has not produced any coherent evidence from which the Court can determine the bases for the hundreds of items she sold in 2004 and 2005 or the expenses she may have paid in the pursuit of her eBay sales activity beyond those respondent already allowed.

III. Accuracy-Related Penalties

Section 7491(c) imposes on the Commissioner the burden of production in any court proceeding with respect to the liability of any individual for penalties and additions to tax. Negligence is defined as any failure to make a reasonable attempt to comply with the provisions of the Internal Revenue Code, and the term "disregard" includes any careless, reckless, or intentional disregard. See sec. 6662(c). Negligence also includes any failure by the taxpayer to keep adequate books and records or to substantiate items properly.

Petitioner's attitude toward the preparation of her tax returns appeared to be cavalier. Petitioner is a revenue officer with the IRS. With this background, she has a wider range of knowledge of tax matters than do members of the general public. Petitioner is, or certainly should be, familiar with the recordkeeping requirements of section 6001, and she had access to a wide range of tax resources relating to the reporting of income and deductions. The Court might not expect for a taxpayer to keep records for a few small items sold on eBay. In view, however, of the large number of transactions in 2004 and 2005 in which petitioner engaged, she should have realized that her activity might be subject to question. Accordingly, respondent's determination is sustained.

Case Questions

1. How did the IRS determine Orellana's income from eBay sales?
2. Why does a taxpayer's subjective belief that she is not engaged in a "business" not relieve the taxpayer's responsibility to report income?
3. Why did the court hold that accuracy-related penalties were appropriate?
4. Based on the holding in *Orellana*, under what circumstances is a seller required to pay income taxes on gains from an online auction?
5. Why was the fact that Orellana worked as a revenue officer with the IRS relevant in the decision? Should this be a relevant consideration?

Although the IRS has explicitly stated that "[a]ll income from auctions, traditional or online . . . is generally taxable unless certain exceptions are met," it is widely known that there is not complete compliance by online sellers.[20] Nonreporting and underreporting of income are major issues stemming from e-commerce. To help online sellers understand their tax responsibilities, the IRS website includes the Online Auction Sellers Tax Center and an IRS Online Auctions video that provides an overview of online auction seller tax responsibilities.

The IRS also makes a distinction between online garage sales and a home-based online auction seller business. If the taxpayer's online auction sales are the Internet equivalent of an occasional garage or yard sale, the taxpayer generally does not have to report the sales. However, sales of appreciated assets at an online auction can be considered income. IRS Fact Sheet 2008-23 contains guidelines for determining whether an activity is engaged in for profit, such as a business or investment activity, or is engaged in as a hobby. Classified as either business income or capital gains, gains from e-commerce must be reported by online sellers on their annual income tax returns. A reportable gain consists of income net of the original cost, known as the "basis" of the item sold.

Where an online seller is operating a "viable online business," the seller may be entitled to deduct business expenses.[21] Under § 162 of the IRC, online sellers who are engaged in a trade or business can deduct ordinary and necessary expenses incurred in carrying on their trade or business. The IRS defines an "ordinary" expense as one that is "common and accepted in a trade or business" and a "necessary" expense as one that is "helpful and appropriate for a trade or business." In order for an online seller to deduct business expenses under § 162, the seller must have the requisite intent to profit.

If a taxpayer uses a portion of his home for an online business, the taxpayer may be able to take a home office deduction. In order to deduct expenses related to the business use of a home, the taxpayer must carry on a "bona fide" business and meet other specific requirements.[22] The home office deduction allows a taxpayer to deduct as an itemized expense that portion of apartment rental or home mortgage costs (and related utility costs and other verifiable upkeep and maintenance expenses) attributable to the amount of the home that is used regularly and exclusively (and the IRS pays attention to "exclusively") as the principal place of business, or for client meetings or business-related storage.

Some U.S. taxpayers who sell items online may try to avoid taxes by using offshore bank accounts. The IRS, however, has issued guidance that U.S. taxpayers must report their worldwide income, including online auctions sales to foreign customers on U.S. tax returns.

The **tax gap** measures the extent to which taxpayers fail to file their federal tax returns and to pay the correct tax on time, which stems from underreporting, underpayment, and nonfiling. The growth of Internet commerce has contributed to the expansion of the tax gap. To address the tax gap that stems from underreporting and nonfiling of income of federal income tax returns by online sellers on websites like eBay, Amazon, and Google Checkout, some have called for increased taxpayer education and enforcement. Others have also called for new IRS regulations, such as requiring Forms 1099 and W-9 for online sellers on websites such as eBay.

Tax Gap
The extent to which taxpayers fail to file their federal tax returns and to pay the correct tax on time that stems from underreporting, underpayment, and nonfiling.

Income Tax from Online Gambling Winnings

The popularity of the Internet has also led to an increased number of individuals who engage in online gambling, especially online poker. According to one report, there are well over 2,000 Internet gambling websites offering various wagering options, including sports betting, casino games, lotteries, and bingo.[23] Conservative estimates show that the industry has grown from $1 billion in profits in 1997 to $10.9 billion in 2006.

Online poker sites try to avoid possible legal issues by setting up their main operations in offshore locations such as Gibraltar or the UK protectorate, the Isle of Man. Online gaming sites, such as Full Tilt Poker and Poker Stars, advertise on television in the United States because they only advertise the practice and learning poker aspect of free play, and allow customers to discover the real money wagering on their own.

Congress adopted the **Unlawful Internet Gambling Enforcement Act of 2006 (UIGEA)** in an effort to curb online gambling.[24] The UIGEA prohibits financial institutions from accepting transactions made in the pursuit of unlawful Internet gambling. Some critics have said that the U.S. effort to prohibit Internet gambling through the UIGEA has done nothing more than force Americans to gamble through illegal and off-shore online wagering operators where gambling earnings are not reported as taxable income. While the UIGEA has been effective in prohibiting publicly held companies

Unlawful Internet Gambling Enforcement Act (UIGEA)
A federal law outlawing unlawful Internet gambling and by providing a safe harbor for certain types of transactions. 31 U.S.C. § 5362.

from operating in the United States, it has been unable to stop privately held companies from providing gambling services to U.S. players.[25]

In 2009, the U.S. Attorney for the Southern District of New York seized $34 million belonging to 27,000 online poker players, but because of the ambiguity of the UIGEA and the feeling among many that online gambling should be regulated and taxed, it is possible that the seizing of these assets will backfire and a court decision will actually support Internet poker.[26]

In July 2010, the House Financial Services Committee approved a bill that would have lifted the ban on Internet gambling by authorizing the Treasury Department to license and regulate web-based nonsports betting operators but the measure failed to receive the necessary votes to become law.[27] If Congress repeals the UIGEA and allows for legalization of domestic online gambling operators in the United States, licensing and regulation would give the IRS a mechanism to collect taxes on gambling deposits, gambling withdrawals, or just net winnings. Winnings by individuals would also be taxed, as regular gambling winnings are now, and gambling losses would also be deductible from gambling winnings. The taxes could yield as much as $42 billion for the government over ten years. States would also have the right to tax the winnings of individual players who participate in Internet gambling within their borders as gambling winnings have traditionally been considered taxable income. Congress and state legislatures will continue to consider the legality and licensing of online gambling sites and income tax issues from online gambling in the coming years.

Tax Consequences of Virtual World Transactions

Along with online gambling winnings, real world income earned in virtual worlds, such as World of Warcraft and Second Life, also raises tax-related questions. A virtual world is a persistent online environment in which users create and control characters (called "avatars").[28] The avatars move through the virtual world, interacting with other avatars, and with the virtual world itself. A vast amount of income-generating activity now occurs in virtual worlds, but it remains unclear whether, and how, income derived from virtual world activity should be taxed.[29] Some countries have already implemented or proposed tax regimes for virtual world income. There are three possible tax regimes: (1) all income generated by in-world activity could be taxed as ordinary income; (2) all income generated in virtual worlds could be taxed as capital gains; or (3) income generated by in-world activity could be taxed as either ordinary income or capital gains based on the nature of activity that produced the income. Some have argued that all virtual world income should be characterized as ordinary income but the IRS has yet to take an official position.[30]

The IRS provides some guidance to taxpayers on the tax consequences of virtual world transactions. The IRS website states, "Cyber-economic activities in the online world may have tax consequences that real world avatar counterparts need to consider. The IRS has provided guidance on the tax treatment of bartering, gambling, business and hobby income—issues that are similar to activities in online gaming worlds. In general, you can receive income in the form of money, property, or services. If you receive more income from the virtual world than you spend, you may be required to report the gain as taxable income. IRS guidance also applies when you spend more in a virtual world than you receive, you generally cannot claim a loss on an income tax return."[31] Like online gambling winnings, virtual world income will continue to be topic of debate in the coming years.

Tax Issues for Telecommuters

Technological advancements, such as smartphones and faster Internet speeds, along with better understanding by management, have increased the mobility of workers and provided more opportunities for workers to telecommute. The number of U.S. employees who worked remotely at least one day per month increased 39 percent from 2006 to 2008, according to one study conducted by WorldatWork, a global human resources association.[32] Another study found that more than 34 million U.S. adults telecommute at least occasionally, and that by 2016, approximately 63 million U.S. adults will telecommute at least some of the time.[33]

This increased mobility of workers and rise in telecommuting raises questions about state income taxes and the ability of a state to impose state income taxes over nonresidents. Most states require payment of personal income taxes, and each state has different tax laws with different taxing authorities. If a person lives in one state and works in another, even temporarily, the worker may have to file a state return in both states. Nonresidents generally have to file a nonresident income tax return with the state, and if the state where they live also imposes a personal income tax, then the individual will also have to file an annual tax return for all income earned, regardless of where it was earned. Some individuals who work in more than one state may have to pay double state income taxes.

Two cases in the State of New York demonstrate the taxing power of a state over a nonresident. In *Huckaby v. N.Y. State Div. of Tax Appeals*, 6 A.D.3d 988, 776 N.Y.S.2d 125 (3d Dep't 2004), a Tennessee resident who telecommuted with a New York employer was required to pay income tax on 100 percent of New York earnings even though he spent only 25 percent of his time in New York. The New York State Department of Taxation and Finance audited Huckaby's tax returns and allocated 100 percent of his income to New York State under the "convenience of the employer test."

The court held that the state satisfied the due process requirement of minimal connection between a taxpayer and the taxing state because the taxpayer had accepted employment from a New York employer and worked in his employer's New York office approximately 25 percent of year.[34] The Court of Appeals determined that, under the relevant New York Tax Law, the legislature intended to tax nonresidents on all income earned while working for a New York employer.

In *Zelinsky v. Tax Appeals Tribunal of the State of New York* (N.Y. 2003), *cert. denied*, 541 U.S. 1009 (2004), law professor Edward Zelinsky challenged New York's ability to tax as "source" income monies he earned while working at his home in Connecticut. Cardozo Law School—the institution for which Zelinsky taught—is located in New York. Zelinsky performed many of his duties, however, at his home in Connecticut. Zelinsky commuted three days each week during the semester, and when school was not in session and during his sabbatical leave in the fall semester of 1995, he worked exclusively at home. Zelinsky argued that New York should be permitted to tax as source income only the percentage of income he earned while he was physically in New York. The court held taxing a nonresident did not violate either the Due Process Clause or the Commerce Clause in the U.S. Constitution. The court stated that "the mere potential for or actual existence of double taxation does not automatically transgress the Commerce Clause if, as here, the challenged tax is in fact fairly apportioned."[35]

A few states have tax reciprocity agreements. For example, all nonresidents who work in the District of Columbia can claim exemption from withholding for the DC income tax. Illinois and Iowa also have a reciprocal agreement for individual income tax purposes. Minnesota and Wisconsin had a reciprocity agreement in place, but that agreement ended effective January 1, 2010.[36] A number of states, including New York with a large number of commuters, have no reciprocity agreements in place. New York, as seen in *Huckaby* and *Zalinksky*, is notorious for its aggressive collection practices.

Along with individual state income taxes, corporate income taxes may also be assessed, even when the corporation only has one employee. Like its sister state New York, New Jersey has also imposed strict rules for telecommuters. In *Telebright Corp., Inc. v. Director, Div. of Taxation*, 25 N.J.Tax 333 (N.J. Tax 2010), the New Jersey Tax Court held that a corporation which had a single employee who lived in New Jersey but who telecommuted on a regular basis from New Jersey was "doing business" in New Jersey and was therefore subject to the New Jersey Corporation Business Tax. The New Jersey court held that a Delaware corporation with offices in Maryland is subject to the New Jersey Corporation Business Tax Act by virtue of the fact that one New Jersey resident employed by the company "telecommutes" by receiving and performing her work assignments each business day at her New Jersey home via computer and telephone. Richard J. Bove, Telebright's lawyer, told *Forbes* magazine that the case would be appealed. "Look at the message this sends to companies in Philadelphia, New York City or Delaware that have a single worker in New Jersey," he said. Bove said he knew of no case from another state premising corporate jurisdiction on one worker, adding, "If there was one, I'm sure it would have been cited in the opinion."[37] As a result of the *Telebright* decision, more companies will likely avoid New Jersey and think twice about allowing telecommuters to work in different states.

Commerce Clause
U.S. Const. art. I, § 8, cl. 3, which gives Congress the exclusive power to regulate commerce among the states, with foreign nations, and with Indian tribes.

Dormant Commerce Clause
The constitutional principle that the Commerce Clause prevents state regulation of interstate commercial activity even when Congress has not acted under its Commerce Clause power to regulate that activity. Also called negative commerce clause.

Privileges and Immunities Clause
The constitutional provision in U.S. Const. art. IV, § 2, cl. 1 prohibiting a state from favoring its own citizens by discriminating against other states' citizens who come within its borders.

Telecommuter Tax Fairness Act
A legislative proposal that would eliminate the punitive tax on telecommuters by prohibiting states from taxing the wages that nonresidents earn in their home states.

Double state income taxes and taxing nonresidents raises some constitutional questions.[38] Congress could pass legislation to prevent double state income taxes under the power of the **Commerce Clause** found in Article I, Section 8, of the U.S. Constitution. Both the Dormant Commerce Clause and Privileges and Immunities Clause provide potential constitutional grounds to invalidate state tax regimes. The **Dormant Commerce Clause** is the constitutional principle that the Commerce Clause prevents state regulation of interstate commercial activity even when Congress has not acted under its Commerce Clause power to regulate that activity. The **Privileges and Immunities Clause** in the Fourteenth Amendment to the U.S. Constitution is a constitutional provision that prohibits a state from favoring its own citizens by discriminating against other states' citizens who come within its borders.

While state income tax may deter telecommuting, telecommuters may be able to claim the home office tax deduction. IRS Publication 587 sets forth the requirements for claiming the home office tax deduction. The term "home" includes a house, apartment, condominium, mobile home, boat, or similar property which provides basic living accommodations.

To address the issues associated with state income taxation of telecommuters, some policy makers have advocated federal legislation. In the 111th Congress (2009–2010), Rep. James Himes (D-Connecticut) sponsored the **Telecommuter Tax Fairness Act** of 2009 (H.R. 2600). The bill would have eliminated the punitive tax on telecommuters by prohibiting states from taxing the wages that nonresidents earn in their home states. The bill would prohibit states from imposing an income tax on the compensation of a nonresident for any period in which a person is not physically present in or working in the state. The Act received some bipartisan support but failed to garner enough support to pass the U.S. House of Representatives. Previous bills aimed at telecommuter tax fairness have also failed.[39] Reducing energy consumption, avoiding the spread of infectious diseases while maximizing productivity, and providing workers with more flexibility are some of the reasons in support of the Telecommuter Tax Fairness Act.

To promote telecommuting by federal employees, Congress passed the Telework Enhancement Act of 2010 (H.R. 1722; Public Law 111-292) that instructs each federal agency to come up with policies to promote telecommuting. Supporters of the Act argue that telecommuting will increase productivity, improve morale, help the government recruit the best people, reduce traffic congestion, and make the environment cleaner. The legislation directs the Office of Personnel Management to come up with teleworking guidelines and requires agencies to establish policies within six months under which employees may be authorized to telework. The Obama administration has set a goal of having 500,000 teleworkers by 2014 for federal government workers.[40]

While Congress and the Obama administration promote telecommuting, some state measures, such as New York's "convenience of the employer" rule, create barriers to telecommuting. Individual states could enter into reciprocity agreements for income taxes in the absence of federal legislation. Time will tell whether Congress will ultimately enact federal legislation to prevent telecommuters from paying double state income taxes. In the meantime, the constitutionality of individual and corporate income tax for telecommuters will likely be a hot issue for courts to consider in the future with our increasingly mobile, and telecommuting, population.

Summary

At the federal level, the Internal Revenue Service (IRS) is responsible for tax collection and tax law enforcement of the Internal Revenue Code (IRC). Each state also has its own agency for tax collection and enforcement. A sales tax is a tax imposed on the sale of goods and services, usually measured as a percentage of their price. Despite its name, the Internet Tax Freedom Act (ITFA) does not prevent state and local governments from imposing sales tax collection requirements on companies selling over the Internet. In *Quill v. North Dakota*, the U.S. Supreme Court ruled that retailers are exempt from collecting sales taxes in states where they have no "nexus" or physical presence, and this substantial nexus test has been applied to online retailers. The Streamlined Sales Tax Project (SSTP) is a multistate initiative to make sales tax laws, rules, and systems more uniform across states and thus easier for vendors to collect states' sales taxes. Nonreporting and underreporting of income is a major issue stemming from e-commerce. Online sellers engaged in a business may be responsible for paying federal and state income taxes, and the IRS and states are increasing efforts to collect income taxes from online transactions. Income taxes imposed from online gambling winnings and virtual world income will continue to be debated in coming years. Telecommuters may also be responsible for paying state income tax, even in states where they are nonresidents.

Key Terms

Commerce Clause *106*
Dormant Commerce Clause *106*
Due Process Clause *98*
income tax *92*
Internal Revenue Code (IRC) *92*
Internal Revenue Service (IRS) *92*
Internet Tax Freedom Act (ITFA) *93*
Privileges and Immunities Clause *106*
sales tax *93*
Streamlined Sales Tax Project (SSTP) *99*
Streamlined Sales and Use Tax Agreement (SSUTA) *99*
Substantial Nexus Test *94*
tax gap *103*
Telecommuter Tax Fairness Act 106
Treasury Regulations *92*
Unlawful Internet Gambling Enforcement Act (UIGEA) *103*
U.S. Tax Court *92*
use tax *98*

Review Questions

1. Where are the sources of the federal tax laws?
2. What is the role of the Internal Revenue Service?
3. What types of cases are decided in the U.S. Tax Court?
4. What is the scope of the Internet Tax Freedom Act (ITFA)?
5. What is the purpose of the Streamlined Sales Tax Project?
6. What is the difference between a sales tax and a use tax?
7. What is the substantial nexus test?
8. When are sellers from online auction sites required to pay income tax?
9. When can an online seller or telecommuter claim the home office tax deduction?
10. What is the purpose of the proposed Telecommuter Tax Fairness Act?

Discussion Questions

1. What are the arguments for and against state sales tax for online purchases? What do you think is the best approach?
2. Some policy makers and politicians have called for a federal value-added tax (VAT) or sales tax levied at a rate of about 15 percent to replace most of the revenues from the federal income taxes. Would you support a federal value-added tax (VAT) or national sales tax to replace federal income taxes? Should the federal value-added tax (VAT) or national sales tax include online purchases? Why or why not?
3. What is the best approach for tax-related issues associated with online gambling winnings and income from virtual world transactions?
4. Would you support federal legislation, such as the Telecommuter Tax Fairness Act, that would prohibit states from collecting state income tax on tax earned by nonresident telecommuters? Why or why not?

Exercises

1. Steve is passionate about rare orchids but can't find them in Minnesota, so he orders his supplies online from an orchid supplier with headquarters in California. The supplier has all of its facilities in California and collects payment in California. Does Steve have to pay either Minnesota or California state sales tax on the orchids? One year later, the supplier opens a warehouse in Minnesota to handle its online orders for the entire country. Is Steve now required to pay Minnesota states tax?
2. Julie runs a home business through which she purchases items at yard and estate sales. She then sells the items for a profit on eBay. In 2010, Julie received income from eBay sales of $85,000. She incurred the following expenses: (1) transportation costs to yard and estate sales; (2) eBay seller fees; and (3) monthly service fee of $50 for high speed Internet that she uses for both personal and business use. Julie also purchased a new computer in 2010 for $700 that she uses for both personal and business use. Go to the IRS website and run a search for "Tax Tips for Online Auction Sellers" and find the page that describes Tax Tips for Online Auction Sellers. Then go to the link for "Business Expenses." After reading these documents, which of the business expenses described above can Julie deduct?
3. Conduct research and find whether the state where you live has any income tax reciprocity agreements with other states. In addition, conduct research to see if there are any proposed income tax reciprocity agreements. Summarize your findings in a memorandum.

Related Internet Sites

http://www.irs.gov/
Official IRS Website

http://taxprof.typepad.com/
Tax Law Prof Blog

http://www.taxfoundation.org/
Tax Foundation

http://www.taxadmin.org/
Federation of Tax Administrators

http://www.streamlinedsalestax.org/
Streamlined Sales Tax Project

http://www.taxlitigation.net/
Tax Law Litigation Blog

http://www.tax.state.ny.us/
New York State Tax Department

http://www.ustaxcourt.gov/
Official website for the U.S. Tax Court

http://www.bankrate.com/taxes.aspx
Bankrate state and federal tax tips

http://www.hbtlj.org/
Houston Business and Tax Law Journal

http://www.jct.gov/
Joint Committee on Taxation

http://www.justice.gov/tax/
U.S. Department of Justice Tax Division

http://www.gpoaccess.gov/uscode/
United States Code (USC). The text Internal Revenue Code (IRC) is codified in Title 26 of the United States Code.

http://www.gpoaccess.gov/cfr/
Code of Federal Regulations (CFR). Tax regulations adopted by the IRS are found in Title 26 of the CFR.

End Notes

1. Chris Cannon, Chris Cannon Quotes, available at http://www.brainyquote.com/quotes/authors/c/chris_cannon.html.
2. IMDB, Memorable Quotes for The Day After Tomorrow, available at http://www.imdb.com/title/tt0319262/quotes.
3. Black's Law Dictionary (9th ed. 2009).
4. Duke University Law Library, Federal Tax Research Guide, available at http://www.law.duke.edu/lib/researchguides/fedtax.
5. Tax Policy Center, The Tax Policy Briefing Book: A Citizen's Guide for the 2008 Election, and Beyond, available at http://www.taxpolicycenter.org/briefing-book/background/numbers/revenue.cfm/.
6. 2 Jerome R. Hellerstein, Walter Hellerstein & John A. Swain, State Taxation P 12.02 (3d ed. 2010).
7. Letter from Benjamin Franklin to Jean-Baptiste Leroy (Nov. 13, 1789), in 10 The Works of Benjamin Franklin 409, 410 (Jared Sparks ed., Hilliard Gray 1840).
8. Internet Tax Freedom Act Amendments Act of 2007, Pub. L. No. 110-108, 121 Stat. 1024 (2007) (codified as amended at 47 U.S.C § 151).
9. See Tex. Tax Code § 151.325.
10. *Borders Online, LLC v. State Bd. of Equalization*, 129 Cal.App.4th 1179, 29 Cal. Rptr. 3d 176, 188 (Cal. Ct. App. 2005).
11. *Amazon.com, LLC v. New York State Dept. of Taxation and Finance*, 81 A.D.3d 183, 913 N.Y.S.2d 129 (1st Dept. Nov. 4, 2010).
12. Michael R. Gordon, *Up the Amazon Without a Paddle: Examining Sales Taxes, Entity Isolation, and the "Affiliate Tax"*, 11 N.C. J. L. & TECH. 299 (2010).
13. 67B Am. Jur. 2d Sales and Use Taxes § 6.
14. See Donald Bruce and William F. Fox, *E-Commerce in the Context of Declining State Sales Tax Bases*, 53 Nat'l Tax J. 1373, 1380, 1380 n. 20 (2000).
15. Robert A. Mikos, State Taxation of Marijuana Distribution and other Federal Crimes, 2010 U. Chi. Legal F. 223, n. 53 (2010).
16. Streamlined Sales Tax Governing Board, available at http://www.streamlinedsalestax.org/.
17. John L. Mikesell, *Commentary*, 63 TAX L. REV. 705, 708 (2010).
18. Harley Duncan, *Administrative Issues in the Adoption of a Federal VAT in Addition to Existing Federal and State Taxes*, 63 TAX L. REV. 713, 725–727 (2010).
19. Amy Feldman and Margaret Collins, *IRS Agent Didn't Report $41,842 in EBay Sales*, Bloomberg News, Apr. 22, 2010, available at http://www.bloomberg.com/news/2010-04-22/irs-agent-found-liable-for-failing-to-report-almost-42-000-in-ebay-sales.html/.
20. Internal Revenue Service, Tax Tips for Online Auction Sellers (2010), available at http://www.irs.gov/businesses/small/industries/article/0,,id=202939,00.html/.
21. Maricel P. Montano, *Can Widening the scope of Information Reporting to Include Income Derived from Online Sales Help to Narrow the Expanding Tax Gap?*, 83 S. CAL. L. REV. 379, 394 (2010).
22. 26 U.S.C. § 280A.
23. Michael Lenhardt, *I'm All In: The Online Poker Industry*, ILLINOIS BUSINESS LAW JOURNAL, Nov. 30, 2009, available at http://www.law.uiuc.edu/bljournal/post/2009/11/30/Im-All-In-The-Online-Poker-Industry.aspx/.
24. Unlawful Internet Gambling Enforcement Act of 2006, Pub. L. No. 109-347, tit. VIII, 120 Stat. 1952 (codified at 31 U.S.C. §§ 5361–5367).
25. See Ross A. Crutchfield, *Folding a Losing Hand: Why Congress Should Replace the Unlawful Internet Gambling Enforcement Act with a Regulatory Scheme*, 45 TULSA L. Rev. 161, 167 (2009); Ian Abovitz, *Why the United States Should Rethink Its Legal Approach to Internet Gambling: A Comparative Analysis of Regulatory Models That Have Been Successfully Implemented In Foreign Jurisdictions*, 22 TEMP. INT'L & COMP. L.J. 437 (2008).
26. Tamara Audi and Amy Schatz, *Online Poker Busts Raise Legal Stakes*, WALL STREET JOURNAL, June 12, 2009, available at http://online.wsj.com/article/SB124476513837208405.html/.
27. Sewell Chan, *Online Betting Barred by U.S. Gets 2nd Look*, N.Y. TIMES, July 29, 2010, at A1.
28. Adam S. Chodorow, *Ability to Pay and the Taxation of Virtual Income*, 75 TENN. L. REV. 695, 699 (2008).
29. Nell A. Beekman, *Virtual Assets, Real Tax: The Capital Gains/Ordinary Income Distinction in Virtual Worlds*, 11 COLUM. SCI. & TECH. L. REV. 152 (2010).
30. Id. at 164.
31. IRS, Tax Consequences of Virtual World Transactions (2010), available at http://www.irs.gov/businesses/small/article/0,,id=215593,00.html/.
32. Ted Schadler, US Telecommuting Forecast, 2009 to 2016, Forrester Research, March 11, 2009, available at http://www.forrester.com/rb/Research/us_telecommuting_forecast,_2009_to_2016/q/id/46635/t/2/.
33. Press Release, PRWeb, Telework Revs Up as More Employers Offer Work Flexibility, Feb. 17, 2009, available at http://www.prweb.com/releases/2009/02/prweb2089024.htm/.
34. See Meredith A. Bentley, *Huckaby v. New York State Division of Tax Appeals: In Upholding the Current Tax Treatment of Telecommuters, the Court of Appeals*

Demonstrates the Need for Legislative Action, 80 St. JOHN'S L. REV. 1147 (2006).

35. *Zelinsky*, 801 N.E.2d at 848.

36. See 701 Iowa Admin. Code 38.13(422); Minn. Stat. 290.081.

37. William P. Barrett, *Bad News for Telecommuters*, FORBES, March 30, 2010, available at http://www.forbes.com/2010/03/30/state-corporate-tax-telecommuters-amazon-personal-finance-new-jersey-tax-grab.html/.

38. See Morgan L. Holcomb, *Tax My Ride: Taxing Commuters In Our National Economy*, 8 FLA. TAX REV. 885 (2008).

39. Telecommuter Tax Fairness Act of 2007 (H.R. 1360), Telecommuter Tax Fairness Act of 2005 (S. 1097; H.R. 2258).

40. Jim Abrams, *Telecommuting Gets Boost from Congress*, BOSTON GLOBE, Jul. 15, 2010, available at http://www.boston.com/business/technology/articles/2010/07/15/telecommuting_gets_boost_from_congress/.

CHAPTER

7 Cybercrimes

Al-Qaeda and other terrorist groups have spoken of their desire to unleash a cyber-attack on our country—attacks that are harder to detect and harder to defend against. In today's world acts of terror could come not only from a few extremists in suicide vests but from a few key strokes of a computer.

PRESIDENT BARACK OBAMA[1]

LEARNING OBJECTIVES

After completing this chapter, you will be able to:

1. Explain the different categories of computer crimes.
2. Discuss the actus reus and mens rea requirements for crimes.
3. Explain the scope of the Fourth Amendment with regard to electronic communications.
4. Explain the jurisdictional requirements for computer crimes.
5. Explain the main federal statutes associated with computer crimes.
6. Describe the challenges in investigating and prosecuting cybercrimes.

COMPUTER CRIME DEFINITION AND CATEGORIES

The Melissa Virus, which spread in March 1999 caused an estimated $80 million in damages to computers worldwide. In the United States alone, the virus made its way through 1.2 million computers in one-fifth of the country's largest businesses.[2] Because each infected computer could infect 50 additional computers, which in turn could infect another 50 computers, the virus proliferated rapidly and exponentially, resulting in substantial interruption or impairment of public communications and services. David Smith, creator of the Melissa Virus, pleaded guilty in 1999 to both state and federal charges with knowingly spreading a computer virus with the intent to cause damage.

Cyberterrorism
The threat of cyberterrorism is one of the most serious global security issues today. For example, when Russian tanks rolled into Georgia in 2008, cyber attacks crippled Georgian government websites.

Computer Crime
Any violations of criminal law that involve a knowledge of computer technology for their perpetration, investigation, or prosecution. Also called cybercrime. Computer Fraud and Abuse Act (CFAA). A federal law establishing civil liability for gaining unauthorized access to a computer and causing damage to that computer. Also called Computer Fraud and Abuse Act or FCFAA. 18 U.S.C. § 1030.

Cybercrime
The term cybercrime is synonymous with "computer crime."

The Melissa Virus brought to light the potential harm associated with computer crimes and cybercrimes. Studies show that Americans are increasingly being victimized by computer crimes. According to Gallup's 2010 crime survey, 11 percent of U.S. adults said they or a household member were the target of a computer crime on their home computer in the past year, up from 6 to 8 percent in recent years.[3] According to estimates, cyber criminals steal intellectual property from businesses worldwide worth up to $1 trillion annually.

The threat of **cyberterrorism** is one of the most serious global security issues today. For example, when Russian tanks rolled into Georgia in 2008, cyber attacks crippled Georgian government websites.[4] Cyberterrorism is defined as terrorism committed by using a computer to make unlawful attacks and threats of attack against computers, networks, and electronically stored information, and actually causing the target to fear or experience harm.[5] Cyberterrorism and cybercrimes threaten the privacy, economic security, and national security of individuals, companies, and countries.

The U.S. Department of Justice broadly defines **computer crime** as "any violations of criminal law that involve a knowledge of computer technology for their perpetration, investigation, or prosecution."[6] Black's Law Dictionary further defines a computer crime as "a crime involving the use of a computer, such as sabotaging or stealing electronically stored data."[7] The term **cybercrime** is synonymous with "computer crime."

The U.S. Department of Justice divides computer-related crimes into three general categories: (1) crimes in which the computer is the "object" of a crime; (2) a computer may be the "subject" of a crime; and (3) a computer may be an "instrument" used to commit traditional crimes.[8]

Object of Crime

First, a computer may be the "object" of a crime. This category primarily refers to theft of computer hardware or software. Under state law, computer hardware theft is generally prosecuted under theft or burglary statutes. Under federal law, computer hardware theft may be prosecuted under 18 U.S.C. § 2314, which regulates the interstate transportation of stolen or fraudulently obtained goods.

Subject of Crime

Second, a computer may be the "subject" of a crime. These are computer crimes for which there is generally no analogous traditional crime and for which special legislation is needed. This category includes spam, viruses, worms, Trojan horses, logic bombs, sniffers, distributed denial of service attacks, and unauthorized web bots or spiders.

Instrument of Crime

Third, a computer may be an "instrument" used to commit traditional crimes. These traditional crimes include identity theft, child pornography, copyright infringement, mail fraud, or wire fraud.

GENERAL PRINCIPLES OF CRIMINAL LAW

Criminal law involves prosecution by the government of a person for an act that has been classified as a crime.[9] Civil cases, on the other hand, involve individuals and organizations seeking to resolve legal disputes. In a criminal case, the state, through a prosecutor, initiates the suit, while in a civil case the victim brings the suit. Persons convicted of a crime may be incarcerated, fined, or both.

A "crime" is generally defined as an act committed, or omitted, in violation of a public law forbidding or commanding it.[10] Though there are some common law crimes, most crimes in the United States are established by federal, state, and local governments. Criminal laws vary significantly from state to state. The Model Penal Code (MPC) serves as a good starting place to gain an understanding of the basic structure of criminal liability.[11]

Crimes include both felonies for more serious offenses and misdemeanors for less serious offenses. Felonies are usually crimes punishable by imprisonment of a year or more, while misdemeanors are less serious crimes usually punishable by fine, penalty, forfeiture, or confinement (usually for a brief term) in a place other than prison—such as a county jail. However, no act is a crime if it has not been previously established as such either by statute or common law.

All statutes describing criminal behavior can be broken down into their various elements. Most crimes consist of two elements: an act (or "actus reus"), and a mental state or ("mens rea").

"Actus reus" refers to the physical aspect of the criminal activity. The term generally includes a voluntary act that causes social harm. In the context of actus reus, "voluntary" may be defined simply as any volitional movement. Habitual conduct—even if the defendant is unaware of what he is doing at the time—may still be deemed voluntary. Acts deemed involuntary may include spasms, seizures, and bodily movements while unconscious or asleep.

Actus Reus
refers to the physical aspect of the criminal activity. The term generally includes a voluntary act that causes social harm. In the context of actus reus, "voluntary" may be defined simply as any volitional movement.

"Mens rea" refers to a mental state, often an element of the offense, which expresses the intent necessary for a particular act to constitute a crime. However, a general intent mens rea also may require that a defendant possessed knowledge with respect to the actus reus of the crime. Mens rea is generally an essential element of any criminal offense unless the legislature has clearly stated otherwise. When a criminal statute does not express a particular mental state, or specific intent, as an element of the crime, then the offense only requires general intent on the part of the perpetrator.

Mens Rea
Latin for "guilty mind." The state of mind that the prosecution, to secure a conviction, must prove that a defendant had when committing a crime; criminal intent or recklessness.

Prosecutors have to prove each and every element of the crime to yield a conviction. "Beyond a reasonable doubt" is the burden of proof in criminal cases used by a jury to determine whether a criminal defendant is guilty. In deciding whether guilt has been proved beyond a reasonable doubt, the jury must begin with the presumption that the defendant is innocent. In civil cases, the plaintiff needs to show a defendant is liable only by a "preponderance of the evidence," or more than 50 percent.

CONSTITUTIONAL ISSUES RELATING TO CYBERCRIMES

Criminal defendants may assert constitutional violations as part of their defense, including cybercrimes. Most constitutional issues related to computer crimes usually fall under either the First Amendment or the Fourth Amendment to the U.S. Constitution. The Commerce Clause, discussed later in this chapter, also applies to some jurisdictional issues.

First Amendment

The First Amendment to the U.S. Constitution provides: "Congress shall make no law respecting an establishment of religion, or prohibiting the free exercise thereof; or abridging the freedom of speech, or of the press; or the right of the people peaceably to assemble, and to petition the government for a redress of grievances." The First Amendment protects the same forms of Internet speech that it does in the tangible world. And just like in the real world, the government may also regulate some speech in cyberspace.

Certain categories of speech are not protected under the First Amendment such as libel or defamation, fighting words, and obscenity. In *Chaplinsky v. New Hampshire*, 315 U.S. 568 (1942), the U.S. Supreme Court noted that categories of unprotected speech such as obscenity and fighting words "are no essential part of any exposition of ideas, and are of such slight social value as a step to truth that any benefit that may be derived from them is clearly outweighed by the social interest in order and morality."

Speech involving fighting words or "true threats" such as sending threatening e-mail messages to a victim or even a public announcement on the Internet of an intention to commit an act that is racially motivated receive no protection under the First Amendment. A similar exception exists for harassment on e-mail or the Internet, as long as it is sufficiently persistent and malicious as to inflict, or is motivated by desire to cause, substantial emotional or physical harm and is directed at a specific person. Child pornography is not protected either, but finding a sufficiently narrow description to prevent its spread on the Internet has proven difficult.

In 2008, the Virginia Supreme Court struck down a Virginia statute in *Jaynes v. Commonwealth*, 666 S.E.2d 303, 313 (Va. 2008), which criminalized the falsification of identifying transmission information in unsolicited bulk e-mail messages or spam as overly broad and infringing on the First Amendment right to engage in anonymous speech. The court emphasized that the statute in question did not distinguish between commercial and non-commercial unsolicited e-mails, including those expressing political and religious messages. Therefore, the statute could not survive strict scrutiny because it was not narrowly tailored to the compelling state interests, as laid out in the federal CAN-SPAM Act of preserving the efficiency and convenience of e-mail.

Fourth Amendment

As the Internet has exploded in scope, courts have also examined how the Fourth Amendment applies to computer crimes. The Fourth Amendment prohibits "unreasonable searches and seizures" by the government. The Fourth Amendment protects legitimate expectations of privacy. (See Figure 7.1.) In the landmark case *Katz v. United States*, 389 U.S. 347, 361 (1967), the U.S. Supreme Court established a general test for determining whether government activity rises to the level of a search: the government conduct must offend the individual's subjective expectation of privacy, and that privacy interest must "be one that society is prepared to recognize as "reasonable." Courts applying the reasonable expectation of privacy test set forth in *Katz* have held that people have a reasonable expectation of privacy in a computer they own in their home, but this is less clear-cut in the workplace.

> The right of the people to be secure in their persons, houses, papers, and effects, against unreasonable searches and seizures, shall not be violated, and no Warrants shall issue, but upon probable cause, supported by Oath or affirmation, and particularly describing the place to be searched, and the persons or things to be seized.

FIGURE 7.1 Fourth Amendment to the U.S. Constitution

Exclusionary Rule

If the government conducts a warrantless search and the individual has a legitimate expectation of privacy, the defendant may seek to have the evidence of the illegal search excluded based on the **exclusionary rule**. The exclusionary rule, which also applies to computer-related crimes, prevents the government from using evidence obtained in violation of an accused person's constitutional rights.

Exclusionary Rule
A rule that excludes or suppresses evidence obtained in violation of an accused person's constitutional rights.

The exclusionary rule applies to evidence gained from an unreasonable search or seizure in violation of the **Fourth Amendment** based on the U.S. Supreme Court ruling in *Mapp v. Ohio*, 367 U.S. 643 (1961). Besides illegal searches, the exclusionary rule also applies to violations of *Miranda* warnings based on the U.S. Supreme Court landmark decision in *Miranda v. Arizona*, 384 U.S. 439 (1966). Under *Miranda*, which has become "part of our national culture" through film and television, a criminal suspect in police custody must be informed of certain constitutional rights before being interrogated. The suspect must be advised of the right to remain silent, the right to have an attorney present during questioning, and the right to have an attorney appointed if the suspect cannot afford one. If the suspect is not advised of these rights or does not validly waive them, any evidence obtained during the interrogation cannot be used against the suspect at trial as stated in *Dickerson v. United States*, 530 U.S. 428, 443-44 (2000).

Fourth Amendment
The constitutional amendment, ratified with the Bill of Rights in 1791, prohibiting unreasonable searches and seizures and the issuance of warrants without probable cause.

The **fruit-of-the-poisonous-tree doctrine**, that stems from the exclusionary rule, provides that evidence derived from an illegal search, arrest, or interrogation is inadmissible because the evidence (the "fruit") was tainted by the illegality (the "poisonous tree").

Fruit-of-the-Poisonous-Tree Doctrine
The rule that evidence derived from an illegal search, arrest, or interrogation is inadmissible because the evidence (the "fruit") was tainted by the illegality (the "poisonous tree").

The fruit-of-the-poisonous-tree doctrine has three important exceptions. The evidence will not be excluded (1) if it was discovered from a source independent of the illegal activity; (2) its discovery was inevitable; or (3) if there is attenuation between the illegal activity and the discovery of the evidence.

In *United States v. Gilkeson*, 431 F. Supp. 2d 270 (N.D. N.Y. 2006), evidence seized from defendant's computer was obtained as a result of police officers' failure to administer *Miranda* warnings, and was thus inadmissible in prosecution on federal child pornography charges despite his consent to the search. After being arrested on basis of probable cause of a violation of New York statute prohibiting endangering the welfare of a child, the defendant in *United States v. Gilkeson* revealed the existence of a computer in a prolonged interrogation, which continued after officers repeatedly ignored his request for an attorney in violation of *Miranda*. The court held that the evidence on the computer must be suppressed pursuant to the fruit doctrine because it was obtained in violation of *Miranda*. The exclusionary rule and the related fruit-of-the-poisonous-tree doctrine are important concepts in protecting the constitutional rights of persons accused of computer-related crimes.

Expectation of Privacy in E-Mail

In a December 2010 decision, in *United States v. Warshak*, 631 F.3d 266 (6th Cir. 2010) (Case 7.1) the U.S. Court of Appeals for the Sixth Circuit ruled that the government must have a search warrant before it can secretly seize and search e-mails stored by e-mail service providers. The court noted that electronic communication "is as important to Fourth Amendment principles today as protecting telephone conversations has been in the past" and therefore held that the defendant had a reasonable expectation of privacy in the content of his e-mails notwithstanding the fact that a third-party provider of Internet communication services had access to those messages.

CASE 7.1

The Case Recognizing a Reasonable Expectation of Privacy in E-mail

United States v. Warshak, ***631 F.3d 266 (6th Cir. 2010)***

Facts

In 2001, Steven Warshak ("Warshak") owned and operated a number of small businesses in the Cincinnati area. Warshak also owned . . . Berkeley Premium Nutraceuticals, Inc. ("Berkeley") [that offered a modest line of so-called nutraceuticals, or herbal supplements].

In the latter half of 2001, Berkeley launched Enzyte, its flagship product. At the time of its launch, Enzyte was purported to increase the size of a man's erection. The product proved tremendously popular, and business rose sharply. By year's end, Berkeley's annual sales topped out at around $250 million, largely on the strength of Enzyte.

The popularity of Enzyte appears to have been due in large part to Berkeley's aggressive advertising campaigns. Around 2004, network television was saturated with Enzyte advertisements featuring a character called "Smilin' Bob," whose trademark exaggerated smile was presumably the result of Enzyte's efficacy. The "Smilin' Bob" commercials were rife with innuendo and implied that users of Enzyte would become the envy of the neighborhood.

A number of advertisements also indicated that Enzyte boasted a 96 percent customer satisfaction rating. Thereafter, the customer-satisfaction statistic cropped up in Berkeley's print advertisements and in the "sales pitches, brochures, [and on the] Internet."

The "life blood" of the business was its auto-ship program, which was instituted in 2001, shortly before Enzyte hit the market. The auto-ship program was a continuity or negative-option program, in which a customer would order a free trial of a product and then continue to receive additional shipments of that product until he opted out. The shipments and charges would continue until the customer decided to withdraw from the program, which required the customer to notify the company.

Procedural History

In September 2006, a grand jury sitting in the Southern District of Ohio returned a 112-count indictment charging Warshak . . . and several others with various crimes related to Berkeley's business. Warshak was charged with conspiracy to commit mail, wire, and bank fraud (Count 1) [and other federal crimes].

Before trial . . . Warshak moved to exclude thousands of e-mails that the government obtained from his Internet Service Providers. That motion was denied.

On August 27, 2008 . . . Warshak received a sentence of 25 years of imprisonment. He was also ordered to pay a fine of $93,000 and a special assessment of $9,300. In addition, he was ordered to surrender $459,540,000 in proceeds-money-judgment forfeiture and $44,876,781.68 in money-laundering-judgment forfeiture.

Following a series of unsuccessful post-trial motions, the defendants timely appealed.

Analysis

Warshak argues that the government's warrantless, ex parte seizure of approximately 27,000 of his private e-mails constituted a violation of the Fourth Amendment's prohibition on unreasonable searches and seizures. The government counters that, even if government agents violated the Fourth Amendment in obtaining the e-mails, they relied in good faith on the Stored Communications Act ("SCA"), 18 U.S.C. §§ 2701 et seq., a statute that allows the government to obtain certain electronic communications without procuring a warrant. The government also argues that any hypothetical Fourth Amendment violation was harmless. We find that the government did violate Warshak's Fourth Amendment rights by compelling his Internet Service

Provider ("ISP") to turn over the contents of his e-mails. However, we agree that agents relied on the SCA in good faith, and therefore hold that reversal is unwarranted.

The Stored Communications Act ("SCA"), "permits a 'governmental entity' to compel a service provider to disclose the contents of [electronic] communications in certain circumstances" [citation omitted].

The compelled-disclosure provisions give different levels of privacy protection based on whether the e-mail is held with an electronic communication service or a remote computing service and based on how long the e-mail has been in electronic storage. The government may obtain the contents of e-mails that are "in electronic storage" with an electronic communication service for 180 days or less "only pursuant to a warrant." 18 U.S.C. § 2703(a). The government has three options for obtaining communications stored with a remote computing service and communications that have been in electronic storage with an electronic service provider for more than 180 days: (1) obtain a warrant; (2) use an administrative subpoena; or (3) obtain a court order under § 2703(d).

E-mail was a critical form of communication among Berkeley personnel. As a consequence, Warshak had a number of e-mail accounts with various ISPs, including an account with NuVox Communications. In October 2004, the government formally requested that NuVox prospectively preserve the contents of any e-mails to or from Warshak's e-mail account. The request was made pursuant to 18 U.S.C. § 2703(f) and it instructed NuVox to preserve all future messages.

In January 2005, the government obtained a subpoena under § 2703(b) and compelled NuVox to turn over the e-mails that it had begun preserving the previous year. In all, the government compelled NuVox to reveal the contents of approximately 27,000 e-mails.

The Fourth Amendment provides that "[t]he right of the people to be secure in their persons, houses, papers, and effects, against unreasonable searches and seizures, shall not be violated, and no Warrants shall issue, but upon probable cause. . . ." U.S. Const. amend. IV. The fundamental purpose of the Fourth Amendment "is to safeguard the privacy and security of individuals against arbitrary invasions by government officials" [citations omitted]. ("The [Fourth] Amendment guarantees the privacy, dignity, and security of persons against certain arbitrary and invasive acts by officers of the Government or those acting at their direction.")

Given the fundamental similarities between e-mail and traditional forms of communication, it would defy common sense to afford e-mails lesser Fourth Amendment protection. . . . E-mail is the technological scion of tangible mail, and it plays an indispensable part in the Information Age. Over the last decade, e-mail has become "so pervasive that some persons may consider [it] to be [an] essential means or necessary instrument[ ] for self-expression, even self-identification." *Quon*, 130 S.Ct. at 2630. It follows that e-mail requires strong protection under the Fourth Amendment; otherwise, the Fourth Amendment would prove an ineffective guardian of private communication, an essential purpose it has long been recognized to serve. . . . As some forms of communication begin to diminish, the Fourth Amendment must recognize and protect nascent ones that arise. See *Warshak I*, 490 F.3d at 473 ("It goes without saying that like the telephone earlier in our history, e-mail is an ever-increasing mode of private communication, and protecting shared communications through this medium is as important to Fourth Amendment principles today as protecting telephone conversations has been in the past.").

If we accept that an e-mail is analogous to a letter or a phone call, it is manifest that agents of the government cannot compel a commercial ISP to turn over the contents of an e-mail without triggering the Fourth Amendment. An ISP is the intermediary that makes e-mail communication possible. E-mails must pass through an ISP's servers to reach their intended recipient. Thus, the ISP is the functional equivalent of a post office or a telephone company. As we have discussed above, the police may not storm the post office and intercept a letter, and they are likewise forbidden from using the phone system to make a clandestine recording of a telephone call-unless they get a warrant, that is [citations omitted]. It only stands to reason that, if government agents compel an ISP to surrender the contents of a subscriber's e-mails, those agents have thereby conducted a Fourth Amendment search, which necessitates compliance with the warrant requirement absent some exception.

As an initial matter, it must be observed that the mere ability of a third-party intermediary to access the contents of a communication cannot be sufficient to extinguish a reasonable expectation of privacy. In Katz, the Supreme Court found it reasonable to expect privacy during a telephone call despite the ability of an operator to listen in.

(Continued)

(Continued)

In this case, the NuVox subscriber agreement tracks that language, indicating that "NuVox may access and use individual Subscriber information in the operation of the Service and as necessary to protect the Service." . . . Thus, under Katz, the degree of access granted to NuVox does not diminish the reasonableness of Warshak's trust in the privacy of his e-mails.

Our conclusion finds additional support in the application of Fourth Amendment doctrine to rented space. Hotel guests, for example, have a reasonable expectation of privacy in their rooms [citation omitted]. This is so even though maids routinely enter hotel rooms to replace the towels and tidy the furniture. Consequently, we are convinced that some degree of routine access is hardly dispositive with respect to the privacy question.

Again, however, we are unwilling to hold that a subscriber agreement will never be broad enough to snuff out a reasonable expectation of privacy. The government may not compel a commercial ISP to turn over the contents of a subscriber's e-mails without first obtaining a warrant based on probable cause. Therefore, because they did not obtain a warrant, the government agents violated the Fourth Amendment when they obtained the contents of Warshak's e-mails. Moreover, to the extent that the SCA purports to permit the government to obtain such e-mails warrantlessly, the SCA is unconstitutional. [. . .]

Even though the government's search of Warshak's e-mails violated the Fourth Amendment, the e-mails are not subject to the exclusionary remedy if the officers relied in good faith on the SCA to obtain them.

[Because agents relied in good faith on provisions of Stored Communications Act (SCA), the exclusionary rule did not apply. The government's violation of SCA provisions was irrelevant to issue of reasonable reliance.]

Conclusion

For the foregoing reasons, we AFFIRM Steven Warshak's convictions. We also AFFIRM the forfeiture judgments against him, but we VACATE his 25-year sentence and REMAND for resentencing.

Case Questions

1. Why did the government argue that the warrantless, ex parte seizure of approximately 27,000 private e-mails did not violate the Fourth Amendment's prohibition on unreasonable searches and seizures.
2. How is e-mail similar to traditional forms of communication for purposes of the Fourth Amendment?
3. Why did the court hold that a subscriber enjoys a reasonable expectation of privacy in the contents of e-mails that are stored with, or sent or received through, a commercial ISP?
4. What part of the Stored Communications Act (SCA) did the court find unconstitutional?
5. Even though the court found that the agents violated the Fourth Amendment, why did the court affirm the conviction for Warshak?

JURISDICTIONAL LIMITS OF CYBERCRIMES

Because of the global reach of the Internet, issues involving the jurisdictional limits of cybercrimes often arise. Issues of jurisdiction over cybercrime come up at both the interstate level (between two or more different states) and at the international level (between two or more different countries).

As a general rule, when a crime is committed in an interstate manner (between two or more different states), the issue becomes a matter of federal jurisdiction. The U.S. Court of Appeals for the Ninth Circuit held in *United States v. Sutcliffe*, 505 F.3d 944, 952-53 (9th Cir. 2007), that the Internet is an instrumentality of interstate commerce and the use of it in furtherance of a crime creates a sufficient nexus for federal subject matter jurisdiction. In *United States v. Sutcliffe*, the defendant was convicted of transmitting interstate threats to injure and transferring Social Security numbers with intent to aid and abet unlawful activity. The court rejected the argument by the defendant that the court lacked jurisdiction and held that the interstate transfer of information by means of the Internet satisfies the jurisdictional elements of the criminal statutes in question.

Most federal statutes relating to computer crimes have been enacted by Congress under the Commerce Clause contained in Article I, section 8, clause 3 of the U.S. Constitution which gives Congress the power "to regulate Commerce . . . among the several States." The U.S. Supreme Court stated in *Reno v. ACLU*, 521 U.S. 844 (1997), that the Internet is "an international network of interconnected computers" similar to—and often using—our national network of telephone lines and is "comparable . . . to both a vast library including millions of readily available and indexed publications and a sprawling mall offering goods and services." The U.S. Supreme Court also held in *Reno v. ACLU* that the Internet is "a valuable tool in today's commerce." Since the Internet is considered to be both a channel and instrumentality of interstate commerce, federal courts have held that Congress has authority under the Commerce Clause to enact criminal statutes aimed at cybercrimes involving the Internet. State court jurisdiction, discussed later in this chapter, can be more problematic.

FEDERAL APPROACHES

Congress has passed legislation targeted specifically at computer-related crimes. The government can charge computer crimes under at least forty different federal statutes and there are also a number of traditional criminal statutes that apply to computer crimes. Moreover, the federal government has sometimes used the United States Sentencing Guidelines to enhance sentences for traditional crimes committed with the aid of computers. This section focuses on the main federal statutes associated with computer crimes.

Computer Fraud and Abuse Act

The **Computer Fraud and Abuse Act of 1986 (CFAA)** makes it a felony to knowingly access a computer without authorization and with intent or reason to believe that the information obtained would be used to injure the United States or to benefit a foreign country.[12] The federal Computer Fraud and Abuse Act (CFAA) serves as the primary means by which unauthorized access to computer systems, including data access and theft cases, are prosecuted.

Computer Fraud and Abuse Act of 1986 (CFAA)
makes it a felony to knowingly access a computer without authorization and with intent or reason to believe that the information obtained would be used to injure the United States or to benefit a foreign country.

A passive receipt of electronic information does not constitute "accessing" a computer from which information is derived, within the meaning of the Computer Fraud and Abuse Act.[13] The word "access," in this context, is an active verb: it means "to gain access to," or "to exercise the freedom or ability to make use of something."

IT Security, a news and information publication covering all aspects of the IT Security marketplace, identified the most famous "black hat" hackers of all time that exploited computer systems.

1. Jonathan James (hacking into U.S. Department of Defense and NSA computers)
2. Adrian Lamo (intrusion of the New York Times and Microsoft networks)
3. Kevin Mitnick (called by the Department of Justice as "the most wanted computer criminal in United States history")
4. Kevin Poulsen (hacking into LA radio's KIIS-FM phone lines, which earned him a brand new Porsche, among other items and dubbed "the Hannibal Lecter of computer crime")
5. Robert Tappan Morris (creator of the Morris worm)

FIGURE 7.2 Most Famous "Black Hat" Hackers of All Time

In 2009, Albert Gonzalez (no relationship to former U.S. Attorney General Alberto R. Gonzales), a former government informant was indicted on charges of conspiracy to gain unauthorized access to computers, to commit fraud in connection with computers and to damage computers, in the process stealing 170 million credit and debit card numbers.[14] The case, *United States v. Rodriguez*, 628 F.3d 1258 (11th Cir. 2010) (Case 7.2), is believed to be the largest hacking and identity theft case ever prosecuted in the United States.

CASE 7.2

The Case of the Prying Former Bureaucrat

United States v. Rodriguez, *628 F.3d 1258 (11th Cir. 2010)*

The main issue in this appeal is whether the prying by a former bureaucrat is criminal: that is, whether the defendant violated the Computer Fraud and Abuse Act, which prohibits "intentionally access[ing] a computer without authorization or exceed[ing] authorized access, and thereby obtain [ing] . . . information from any department or agency of the United States." 18 U.S.C. § 1030(a)(2)(B). Roberto Rodriguez, a former employee of the Social Security Administration, appeals his conviction for violating the Act on the grounds that he did not exceed his authorized access to his former employer's databases and that he did not use the information to further another crime or to gain financially. The Administration prohibits accessing information on its databases for nonbusiness reasons, and Rodriguez at trial admitted that he accessed information for nonbusiness reasons when he obtained personal identifying information, such as birth dates and home addresses, of 17 persons he knew or their relatives. Rodriguez also appeals his sentence of 12 months of imprisonment on the ground that it is unreasonable. Because the record establishes that Rodriguez exceeded his authorized access and the Act does not require proof that Rodriguez used the information to further another crime or to gain financially, we AFFIRM his conviction. We also conclude that Rodriguez's sentence is reasonable.

Background

From 1995 to 2009, Roberto Rodriguez worked as a TeleService representative for the Social Security Administration. Rodriguez's duties included answering questions of the general public about social security benefits over the telephone. As a part of his duties, Rodriguez had access to Administration databases that contained sensitive personal information, including any person's social security number, address, date of birth, father's name, mother's maiden name, amount and type of social security benefit received, and annual income.

The Administration established a policy that prohibits an employee from obtaining information from its databases without a business reason. The Administration informed its TeleService employees about its policy through mandatory training sessions, notices posted in the office, and a banner that appeared on every computer screen daily. The Administration also required TeleService employees annually to sign acknowledgment forms after receiving the policies in writing. The Administration warned employees that they faced criminal penalties if they violated policies on unauthorized use of databases. From 2006 to 2008, Rodriguez refused to sign the acknowledgment forms. He asked a supervisor rhetorically, "Why give the government rope to hang me?" To monitor access and prevent unauthorized use, the Administration issued unique personal identification numbers and passwords to each TeleService employee and reviewed usage of the databases.

In August 2008, the Administration flagged Rodriguez's personal identification number for suspicious activity. Administration records established that Rodriguez had accessed the personal records of 17 different individuals for nonbusiness reasons. The Administration informed

Rodriguez that it was conducting a criminal investigation into his use of the databases, but Rodriguez continued his unauthorized use. None of the 17 victims knew that Rodriguez had obtained their personal information without authorization until investigators informed them of his actions.

On April 2, 2009, a grand jury indicted Rodriguez with 17 misdemeanor counts of violating the Computer Fraud and Abuse Act. The indictment charged Rodriguez with "intentionally access[ing] a computer without authorization or exceed[ing] authorized access, and thereby obtain[ing] . . . information from any department or agency of the United States." 18 U.S.C. § 1030(a)(2)(B). Trial commenced on July 27, 2009.

On July 29, 2009, the jury rejected Rodriguez's argument about his conduct and returned a guilty verdict on all 17 counts.

After considering the statutory factors for sentencing . . . the district court varied upward and sentenced Rodriguez to 12 months of imprisonment and 12 months of supervised release.

Discussion

Rodriguez argues that he did not violate section 1030(a)(2)(B) because he accessed only databases that he was authorized to use as a TeleService representative, but his argument ignores both the law and the record. The Computer Fraud and Abuse Act makes it a crime to "intentionally access [ ] a computer without authorization or exceed[ ] authorized access, and thereby obtain[ ] information from any department or agency of the United States." 18 U.S.C. § 1030(a)(2)(B). The Act defines the phrase "exceeds authorized access" as "to access a computer with authorization and to use such access to obtain or alter information in the computer that the accesser is not entitled to obtain or alter." Id. at § 1030(e)(6). The policy of the Administration is that use of databases to obtain personal information is authorized only when done for business reasons. Rodriguez conceded at trial that his access of the victims' personal information was not in furtherance of his duties as a TeleService representative and that "he did access things that were unauthorized." In the light of this record, the plain language of the Act forecloses any argument that Rodriguez did not exceed his authorized access.

Rodriguez also argues that his conviction cannot stand because he never used the personal information he accessed without authorization to defraud anyone or to gain financially, but this argument is foreclosed by the plain language of the Act. "The starting point for all statutory interpretation is the language of the statute itself[,]" and "we look to the entire statutory context." *United States v. DBB, Inc.*, 180 F.3d 1277, 1281 (11th Cir.1999). Sections 1030(c)(2)(B)(i) and (ii) of the Act provide a punishment of up to five years of imprisonment if "the offense was committed for purposes of commercial advantage or private financial gain [or if] the offense was committed in furtherance of any criminal or tortious act." 18 U.S.C. § 1030(c)(2)(B)(i), (ii). The misdemeanor penalty provision of the Act under which Rodriguez was convicted does not contain any language regarding purposes for committing the offense. See Id. § 1030(c)(2)(A). Rodriguez's argument would eviscerate the distinction between these misdemeanor and felony provisions. That Rodriguez did not use the information to defraud anyone or gain financially is irrelevant.

Conclusion

The judgment of the district court is AFFIRMED.

Case Questions

1. What was the criminal act, or actus reus, that Rodriguez committed?
2. Why did the government charge Rodriguez with 17 misdemeanor counts of violating the Computer Fraud and Abuse Act?
3. Why did the court reject the argument by Rodriguez that his conviction cannot stand because he never used the personal information he accessed without authorization to defraud anyone or to gain financially?

Communications Decency Act (CDA)
A federal law aimed at combating child pornography. In *Reno v. American Civil Liberties Union*, 521 U.S. 844 (1997), the U.S. Supreme Court struck down those portions of the act as unconstitutional, but provisions banning transmission of obscene speech to minors, remain in effect. 47 U.S.C. § 223.

PROTECT Act
The Prosecutorial Remedies and Other Tools to End the Exploitation of Children Today Act of 2003 (PROTECT Act) is a federal law that establishes stronger laws to combat child pornography and exploitation by revising and strengthening the prohibition on computer-generated child pornographic images, prohibiting any obscene materials that depict children, and providing tougher penalties compared to existing law. 18 U.S.C. § 2252A.

Child Pornography Statutes

Congress has attempted to limit online child pornography several times but these legislative attempts have faced constitutional challenges. The advent of new technology has presented challenges for Congress in constructing a law that effectively minimizes the societal harms caused by child pornography without violating First Amendment rights guaranteed by the Constitution. In its first attempt to limit online child pornography, Congress passed the **Communications Decency Act of 1996 (CDA)**, but the U.S. Supreme Court ruled that portions of the CDA infringed on First Amendment rights.[15] In *Reno v. American Civil Liberties Union*, 521 U.S. 844 (1997), the U.S. Supreme Court struck down those portions of the CDA that banned "indecent" and "patently offensive" images as being unconstitutionally vague and overbroad. The rest of the CDA banning transmission of obscene speech to minors, remains in effect.

Congress also passed the Child Pornography Prevention Act of 1996 (CPPA)[16] that regulated computer-generated images but the U.S. Supreme Court rejected the ban on "virtual child pornography" in *Ashcroft v. Free Speech Coal.*, 535 U.S. 234, 249-50 (2002), striking down the CPPA as overbroad and unconstitutional.[17]

After the U.S. Supreme Court invalidated the CPPA, Congress passed the **Prosecutorial Remedies and Other Tools to End the Exploitation of Children Today Act of 2003 (PROTECT Act).**[18] The PROTECT Act establishes stronger laws to combat child pornography and exploitation by revising and strengthening the prohibition on computer-generated child pornographic images, prohibiting any obscene materials that depict children, and providing tougher penalties compared to existing law. (See Figure 7.3.) After a number of circuit courts questioned the constitutionality of the

Section 503 of the Prosecutorial Remedies and Other Tools to End the Exploitation of Children Today Act of 2003 (PROTECT Act), codified in 18 U.S.C. § 2252A, states:

"(a) Any person who-

"(3) knowingly-

. . . .

"(B) advertises, promotes, presents, distributes, or solicits through the mails, or in interstate or foreign commerce by any means, including by computer, any material or purported material in a manner that reflects the belief, or that is intended to cause another to believe, that the material or purported material is, or contains-

"(i) an obscene visual depiction of a minor engaging in sexually explicit conduct; or

"(ii) a visual depiction of an actual minor engaging in sexually explicit conduct,

. . . .

"shall be punished as provided in subsection (b)." § 2252A(a)(3)(B) (2000 ed., Supp. V).
Section 2256(2)(A) defines "sexually explicit conduct" as
"actual or simulated-

"(i) sexual intercourse, including genital-genital, oral-genital, anal-genital, or oral-anal, whether between persons of the same or opposite sex;

"(ii) bestiality;

"(iii) masturbation;

"(iv) sadistic or masochistic abuse; or

"(v) lascivious exhibition of the genitals or pubic area of any person."

Violation of § 2252A(a)(3)(B) incurs a minimum sentence of 5 years imprisonment and a maximum of 20 years. 18 U.S.C. § 2252A(b)(1).

FIGURE 7.3 Pandering Provision under the PROTECT Act

PROTECT ACT, the U.S. Supreme Court upheld the PROTECT Act, which bans the distribution of certain child pornography involving the use of actual children, as constitutional in *United States v. Williams*, 553 U.S. 285 (2008). In *United States v. Williams*, the U.S. Supreme Court upheld convictions of the defendant for one count of pandering child pornography under 18 U.S.C. § 2252A(a)(3)(B) and one count of possessing child pornography. Williams received concurrent 60-month prison terms on the two counts. For the time being, the PROTECT Act is a valuable tool for prosecutors in combating child pornography. However, like the child pornography statutes that came before it, the PROTECT Act will continue to face constitutional challenges.

CAN-SPAM Act

In an effort to combat unsolicited e-mail, Congress adopted the Controlling the Assault of Non-Solicited Pornography and Marketing Act of 2003 (CAN-SPAM Act).[19] Spam is unsolicited bulk commercial e-mail from a party with no preexisting business relationship. "Spam" is typically understood to refer broadly to unsolicited e-mail messages (or "junk" e-mail), typically commercial in nature. The CAN-SPAM Act has several key provisions that affect persons or companies that send spam or unsolicited commercial e-mail sent to a large number of addresses. The CAN-SPAM Act applies to "multiple" e-mails defined as more than 100 electronic mail messages during a 24-hour period, more than 1,000 electronic mail messages during a 30-day period, or more than 10,000 electronic mail messages during a one-year period.

The CAN-SPAM Act prohibits a number of well-known deceptive and/or fraudulent practices commonly used in commercial e-mails. For example, the CAN-SPAM Act prohibits using deceptive subject lines, false or misleading header information, and using another computer to relay e-mail messages without authorization to prevent anyone from tracing the e-mail back to its sender. The Act also requires that a commercial e-mail include a method for the recipient to "opt-out" of future solicitations and that the subject line warn if the e-mail contains sexually oriented material. To comply with this provision, most commercial e-mail messages will now contain a link to "unsubscribe" from future e-mail solicitation. Both the U.S. Department of Justice and the Federal Trade Commission (FTC) enforce the CAN-SPAM Act. A person found guilty for violations of the CAN-SPAM Act can receive a maximum sentence of up to five years in prison, a fine, or both imprisonment and a fine. The criminal provisions of CAN-SPAM are for the most egregious violations and prohibit sexually explicit e-mail that fails to include a label designating it as sexually explicit. Chapter 11 provides additional discussion of civil actions under the CAN-SPAM Act. For the text of the CAN-SPAM Act, see Appendix C.

A federal appeals court, in *United States v. Kilbride*, 584 F.3d 1240 (9th Cir. 2009), upheld convictions for Jeffrey Kilbride who was sentenced to 78 months and Robert Schaffer who was sentenced to 63 months for violating the CAN-SPAM Act. The court rejected a constitutional challenge brought by Schaffer and Kilbride to the CAN-SPAM Act for vagueness. The convictions arose from conduct relating to their business of sending unsolicited bulk e-mail or spam advertising adult websites. Companies and individuals that engage in e-mail solicitation and marketing should ensure that they comply with requirements under the CAN-SPAM Act.

SAFE WEB Act The Undertaking Spam, Spyware, and Fraud with Enforcers Beyond Borders Act of 2006 (SAFE WEB Act) is a federal law that strengthens the ability of the Federal Trade Commission (FTC) to enforce the CAN-SPAM Act outside of U.S. borders.

Congress enacted the **Undertaking Spam, Spyware, and Fraud with Enforcers Beyond Borders Act of 2006 (SAFE WEB Act)** to strengthen the ability of the Federal Trade Commission (FTC) to enforce the CAN-SPAM Act outside of U.S. borders.[20] The SAFE WEB Act provides new routes for international cooperation on Internet investigations, but cross-border enforcement still remains a challenge for law enforcement officials.

Criminal Copyright Infringement and the Digital Millennium Copyright Act

Along with civil liability for copyright infringement, those who infringe on copyrights may also face prosecution for criminal copyright infringement. Although the common remedy for infringement is by a civil action for infringement, the federal government may also bring criminal charges for criminal copyright infringement.[21] In recent years, the FBI has increased its efforts in fighting piracy and prosecuting criminal copyright infringement. Unlike civil copyright infringement, proving criminal infringement requires a showing of willful infringement on the part of the defendant.[22] The majority of courts have required the government to prove the defendant intentionally violated a known legal duty to satisfy the mens rea or criminal intent element of the crime.[23]

Criminal penalties under the Copyright Act, codified in 18 U.S.C. § 2319, include anywhere from one to ten years imprisonment or in certain circumstances, the imposition of both fines and imprisonment. Most movies include the FBI warning at the beginning that "criminal copyright infringement, including infringement without monetary gain, is investigated by the FBI and is punishable by up to five years in federal prison and a fine of $250,000."[24]

Two California cases in 2010 represent the increased efforts by law enforcement in combating copyright infringement. In January 2010, a man from Irvine, California, pleaded guilty to uploading an advanced copy of the film *The Love Guru* to a piracy group's website that made it available on the Internet. According to the plea agreement, the defendant Mischa Wynhausen received a copy of the film from a group of people who had received the film from a man who had illegally copied it—Jack Yates, of Los Angeles. Yates worked at a company hired by Paramount to make an advanced copy, called a "screener," for NBC-TV's *The Tonight Show*. Because Wynhausen cooperated with investigators, prosecutors recommended a sentence of three years of probation for Wynhausen.[25] Yates was sentenced to six months in prison after pleading guilty to a misdemeanor offense of criminal copyright infringement. In a separate case in December 2010, a man from El Cerrito, California, Julius Chow Lieh Lui, was sentenced to four years in prison for criminal copyright infringement for replicating and/or selling thousands of counterfeit copies of Norton Anti-Virus, CDs, and DVDs through his company, SuperDVD.[26] With the rise of copyright infringement via the Internet, the Computer Crime & Intellectual Property Section of the U.S. Department of Justice continues its efforts to investigate and prosecute criminal copyright infringement.

Digital Millennium Copyright Act (DMCA) A 1998 federal law harmonizing United States copyright protection with international law, limiting copyright liability for Internet service providers, and expanding software owners' ability to copy programs.

The **Digital Millennium Copyright Act of 1998 (DMCA)** provides civil liability limitations for transmitting copyrighted material online.[27] The DMCA also provides criminal penalties for circumvention of copyright protection systems and for compromising the integrity of copyright management information. The DMCA's primary focus is to criminalize the circumvention of technologies that secure digital copies of software, music and videos and literary works. The U.S. Department of Justice has successfully obtained convictions for violations of the Digital Millennium Copyright Act in a number of cases. Federal prosecutors obtained their first indictment under the DMCA in August 2001 and the first jury trial conviction in 2003.[28] Through Operation Copycat, the U.S. Attorney's Office secured convictions against thirty-six individuals for unauthorized camcording of movies in a theater and for violating the Digital Millennium Copyright Act. In Operation Copyright, one of the defendants pleaded guilty for illegally distributing many prerelease and new release movies and software, including *Benchwarmers*, *XMen*, *Cars*, and *Click*. He then distributed copies of the cammed movies to others on the Internet.

Federal prosecutors in San Diego, California, also reached a plea agreement with three defendants in October 2009 to a one-count indictment for violating the

FIGURE 7.4 FBI's Anti-Piracy Warning Seal

DMCA.[29] The defendants who pleaded guilty admitted to hiring computer hackers to break the latest DISH Network encryption scheme. One defendant was sentenced to 18 months in custody followed by three years of supervised release. The other two defendants were each sentenced to one month of custody and five months of house arrest.

FBI's Anti-Piracy Warning Seal

The FBI's Anti-Piracy Warning Seal (see Figure 7.4.) was specifically created to deter illegal practice and to increase public awareness of the penalties associated with piracy. Since August 2006, the FBI has authorized use of the FBI Anti-Piracy seal and warning by members of the Motion Picture Association of America (MPAA), the Recording Industry Association of America (RIAA), the Software & Information Industry Association (SIIA), the Business Software Alliance (BSA), and the Entertainment Software Association (ESA). Along with the FBI's Anti-Piracy Warning Seal, many copyrighted works include the following warning: "Warning: The unauthorized reproduction or distribution of this copyrighted work is illegal. Criminal copyright infringement, including infringement without monetary gain, is investigated by the FBI and is punishable by up to five years in federal prison and a fine of $250,000."

Electronic Communications Privacy Act

The **Electronic Communications Privacy Act of 1986 (ECPA)** makes it illegal to intentionally intercept electronic transmissions and regulates crimes with no close "traditional crime" analog, such as hacking.[30] The ECPA originally applied to cell phone communication, but it was amended in 1994 to apply to cordless telephone communication and e-mail.[31] Unlike the CFAA, the ECPA approaches such crimes by updating existing federal prohibitions against intercepting wire and electronic communications. The ECPA attempts to curb hacking activities by fortifying the privacy rights of computer users and enabling law enforcement officers to employ electronic surveillance in the course of investigating computer crimes. The government has used the ECPA to prosecute hackers, although they generally rely on the CFAA. Prosecutors have invoked the ECPA against piracy of electronically encrypted, satellite-transmitted television broadcasts.

Electronic Communications Privacy Act (ECPA) A federal law that regulates surveillance of electronic communications. 18 U.S.C. §§ 2701–2712.

Current and ongoing Internet trends and schemes identified by the Internet Crime Complaint Center.

Auction Fraud
Auction Fraud—Romania
Counterfeit Cashier's Check
Credit Card Fraud
Debt Elimination
Parcel Courier E-mail Scheme
Employment/Business Opportunities
Escrow Services Fraud
Identity Theft
Internet Extortion
Investment Fraud
Lotteries
Nigerian Letter or "419"
Phishing/Spoofing
Ponzi/Pyramid
Reshipping
Spam
Third Party Receiver of Funds

FIGURE 7.5 Current Internet Crime Schemes

Identity Theft

Identity Theft
The unlawful taking and use of another person's identifying information for fraudulent purposes.

The advent of the Internet has greatly increased the incident rate of **identity theft**. The Federal Trade Commission (FTC) estimates that as many as 9 million Americans have their identities stolen each year.[32] Identity theft occurs when someone uses another person's personally identifying information, such as a name, Social Security number, or credit card number, without permission, to commit fraud or other crimes. Because of the nature of the crime, law enforcement agencies have faced challenges in investigating cases of identity theft and in prosecuting the offenders.

The federal identity theft statute, codified in 18 U.S.C. § 1028, prohibits the knowing transfer, possession, or use of a means of identification, such as names, Social Security numbers, and dates of birth, to commit a crime. The federal statute also prohibits the production, transfer, or possession, in certain circumstances, of false or illegally issued identification documents. It further prohibits production, transfer, or possession of a "document-making implement," specifically including computers, with the intent to use it in the production of a false identification document. The term *transfer* includes making either false identification documents or the software or data used to make them available online. The federal identity theft statute was enacted in 1998 as part of the Identity Theft and Assumption Deterrence Act, which penalizes fraud in connection with the unlawful theft and misuse of personal identifying information, regardless of whether the information appears or is used in documents.

With the enactment of the Identity Theft Penalty Enhancement Act of 2004, Congress created a new statutory crime: aggravated identity theft.[33] The statute provides for a mandatory two-year sentence for any identity fraud crime where the identity in question belonged to another person. The Identity Theft Penalty

Enhancement Act, codified in 18 U.S.C. § 1028A, states: "Whoever, during and in relation to any [predicate identity fraud crime], knowingly transfers, possesses, or uses, without lawful authority, a means of identification of another person shall, in addition to the [sentence for the predicate crime], be sentenced to a term of imprisonment of 2 years."

In 2009, the U.S. Supreme Court unanimously held in *Flores-Figueroa v. United States*, 129 S. Ct. 1886, 1888 (2009) that in order to convict a defendant of aggravated identity theft, the government had to prove that the defendant had actual knowledge that the identity in question belonged to another person. While the Identity Theft Penalty Enhancement Act often involves the use of falsified Social Security numbers by illegal aliens, the statute also applies to other individuals that engage in identity theft, including identity theft using a computer.

Criminals often use phishing as a common form of identity theft. Phishing is the sending of a fraudulent electronic communication that appears to be a genuine message from a legitimate entity or business for the purpose of inducing the recipient to disclose sensitive personal information. Phishing may be prosecuted under the federal identity theft statute, codified in 18 U.S.C. § 1028. Other federal crimes that could be committed through a phishing scheme are wire fraud (18 U.S.C. § 1343), credit card fraud (18 U.S.C. § 1029), bank fraud (18 U.S.C. § 1344), and computer fraud (18 U.S.C. § 1030(a)(4)).

The Federal Trade Commission (FTC) and the U.S. Department of Justice aggressively investigate phishing. The U.S. Department of Justice prosecutes the criminal case and the FTC has authority to bring a civil action. In 2004, Zachary Hill, age 20, was sentenced to almost four years in prison (46 months) for orchestrating a scheme to defraud consumers of personal financial information via spam e-mail.[34] Hill was accused of fraudulently obtaining credit card numbers, usernames, and passwords of Internet accounts. Hill sent e-mails supposedly from AOL and PayPal with the subject line that read "AOL Billing Error Please Read Enclosed E-mail" or "Please Update Account Information Urgent!" E-mail recipients were directed to click on a hyperlink that led to a look-a-like AOL page that prompted them to input personal and financial information. Hill agreed to a plea resulting in a sentence of forty-six months. In a related civil action, the FTC brought a civil complaint against Hill seeking an injunction and damages for his fraudulent conduct.

In May 2006, President George W. Bush signed an Executive Order creating the first ever "Identity Theft Task Force." The President's Task Force on Identity Theft was established by Executive Order 13402 launching a new era in the fight against identity theft. Recognizing the heavy financial and emotional toll that identity theft exacts from its victims, and the severe burden it places on the economy. President Bush called for a coordinated approach among government agencies to combat this crime. This Task Force helps law enforcement investigate and prosecute identity theft.

Federal prosecutors in Kansas City reached a plea agreement involving aggravated identity theft in August 2008. Jerry Bagby, 51, of Kansas City, pleaded guilty that he and co-defendant Kimberly Ann Mavis, 30, of Kansas City, participated in a conspiracy to commit aggravated identity theft in 2007 in a conspiracy that resulted in a total loss of $62,742.[35] Mavis used a computer to illegally access customer databases at Premier Bank to steal personal identity information and credit bureau reports of the bank's customers. Bagby and Mavis made fraudulent credit purchases at area retail stores such as Lowe's, Sears, Best Buy, and Kohl's. Bagby and Mavis then sold the items to others and split the proceeds equally.

With the new aggravated identity theft crime and implementing the president's Identity Theft Task Force, federal law enforcement have more tools to prevent, investigate, and prosecute identity theft crimes.

> Whoever, having devised or intending to devise any scheme or artifice to defraud, or for obtaining money or property by means of false or fraudulent pretenses, representations, or promises, transmits or causes to be transmitted by means of wire, radio, or television communication in interstate or foreign commerce, any writings, signs, signals, pictures, or sounds for the purpose of executing such scheme or artifice, shall be fined under this title or imprisoned not more than 20 years, or both. If the violation occurs in relation to, or involving any benefit authorized, transported, transmitted, transferred, disbursed, or paid in connection with, a presidentially declared major disaster or emergency (as those terms are defined in section 102 of the Robert T. Stafford Disaster Relief and Emergency Assistance Act (42 U.S.C. 5122)), or affects a financial institution, such person shall be fined not more than $1,000,000 or imprisoned not more than 30 years, or both.

FIGURE 7.6 Text of the Federal Wire Fraud Statute (codified in 18 U.S.C. § 1343)

Wire Fraud

The federal wire fraud statute, codified in 18 U.S.C. § 1343, prohibits the use of interstate wire communications to further a fraudulent scheme to obtain money or property. Courts have held that the federal wire fraud statute applies to computer crimes.

Wire Fraud
An act of fraud using electronic communications, as by making false representations on the telephone to obtain money. The federal Wire Fraud Act provides that any artifice to defraud by means of wire or other electronic communications (such as radio or television) in foreign or interstate commerce is a crime. 18 U.S.C. § 1343.

Persons convicted under the federal **wire fraud** statute can face severe punishment. (See Figure 7.6.) Violations of the wire fraud statute are punishable by fines, imprisonment of up to twenty years, or both. If the violation affects a financial institution, the punishment is a fine of not more than $1,000,000, imprisonment of not more than thirty years, or both.

In *United States v. Farrington*, 449 F.3d 854 (8th Cir. 2007), a federal appeals court considered the appeal brought Byron Farrington involving his conviction of 34 counts of wire fraud for wireless Internet services paid for by subscribers whose credit cards were charged multiple times for services never received. Farrington was sentenced to 63 months' imprisonment and ordered to pay $258,566.76 in restitution. The appeals court affirmed the decision by the federal court holding that the calculation of the restitution was proper and that the sentencing was reasonable.

Federal Wiretap Act (Title III)

Federal Wiretap Act (Title III)
A federal law that prohibits any person from intercepting or attempting to intercep any wire, oral, or electronic communication. 18 U.S.C. § 2511.

The ECPA extended the prohibitions in Title III of the Omnibus Crime Control and Safe Streets Act of 1968 ("Title III") on intercepting oral and wire communication to include electronic communications intercepted during transmission. The **Federal Wiretap Act**, also called Title III or the federal wiretap statute, codified in 18 U.S.C. § 2511(1)(a), prohibits any person from intercepting or attempting to intercept any "wire, oral, or electronic communication."[36]

To comply with the "necessity requirement" of Title III, wiretap applications must include a "full and complete statement" explaining if alternative investigative techniques have been tried and failed, why they "reasonably appear" unlikely to succeed if tried, or that they are too dangerous. 18 U.S.C. § 2518(1)(c). To be adequate, the statement must provide some basis for concluding that less intrusive investigative procedures are not feasible. Criminal defendants may claim that the government has violated the wiretap statute in Title III to exclude damaging evidence. The contents of intercepted wiretaps or any evidence derived from the wiretap cannot be used at trial if the disclosure of those contents would violate the wiretap act.

STATE APPROACHES

While federal officials often investigate and prosecute cybercrimes, states officials can also prosecute computer crimes under a variety of state laws.[37] Like the federal statutes, many of the state statutes divide computer crimes into the same three categories: "crimes where a computer is the target, crimes where a computer is a tool of the crime, and crimes where a computer is incidental."[38] Many traditional state crimes can be extended into the digital world. For instance, the alteration of public computer records has been held to constitute forgery despite the absence of a traditional writing on paper. Computer activities may also be used as evidentiary support for traditional crimes.

Both federal and state prosecutors can charge a defendant without violating the Double Jeopardy Clause because the states and federal government can each charge the same conduct under the dual sovereignty doctrine. But a U.S. Department of Justice policy, known as the "Petite Policy," discourages federal actions when state prosecutions have already been brought.[39]

Along with traditional crimes like fraud, theft, and child pornography that are facilitated and enabled by a computer, states have enacted legislation specifically aimed at cybercrimes. Over 40 states have computer crime laws that criminalize conduct in similar ways to the federal Computer Fraud and Abuse Act (CFAA).[40] A growing number of states have also passed legislation to protect against theft of trade secrets or against unauthorized access to, destruction or transmission of computerized data. Thirty-nine states have also enacted anti-spam laws regulating the use of Internet communications to send unsolicited advertisements for the purpose of promoting real property, goods, or services for sale or lease. Furthermore, many states have passed "anti-spyware" legislation with criminal penalties.

Jurisdiction and the global reach of the Internet are significant challenges for state officials in prosecuting computer crimes. The patchwork of state laws addressing cybercrimes is often ineffective due to the difficulty in tracking cybercrime and enforcing laws across jurisdictions. Jurisdictional problems arise for state prosecutors when criminal acts are committed out of state since the jurisdictional rules of criminal law require the prosecutor to prove that the defendant intended to cause harm within his state. Therefore, many states have broadened their jurisdictional rules to address the new concerns that arise from the global nature of the Internet.

Funded through a cooperative effort between the National Association of Attorneys General (NAAG) and the National Center for Justice and the Rule of Law at the University of Mississippi, the Cyber Crime Project works to provide the necessary training and technical assistance to prosecutors in Attorney General Offices to enable them to successfully investigate and prosecute computer-based crimes.[41] The Cyber Crime Project develops and conducts training seminars throughout the year at the University of Mississippi and also produces a bi-monthly Cyber Crime e-newsletter for prosecutors and civil enforcement attorneys covering recent case law, federal and state legislation, Attorneys General initiatives, and other computer crime issues.

Cyberbullying and Sexting

In recent years, federal and state officials have needed to address "sexting" and the related problem of "cyberbullying," especially among adolescents and young adults. **Sexting** is defined as "the practice of sending or posting sexually suggestive text messages and images, including nude or semi-nude photographs, via cellular telephones or over the Internet."[42] Nearly 40 percent of teens say they have sent or posted sexually suggestive messages, according to a 2008 national survey.[43] A Kansas statute, Kan. Stat. §72-8256(a)(2), for example, defines **cyberbullying** as "bullying by use of any electronic device through means including, but not limited to, e-mail, instant messaging, text messages, blogs, mobile phones, pagers, online games and websites."

In the first federal sexting case, *Miller v. Mitchell*, 598 F.3d 139 (3rd Cir. 2010), the U.S. Court of Appeals for the Third Circuit issued a preliminary injunction that barred

Sexting
The practice of sending or posting sexually suggestive text messages and images, including nude or semi-nude photographs, via cellular telephones or over the Internet.

Cyberbullying
Bullying by use of any electronic device through means including, but not limited to, e-mail, instant messaging, text messages, blogs, mobile phones, pagers, online games, and websites.

the District Attorney from bringing retaliatory criminal charges against minors who engaged in sexting with distributing child pornography. In October 2008, several teenagers in Pennsylvania were caught sending sexually suggestive text messages at school. The District Attorney informed the parents of youth involved that unless their children attended a six-to-nine-month education program, they would be prosecuted for "sexting" by minors. After three of the students refused to attend the program, the District Attorney threatened to prosecute the students on child pornography charges. The students and their parents filed suit against the District Attorney in federal court, alleging retaliation in violation of their constitutional rights. The appellate court found that the plaintiffs had reasonably established that compelling completion of the educational program under threat of prosecution might violate the minors' First Amendment right against compelled speech and the parents' Fourteenth Amendment right to parental autonomy.

Some states, such as Kansas, have passed legislation to address sexting. In 2009, the Vermont Legislature passed a law legalizing the consensual exchange of graphic images between two people ages 13 to 18 but forwarding or disseminating images to others remains a crime. Other states have proposed legislation to address sexting.

Some states and individual school districts have also implemented programs to educate minors, parents, and school faculty and administrators about the dangers of sexting. For example, the Pennsylvania Attorney General's Office launched a new educational program aimed at preventing cyberbullying and to address sexting.

With the pervasive problem of sexting of cyber-bullying among youth today, judges, legislatures, parents, and school official will need to continue to develop appropriate standards and programs to help protect minors.

ENFORCEMENT OF CYBERCRIMES

Law enforcement officials and prosecutors face challenges in the investigation and prosecution of computer crimes. Cybercrimes are often not enforced because of jurisdictional problems, the lack of information sharing among enforcement agencies, lack of technological resources and experience among local enforcement agencies, and resistance to devoting time and resources to a problem in which most of the victims are outside any one jurisdiction. Many companies and individuals may also be reluctant to report offenses due to the potential for negative publicity. Criminals may encrypt data so that even if law enforcement seizes or intercepts the data, they will be unable to understand its contents or use it as evidence. Finding the true identity of criminals from online criminal conduct can also be a difficult task for investigators.

A host of federal agencies deal with cybercrimes and cyber-terrorism. The FBI and the U.S. Department of Justice (DOJ) have created numerous programs and deployed new technologies to aid in the investigation and prosecution of computer crime. The Computer Crime and Intellectual Property Section (CCIPS) of the U.S. Department of Justice is responsible for implementing the Department's national strategies in combating computer and intellectual property crimes worldwide. CCIPS prevents, investigates, and prosecutes computer crimes by working with other government agencies, the private sector, academic institutions, and foreign counterparts. The Child Exploitation and Obscenity Section (CEOS) of the U.S. Department of Justice enforces federal child exploitation laws and works to prevent the exploitation of children, including online child pornography.

The Internet Crime Complaint Center (IC3) is a partnership between the Federal Bureau of Investigation (FBI), the National White Collar Crime Center (NW3C), and the Bureau of Justice Assistance (BJA) to serve as a means to receive Internet-related criminal complaints and to further research, develop, and refer the criminal complaints to federal, state, local, or international law enforcement and/or regulatory agencies for any investigation they deem to be appropriate. Victims of computer crimes can submit complaints through the Internet Crime Complaint Center.

Because of the global reach of the Internet, an international solution aimed at preventing and enforcing computer crimes is needed. In 2000, Onel de Guzman sent out the "Love Bug" virus from the Philippines. Although the virus caused billions of dollars in damage worldwide, de Guzman was never charged because the Philippines did not have a computer crime law that allowed extradition.[44]

International treaties generally govern the extradition of suspected criminals, including suspects of cybercrimes. **Extradition** is defined as the official surrender of an alleged criminal by one state or nation to another having jurisdiction over the crime charged.

Extradition
The official surrender of an alleged criminal by one state or nation to another having jurisdiction over the crime charged; the return of a fugitive from justice, regardless of consent, by the authorities where the fugitive is found.

Several international organizations have recognized the need for international cooperation in addressing computer crimes and cyberterrorism. Interpol, the world's largest international police organization with 188 member countries, is actively involved in combating computer crimes or information technology crime. Created in 1923, Interpol facilitates cross-border police co-operation, and supports and assists all organizations, authorities, and services whose mission is to prevent or combat international crime, including computer crimes. The Council of Europe enacted the Convention on Cybercrime in 2004, which requires parties to enact substantive and procedural legislation to criminalize certain computer crimes and facilitates extradition of those charged with committing such crimes. The Convention on Cybercrime is significant because it is the first multilateral treaty to address the issues of computer crime and electronic gathering of evidence related to such crimes. The European Union launched the Critical Information Infrastructure Protection Initiative (CIIPI) that calls for greater international cooperation on the subject of infrastructure protection. The Organization for Security and Cooperation in Europe (OSCE), a branch of the United Nations, has developed numerous counter-terrorism technical assistance programs, one of which is the Action against Terrorism Unit (ATU).[45] Despite the strides in international cooperation to address cybercrime and cyberterrorism, none of the programs are capable of completely securing the Internet, and more international cooperation is needed.

Summary

A computer crime or cybercrime is a crime involving the use of a computer, such as sabotaging or stealing electronically stored data. Computer crimes include violations of criminal law that involve a knowledge of computer technology for their perpetration, investigation, or prosecution. The three general categories of cybercrimes are (1) crimes in which the computer is the "object" of a crime; (2) a computer may be the "subject" of a crime; and (3) a computer may be an "instrument" used to commit traditional crimes. Most crimes consist of two elements: an act (or "actus reus"), and a mental state or ("mens rea"). "Actus reus" refers to the physical aspect of the criminal activity. "Mens rea" refers to a mental state, often an element of the offense, which expresses the intent necessary for a particular act to constitute a crime. Most constitutional issues related to computer crimes usually fall under either the First Amendment or the Fourth Amendment to the U.S. Constitution. The exclusionary rule, which also applies to computer-related crimes, prevents the government from using evidence obtained in violation of an accused person's constitutional rights, including the Fourth Amendment prohibition against unreasonable searches and seizures. Persons have a reasonable expectation of privacy in the content of their e-mails under the Fourth Amendment. Congress has passed legislation targeted specifically at computer related crimes. The government can charge computer-related crimes under at least forty different federal statutes, and there are also a number of traditional criminal statutes that apply to computer crimes. While federal officials often investigate and prosecute cybercrimes, states officials can also prosecute computer crimes under a variety of state laws. Law enforcement officials and prosecutors face challenges in the investigation and prosecution of computer crimes, and cooperation is needed at the state, federal, and international levels.

Key Terms

actus reus *113*
Communications Decency Act (CDA) *122*
computer crime *112*
Computer Fraud and Abuse Act (CFAA) *119*
Copyright Act *124*
cyberbullying *129*
cybercrime *112*
cyberterrorism *112*
Digital Millennium Copyright Act (DMCA) *124*
Electronic Communications Privacy Act (ECPA) *125*
exclusionary rule *115*
extradition *131*
Federal Wiretap Act (Title III) *128*
Fourth Amendment *115*
fruit-of-the-poisonous-tree doctrine *115*
identity theft *126*
mens rea *113*
PROTECT Act *122*
SAFE WEB Act *123*
sexting *129*
wire fraud *128*

Review Questions

1. What is the definition of cybercrime?
2. What are the three general categories of computer-related crimes?
3. What is the name of the landmark U.S. Supreme Court case that established the expectation of privacy test under the Fourth Amendment?
4. Which statutes passed by Congress aimed at fighting child pornography has the U.S. Supreme Court found unconstitutional?
5. Which statutes aimed at fighting child pornography have federal courts upheld as constitutional?
6. What does the CAN-SPAM Act provide?
7. What are the penalties for violating the federal wire fraud act?
8. What does the federal wiretap act provide?
9. Why are cybercrimes difficult to investigate and prosecute?
10. Why is international cooperation needed in addressing cybercrimes and cyberterrorism?

Discussion Questions

1. When imposing criminal sentences, courts may impose special conditions for offenders on supervisory release including restrictions on computer and Internet usage. Should convicted sex offenders on probation be required to obtain their probation officer's permission before accessing the Internet? Should courts be able to impose an absolute ban on computers and the Internet, or should courts allow for a broad-but-not-absolute ban on computer and Internet usage? See *United States v. Granger*, 117 F. App'x 247, 248-49 (4th Cir. 2004) and *United States v. Paul*, 274 F.3d 155, 167-70 (5th Cir. 2001) for cases upholding absolute bans on computer and Internet usage for convicted sex offenders.
2. States have increasingly utilized specialized drug courts to deal with a significant segment of those charged with violating criminal drug statutes. Should specialized courts for computer related crimes be created? If so, which categories of cybercrimes should fall under the jurisdiction of cybercrime courts? Why or why not?
3. In a case involving Craigslist's alleged inducement of prostitution, a federal court in Illinois held that Craigslist's popular Internet classifieds service could not be held liable for facilitating prostitution because its "adult" category was not inherently unlawful as compared to a site that required users to express unlawful preferences. See *Dart v. Craigslist, Inc.*, No. 09 C 1385, 2009 WL 3416106 (N.D. Ill. Oct. 20, 2009). After a long-running battle with lawmakers and human-rights groups, Craigslist removed its paid adult-service category in September 2010. Subsequently, Village Voice Media's backpage.com has also been criticized by prosecutors around the country for allegedly facilitating the human trafficking of minors and prostitution. Under what circumstances, if any, could a website owner or operator be found responsible for facilitating the human trafficking of minors or prostitution? What can law enforcement do to prevent the facilitation of human trafficking of minors or prostitution via the Internet?
4. In April 2009, Boston police officers arrested a twenty-two-year-old medical school student named Philip Markoff—better known as the "Craigslist killer"—in connection with several crimes. First, Markoff allegedly robbed a woman at gunpoint at a Westin hotel after he arranged to receive a massage from her through a Craigslist "Erotic Services" posting online. According to police, four days later, Markoff murdered Julissa Brisman, another masseuse he had solicited through Craigslist's "Erotic Services." While in custody, Markoff committed suicide. What category of computer-related crimes

discussed in this chapter did Markoff allegedly commit? What is your reaction to the Craigslist killer case?

5. The Direct Marketing Association (DMA) adjusted the Guidelines for Ethical Business Practices to address issues concerning e-mail and the CAN-SPAM Act. What can private industry and trade associations do to prevent, investigate, and detect cybercrimes? Is self-regulation a better alternative than government regulation? Is the private sector better equipped than the government in responding to cybercrimes?

Exercises

1. You are working as a manager for a technology company. First, visit the website for the Computer Crime & Intellectual Property Section of the United States Department of Justice at www.cybercrime.gov and find a recent press release involving a cybercrime. After reading the press release, conduct additional research about this case on Google News or a news database. After conducting research, write a memorandum to employees at your company based on the information you find with a caution on how the employees should be careful about potential criminal conduct.
2. Jane, an at-will employee, is asked be her supervisor, Dan, to copy software to another computer, but Jane refuses because she has a good-faith belief that copying the software is illegal. Jane is terminated for refusing to copy the software, and she brings a wrongful discharge case against the employer, arguing that it is against public policy of a state to mandate an employee to be terminated for refusing to perform or participate in illegal or wrongful acts. How should the court decide the wrongful discharge case? Could Dan, the supervisor, be prosecuted for criminal copyright infringement? For more information on retaliatory discharge, see Common-Law Retaliatory Discharge of Employee for Refusing to Perform or Participate in Unlawful or Wrongful Acts, 104 A.L.R.5th 1.
3. The government obtains a search warrant, and the warrant authorizes police to search for instrumentalities of computer harassment and photographs indicative of this offense, which involves communicating "obscene, vulgar, profane, lewd, lascivious, or indecent language," or making a "suggestion or proposal of an obscene nature," or threatening an "illegal or immoral act." During the search, the police find child pornography on the defendant's computer. The defendant argues that the seizure of child pornography during a computer search for evidence of harassment should be excluded under the Fourth Amendment because the evidence was beyond the scope of the search warrant. How should the court decide the case? See *United States v. Williams*, 592 F.3d 511, 521–22 (4th Cir. 2010).
4. *Hypothetical:* John uses a small camcorder and secretly records a movie shown at his local theater. He then uploads the movie to a website and sends out the link to his friends and family. Which federal laws has John violated? What are the potential penalties that John could face?

Related Internet Sites

http://www.cybercrime.gov/
Computer Crime & Intellectual Property Section of the United States Department of Justice

http://www.fbi.gov/about-us/investigate/cyber/cyber
Federal Bureau of Investigation (FBI) Cyber Crimes Division

http://www.secretservice.gov/ectf.shtml
Secret Service Electronic Crimes Task Forces

http://www.ic3.gov
Internet Crime Complaint Center (IC3)

http://www.ftc.gov/bcp/menus/consumer/tech.shtm
FTC Consumer Publications on Computers & Internet

http://www.idtheft.gov/
One-stop resource for government information about identity theft

http://www.justice.gov/criminal/ceos/index.html
U.S. Department of Justice Child Exploitation and Obscenity Section (CEOS)

http://law.findlaw.com/state-laws/computer-crimes/
State Computer Crimes Laws

http://www.interpol.int/public/TechnologyCrime/default.asp
Interpol—Information Technology Crime

http://www.justice.gov/criminal/fraud/websites/idtheft.html
Department of Justice Fraud Identity Theft Website

http://www.justice.gov/dag/iptaskforce/
Department of Justice Task Force on Intellectual Property

End Notes

1. Press Release, White House, Remarks by the President on Securing Our Nation's Cyber Infrastructure (May 29, 2009), available at http://www.whitehouse.gov/the_press_office/Remarks-by-the-President-on-Securing-Our-Nations-Cyber-Infrastructure/.
2. Press Release, U.S. Dep't of Justice, Creator of "Melissa" Computer Virus Pleads Guilty to State and Federal Charges (Dec. 9, 1999), available at http://www.cybercrime.gov/melissa.htm/.
3. UPI, Survey: Computer crime rising in U.S., Dec. 13, 2010, available at http://www.upi.com/Top_News/US/2010/12/13/Survey-Computer-crime-rising-in-US/UPI-27911292255506/.
4. *Marching Off to Cyberwar*, THE ECONOMIST, Dec. 4, 2008, available at http://www.economist.com/node/12673385/.
5. Black's Law Dictionary (9th ed. 2009).
6. Nat'l Inst. of Justice, Dept. of Justice, Computer Crime: Criminal Justice Resource Manual 2 (1989).
7. Black's Law Dictionary (9th ed. 2009).
8. Jessica L. McCurdy, *Computer Crimes*, 47 AM. CRIM. L. REV. 287, 300 (2010).
9. Legal Information Institute, Criminal law: an overview, available at: http://topics.law.cornell.edu/wex/Criminal_law/.
10. Black's Law Dictioanry (9th ed. 2009).
11. Model Penal Code § 1.12.
12. Computer Fraud and Abuse Act (CFAA); Pub. L. No. 99-474, 100 Stat. 1213 (codified as amended at 18 U.S.C. § 1030).
13. *Role Models America, Inc. v. Jones*, 305 F. Supp. 2d 564, 186 Ed. Law Rep. 227 (D. Md. 2004).
14. *United States v. Gonzalez*, 2009 U.S. Dist. LEXIS 50791 (D. Mass. May 26, 2009).
15. Communications Decency Act of 1996, Pub. L. No. 104-104, 110 Stat. 56, 133-43 (1996) (codified in scattered sections of 47 U.S.C.).
16. Child Pornography Prevention Act of 1996, Pub. L. No. 104-208, 110 Stat. 3009-26 (codified as amended in scattered sections of 18 U.S.C.).
17. Taylor McNeill, *Protecting Our Children or Upholding Free Speech: Does One Exclude the Other? United States v. Williams*, 60 MERCER L. REV. 1059 (2009).
18. Prosecutorial Remedies and Other Tools to End the Exploitation of Children Today Act of 2003 ("PROTECT Act"), Pub. L. No. 108-21, 117 Stat. 650 (codified as amended in scattered sections of 18 U.S.C. and 28 U.S.C.).
19. Controlling the Assault of Non-Solicited Pornography and Marketing Act of 2003 (CAN-SPAM Act of 2003), Pub. L. No. 108-187, 117 Stat. 2699 (2003); codified at 15 U.S.C. §§ 7701–7715.
20. U.S. SAFE WEB Act of 2006, Pub. Law 109-455, 120 Stat. 3372 (2006) (amending various sections of the FTC Act, 15 U.S.C.A. §§ 41, 45–46, 56–58).
21. 18 AM. Jur. 2d Copyright and Literary Property § 267.,
22. Sharon B. Soffer, *Criminal Copyright Infringement*, 24 AM. CRIM. L. REV. 491, 491 (1987).
23. See *United States v. Moran*, 757 F. Supp. 1046, 1049 (D. Neb. 1991); *United States v. Sherman*, 576 F.2d 292, 297 (10th Cir. 1978).
24. 18 U.S.C. § 2319.
25. Rachanee Srisavasdi, *Local Admits to Uploading Screener to Internet*, ORANGE COUNTY REG., Jan. 2, 2010, *available at* 2010 WLNR 86989.
26. Press Release, U.S. Dep't of Justice, El Cerrito Man Sentenced to 48 Months for Criminal Copyright Infringement, (December 14, 2010), available at http://sanfrancisco.fbi.gov/dojpressrel/pressrel10/sf121410.htm/.
27. Digital Millennium Copyright Act, Pub. L. No. 105-304, 112 Stat. 2860 (codified as amended in scattered sections of 17 U.S.C.).
28. Press Release, U.S. Dep't of Justice (July 31, 2007), Third Conviction for Camcording Movies in a Theater and Third Conviction for Violating the Digital Millennium Copyright Act as Part of Operation Copycat, available at http://www.justice.gov/criminal/cybercrime/madhaniPlea.htm/.
29. Press Release, U.S. Dep't of Justice, (January 29, 2010), available at http://www.justice.gov/usao/cas/press/cas10-0129-Kwak.pdf/.
30. Electronic Communications Privacy Act of 1986 (ECPA), Pub. L. No. 99-508, 100 Stat. 1848 (1986).
31. *Supra*, note 7 at 313–314.
32. Federal Trade Commission, About Identity Theft, available at: http://www.ftc.gov/bcp/edu/microsites/idtheft/consumers/about-identity-theft.html/.
33. Identity Theft Penalty Enhancement Act, Pub. L. No 108-275, 118 Stat. 831, 831–32 (2004), codified at 18 USC § 1028A.
34. Press Release, U.S. Department of Justice, Fraudster Sentenced to Nearly Four Years in Prison in Internet "Phishing" Case (May 18, 2004), available at http://www.usdoj.gov/opa/pr/2004/May/04_crm_336.htm/.
35. Press Release, U.S. Department of Justice, KC Man Pleads Guilty to Identity Theft, Credit Card Fraud (August 19, 2008), available at http://www.justice.gov/criminal/cybercrime/bagbyPlea.pdf/.
36. The Wiretap Act was passed as Title III of the Omnibus Crime Control and Safe Streets Act of 1968, Pub. L. No. 90–351, §§ 2510-2519, 82 Stat. 212, 212–25 (codified as amended at 18 U.S.C. §§ 2510–2522).
37. Andrew B. Serwin, *Poised on the Precipice: A Critical Examination of Privacy Litigation*, 25 SANTA CLARA COMPUTER & HIGH TECH. L.J. 883, 895 (2009).

38. Marc. D. Goodman, *Why the Police Don't Care About Computer Crime*, 10 HARV. J. L. & TECH. 465, 468–69 (1997).
39. United States Attorneys' Manual, § 9-2.031.
40. Serwin, *supra* note 36.
41. Hedda Litwin, Cyber Crime Training Collaboration with the National Center for Justice and the Rule of Law, available at http://www.naag.org/cybercrime.php/.
42. Black's Law Dictionary (9th ed. 2010).
43. Elizabeth M. Ryan, *Sexting: How the State Can Prevent a Moment of Indiscretion from Leading to a Lifetime of Unintended Consequences for Minors and Young Adults*, 96 IOWA L. REV. 357, 359 (2010).
44. Orin S. Kerr, *Enforcing Law Online* 74. U. CHI L. REV. 745, 758 (2007).
45. Kelly A. Gable, *Cyber-Apocalypse Now: Securing the Internet Againstagainst Cyberterrorism and Using Universal Jurisdiction as a Deterrent*, 43 Vand. J. Transnat'l L. 57, 88–93 (2010).

CHAPTER

8 Tort Law in Cyberspace

The privacy right is "the right to be let alone"—the most comprehensive of rights and the right most valued by civilized men.

U.S. Supreme Court Justice LOUIS BRANDEIS[1]

LEARNING OBJECTIVES

After completing this chapter, you will be able to:

1. Explain general principles of tort law.
2. Describe the different tort actions available to injured persons relating to online conduct.
3. Explain the different types of invasion of privacy by the Internet.
4. Describe the right of publicity.
5. Discuss the application of intentional infliction of emotional distress and negligent infliction of emotional distress in the online environment.
6. Discuss the remedies available in tort cases related to the Internet.
7. Explain the different defenses in Internet tort cases.

OPENING SCENARIO AND OVERVIEW

Erin Andrews became aware in July 2009 that she had been surreptitiously videotaped without her knowledge or consent by a stalker while staying in various hotel rooms across the country to perform her job as an ESPN reporter. After national media coverage, Michael David Barrett pleaded guilty to videotaping Andrews in the nude through peepholes in hotel rooms and posting those videos on the Internet. Barrett was sentenced to $2\frac{1}{2}$ years in prison for stalking Andrews. Andrews subsequently filed civil lawsuits in Tennessee and Illinois against various hotels saying they negligently helped Barrett rent rooms next to her without her permission and failed to catch him creating peepholes. "I've filed this lawsuit to hold accountable those who put my personal safety at risk and who allowed my privacy to be invaded while I was a guest at their hotel, as well as for actually stalking me and making my most personal moments public," Andrews said in a statement.[2]

In the civil complaint filed in Illinois, Andrews alleged that Barrett called the defendant hotels seeking to determine if Andrews had made reservations to stay there.[3] Not only did the hotels confirm that Andrews was intending to register as a guest, but they also released, without Andrews' consent, her room number. The hotels then provided Barrett a hotel room immediately adjacent to hers. Barrett subsequently checked in to the room next to Andrews, modified the peephole device in Andrews' hotel room door, and filmed Andrews through the altered peephole while she was getting dressed and without her consent or knowledge. Barrett ultimately disseminated these videos of Andrews over the Internet. Andrews alleged that the actions of the hotel defendants directly facilitated Barrett's conduct.

Andrews's suit claims a variety of torts including negligence, negligent infliction of emotional distress, and invasion of privacy against the hotel entities. The suit also claims intentional infliction of emotional distress against Barrett. Andrews asked for damages in excess of $1 million from the hotels, saying they negligently helped a stalker rent rooms next to her without her permission and failed to catch him creating peepholes.

The incident involving Andrews shows the potential tort liability for tortious conduct relating to the Internet.

Tort
A civil wrong, other than breach of contract, for which a remedy may be obtained, usually in the form of damages; a breach of a duty that the law imposes on persons who stand in a particular relation to one another.

GENERAL PRINCIPLES OF TORT LAW

Torts are civil wrongs recognized by law as grounds for a lawsuit. These wrongs result in an injury or harm constituting the basis for a claim by the injured party. While some torts are also crimes punishable with imprisonment, the primary aim of tort law is to provide relief for the damages incurred and deter others from committing the same harms.[4] A tort is a breach of a duty that the law imposes on persons who stand in a particular relation to one another. One who commits a tort or the wrongdoer is called a **tortfeasor**. A "tort," which is a civil wrong, should not be confused with a "torte," which is a cake made with many eggs and often grated nuts or dry bread crumbs and usually covered with a rich frosting.[5]

Tortfeasor
One who commits a tort; a wrongdoer.

Negligence
The failure to exercise the standard of care that a reasonably prudent person would have exercised in a similar situation; any conduct that falls below the legal standard established to protect others against unreasonable risk of harm, except for conduct that is intentionally, wantonly, or willfully disregardful of others' rights.

In the United States, legal actions for injuries are generally based in tort law, the branch of the law that allows injured persons to seek monetary compensation from those responsible for the injury. Tort law is generally the province of state law (rather than federal law) created through state legislation and state judicial decisions, known as the common law.[6] Variations exist among the states, but state tort rules are similar enough that generalized statements of liability can be made. Many judges and states utilize the Restatement (Second) of Torts and the Restatement (Third) of Torts: Products Liability, the American Law Institute's synthesis of the major principles of contemporary tort law, as influential guides. Some judges that examine tort cases also look to the legal treatise *The Law of Torts* by Dan B. Dobbs and its predecessor Prosser and Keaton's *Law of Torts* as persuasive authority on tort law.

Strict Liability
Liability that does not depend on actual negligence or intent to harm, but that is based on the breach of an absolute duty to make something safe.

Torts generally fall into three categories: (1) intentional torts, which are based on results intended by the wrongdoer; (2) negligent torts (or negligence), which are unintentional wrongs; and (3) strict liability, which is imposed without fault. Intentional torts are those wrongs that the defendant knew or should have known would occur through their actions or inactions. **Negligence** occurs when the defendant's actions were unreasonably unsafe. **Strict liability** wrongs do not depend on the degree of carefulness by the defendant, but are established when a particular action causes damage.[7] There are also separate areas of tort law including invasion of privacy and economic torts.

Internet torts are considerably different from torts in traditional civil litigation. One major difference between traditional tort claims and Internet tort claims is the nature of injuries suffered by the plaintiffs. In the brick-and-mortar world, negligence and personal injury cases are the most common types of tort cases.[8] Most cases involving the Internet involve financial loss. Based on one study, 97 percent of Internet torts are intentional torts, while traditional torts are predominately negligence.[9] Most torts involving the Internet are publication or informational torts where people can make their voices heard.

Cybertort
A cause of action that exists due to harmful Internet contact. Any tort action that involves the Internet or use of a computer.

The term "**cybertort**" is defined in secondary legal sources as "a cause of action that exists due to harmful Internet contact."[10] Basically, any tort action that involves the Internet or use of a computer can be considered a cybertort. While some commentators and legal scholars often use the term "cybertort," only one judge has used the term "cybertorts" in a published judicial opinion.[11]

This chapter focuses on the torts of invasion of privacy, negligent and intentional infliction of emotional distress, economic torts, and strict liability involving the Internet. Remedies and defenses in online tort cases will also be discussed. Defamation and online speech are discussed in Chapter 9 and privacy-related statutes are covered in Chapter 10.

INVASION OF PRIVACY

Invasion of Privacy
An unjustified exploitation of one's personality or intrusion into one's personal activities, actionable under tort law and sometimes under constitutional law.

As illustrated by the civil suit filed by Erin Andrews, one of the potential torts involving the Internet is **invasion of privacy**. Beginning in 1905, American courts began to recognize an independent tort for invasion of privacy, providing clear protection for the kinds of informational concerns that have become incredibly valuable in the modern economic landscape. By 1960, shortly before the tort of invasion of privacy was recognized by the Restatement (Second) of Torts, the majority of jurisdictions had acknowledged the existence of some form of the claim.[12] One who invades the privacy of another is subject to tort liability for the resulting harm to the interests of the other. The tort of invasion of privacy encompasses four causes of action: (1) unreasonable intrusion upon the seclusion of another; (2) misappropriation of a person's name or likeness; (3) public disclosure of private facts; or (4) publicity that unreasonably places a person in a false light before the public.[13]

The Restatement (Second) of Torts provides that the acts constituting invasion of privacy must be highly offensive to a reasonable person for all forms of invasion of privacy except misappropriation of a person's name or likeness. While most courts provide for liability when the act constituting the invasion of privacy is "highly offensive to a reasonable person," some courts have applied or recognized an even more stringent requirement of outrageous conduct.[14] Outrageous conduct is conduct that so is outrageous in character, and so extreme in degree, as to go beyond all possible bounds of decency, and to be regarded as atrocious and utterly intolerable in a civilized community.

Intrusion upon Seclusion

The first type of invasion of privacy is intrusion upon seclusion. The Restatement (Second) of Torts § 652B describes this type of torts as "[o]ne who intentionally intrudes, physically or otherwise, upon the solitude or seclusion of another or his private affairs or concerns, is subject to liability to the other for invasion of his privacy, if the intrusion would be highly offensive to a reasonable person."

The elements for intrusion upon a plaintiff's seclusion or solitude are (1) an intentional intrusion by the defendant; (2) into a matter which the plaintiff has a right to keep private; and (3) by the use of a method which is objectionable to the reasonable person. The tort of intrusion into private matters is proven only if the plaintiff had an objectively reasonable expectation of seclusion or solitude in the invaded place, conversation, or data source. To prove actionable intrusion, the plaintiff must show that the defendant penetrated some zone of physical or sensory privacy surrounding, or obtained unwanted access to, data about the plaintiff, and the tort is proven only if the plaintiff had an objectively reasonable expectation of seclusion or solitude in the place, conversation, or data source.

Google's Street View, which allows a person to search for street level images, has led to a number of privacy concerns, including legal actions in Europe. In Pennsylvania, private road residents brought an action against Google asserting a claim for invasion of privacy arising from the presence of images of their residence as part of an online map in *Boring v. Google Inc.*, 362.

Fed. Appx. 273 (3rd Cir. 2010). The federal appeals court found that the existence of an image did not in itself rise to the level of an intrusion that could reasonably be called highly offensive. Thus, the court affirmed the lower court's ruling that for purposes of Pennsylvania law, the residents did not suffer a substantial and highly offensive intrusion upon seclusion arising from the presence on the Internet search engine of street level images of their residence, outbuildings, and swimming pool, taken from a continuously filming digital panoramic camera mounted on a vehicle in their driveway off a private unpaved road.

Under the current law, plaintiffs will usually not prevail when bringing an action for the tort of intrusion upon seclusion when a photo is taken in a public place and then uploaded to the Internet, but some have called for a change in the law and to provide more protections against invasion of privacy.

Misappropriation of a Person's Name or Likeness/Right of Publicity

The next type of invasion of privacy is misappropriation of a person's name or likeness. This type of invasion of privacy is sometimes called appropriation of a person's name or likeness. The Restatement (Second) of Torts § 652C states "[o]ne who appropriates to his own use or benefit the name or likeness of another is subject to liability to the other for invasion of his privacy."

The **right of publicity**, which is a separate tort action, is related to the privacy tort for misappropriation. The right of publicity is the right of a person to control the commercial use of their identity. In a number of states, including California, which is home to many celebrities in the entertainment industry, the right of publicity is defined by statute, but courts have also recognized many common-law rights. Approximately thirty states recognize some form of the right of publicity. Under the right of publicity, a person can bring a claim when someone else uses the person's identity for commercial purposes without the person's consent.

Right of Publicity
The right to control the use of one's own name, picture, or likeness and to prevent another from using it for commercial benefit without one's consent.

The right of publicity is different from the privacy tort for misappropriation because the right of publicity protects a person's pecuniary and proprietary interests rather than emotional interests. Meanwhile privacy rights are personal rights, and any damage is measured primarily by the existence of mental distress or degree of mental distress. The elements for both the privacy tort and right of publicity are (1) the defendant's use of the plaintiff's identity; (2) the appropriation of plaintiff's name or likeness to defendant's advantage; (3) lack of consent; and (4) resulting injury.[15]

Celebrities may bring a tort claim for misappropriation or right of privacy for unauthorized use of their name or likeness. For example, golfer John Daly sued a golf company for misappropriation of his name and likeness in *John Daly Enterprises, LLC v. Hippo Golf Co., Inc.*, 646 F. Supp. 2d 1347 (S.D. Fla. 2009). The court held that Daly's name and likeness were commercially exploited to promote the defendant golf company's equipment and that the website used Daly's name and likeness to directly promote the golf equipment without obtaining consent from the golfer.

Sometimes the First Amendment free of speech may outweigh the right of publicity or privacy rights. In *C.B.C. Distr. & Mktg., Inc. v. Major League Baseball Adv. Media, L.P.*, 505 F.3d 818, 823-24 (8th Cir. 2007), the U.S. Court of Appeals for the Eighth Circuit concluded that freedom of speech outweighed the state interest in according publicity rights to the objecting athletes in a case brought involving Major League Baseball and a company that distributes and sells fantasy sports products, including fantasy baseball games accessible over the Internet.

Similarly, a federal court in Minnesota held in *CBS Interactive Inc. v. Nat'l Football Players Ass'n*, 259 F.R.D. 398 (D. Minn. 2009), that the First Amendment superseded the publicity rights of National Football League players in a case involving an operator of a fantasy sports website. These cases set forth a precedent for other online fantasy sports leagues, which is a multimillion dollar industry in the United States.

California's Right of Publicity Statute

In addition to the common law cause of action for misappropriation, California has a statutory remedy for commercial misappropriation. Under the statute, a plaintiff must prove all the elements of the common-law cause of action. In addition, the plaintiff must allege a knowing use by the defendant as well as a direct connection between the alleged use and the commercial purpose. *Downing v. Abercrombie & Fitch*, 265 F.3d 994, 1001 (9th Cir. 2001). The text of the Cal. Civil Code § 3344 provides:

> Any person who knowingly uses another's name, voice, signature, photograph, or likeness, in any manner, on or in products, merchandise, or goods, or for purposes of advertising or selling, or soliciting purchases of, products, merchandise, goods or services, without such person's prior consent, or, in the case of a minor, the prior consent of his parent or legal guardian, shall be liable for any damages sustained by the person or persons injured as a result thereof. In addition, in any action brought under this section, the person who violated the section shall be liable to the injured party or parties in an amount equal to the greater of seven hundred fifty dollars ($750) or the actual damages suffered by him or her as a result of the unauthorized use, and any profits from the unauthorized use that are attributable to the use and are not taken into account in computing the actual damages. In establishing such profits, the injured party or parties are required to present proof only of the gross revenue attributable to such use, and the person who violated this section is required to prove his or her deductible expenses. Punitive damages may also be awarded to the injured party or parties. The prevailing party in any action under this section shall also be entitled to attorney's fees and costs.

Misappropriation of a person's name or likeness or right of publicity is not limited to celebrities. The Florida legislature enacted Fla. Stat. § 540.08 to expand the remedies available under the common law right against misappropriation. Courts have interpreted the Florida statute's commercial purpose requirement to require that a defendant's unauthorized use "directly promote" a product or service.

In *Almeida v. Amazon.com, Inc.*, 456 F.3d 1316 (11th Cir. 2006), a woman who had been photographed for an artistic exhibit when she was a minor with her mother's consent brought an action against the online retailer Amazon.com, which sold copies of a book displaying her photograph on its cover claiming invasion of privacy based on misappropriation. The court concluded that the online retailer had not used the woman's image for purposes of trade or for any commercial or advertising purpose since the retailer did not make editorial choices as to the cover images it displayed on its website, and its use of those images was not an endorsement or promotion of any product or service but was merely incidental to and customary for the business of Internet book sales.

Unauthorized product celebrity endorsements are common with the proliferation of websites and new media. After the dietary supplement esveratrol received attention on *60 Minutes* and *The Oprah Winfrey Show*, the Internet swelled with websites making unproven health claims and using false celebrity product endorsements for anti-aging and weight-loss pills made from resveratrol. The *New York Times* reported in 2009 that in response to the misuse of their names, Oprah Winfrey and her regular guest Dr. Mehmet Oz, along with Barbara Walters, publicly denounced the websites and said they do not endorse the products.[16]

Companies should ensure that endorsements from celebrities along with photographs and images used in advertising and displayed on websites are authorized. Otherwise, website owners or operators can face potential tort liability for misappropriation of a person's name and likeness and the right of publicity.

William Prosser (1898–1972): The Real King of Torts

William Prosser is considered a giant of tort law. One legal scholar observed that "[r]arely in the history of American legal education has one author's name been so clearly identified with his subject as the name of William L. Prosser is with the law of torts." The *Washington Post* described Prosser as "a scholar and author who was to torts what Dr. Spock is to child care." When Prosser died in 1972, his colleagues heralded him as "a great Master of Torts." After graduating from the University of Minnesota Law School, Prosser joined the law firm Dorsey, Colman, Barker, Scott & Barber (now Dorsey & Whitney). He taught at the University of Minnesota from 1931 until 1940 and then became the Minnesota counsel for the Roosevelt Administration's Office of Price Administration. In 1947, Prosser became a professor at Harvard Law School, and one year later he joined the law school at the University of California at Berkeley (Boalt Hall) where was served as dean from 1948 to 1961. Prosser wrote the legal treatise Prosser on Torts, which has been cited by judges in thousands of judicial opinions. Prosser was also Reporter for the Restatement (Second) of Torts, which has been described as the most influential of the American Law Institute's volumes restating and reshaping American law. He also wrote a textbook on tort law that has gone through eleven editions and remains a popular choice among law school professors today. Although John Grisham wrote the legal/suspense novel *The King of Torts* based on a fictional character, Prosser should be considered the real King of Torts.[17]

Public Disclosure of Private Facts

Public disclosure of private facts is another form of invasion of privacy under tort law. The Restatement (Second) of Torts § 652D provides:

> One who gives publicity to a matter concerning the private life of another is subject to liability to the other for invasion of his privacy, if the matter publicized is of a kind that
>
> **a.** would be highly offensive to a reasonable person, and
> **b.** is not of legitimate concern to the public.

The three basic elements of the cause of action for invasion of privacy based on public disclosure of private facts are (1) there must be a public disclosure; (2) the facts disclosed must be private facts, rather than public ones; and (3) the matter made public must be one which would be offensive and objectionable to a reasonable person of ordinary sensibilities.[18]

Public disclosure of private facts constitutes a tort if both parties believe that the embarrassing matter is true and the plaintiff's injury resulted from that assumption. The cases about public disclosure of private facts do not seem to pay much attention to whether it occurs in newspapers, radio, television, or the Internet.[19] The tort has developed and been refined unaffected by how the media has grown and changed. Cases of public disclosure of private facts sometimes involve a situation where the defendant has revealed a private medical condition about the plaintiff to a third party. When a rape victim's name appears on the Internet, the tort of public disclosure of private facts may be the best available option.[20]

Posting private information on the Internet satisfies the "public disclosure" element in a public disclosure of private facts case.[21] In *Yath v. Fairview Clinics, N.P.*, 767 N.W.2d 34 (Minn. Ct. App. 2009), a patient brought an action against a health care provider and employees after the plaintiff's private health information was posted on the Internet. The invasion of privacy case involved the Internet posting of embarrassing personal information taken surreptitiously from a patient's medical file. A medical clinic employee saw a personal acquaintance at the clinic and read her medical file, learning that she had a sexually transmitted disease and a new sex partner other than her husband. The employee disclosed this information to another employee, who then disclosed it to others, including the patient's estranged husband. Then someone posted the information on the social networking website MySpace.com. The court held that the temporary posting of information from the patient's medical file on a public social networking website for anyone to view satisfied the publicity element for such a claim, and the number of actual viewers was irrelevant.

A 2009 California state court examined a public disclosure of private facts case involving a post on the social networking website MySpace.com in *Moreno v. Hanford Sentinel, Inc.*, 172 Cal. App. 4th 1125, 91 Cal. Rptr. 3d 858 (2009). An online journal entry posted on the author's MySpace.com website disparaging the author's hometown was not a private fact and therefore did not constitute the tort of invasion of privacy through public disclosure of private fact. Even though the author posted the journal entry to the website under her first name only and removed the entry from the website before learning it had been submitted to a newspaper, the author's identity was readily ascertainable from the website and the author's affirmative act made the entry available to anyone with a computer. The court in *Moreno v. Hanford Sentinel* held that once the ode or journal entry was published on MySpace.com, the facts were not private.

Revealing private information on online social networking sites, such as Facebook and Twitter, creates potential liability when disclosure of the private facts would be offensive and objectionable to a reasonable person.

False Light
In an invasion-of-privacy action, a plaintiff's allegation that the defendant attributed to the plaintiff views that he or she does not hold and placed the plaintiff before the public in a highly offensive and untrue manner.

False Light

Publicly placing a person in **false light** is another form of invasion of privacy. The majority of jurisdictions have recognized false light as a separate actionable tort. Most jurisdictions have adopted either the analysis of the tort of false light given by Dean Prosser in the legal treatise Prosser and Keaton's *Law of Torts* or the definition provided by the Restatement (Second) of Torts. A minority of jurisdictions, on the other hand, have refused to recognize the tort of false light invasion of privacy. In an invasion-of-privacy action, false light is the plaintiff's allegation that the defendant attributed to the plaintiff views that he or she does not hold and placed the plaintiff before the public in a highly offensive and untrue manner. If the matter involves the public interest, the plaintiff must prove the defendant's malice.

The Restatement (Second) of Torts § 652E states:

> One who gives publicity to a matter concerning another that places the other before the public in a false light is subject to liability to the other for invasion of his privacy, if
>
> **a.** the false light in which the other was placed would be highly offensive to a reasonable person, and
>
> **b.** the actor had knowledge of or acted in reckless disregard as to the falsity of the publicized matter and the false light in which the other would be placed.

In *Meyerkord v. Zipatoni Co.*, 276 S.W.3d 319 (Mo. Ct. App. 2008) (Case 8.1), the Missouri Court of Appeals recognized false light as a separate tort for the first time in a case involving an online viral marketing scheme for Sony's PlayStation Portable or PSP. Missouri followed the majority of jurisdictions in recognizing false light as a separate actionable tort although a few states have not recognized false light as a separate tort.

CASE 8.1

The Case of the Online Viral Marketing Scheme

Meyerkord v. Zipatoni Co., *276 S.W.3d 319 (Mo. Ct. App. 2008)*

Plaintiff, Greg Meyerkord ("Meyerkord"), appeals from the judgment dismissing Meyerkord's action for false light invasion of privacy against defendant, The Zipatoni Co. ("Zipatoni"). Meyerkord contends his claim represents the "classic case" of false light invasion of privacy. We vacate and remand.

Some time prior to early 2003, Meyerkord was employed by Zipatoni, a Missouri corporation that provides marketing services to businesses, and was listed as the "registrant" for Zipatoni's account with Register.com for the purpose of the registration of websites. Meyerkord's employment with Zipatoni ended in 2003.

In 2006, Zipatoni registered www.alliwantforxmasisapsp.com through Register.com. Meyerkord was listed as the registrant for www.alliwantforxmasisapsp.com, but had no involvement in the creation, registration, or marketing of the website, which was used during a viral marketing campaign initiated by Sony to sell its Play Station Portable ("PSP"). Shortly after the PSP campaign became active, bloggers, consumers, and consumer activist groups began voicing on blogs and websites their concern, suspicion, and accusations over the campaign and those associated with it, including Zipatoni and Meyerkord.

Thereafter, Meyerkord filed an action against Zipatoni for false light invasion of privacy because Zipatoni failed to remove him as the registrant for its account with Register.com and registered www.alliwantforxmasisapsp.com with Meyerkord listed as the registrant when he no longer worked for Zipatoni. As a direct result of the "negligence" of Zipatoni, Meyerkord alleged the content of www.alliwantforxmasisapsp.com was "publicly attributed" to Meyerkord, and his "privacy has been invaded, his reputation and standing in the community has been injured, and he has suffered shame, embarrassment, humiliation, harassment, and mental anguish." Meyerkord also alleged these injuries will continue because the blogs and websites criticizing him will remain "on the [i]nternet and open for searching/viewing for an indefinite period of time." Meyerkord requested a judgment in excess of $25,000.

Zipatoni filed a motion to dismiss in which it argued no Missouri court had recognized the "false light" tort as an action separate from defamation, and Meyerkord failed to plead a claim for defamation. The trial court granted Zipatoni's motion to dismiss. This appeal follows.

(*Continued*)

(Continued)

Since the early twentieth century, Missouri has recognized a cause of action for an "invasion of privacy" [citation omitted]. In *Barber v. Time, Inc.,* 348 Mo. 1199, 159 S.W.2d 291 (1942), the Supreme Court acknowledged the general "right of privacy" not to have certain private affairs made public.

An "invasion of privacy" is a general term used to describe four different torts.[. . .]

We have acknowledged this Restatement classification, but we have yet to recognize a cause of action for false light invasion of privacy.

Meyerkord argues the false light invasion of privacy tort should be recognized in this case because this case meets the elements of the tort and represents the "classic case" discussed in *Sullivan v. Pulitzer Broadcasting Co.,* 709 S.W.2d 475 (Mo. banc 1986), the key case dealing with the question of whether Missouri courts should adopt a cause of action for false light invasion of privacy. In *Sullivan*, the court looked at the issue of whether a plaintiff could sue for false light invasion of privacy and avoid the two year statute of limitations for defamation actions. In deciding that question, the court noted it had not yet recognized a cause of action apart from defamation for false light invasion of privacy. However, it went on to say that: [i]t may be possible that in the future Missouri courts will be presented with an appropriate case justifying our recognition of the tort of "false light invasion of privacy."

The court also noted the difference between false light and defamation was that the latter protects one's interest in his or her reputation, while the former protects one's interest in the right to be let alone. An action for false light invasion of privacy does not require one to also be defamed; it is enough that he or she is given unreasonable and highly objectionable publicity that attributes to him or her characteristics, conduct, or beliefs that are false, and so is placed before the public in a false position. Restatement (Second) of Torts Section 652E, cmt. B (1977). When this is the case and the matter attributed to the plaintiff is not defamatory, the rule here affords a different remedy not available in an action for defamation.

Section 652(E) of the Restatement (Second) of Torts spells out the elements of the tort of false light invasion of privacy as follows:

> One who gives publicity to a matter concerning another that places the other before the public in a false light is subject to liability to the other for invasion of his privacy, if (a) the false light in which the other was placed would be highly offensive to a reasonable person, and (b) the actor had knowledge of or acted in reckless disregard as to the falsity of the publicized matter and the false light in which the other would be placed.

This section applies only when the publicity given to the plaintiff has placed him in a false light before the public, of a kind that would be highly offensive to a reasonable person. In other words, it applies only when the defendant knows the plaintiff, as a reasonable person, would be justified in the eyes of the community in feeling seriously offended and aggrieved by the publicity. On the other hand, the plaintiff's privacy is not invaded when unimportant false statements are made, even when they are made deliberately. It is only when there is such a major misrepresentation of one's character, history, activities, or beliefs that serious offense may reasonably be expected to be taken by a reasonable person in his or her position, that there is a cause of action for invasion of privacy.

In deciding whether to adopt the tort of false light invasion of privacy, we note the majority of jurisdictions addressing false light claims have chosen to recognize false light as a separate actionable tort. Further, of these jurisdictions most have adopted either the analysis of the tort given by Dean Prosser or the definition provided by the Restatement (Second) of Torts. On the other hand, a minority of jurisdictions have refused to recognize the tort of false light invasion of privacy.

The rationales commonly supporting a court's refusal to recognize false light invasion of privacy are that: (1) the protection provided by false light either duplicates or overlaps the interests already protected by the defamation torts of slander and libel; (2) to the extent it would allow recovery beyond that permitted for libel or slander, false light would tend to exacerbate the tension between the First Amendment and these cases; and (3) it would require courts to consider two claims for the same relief, which, if not identical, at least would not differ significantly.

As to the first rationale, we find false light invasion of privacy is sufficiently distinguishable from defamation torts. In defamation law, the interest sought to be protected is the objective one of reputation, either economic, political, or personal, in the outside world. On the other hand, in privacy cases, the interest affected is the subjective one of injury to the person's right to be let alone. Further, where the issue is truth or falsity, the marketplace of ideas provides a forum where the answer can be found, while in privacy cases, resort to the marketplace merely accentuates the injury. Thus, we find the interests at stake are sufficiently distinct for a separate remedy for false light invasion of privacy to exist.

The second rationale for refusing to recognize false light invasion of privacy can be easily mitigated through the adoption of a heightened standard like actual malice or recklessness. Some courts have adopted an actual malice standard for claims involving public officials or figures or claims asserted by private individuals about matters of public concern and a negligence standard for claims by private individuals about matters of private concern. However, we find that adhering to the actual malice standard in the Restatement for all types of cases strikes the best balance between allowing false light claims and protecting First Amendment rights. . . . Moreover, the Restatement's requirement that the statement must be "highly offensive to a reasonable person" reduces the possibility that the recognition of the false light tort will result in unnecessary litigation.

As noted earlier, the Missouri Supreme Court has considered the issue of whether Missouri courts should adopt the tort of false light invasion of privacy, but the Supreme Court concluded it had not yet been confronted with a factually suitable case. We now find that the facts of the present case properly present the issue of false light invasion of privacy and we hold that a person who places another before the public in a false light may be liable in Missouri for the resulting damages. In recognizing this cause of action, we note that as a result of the accessibility of the internet, the barriers to generating publicity are quickly and inexpensively surmounted. Moreover, the ethical standards regarding the acceptability of certain discourse have been diminished. Thus, as the ability to do harm grows, we believe so must the law's ability to protect the innocent.

We now turn to Zipatoni's third argument for not recognizing a cause of action for false light invasion of privacy in this case. In his petition, Meyerkord alleged Zipatoni was "negligent and careless" in failing to remove him as the registrant for its account with Register.com and in registering www.alliwantforxmasis apsp.com with Meyerkord listed as the registrant. Because we have adopted the tort of false light invasion of privacy and have found that the proper standard for liability is actual malice, we find Meyerkord has failed to plead the essential elements for a claim of false light invasion of privacy. Therefore, the trial court did not err in granting Zipatoni's motion to dismiss because Meyerkord's petition failed to state a claim upon which relief may be granted.

However, because of the developing status of this area of the law, and because no previous cases have discussed pleading requirements in Missouri, we will remand this case and give Meyerkord an opportunity to amend his petition to plead the correct standard for his claim of false light invasion of privacy as adopted above.

Case Questions

1. Why is accessibility of the Internet a consideration in a claim for false light?
2. What were the reasons give by Zipatoni against recognizing a cause of action for false light invasion of privacy?
3. Why did the court reject these reasons and recognize the false light invasion of privacy tort?

INTENTIONAL AND NEGLIGENT INFLICTION OF EMOTIONAL DISTRESS

The growth and popularity of electronic communication has led to a number of cases involving intentional and negligent infliction of emotional distress. Posting derogatory, profane, and offensive comments about a person on a website or in an e-mail can lead to potential tort liability for intentional and negligent infliction of emotional distress.

Tort law provides that a person who by extreme and outrageous conduct intentionally or recklessly causes severe emotional distress to another is subject to liability for such emotional distress and bodily harm. **Intentional infliction of emotional distress** is sometimes abbreviated with the acronym IIED.

Intentional Infliction of Emotional Distress (IIED) The tort of intentionally or recklessly causing another person severe emotional distress through one's extreme or outrageous acts.

The tort of the intentional infliction of emotional distress consists of the following four elements: (1) the defendant must have acted intentionally or with reckless disregard of the consequences; (2) the defendant's conduct must have been extreme or outrageous; (3) the plaintiff must have suffered severe emotional distress; and (4) the defendant's conduct must have been the cause of such emotional distress. For intentional infliction of emotional distress, the conduct must be so extreme as to exceed all bounds usually tolerated in a civilized community.

Negligent Infliction of Emotional Distress The tort of causing another severe emotional distress through one's negligent conduct.

Although the tort of the **negligent infliction of emotional distress** is similar to the tort of intentional infliction of emotional distress, there is an important distinction. Intentional infliction requires that the defendant's behavior be extreme and outrageous, whereas negligent infliction requires only that the defendant's conduct be unreasonable and create an unreasonable risk of foreseeable harm. In other words, negligent infliction of emotional distress does not require a showing of outrageous conduct. Instead, a plaintiff in a negligent infliction of emotional distress case must prove that the defendant should have realized that its conduct involved an unreasonable risk of causing emotional distress, and that distress, if it were caused, might result in illness or bodily harm. Eight states have adopted negligent infliction of emotional distress as an independent tort. But tort law on the negligent infliction of emotional distress remains highly unstable, varying from state to state, and lacking any consensus among courts and commentators.[22]

A number of cases have recognized vicarious and individual liability for intentional infliction of emotional distress from Internet and electronic communications. In *Delfino v. Agilent Technologies, Inc.*, 145 Cal. App. 4th 790, 52 Cal. Rptr. 3d 376 (6th Dist. 2006), a California state court held that repeated threats of physical harm directed to plaintiffs, stated in graphic terms in e-mails and Internet bulletin board postings on Yahoo!, were sufficient acts of "extreme and outrageous conduct" to support a claim of intentional infliction of emotional distress.

Cyberbullying Bullying by use of any electronic device through means including, but not limited to, e-mail, instant messaging, text messages, blogs, mobile phones, pagers, online games, and websites.

Cyberstalking Similar to cyberbullying, involves publicly viewed threats and harassment over the Internet, protecting the perpetrator behind a veil of anonymity. The primary difference is cyberstalking takes place over an extended period of time, whereas cyberbullying can be one isolated incident, or if repeated through a series of incidents, within a short period of time. Cyberstalking is often committed by one perpetrator, whereas the victim of cyberbullying can be the target of one person or a group of people.

Where supervisors or other workers send offensive e-mails to another employee, both the employer and the supervisor can be found liable for intentional or negligent infliction of emotional distress. For example, in *McNeail-Tunstall v. Marsh USA*, 307 F. Supp. 2d 955 (W.D. Tenn. 2004) (applying Tennessee law), the court held that a supervisor's alleged racially discriminatory conduct of sending an employee various e-mails raised genuine issues of material fact precluding summary judgment for the employer and supervisor on the employee's claim of the negligent infliction of emotional distress.

Intentional infliction of emotional distress may also be used for **cyberbullying** and **cyberstalking.** Numerous news articles have described a rise in cyberbullying, especially in schools. Cyberbullying occurs when a person uses an electronic device to inflict emotional or mental abuse.[23] The federal government defines cyberbullying as any type of harassment or bullying (e.g., teasing, telling lies, making fun of someone, making rude or mean comments, spreading rumors, or making threatening or aggressive comments) that occurs through e-mail, a chat room, instant messaging, a website (including blogs), text messaging, videos, or pictures posted on websites or sent through cell phones.[24]

Cyberstalking, similar to cyberbullying, involves publicly viewed threats and harassment over the Internet, protecting the perpetrator behind a veil of anonymity. The primary difference is cyberstalking takes place over an extended period of time, whereas cyberbullying can be one isolated incident, or if repeated through a series of incidents, within a short period of time. Cyberstalking is often committed by one perpetrator, whereas the victim of cyberbullying can be the target of one person or a group of people.

Teachers and school administrators may be able to recover under intentional infliction of emotional distress if students post inappropriate material online. For example, a high school teacher in Pennsylvania targeted by a website created by a student obtained a $500,000 judgment for intentional infliction of emotional distress and invasion of privacy. The student made a website that included derogatory, profane, and offensive comments about the student's algebra teacher and principal, listing reasons why the teacher should die, and soliciting donations to pay for a hitman to kill the teacher.[25]

Although there may be disputes about what is considered outrageous conduct tolerated in a civilized community, especially in the Internet age, intentional and negligent infliction of emotional distress are possible torts for individuals who have been the victims of cyberbullying and other harmful electronic communication.

ECONOMIC TORTS

Along with negligent and intentional infliction of emotional distress, plaintiffs who have been injured from electronic communication may seek redress in the courts by filing a cause of action for an **economic tort**. Potential economic torts include fraud, negligent misrepresentation, interference with contractual relations, and interference with prospective economic relations. Judge Richard Posner, perhaps the most influential legal thinker in America today and the leading advocate of the conservative law and economics approach to the study of law, defines economic tort as "tort claims that do not allege physical contact with the victim or his property or harm to such nonfinancial, or at least noncommercial, goods as business reputation and personal privacy."[26] Harm to personal privacy and the reputation of a business are common in economic tort cases.

Economic Tort
A tort that impairs some aspect of an economic interest or business relationship and causes economic loss rather than property damage or bodily harm. Business torts include tortious interference with contractual relations, intentional interference with prospective economic advantage, unfair business practices, misappropriation of trade secrets, and product disparagement.

Fraud and Misrepresentation

Fraudulent activities are rampant with the Internet. Fraud is usually a tort, but in some cases, fraud may also be a crime. When fraud is a tort rather than a crime, it is often called common-law fraud. Black's Law Dictionary (9th ed. 2009) defines fraud as "a knowing misrepresentation of the truth or concealment of a material fact to induce another to act to his or her detriment." Fraud is a tort arising from a knowing misrepresentation, concealment of material fact, or reckless misrepresentation made to induce another to act to his or her detriment. Common-law fraud is sometimes called intentional misrepresentation or fraudulent misrepresentation.

Although the elements vary somewhat from state to state, as a general rule, the plaintiff must prove the following elements for common law fraud: (1) false representation or concealment of a material fact; (2) reasonably calculated to deceive; (3) made with the intent to deceive; and (4) resulting in injury or detrimental reliance.[27]

Proving and successfully collecting a judgment in an Internet fraud case can be challenging. Potential plaintiffs may not be able to discover the true identity of those who engage in Internet fraud. Jurisdictional challenges exist since many fraudulent activities are conducted outside the United States or in a different state. Even if the plaintiff can identify the true identity and obtain personal jurisdiction over the defendant, other hurdles in a fraud case must be overcome.

For example, the presence of a contract can be problematic for plaintiffs in a common-law fraud case. In *Duffy v. Ticketreserve, Inc.*, 722 F. Supp. 2d 977 (N.D. Ill. 2010), customers of an online marketplace asserted various fraud and breach of contract claims, including common-law fraud, against the defendant The Ticket Reserve, Inc., doing business as FirstDIBZ.com, which operates an online marketplace where Internet users can buy, sell, and trade options to purchase tickets to sporting events. In *Duffy v. Ticketreserve*, the plaintiffs paid the defendant a fee for each transaction, and the customers attempted to secure tickets to the 2009 SuperBowl. The court rejected the common-law fraud claim because the customers' reliance on sales and promotional representations made by the operator of the website was not reasonable. The contractual language specifically excused the website operator from any legal duty to provide substitute tickets or other compensation in the event of a seller's default.

In a common-law fraud case, the plaintiffs are required to satisfy heightened pleading requirements for the complaint. Federal Rule of Civil Procedure 9(b) requires that "[i]n all averments of fraud or mistake, the circumstances constituting fraud or mistake shall be stated with particularity." The circumstances constituting the alleged fraud should be specific enough to give defendants notice of the particular misconduct so that they can defend against the charge and not just deny that they have done anything wrong.

At least one court has recognized a fraud and negligent misrepresentation case against a website. In *Anthony v. Yahoo Inc.*, 421 F. Supp. 2d 1257, 1263 (N.D. Cal. 2006), involving the online personal dating service for Yahoo!, the court stated that although the complaint must specify such facts as the times, dates, places, benefits received, and other details of the alleged fraudulent activity, this rule may be relaxed with respect to matters within the opposing party's knowledge. The court held that the plaintiff listed twenty-three concrete examples of false profiles, including user names and excerpts from each posting, to satisfy the heightened pleading requirements for the fraud and negligent misrepresentation causes of action. After denying the motion to dismiss the case and approving the class-action suit, Yahoo! entered into a $4 million settlement involving its online dating service.[28] Yahoo! agreed to a one-time payment of $35 for each member of the class-action who viewed a profile during his or her subscription period that the user believed was posted for purposes other than dating. In July 2010, Yahoo! discontinued its online dating service after striking a deal with Match.com for Match.com to become the exclusive online dating site on Yahoo.[29]

Negligent misrepresentation, or sometimes called misrepresentation, is akin to fraud. As illustrated in the case involving Yahoo!'s online dating service, plaintiffs will often allege both fraud and negligent misrepresentation in the same case. Generally, the elements of fraud and misrepresentation are similar. The difference between fraud and negligent misrepresentation is that negligent misrepresentation only requires that the statement or omission was made without a reasonable basis for believing its truthfulness, rather than an actual knowledge of its falsity.[30]

With the growth of technology and globalization, the Internet has facilitated opportunities for securities fraud involving investment schemes. Along with a traditional tort action, investors may bring claims under federal and state securities statutes for fraudulent statements involving investments, which are common in online bulletin boards and other online communication. In addition, the Securities and Exchange Commission (SEC) may bring an action against those who engage in securities fraud. The SEC Internet Enforcement Office, created in 1998, deals exclusively with fraud conducted over the Internet. Common securities fraud techniques involving the Internet include microcap fraud, false promises of imminent IPOs, baseless financial projections, false track records, inflated performance claims, and fake testimonials.[31]

With so many online fraud schemes, one approach is to focus on preventing and avoiding fraud. President Obama established the Financial Fraud Enforcement Task Force in November 2009 to hold accountable those who helped bring about the last financial crisis as well as those who would attempt to take advantage of the efforts at economic recovery. The Financial Fraud Enforcement Task Force maintains a wide list of resources and information dedicated to helping find and report suspected cases of financial fraud. For more information about the Financial Fraud Enforcement Task Force and tips for avoiding fraud, visit the task force website at www.stopfraud.gov. While fraudulent activities involving the Internet cannot be completely prevented, individuals and companies can educate themselves to avoid online scams. The axiom "if it sounds too good to be true, it probably is" certainly applies to online activities and individuals and companies should use sound judgment to avoid becoming the victims of fraud.

Interference with Contractual Relations

Another potential economic tort involving the Internet is tortious interference with contractual relations. A claim for tortious interference with contractual relations may also involve claims for defamation and trademark infringement.

Tortious interference with contractual relations is a third party's intentional inducement of a contracting party to break a contract, causing damage to the relationship between the contracting parties. Tortious interference with contractual relations is sometimes called tortious interference, unlawful interference with contractual relations, interference with a contractual relationship, interference with contract, inducement of breach of contract, procurement of breach of contract, or tortious interference with business relationships.

Since tortious interference is a state action, there are some variations among the states. The basic elements of tortious interference are essentially the same in every jurisdiction. To make a prima facie case for tortious interference with contractual relations, the plaintiff must prove (1) the existence of a business relationship under which the claimant has rights; (2) the defendant's knowledge of the relationship; (3) an intentional and unjustified interference with the relationship; (4) by a third party; and (5) damage to the claimant caused by the interference. Some jurisdictions also require that the interference actually result in a termination or breach of the contract.

In *Indiaweekly.com, LLC v. Nehaflix.com, Inc.*, 596 F. Supp. 2d 497 (D. Conn. 2009), a federal court judge in Connecticut held that the plaintiff sufficiently stated a claim for tortious interference of contractual relations to survive a motion to dismiss involving two competing businesses that sold videos online. The court held that under Connecticut law, the complaint alleged that the competing online video seller deprived the plaintiff of the benefit of its agreement to place its logos on DVDs. The actual loss was money paid for the frustrated advertising and the loss of goodwill the advertisement would have brought.

Tortious interference with contractual relations might also be a possible cause of action with ad-blocking software. Internet advertising and the use of software that blocks Internet advertisements is becoming more effective and experiencing wider distribution. Although no known cases have been filed, tortious interference with contractual relations could potentially be used with ad-blocking software. Tortious interference with contractual relations, still in a formative stage, is a possible theory of recovery involving the Internet.

Interference with Prospective Economic Relations

Tortious interference with prospective economic relations is another potential economic tort in the online environment. Tortious interference with prospective advantage is intentional, damaging intrusion on another's potential business relationship, such as the opportunity of obtaining customers or employment. Some courts also call this tort interference with a business relationship, tortious interference with a business advantage, or tortious interference with prospective advantage.

In order to recover damages, the plaintiff must prove (1) that the defendant intentionally interfered with the plaintiff's existing or potential economic relations; (2) for an improper purpose or by improper means; and (3) causing injury to the plaintiff.[32]

The Utah Supreme Court considered a tortious interference with prospective economic advantage case involving the online retailer Overstock.com in 2008. In *Overstock.com, Inc. v. SmartBargains, Inc.*, 192 P.3d 858 (Utah 2008), Overstock.com sued a competitor for violation of the 2004 Utah Spyware Control Act, common-law unfair competition, and tortious interference with prospective economic advantage, complaining that pop-up advertisements of a competitor unlawfully appeared when customers accessed the online store's website. The Utah Supreme Court held that the pop-up advertisements did not present an improper purpose or an improper means, and thus the online retailer failed to satisfy the "improper purpose or by improper means" element to recover damages in the tortious interference with prospective economic advantage case.

Finding the true identity of potential defendants can also be a challenge in a tortious interference with prospective economic relations case. In *Solers, Inc. v. Doe*, 977 A.2d 941 (D.C. 2009), a software developer brought suit against a "John Doe" defendant, alleging defamation and tortious interference with prospective advantageous business opportunities based on an anonymous Internet report to a trade association that claimed the developer was using unlicensed software. The plaintiff subpoenaed the trade association to compel disclosure of the defendant's identity, but the D.C. Court of Appeals ruled that the First Amendment right to anonymous Internet speech warranted application of a rigorous five-part discoverability test before the defendant's true identity could be discovered.

While challenges may exist for plaintiffs in a tortious interference with prospective economic relations case, these hurdles can be overcome in the right case. For plaintiffs that have suffered injuries, tortious interference with prospective economic relations is another arrow in the quiver of tort law. The economic torts of fraud, negligent misrepresentation, tortious interference with contractual relations, and tortious interference with prospective economic relations are potential theories of recovery for individuals and companies that have suffered online attacks.

STRICT LIABILITY

Strict liability is another potential tort to consider in the online marketplace, especially for online sellers. Strict liability is defined as liability that does not depend on actual negligence or intent to harm, but on the breach of an absolute duty to make something safe.[33] Strict liability most often applies either to ultrahazardous activities or in products liability cases.

Examples of strict liability for ultrahazardous activities include roadway blasting, the use of atomic energy, the manufacture and storage of explosives, the operation of oil and gas wells, the operation of high voltage power lines, and the use of large storage tanks for flammable materials.[34]

While strict liability for ultrahazardous activities is probably not a major concern for most companies that have an online presence, products liability should foster some attention for online sellers. A products liability claim may be brought under several theories, including strict liability, breach of warranty, and negligence. A plaintiff is allowed to submit multiple theories of products liability, so long as the plaintiff meets the requirements for each theory. A seller or manufacturer is strictly liable in tort when an article he or she places on the market, knowing that the article is to be used without inspection for defects.[35] The purpose of imposing strict liability is to insure that the costs of injuries resulting from defective products are borne by the manufacturers who put such products on the market, rather than by the injured persons, who are powerless to protect themselves.

The Restatement Third, Torts: Products Liability recognizes three distinct categories of product defects for strict products liability: (1) manufacturing defects; (2) design defects; and (3) inadequate instructions or warnings defects.

A retailer, including an online retailer, who sells a product in a defective condition, may be held liable in a products liability action. Furthermore, a retailer, along with others engaged in distributing a defective product, may be held strictly liable for personal injuries caused by the product's defects, even though the retailer has no control as to hidden or latent defects such as where the product is prepackaged.

Although liability under strict products liability for online sellers is uncommon, the possibility for liability exists. Based on an empirical study involving successful Internet cases decided between January 1, 1992, and July 1, 2004, only one company was forced by a court to make any restitution for the sale of defective goods on its website.[36] The sole successful products liability action involved the online sale of a field-monitoring device for tracking criminals under house arrest in *Kirby v. B.I. Inc.*, No. CIV.A.4:98-CV-1136-Y, 2003 U.S. Dist. LEXIS 16964, at *49-50 (N.D. Tex. Sept. 26, 2003). The manufacturer's website advertised that its field-monitoring unit in the offender's home would detect any tampering. However, when a murderer cut off the ankle device, he was out of range of the monitoring unit, so the home unit did not detect the tampering. The victim's estate successfully brought an action for misrepresentation based on false statements about the field-monitoring unit on the company's website. Strict liability for misrepresentations are based on a misrepresentation of a material fact concerning the character or quality of the product sold that is made to the public by one that is engaged in the business of selling the product. The fact misrepresented must be a material fact.[37] If a consumer justifiably relies on the misrepresentation and suffers physical harm by reason of the fact misrepresented, strict liability may be imposed.

A number of cases involving strict products liability for online sellers question whether there are sufficient contacts to maintain jurisdiction. Maintaining a website by a manufacturer or other defendant in a products liability case can be a factor when determining whether the defendant has purposefully availed itself of the privileges of doing business in the forum state.[38] Personal jurisdiction in cases involving interactive websites is determined by the degree of interaction. In *Matthews v. Brookstone Stores, Inc.*, 469 F. Supp. 2d 1056 (S.D. Ala. 2007), a nonresident distributor's establishment of a purely passive website to provide information about products does not provide the basis for establishing personal jurisdiction in a products liability suit. On the other hand, the U.S. Supreme Court has held that maintaining corporate employees or agents in the state to conduct corporate activities establishes sufficient "minimum contacts" under the Due Process Clause to establish personal jurisdiction in state courts.[39]

Online companies that sell defective products and put those products into the stream of commerce can potentially face lawsuits for products liability and should take measures to limit their liability such as providing warnings on packages.

REMEDIES IN TORT CASES

A remedy is anything a court can do for a litigant who has been wronged or is about to be wronged.[40] The two most common remedies are money damages (legal remedies) and injunctions (equitable remedies). An injunction is a court order commanding or preventing an action by the defendant. Monetary damages, including compensatory damages, are generally available in tort cases, including Internet tort cases. Compensatory damages in tort cases generally include reimbursement for monetary loss as well as damages for intangible elements of injury such as pain and suffering, emotional distress, and humiliation.

To obtain an injunction, the plaintiff must show that monetary damages are insufficient and that an irreparable injury will result unless an injunction is granted. A court may issue an injunction to take down a website or to remove specific content from a website. In *Bosley v. Wildwett.com*, 310 F. Supp. 2d 914 (N.D. Ohio 2004), a court issued a preliminary injunction against a website that displayed a video of a local television news anchor participating in a wet T-shirt contest. The video and images were posted on the Internet and due to the controversy, the news anchor resigned from her position. In awarding the injunction, the court held that the news anchor established a likelihood of success on the merits of her claim that her rights of privacy and publicity were violated.

Unlike breach of contract cases, in tort cases the plaintiff may recover punitive damages. Punitive damages may be awarded in addition to actual damages if the defendant acted with recklessness, malice, or deceit. Punitive damages are assessed to punish the wrongdoer or to deter wrongful conduct. Punitive damages are also called exemplary damages. The U.S. Supreme Court has held that three guidelines help determine whether a punitive-damages award violates constitutional due process: (1) the reprehensibility of the conduct being punished; (2) the reasonableness of the relationship between the harm and the award; and (3) the difference between the award and the civil penalties authorized in comparable cases.[41]

Punitive damages are rarely awarded in Internet cases. When punitive damages are awarded, they are generally proportional to compensatory damages. Punitive damage awards are also frequently reduced on appeal. The lack of effectiveness in awarding punitive damage awards in Internet cases is based in part on the difficulties in obtaining personal jurisdiction, choice of law and choice of forum clauses in the terms of service agreements, and immunity provision in the Communications Decency Act (CDA).[42]

DEFENSES IN INTERNET TORT CASES

Defendants in Internet tort cases may assert a variety of defenses, such as lack of jurisdiction, consent, the "Good Samaritan" provision under the **Communications Decency Act (CDA)**, sovereign immunity, the First Amendment, and the statute of limitations.

Communications Decency Act (CDA)
A federal law aimed at combating child pornography. In *Reno v. American Civil Liberties Union*, 521 U.S. 844 (1997), the U.S. Supreme Court struck down those portions of the act as unconstitutional, but provisions banning transmission of obscene speech to minors, remain in effect. 47 U.S.C. § 223.

Jurisdiction

Because of the anonymous nature of the Internet, identifying the true identity of a person who posts content on the Internet may be challenging. Even if a victim in a potential tort case is able to discover the true identity of a potential defendant, courts may hold that there are not sufficient contacts to establish personal jurisdiction over a particular defendant. Jurisdictional issues, discussed in greater detail in Chapter 1, create challenges for plaintiffs in tort cases involving the Internet.

Consent

Consent is a defense in most tort cases. In fact, consent is an absolute defense to the tort of invasion of privacy. Consent is agreement, approval, or permission as to some act or purpose, given voluntarily by a competent person. Consent is often implied rather than expressed. Consent may be implied from custom, local or general, from usage or from the conduct of the parties, or some relationship between them. For example, an employer that institutes a computer use policy for employees may use the policy as a defense in a potential claim for invasion of privacy brought by the employee. In *TBG Ins. Services Corp v. Superior Court*, 117 Cal. Rptr. 2d 155, 161 (Cal. Ct. App. 2002), a California court held that an employer's written electronic and computer use policy gave advance notice to the employee and the employee's written consent to the policy defeated the employee's claim to a reasonable expectation of privacy. Companies should adopt an Internet and computer use policy for employees and notify employees of this policy to protect themselves from possible invasion of privacy tort actions brought by employees.

Communications Decency Act

Section 230 of the federal Communications Decency Act (CDA), codified in 47 U.S.C. § 230, grants broad immunity to providers of "interactive computer services" (website owners and Internet service providers) for tort claims from liability arising out of their publication of user-generated content. The so-called Good Samaritan provision under section 230 of the CDA states that "[n]o provider or user of an interactive computer service shall be treated as the publisher or speaker of any information provided by another information content provider" and that "[n]o cause of action may be brought and no liability may be imposed under any State or local law that is inconsistent with this section." For example, in *Carafano v. Metrosplash.com, Inc.*, 339 F.3d 1119, 1123–24 (9th Cir. 2003), the Ninth Circuit held that a web-based dating-service provider was not liable when an unidentified party posted a false online personal profile for a popular actress, causing her to receive sexually explicit phone calls, letters, and faxes at her home.

Section 230 of the Communications Decency Act also prevents the website owner from being held liable for removing or blocking access to material it considers harmful. In the face of section 230 immunity, a claim against a website owner will survive only if the plaintiff can show that the website owner was personally involved in creating or developing the allegedly illegal content. The immunity provision under section 230 of the Communications Decency Act is discussed in greater detail in Chapter 9 on defamation.

Sovereign Immunity

In tort cases filed against federal, state, or local governments, sovereign immunity applies. The United States, as a sovereign country, is immune from suit unless it consents to be sued. The Federal Tort Claims Act (FTCA), codified in 28 U.S.C. §§ 1346(b), 2679(a), is a limited waiver of sovereign immunity, and the exclusive remedy for tort claims brought against the United States for money damages for tort claims arising from wrongful acts or omissions of federal employees while acting within the scope of their employment or office.

Common-law tort claims require a showing of culpability on the part of the government, which is often extremely difficult for plaintiffs to establish. Governmental entities and their employees are likely to be shielded from liability for tort actions by the FTCA or equivalent state tort claims acts, as long as the challenged act or omission relates to a discretionary function.

In *Doe v. United States*, 83 F. Supp. 2d 833 (S.D. Tex. 2000), various temporary labor companies, who were falsely identified in a government news release posted on a government website that the labor companies had been indicted by a federal grand jury on charges of mail fraud and money laundering, filed a tort action against the U.S. government. The court granted the government's motion to dismiss finding that the allegations did not state a cause of action under Texas law for invasion of privacy by publication of private facts. Indeed, it is exceptionally difficult for plaintiffs to succeed in a federal tort claims proceeding against the U.S. Government. Similarly, many tort actions against state and local governments are also unsuccessful.

First Amendment Freedom of Speech

As seen in the cases involving online fantasy sports, the First Amendment may be a valid affirmative defense in tort cases. Courts must balance First Amendment rights with individual rights such as the right of privacy or the right of publicity. In *C.B.C. Distribution and Marketing, Inc. v. Major League Baseball Advanced Media, L.P.*, 505 F.3d 818 (8th Cir. 2007), the court held that the First Amendment speech rights of a company that sold fantasy sports products via the Internet to use professional baseball players' names and statistical information took precedence over the publicity rights of the players. The First Amendment may be used by other individuals and companies as a defense in tort cases involving the Internet.

Statute of Limitations

Passage of time and the statute of limitations is another potential affirmative defense in Internet tort cases. Since tort actions are based on state law claims, the time period for filing a complaint depends upon the type of injury asserted and state law. The time period generally begins to run when the plaintiff suffers an injury, or in the case of latent injuries, until the plaintiff discovers, or should have discovered, that an injury has occurred. In tort cases, the statute of limitations period is typically two years.

Summary

Torts are civil wrongs recognized by law as grounds for a lawsuit. The term "cybertort" is defined as a cause of action that exists due to harmful Internet contact. Basically, any tort action that involves the Internet can be considered a cybertort. There are a variety of different torts available for injuries related to the Internet including invasion of privacy, intentional and emotional infliction of emotional distress, defamation, economic torts, and strict liability. The tort of invasion of privacy encompasses four causes of action: (1) unreasonable intrusion upon the seclusion of another; (2) misappropriation of a person's name or likeness; (3) public disclosure of private facts; or (4) publicity that unreasonably places the other in a false light before the public. Cyberbullying and cyberstalking, where persons post harmful comments about another person on a website or in another form of electronic communication, can lead to potential tort liability for intentional and negligent infliction of emotional distress. Intentional infliction requires that the defendant's behavior be extreme and outrageous, whereas negligent infliction requires only that the defendant's conduct be unreasonable and create an unreasonable risk of foreseeable harm. Potential economic torts in the online environment include fraud, negligent misrepresentation, interference with contractual relations, and interference with prospective economic relations. Both money damages and injunctive relief are potential remedies in Internet tort cases. Punitive damages may also be awarded if the defendant acted with recklessness, malice, or deceit. Lack of jurisdiction, consent, the Good Samaritan provision under the Communications Decency Act (CDA), sovereign immunity, the First Amendment, and the statute of limitations are among potential defenses in Internet tort cases.

Key Terms

Communications Decency Act (CDA) *152*
cyberbullying *146*
cyberstalking *146*
cybertort *138*
economic tort *147*
false light *142*
Intentional Infliction of Emotional Distress (IIED) *145*
invasion of privacy *138*
negligence *137*
negligent infliction of emotional distress *146*
right of publicity *139*
strict liability *137*
tort *137*
tortfeasor *137*

Review Questions

1. What is a cybertort?
2. What are the four types of invasion of privacy?
3. Which torts are available to a celebrity whose name and likeness are used in an unauthorized endorsement on a website?
4. What are the elements for the tort of intentional infliction of emotional distress?
5. What is the difference between negligent infliction of emotional distress and intentional infliction of emotional distress?
6. What are the possible economic torts available to individuals and companies for injuries sustained in the online environment?
7. Why should an online seller be concerned with strict products liability?
8. What are the potential remedies available in Internet tort cases?
9. When should punitive damages be awarded in a case for intentional infliction of emotional distress involving harmful content on the Internet?
10. What are the potential affirmative defenses in Internet tort cases?

Discussion Questions

1. Run a search on the Internet and find the website for the Facebook Privacy Policy. After reading the Facebook Privacy Policy, summarize the policy in your own words. If you have a Facebook account, discuss how you control your privacy settings. What information and content do you not post on Facebook?
2. The TRUSTe certification mark certifies that participating e-commerce companies employ adequate privacy protections for consumer data and is awarded based on compliance with a set of "reasonable privacy practices." Companies are allowed to self-certify compliance and display the TRUSTe certification mark on their website after payment of a fee. One survey purported to show that websites displaying the TRUSTe mark were 50 percent more likely to violate privacy norms than those that did not. One commentator notes that consumers have reached the conclusion that trustmarks did not sufficiently monitor, enforce, or inform about, the promises they were intended to enforce. See Gary E. Marchant, Douglas J. Sylvester, and Kenneth W. Abbott, *A New Soft Law Approach to Nanotechnology Oversight: A Voluntary Product Certification Scheme*, 28 UCLA J. Envtl. L. & Pol'y 123, 145 (2010). What are the advantages and disadvantages of self-certification programs, such as the TRUSTe certification program, over civil torts actions in dealing with online privacy issues?
3. On October 31, 2006 (Halloween night), California Highway Patrol (CHP) officers placed accident scene images of Nikki Catsouras' corpse on the Internet for the lurid titillation of persons unrelated to official CHP business. The images were disseminated via e-mail for shock value and forwarded to thousands of Internet users resulting in serious emotional distress to family members of the deceased. The family then sued the CHP for invasion of privacy, intentional infliction of emotional distress, and negligence. (See *Catsoura s v. Department of California Highway Patrol*, 181 Cal. App. 4th 856, 104 Cal. Rptr. 3d 352 (4th Dist. 2010).) If you were a juror on the case, how would you decide? Should the family also be entitled to punitive damages for outrageous conduct? Explain.

Exercises

1. John, an at-will employee, works as a custodian at a private high school. After work one day, John visits an exotic dance club. At the dance club, John's photograph is taken where he is sitting next to the star of a prime-time television show. In the photograph, both John and the celebrity appear intoxicated at the dance club with a female dancer. The photographer sells the photograph to a celebrity tabloid website, and the photo is posted on the Internet. The principal of the high school where John works sees the photograph of John on the celebrity tabloid website and then fires John for violating the school's personal conduct policy. John finds another custodian job two months later. What tort actions, if any, could John potentially file? Who are the potential defendants? What would be John's damages in a civil tort action?
2. Troy Vargas, president and CEO of Acme Corp. (a fictitious company), sends a company-wide e-mail to all employees that he has fired Jane Anderson, a senior vice president. In the e-mail, Troy Vargas discloses that Jane is a lesbian. Anderson files a civil action against Vargas and Acme Corp. What tort actions, if any, could Jan potentially file? What damages would Jane be able to recover? See *Borquez v. Robert C. Ozer, P.C.*, 923 P.2d 166 (Colo. Ct. App. 1995) (employer disclosed to other employees that plaintiff was homosexual).

3. John, a seventeen-year-old high school student, is teased online by a group of female cheerleaders from his high school for being short. When the boy mentions thoughts of suicide, the cheerleaders encourage John to take his own life by posting comments on John's Facebook account using computers in the school library. John then sends a text message that says, "After I kill myself, maybe you will respect me." The next day, John kills himself with a shotgun. John's parents sue the cheerleaders, the cheerleaders' parents, the school, and school officials for wrongful death and intentional infliction of emotional distress. How would a court decide on a claim for intentional infliction of emotional distress?
4. You are working as a project manager for ABC LLC, a new limited liability company (LLC) that currently has fifteen employees. The owner of the company, Fred Liddle, tells you that a company employee has been fired for sending harassing e-mails to another company employee. Since ABC LLC is a new company, there is no existing company e-mail policy. Conduct research on the Internet and find a sample company e-mail policy that you think is appropriate. Then write a memorandum to Fred Liddle explaining why the company should adopt a company e-mail policy and how the policy could limit the company's potential tort liability. To begin your research, consider running a search on Google, Yahoo!, or another Internet search engine for "sample internet and e-mail policy" or something similar.
5. The widow of a company manager killed in a terrorist attacks receives a call and e-mail from her husband's employer informing her that her husband is among those "accounted for" as having escaped the terrorist attack. A website maintained by the company also lists the manager as among the survivors, but several days after the initial call and e-mail, a representative called again and informed the widow that there had been a mistake, and that the widow's husband was missing. How would a court rule in a case for intentional infliction of emotional distress brought by the widow? See *Greene-Wotton v. Fiduciary Trust Co. Intern.*, 324 F. Supp. 2d 385 (S.D. N.Y. 2003).

Related Internet Sites

http://cyber.law.harvard.edu/privacy/module2.html
Privacy in Cyberspace Tutorial provided by the Berkman Center for Internet & Society at Harvard Law School

http://lawprofessors.typepad.com/tortsprof/
Law Professor Tort Law Blog

http://www.lexisnexis.com/lawschool/study/outlines/html/torts/index.asp
LexisNexis Capsule Summary on Torts

http://www.dayontorts.com/
Daily Tort Law Blog

http://caselaw.findlaw.com/summary/
FindLaw Case Summaries (look under the topics for "Cyberspace Law" and "Injury And Tort Law")

http://www.law.cornell.edu/uscode/
Text of the Federal Tort Claims Act in the United States Code (Go to Title 28 >Part VI >Chapter 171)

http://www.stopfraud.gov/
Financial Fraud Enforcement Task Force website

End Notes

1. *Olmstead v. United States*, 277 U.S. 438, 478 (1928) (Brandeis, J., dissenting).
2. Barbara De Lollis, *ESPN's Erin Andrews Files Suit Against Marriott, Radisson and Stalker, USA Today*, July 15, 2010, available at http://travel.usatoday.com/hotels/post/2010/07/espns-erin-andrews-files-suit-against-marriott-radisson-and-stalker/100089/1#uslPageReturn/.
3. Complaint, *Andrews v. Marriott Int'l, Inc.*, et. al., No. 2010-L-008186 (Ill. Cir. Cook Co. July 15, 2010), available at http://www.usatoday.com/travel/pdf/erinandrewscivilsuit.pdf/.
4. Anna C. Mastroianni, *Liability, Regulation and Policy in Surgical Innovation: The Cutting Edge of Research and Therapy*, 16 HEALTH MATRIX 351 (2006) (citing Robert E. Keeton et al., Tort and Accident Law: Cases and Materials 1 (3d ed. 1998)).
5. Merriam-Webster's Online Dictionary, available at http://www.merriam-webster.com/dictionary/torte (last visited Feb. 4, 2011).
6. Legal Information Institute, Tort Law: An Overview, available at http://topics.law.cornell.edu/wex/tort/.
7. Black's Law Dictionary (9th ed. 2009).
8. Bradley Kay, *Extending Tort Liability to Creators of Fake Profiles on Social Networking Websites*, 10 CHI.-KENT J. INTELL. PROP. 1, 14 (2010).
9. Daniel P. Schafer, *Canada's Approach to Jurisdiction over Cybertorts: Braintech v. Kostiuk*, 23 FORDHAM INT'L L.J. 1186, 1190 n.28 (2000) (citing Rosalind Resnick, *Cybertort: The New Era*, Nat'l L.J., July 18, 1994, at A1).
10. Michael L. Rustad and Thomas H. Koenig, *Rebooting Cybertort Law*, 80 Wash. L. Rev. 335, 358 (2005).
11. See *Huggins v. Boyd*, 304 Ga. App. 563, 697 S.E.2d 253 (Ga. Ct. App. 2010).

12. Geoffrey Christopher Rapp, *Defense against Outrage and the Perils of Parasitic Torts*, 45 Ga. L. Rev. 107, 199–200 (2010).
13. Restatement (Second) of Torts § 652A.
14. 62A Am. Jur. 2d Privacy §§ 32–4.
15. Jessica K. Baranko, *It's My Name and Mine Alone: How Chad Ocho Cinco Affects the Right of Publicity*, 20 MARQ. SPORTS L. REV. 463, 465 (2010).
16. Sarah Arnquist, *With Resveratrol, Buyer Beware*, N.Y. Times, Aug. 18, 2009, at D4.
17. Christopher J. Robinette, *The Prosser Notebook: Classroom as Biography and Intellectual History*, 2010 U. Ill. L. Rev. 577, 583–85 (2010) (citing Craig Joyce, *Keepers of the Flame: Prosser and Keeton on the Law of Torts (Fifth Edition) and the Prosser Legacy*, 39 Vand. L. Rev. 851, 852 (1986) (book review); T.R. Reid, *The Liability Crisis: Litigation Loosens the Stiff Upper Lip*, Washington Post, Feb. 24, 1986, at A1).
18. 62A Am. Jur. 2d Privacy § 92.
19. Erwin Chemerinsky, *Tucker Lecture, Law and Medium Symposium*, 66 Wash. & Lee L. Rev. 1449, 1453–54 (2009).
20. See Moira McDonough, *Internet Disclosures of a Rape Accuser's Identity*, 3 VA. SPORTS & ENT. L. J. 284, 297 (2004).
21. Claims for Vicarious and Individual Liability for Infliction of Emotional Distress Derived from Use of Internet and Electronic Communications, 30 A.L.R.6th 241 (2008).
22. Ira Mark Ellman and Stephen D. Sugarman, *Spousal Emotional Abuse as a Tort?*, 55 Md. L. Rev. 1268, 1299 (1996).
23. Electronic Aggression/Cyberbullying, FindYouth Info.gov, available at http://www.findyouthinfo.gov/spotlight_cyberBullying.shtml/.
24. Kristopher Accardi, Comment, *Is Violating an Internet Service Provider's Terms of Service an Example of Computer Fraud and Abuse? An Analytical Look at the Computer Fraud and Abuse Act, Lori Drew's Conviction and Cyberbullying*, 37 W. ST. U. L. REV. 67 (2009).
25. *J.S. v. Bethlehem Area School District*, 807 A.2d 847 (Pa. 2002); Kathryn Balint, *Personal Fouls: Students Get Rude and Crude with Internet Slambooks*, SAN DIEGO UNION-TRIB., Nov. 3, 2001, at El.
26. Richard A. Posner, *Common-Law Economic Torts: An Economic and Legal Analysis*, 48 ARIZ. L. REV. 735, 745–47 (2006).
27. 37 Am. Jur. 2d Fraud and Deceit § 475.
28. *Anthony, et al. v. Yahoo!, Inc.* Settlement, available at http://www.anthonysettlement.com/.
29. Wailin Wong, *Connecting Hearts Online: Web-based Dating Services Shed Stigma, Pierce Mainstream*, CHICAGO TRIBUNE, July 23, 2010, at 2010 WLNR 14697929.
30. 37 C.J.S. Fraud § 77.
31. Palmer T. Heenan, Jessica L. Klarfeld, Michael Angelo Roussis, and Jessica K. Wash, *Securities Fraud*, 47 AM. CRIM. L. REV. 1015, 1084–85 (2010).
32. Andrew Saluke, *Ad-Blocking Software as Third-Party Tortious Interference with Advertising Contracts*, 7 FLA. ST. U. BUS. REV. 87, 99, note 87 (2008).
33. Black's Law Dictionary (9th ed. 2009).
34. Colin K. Kelly, Note, *Hamilton v. Accu-Tek: Collective Liability for Handgun Manufacturers in the Criminal Misuse of Handguns*, 103 W. VA. L. REV. 81, note 44 (2000).
35. 63 Am. Jur. 2d Products Liability § 91.
36. Michael L. Rustad and Thomas H. Koenig, *Rebooting Cybertort Law*, 80 WASH. L. REV. 335, 359 (2005).
37. 63A Am. Jur. 2d Products Liability § 849.
38. 63B Am. Jur. 2d Products Liability § 1538.
39. See *Int'l Shoe Co. v. Washington*, 326 U.S. 310 (1945).
40. Black's Law Dictionary (9th ed. 2009).
41. *BMW of North America, Inc. v. Gore*, 517 U.S. 559 (1996).
42. Alvin C. Harrell and Kurt Eggert, *Chapman University Presents Consumer Law Symposium on Responsibility and Reform*, 58 CONSUMER FIN. L. Q. REP. 214, 215 (2004).

CHAPTER

9 Regulating Online Speech

Congress shall make no law respecting an establishment of religion, or prohibiting the free exercise thereof; or abridging the freedom of speech, or of the press; or the right of the people peaceably to assemble, and to petition the government for a redress of grievances.

First Amendment to the United States Constitution

LEARNING OBJECTIVES

After completing this chapter, you will be able to:

1. Explain the scope of the First Amendment freedom of speech and the press in the Internet age.
2. Define libel, slander, and defamation.
3. Discuss the elements in a defamation action involving online speech.
4. Identify and explain the defenses in an online defamation case, including the immunity provision in Section 230 of the Communications Decency Act.
5. Describe the issues involving criminal prosecution for online speech.
6. Explain the elements of business disparagement in the online environment.

OPENING SCENARIO AND OVERVIEW

Sarah Jones, a high school teacher and a cheerleader for the Cincinnati Bengals professional football team, won a judgment in August 2010 in an online defamation suit for $11 million against Dirty World Entertainment Recordings, LLC, which runs the website www.thedirty.com. Jones claimed that the defendant, who operates an interactive website, caused injury to her reputation based on certain harmful statements posted on the defendant's website.[1] The court entered a default judgment after the defendant failed to respond to the lawsuit, In January 2011, the court denied the defendant's motion to dismiss the case based on lack of personal jurisdiction. Jones, however, has yet to collect on the $11 million judgment.

In another high profile case, a federal appeals court affirmed an $11.3 million verdict against a Florida woman in 2006 stemming from defamatory statements posted on an online bulletin board.[2] The plaintiff failed to collect any money from the $11.3 million verdict and ultimately lost money pursuing the case because the blogger was effectively judgment-proof due to the blogger's lack of financial resources.

As illustrated by these two cases, the possibility of liability and damages with online defamation exists, but collecting and enforcing a judgment against a website owner or blogger can be challenging. Defamation via the Internet is a growing concern, especially as Google and other search engines become more effective at retrieving information about people. To compound the problem, defendants have a number of possible defenses in online defamation actions, such as the First Amendment and the immunity provision in § 230 of the Communications Decency Act (47 U.S.C. § 230).

This chapter focuses on the issues involved associated with online speech, including First Amendment considerations, civil liability and defenses involving alleged defamatory statements made online, criminal defamation, and business disparagement.

FIRST AMENDMENT FREEDOMS OF SPEECH AND PRESS

The **First Amendment** to the U.S. Constitution provides: "Congress shall make no law respecting an establishment of religion, or prohibiting the free exercise thereof; or abridging the freedom of speech, or of the press; or the right of the people peaceably to assemble and to petition the Government for a redress of grievances."[3] The First Amendment was adopted to curtail the power of Congress to interfere with an individual's freedom to express himself or herself in accordance with the dictates of his or her own conscience.[4]

First Amendment The constitutional amendment, ratified with the Bill of Rights in 1791, guaranteeing the freedoms of speech, religion, press, assembly, and petition.

The First Amendment originally applied just to the federal government and did not apply to state governments. With the adoption of the Fourteenth Amendment, the First Amendment guarantees of speech and press now apply not just to the federal government, but also to state and local governments.[5]

The U.S. Constitution, and specifically the First Amendment, applies only to government conduct and does not govern private conduct. Application of the U.S. Constitution to government actions is called the "state action" or "state actor" requirement under constitutional law.[6] The First Amendment does not regulate the conduct of private parties.[7] A party may not, therefore, allege a constitutional violation without alleging the conduct of a state actor.

Under the power of judicial review, federal courts can declare that acts of Congress and state legislatures, decisions of state and federal courts, and acts of the president are unconstitutional. With judicial review, courts may find that legislation passed by Congress violates the First Amendment **Speech Clause** under the First Amendment that Congress shall make no law "abridging the freedom of speech." Application of the Free Speech Clause tends to be case-specific, with each type of government regulation receiving a level of scrutiny appropriately tailored to the specific type of speech and the context in which that speech operates.[8]

Speech Clause The First Amendment provision that "Congress shall make no law . . . abridging the freedom of speech."

Vagueness or Overbreadth

Courts may find that legislation violates the U.S. Constitution based on either vagueness or overbreadth. A law or regulation is "void for vagueness" under the First Amendment if its prohibitions are not clearly defined and if does not give the person of ordinary intelligence a reasonable opportunity to know what is prohibited.[9] Under the overbreadth doctrine, a plaintiff may challenge an overbroad statute or regulation by showing that it may inhibit the First Amendment rights of parties not before the court, even if their own conduct is not protected.[10] For example, in *Reno v. ACLU*, 521 U.S. 844, 874–81 (1997), the U.S. Supreme Court held that that certain portions of the federal Communications Decency Act of 1996 (CDA), 47 U.S.C. § 223, violated the First Amendment based on the overbreadth doctrine because in trying to prevent minors from receiving certain sexual content via the Internet, the legislation interfered with communications that would only reach adults. Legislation that is overbroad can suppress or chill protected speech. The U.S. Supreme Court supported the proposition that the First Amendment applies to speech on the Internet.[11] Courts may declare a vague or overbroad statute as unconstitutional in violation of the First Amendment.

Unprotected Speech

While speech is generally protected by the First Amendment, some types of speech are not protected. Examples of unprotected speech include obscenity, fighting words, defamation, child pornography, perjury, blackmail, incitement to imminent lawless action, true threats, and solicitations to commit crimes.[12] The right of free speech is not absolute at all times.

In *Miller v. California*, 413 U.S. 15, 24 (1973), the U.S. Supreme Court established a three-part test for determining whether material is "obscene" and therefore falls outside the scope of First Amendment protections. The *Miller* test questions (a) whether the average person, applying contemporary community standards would find that the work, taken as a whole, appeals to the prurient interest; (b) whether the work depicts or describes, in a patently offensive way, sexual conduct specifically defined by the applicable state law; and (c) whether the work, taken as a whole, lacks serious literary, artistic, political, or scientific value. If the court regards the material as obscene, then no First Amendment protection applies. A common situation arises when a person is convicted to online distribution of obscene materials. For example, in *United States v. Little*, 365 Fed. Appx. 159 (11th Cir. 2011), a federal appeals court held that the U.S. District Court did not err in applying the *Miller* standard for determining obscenity, with respect to defendants' prosecution for online distribution of obscene materials, since the "local community" standard was applicable to Internet-based as well as print materials. Like obscenity in the material world, the government may regulate obscenity transmitted online without violating the First Amendment. Obscenity and child pornography are covered in greater detail in Chapter 7 in the discussion on cybercrimes.

True threats are another area of unprotected speech. For example, the court in *United States v. Sutcliffe*, 505 F.3d 944 (9th Cir. 2007), held that the defendant's statements on his website explicitly threatening certain named individuals with bodily harm were "true threats" falling outside of First Amendment speech protections, where the statements were made in the context of a labor dispute after the defendant was fired by his employer. Similarly, in *Myers v. Loudoun County School Bd.*, 500 F. Supp. 2d 539 (E.D. Va. 2007), the court held that school authorities could decline, on grounds of vulgarity and consistent with the First Amendment, to accept a proposed advertisement in a school athletic program referring readers to Internet websites named, "www.CivilReligionSucks.com," or "www.CivilReligionSux.com."

A website that incites others to violate the law is also not protected speech. In *United States v. Rivera*, 92 A.F.T.R.2d 2003-6844, 2003 WL 22429482 (C.D. Cal. July 18, 2003), the court found that the defendant maintained a website that sold abusive tax scheme promotional materials in violation of the Internal Revenue Code, and ordered that the defendant to remove from the website all false commercial speech designed to incite others to violate the law.

If the speech involves obscenity, fighting words, defamation, child pornography, perjury, blackmail, incitement to imminent lawless action, true threats, and solicitations to commit crimes, then the speech receives no protection under the First Amendment.

Commercial Speech

Commercial speech is entitled to limited protection under the First Amendment, but the protection afforded to commercial speech is somewhat less than the protection afforded to other forms of noncommercial speech. Only truthful advertising related to lawful activities is entitled to the protection of the First Amendment.[13] In order for commercial speech to be entitled to any First Amendment protection, the speech must first concern a lawful activity and must not be misleading. False or misleading commercial speech receives no protection under the First Amendment. For example, the U.S. Court of Appeals for the Second Circuit held in *Alexander v. Cahill*, 598 F.3d 79 (2nd Cir. 2010), that a New York rule establishing a 30-day moratorium on attorney advertising and solicitations, including Internet solicitations, was narrowly tailored under the First Amendment to further state interest in protecting privacy and tranquility of personal injury victims and their loved ones.

Expressive Conduct

The First Amendment affords protection to expressive conduct as well as actual speech. For conduct to be considered protected speech, a person must have the intent to convey a particularized message in circumstances where it is likely that the message would be understood. To determine whether conduct is speech, one must look at the conduct that actually occurred and the context in which it occurred.

In *Junger v. Daley*, 209 F.3d 481 (6th Cir. 2000), the court held that since computer source code is an expressive means for the exchange of information and ideas about computer programming, it is protected by the First Amendment. In *Butler v. Adoption Media, LLC*, 486 F. Supp. 2d 1022 (N.D. Cal. 2007), same-sex domestic partners brought an action against former operators of an adoption website stemming from rejection of their application to have their profile posted on the website. The court determined that the defendants were in the business of selling adoption-related services, thus, the website was not expressive speech afforded to protection under the First Amendment, but rather a commercial enterprise where prospective parents post profiles for a fee. In some circumstances, courts may recognize the First Amendment protects expressive conduct as well as actual speech.

Public Forum and Time-Place-and-Manner Restrictions

If the speech involves government property, public forum analysis and time-place-and-manner restrictions may apply. A public forum, typically a public park or street, is a public place where people traditionally gather to express ideas and exchange views. To be constitutional, the government's regulation of a public forum must be narrowly tailored to serve a significant government interest.[14] The government may only enact content-neutral, time, place, and manner restrictions. As long as the restrictions are narrowly tailored to achieve a legitimate governmental interest, they do not violate the First Amendment.

Government websites are not considered public forums and as such, governments do not have to give certain groups access to official government websites. In *Sutliffe v. Epping School Dist.*, 584 F.3d 314 (1st Cir. 2009), the First Circuit held that a town's website was not a traditional public forum for purposes of determining whether town officials violated the free speech rights of a citizens group by refusing to place a hyperlink on the town website to the group's website. Similarly, in *Vargas v. City of Salinas*, 46 Cal. 4th 1, 205 P.3d 207 (Cal. 2009), the California Supreme Court held that a city's official website was not a public forum and the city had no obligation to provide proponents of a ballot measure with special access to the city's official website to enable them to post material of their own choosing. Also in *United States v. American Library Ass'n, Inc.*, 539 U.S. 194, 203–07 (2003), the U.S. Supreme Court held that Internet access in a public library does not constitute a public forum. Courts have refused to expand the definition of "traditional public forum" beyond streets and parks to official government websites and Internet access in public libraries.

Prior Restraint

Prior Restraint
A governmental restriction on speech or publication before its actual expression.

The early U.S. Founders were adamantly opposed to prior restraints, and this opposition was at the forefront of their minds when drafting the First Amendment. A **prior restraint** is formal censorship by the government before publication. A prior restraint is defined as a governmental restriction on speech or publication before its actual expression.[15] Prior restraints violate the First Amendment unless the speech is obscene, is defamatory, or creates a clear and present danger to society. The legal doctrine of prior restraint (or formal censorship before publication) is probably the oldest form of press control. The First Amendment's guarantee of "the freedom of speech, or of the press" prohibits a wide assortment of government restraints upon expression, but the main focus was directed at laws implemented by the monarch and parliament in England during the sixteenth and seventeenth centuries to restrict the "evils" of the printing press.

At least one court has held that filtering websites on library computers is not considered a prior restraint. The Washington Supreme Court held in *Bradburn v. North Cent. Regional Library Dist.*, 168 Wash. 2d 789, 231 P.3d 166 (Wash. 2010) that a library district's policy to filter websites on library computers provided by the district for public use did not constitute an unlawful prior restraint since the policy did not prevent speech and did not ban or attempt to ban speech before it occurred, but rather constituted a standard for the district to make determinations about what materials would be included in its collection available to library patrons.

On the other hand, some courts have determined that an injunction that prohibits a party from posting certain information on the Internet is an impermissible prior restraint on free speech. In *Evans v. Evans*, 162 Cal. App. 4th 1157, 76 Cal. Rptr. 3d 859 (2008), a California court held that a preliminary injunction prohibiting a deputy sheriff's former wife from publishing any "false and defamatory" statements on the Internet was constitutionally invalid as a prior restraint. Indeed, a prior restraint on speech is the most serious and least tolerable infringement on First Amendment rights.

Freedom of the Press

The First Amendment not only protects the freedom of speech, but also the freedom of the press. The First Amendment "Press Clause" provides that "Congress shall make no law . . . abridging the freedom . . . of the press." The primary purpose of the guarantee of freedom of the press is to prevent prior restraints on publication. The Framers did not design, nor has the U.S. Supreme Court recognized, a protection for the press that extends beyond the protection of other speech. In his concurring opinion in *First National Bank v. Bellotti*, 435 U.S. 756 (1978), for example, Chief Justice Warren Burger stated that "the history of the [Press] Clause does not suggest that the authors contemplated a 'special' or 'institutional' privilege."

The broad parameters of the prior restraint doctrine were further explained in the Pentagon Papers case, *New York Times Co. v. United States*, 403 U.S. 713 (1971). In the Pentagon Papers case, the federal government sought to enjoin the *New York Times* and the *Washington Post* from publishing a classified study on U.S. policy-making in Vietnam. The Vietnam conflict was ongoing, and the government argued that the publication of the classified information might damage the national interest.

The Court observed that, because any prior restraint on speech is presumptively invalid under the First Amendment, the government bore a heavy burden of showing a justification for the restraint. Finding that the government had not met its burden, the Court denied the injunction.

One growing concern involving the freedom of the press involves jail time for journalists who refuse to disclosure their sources. For example, video blogger Josh Wolf spent more than seven months in jail for refusing to comply with a subpoena seeking his testimony and video footage about a violent protest that he had covered.[16] His attempts to quash the subpoena failed, and his appeal was denied.

Some have called for reporter's shield laws to protect journalists, including online journalists. Reporter's shield laws are statutes that protect a newsgatherer from compulsory disclosure of confidential information. Thirty-five states and the District of Columbia have enacted reporter's shield laws, but there is not a federal reporter's shield law.[17]

In a case involving Apple's audio interface for GarageBand, a California Court of Appeals held that online journalists have the same right to protect the confidentiality of their sources as print journalists. The court in *O'Grady v. Superior Court*, 139 Cal. App. 4th 1423 (Cal. App. 2006), held that California's reporter shield law protecting confidential sources applied to a news-oriented website that gathered, selected, and prepared, for purposes of publication to a mass audience, information about current events of interest and concern to that audience. Although some states have reporter's shield laws, until other states and Congress adopt a reporter's shield law, journalists, including online journalists, may face jail time for failing to comply with court orders to disclose confidential sources.

The First Amendment to the Constitution which provides that "Congress shall make no law . . . abridging the freedom of speech . . ." is one of the most revered and fiercely protected rights enjoyed by American citizens.[18] Consequently, the First Amendment freedom of speech, and its application to online speech, is one of the most litigated and debated parts of the Bill of Rights.

CIVIL LIABILITY FOR DEFAMATION

The Internet has become the dominant form of media today, and the increased use of the Internet and e-mail has resulted in a number of defamation cases involving online speech.

Defamation is the act of harming the reputation of another by making a false statement to a third person.[19] A statement is **defamatory** when it tends to injure a person's reputation and consequently exposes the person to public hatred, contempt, ridicule, or financial injury, or where it impeaches any person's honesty, integrity, virtue, or reputation. The law of defamation includes the twin torts of libel and slander. Historically, courts divided defamation into two categories: **libel** (written defamation) and **slander** (oral defamation). Most modern defamation cases involve libel, and modern writers have come to use the term "defamation" to describe both libel and slander. Defamatory material posted to Internet websites constitutes libel.

There are two forms of defamation, depending on the subject matter of the statement: **defamation per se** and **defamation per quod**. Defamation per se involves a statement that is defamatory in and of itself and is not capable of an innocent meaning. Defamation per se may involve a statement about criminal conduct, a loathsome disease, sexual misconduct, or misconduct in a person's trade, profession, office, or occupation. Defamation per quod involves defamation that either is not apparent but is proved by extrinsic evidence showing its injurious meaning or is apparent but is not a statement that is actionable per se. A per quod plaintiff must actually prove such damages.

Defamation
The act of harming the reputation of another by making a false statement to a third person. A false written or oral statement that damages another's reputation.

Defamatory
Tending to harm a person's reputation, usually by subjecting the person to public contempt, disgrace, or ridicule, or by adversely affecting the person's business.

Libel
A defamatory statement expressed in a fixed medium, especially writing but also a picture, sign, or electronic broadcast. *See also* defamation.

Slander
A defamatory assertion expressed in a transitory form, especially speech.

Defamatory Per Se
A statement that is defamatory in and of itself and is not capable of an innocent meaning.

Defamation Per Quod
Defamation that either (1) is not apparent but is proved by extrinsic evidence showing its injurious meaning or (2) is apparent but is not a statement that is actionable per se.

While the elements of defamation are governed by state law, nearly every state uses a definition that mirrors the Restatement (Second) of Torts. To establish a defamation claim, most states require the plaintiff to prove four elements. For example, under Nevada law, the elements of a defamation claim are (1) that defendant made a defamatory communication to a third person, (2) that the statement was false, (3) that defendant was at fault in communicating the statement, and (4) that plaintiff suffered harm.[20]

A defamatory statement must be about the plaintiff or "of and concerning the plaintiff."[21] The Restatement (Second) of Torts § 564 states "[a] defamatory communication is made concerning the person to whom its recipient correctly, or mistakenly but reasonably, understands that it was intended to refer." In other words, plaintiffs are required to demonstrate that the communication was specifically directed towards them.

The defamatory statement must also be communicated or "published" to a third party. Publication to even one other person is sufficient to maintain a defamation action. It is well-settled that posting material to a website satisfies the publication requirement for defamation. E-mail sent to third parties also meets the publication requirement.[22] In the case *In re Perry*, 423 B.R. 215, 267 (Bkrtcy. S.D.Tex. 2010), the court concluded that an e-mail, just like a letter or a note, sent to third parties constitutes publication for defamation purposes. On the other hand, there is no publication, as required to support defamation claim, where a defendant communicates a statement directly to a plaintiff, who then communicates it to a third person.

Actual Malice Requirement for Public Figures

The level of fault in a defamation case depends on the type of plaintiff. In the landmark decision *New York Times Co. v. Sullivan*, 376 U.S. 254 (1964), the U.S. Supreme Court imposed the constitutional requirement that a public figure plaintiff must prove "actual malice" to prevail on a defamation claim. **Actual malice** is defined as knowledge of falsity or reckless disregard for the truth. Proof of falsity is necessary but not sufficient. If the plaintiff is a public figure, the plaintiff must also prove actual malice. Private plaintiffs only need to prove that the defendant acted negligently regarding the truth of the allegedly defamatory statement. Plaintiffs that are public figures must establish a higher degree of fault.

Actual Malice
Knowledge (by the person who utters or publishes a defamatory statement) that a statement is false, or reckless disregard about whether the statement is true.

There are two types of public figures: (1) general-purpose public figures, and (2) limited-purpose public figures.[23] A defendant in a defamation case will try to argue that the plaintiff is considered a public figure.

General-purpose public figures are people who achieve such pervasive fame or notoriety that they become public figures for all purposes and in all contexts.[24] To be classified as a general-purpose public figure, an individual must be found to have general fame and notoriety in the community. Examples of public figure include actors, sports figures, entertainers, public officers, inventors, explorers, and war heroes.

Limited-purpose public figures are people who thrust themselves to the forefront of particular public controversies in order to influence the resolution of the issues involved. If a person voluntarily injects themselves or is drawn into a particular public controversy, he or she becomes a limited-purpose public figure for that particular issue.

In *D.C. v. R.R.*, 182 Cal. App. 4th 1190, 106 Cal. Rptr. 3d 399 (Cal. App. 2010), a California court held that a high school student who established a website to promote his entertainment career was not a public figure or a limited public figure. The court determined that the student was not in the public eye when the fellow student posted the message, there was not widespread public interest in the student's life, and the message was not part of an ongoing controversy, dispute, or discussion.

In *Atlanta Humane Soc. v. Mills*, 618 S.E.2d 18 (Ga. Ct. App. 2005), the director of an association providing animal control services to county governments was a

Plaintiff	Level of Fault Required
General Purpose Public Figure	Actual Malice
Limited Purpose Public Figure	Actual Malice
Private Plaintiff	At Least Negligence

FIGURE 9.1 Fault Required in Defamation Cases

limited-purpose public figure in controversy surrounding the association's performance of the county's animal control duties, for purposes of the director's action against an individual who posted allegedly defamatory messages on an Internet message board. The controversy had been the focus of a television series on animal cruelty, the director had issued many press releases and given numerous interviews on behalf of association, and the individual's Internet comments were germane to the director's participation in the controversy.

If a person voluntarily injects themselves into a public controversy, or is drawn into a particular public controversy, then the person is a limited-purpose public figure for that particular issue, and the plaintiff must prove actual malice. If the court determines that the plaintiff is not a public figure, then the plaintiff need to only prove negligence.

Damages and Remedies in Defamation Actions

The plaintiff in a defamation action must also demonstrate resulting harm or damages. A variety of damages may be recoverable in an action for defamation, including nominal damages, general compensatory damages for harm to reputation, special compensatory damages for demonstrable special harm to the plaintiff's reputation, damages for any resulting bodily harm, emotional distress or mental anguish damages, and punitive or exemplary damages.[25] The plaintiff may also be entitled to an injunction. For example, an injunction issued by a court may order the defendant to remove defamatory statements posted on a website.

Only fair and reasonable compensation shall be awarded in a defamation action. Usually, the plaintiff will only recover actual or compensatory damages commensurate with the harm suffered. Punitive damages may be awarded in exceptional cases to punish a person for outrageous conduct which is malicious, wanton, reckless, or in willful disregard for another's rights.[26]

When the defamation is a libel, most jurisdictions agree that the defamation is actionable per se. In a libel case, a plaintiff is not required to demonstrate that he or she suffered any special harm or actual damages. Rather, the jury can infer that harm to reputation was sustained and award general compensatory damages at its discretion for the libel.

The U.S. Supreme Court held in *Gertz v. Welch,* 418 U.S. 323 (1974), that states may allow private individuals to recover for defamation without showing knowledge of falsity or reckless disregard for the truth, but that the recovery must be limited to damages for actual injury. Where a plaintiff does not show that a defamatory statement was made with actual malice or reckless disregard for the truth, a plaintiff may recover damages only upon and to the extent of proof of actual injury.

In *Too Much Media, LLC v. Hale,* 413 N.J. Super. 135, 993 A.2d 845 (N.J. Super. Ct. App. Div. 2010), an allegation in a software company's complaint against a website operator that the company had been extremely damaged by the operator's alleged defamatory comments on Internet message boards was sufficient to state a claim for defamation.

The court held that the law of evidence of damages to the company's reputation provided did not justify dismissal of the complaint.

The trial court judge or appellate can may reduce a jury's award for damages if the award is excessive. In *Cretella v. Kuzminski*, 640 F. Supp. 2d 741 (E.D.Va. 2009), a jury award of $24,000 in actual damages stemming from a defamatory statement in a copy of an e-mail sent to a state bar association's ethics committee was reduced to $6,000 since the attorney did not claim that the e-mail itself was defamatory and there was no evidence that the statement was likely to be found by friends, family, or potential employers.

Defamatory statements can damage reputations, harm job prospects, result in the loss of business, and inflict serious emotional harm. Plaintiffs may recover for lost profits, lost employment opportunities, incurred costs, lost time value, and future injury.

Subpoena Requests for Identity of Anonymous Internet Users

Because of the anonymous nature of the Internet and online communication, one of the obstacles for a plaintiff in an online defamation action is discovering the true identity of the potential defendant or defendants. Many blogs are anonymous, which creates an additional challenge for plaintiffs in defamation actions. If the identity of the person or persons who made the allegedly defamatory statement is unknown, the plaintiff may file an action and name "John Doe" as the defendant. During the discovery process, the plaintiff may then request the court to issue a subpoena against an Internet Service Provider (ISPs) for the disclosure of the identity of those who, acting anonymously or pseudonymously on the Internet, have allegedly caused harm.

Many courts have considered whether the ISP is required to disclose the identity of the individuals and the results are somewhat mixed.[27] As a general rule, in order to compel discovery of an anonymous Internet speaker's identity, the requesting party must show that (1) the speaker has been given adequate notice and a reasonable opportunity to respond to the discovery request, (2) the requesting party's cause of action could survive a motion for summary judgment on elements not dependent on the speaker's identity, and (3) a balance of the parties' competing interests favors disclosure.[28] In *Richerson v. Beckon*, No. C07-5590 JKA, 2008 WL 833076, at *4 (W.D. Wash. March 27, 2008), a California court found that speech on an employee blog about a school administrator was not of "public concern" and was not protected. But in *Krinsky v. Doe 6*, 159 Cal. App. 4th 1154, 1168–73 (2008), the plaintiff was required to make a prima facie showing of libel before enforcing a subpoena seeking the identity of an Internet blogger. Courts must balance the First Amendment right to anonymity and the right of plaintiffs to recover damages arising from defamatory statements.[29]

Alleged defamatory statements can be made in a variety of different ways through online communication. Websites, online discussion boards, online chat rooms, e-mail, blogs, and social networking sites such as Facebook and Twitter are potential forums for defamation in the online environment.[30]

The pervasiveness of the Internet and social media has heightened the opportunities for publication of potentially defamatory statements.[31] In fact, the rise of blogging has even created a market for bloggers' liability insurance, to protect against potential defamation claims, as well as copyright and other actions. Defamation suits are difficult to win, and even if the plaintiff wins, defendants may not have the assets to satisfy a judgment. Defamation suits are often about exposing the critic. The exposure or threat of litigation is enough to stop the criticism and defamatory statements. The exposure, and not the judgment, is often the real outcome in John Doe defamation suits.

DEFENSES IN ONLINE DEFAMATION CASES

Even if the plaintiff in a defamation suit can find the true identity of a person who makes an allegedly defamatory statement, defendants in online defamation cases have a variety of potential defenses available to them. These potential defenses include immunity under § 230 (Section 230) of the Communications Decency Act (CDA), privileges, opinion, truth, consent, and anti-SLAPP (strategic lawsuit against public participation) legislation. Defendants may also argue that the plaintiff is a public figure requiring the plaintiff to prove actual malice under the *New York Times Co. v. Sullivan* standard discussed above.

Immunity under Section 230 of the Communications Decency Act

The statutory protections found in § 230(c) of the Communications Decency Act (CDA), codified at 47 U.S.C. § 230(c), provide immunity from defamation lawsuits for Internet service providers (ISPs), and to a certain extent website owners from liability for the defamatory content others post on their websites.

Although the U.S. Supreme Court in *Reno v. ACLU*, 521 U.S. 844 (1997), held the indecency provisions of the Communications Decency Act (CDA) unconstitutional, the immunity provision under the CDA remains in force. The Communications Decency Act was part of the Telecommunications Act of 1996, Pub. L. No. 104-104, 110 Stat. 137. Some argue that the immunity provisions breed an online culture where people are more apt to publish low value, private, or defamatory speech. Other groups defend the immunity provision to encourage the freedom of speech protected under the First Amendment.

Courts construing Section 230 of the CDA frequently have employed a three-pronged test asking whether (1) the online entity uses or provides interactive computer services; (2) the entity is an information content provider with respect to the disputed activity or objectionable content; and (3) the plaintiff seeks to treat it as the "publisher or speaker" of information originating with a third party.[32]

Internet service providers (ISPs) are generally considered providers of an "interactive computer service" within the meaning of the Communications Decency Act and entitled to immunity. Website owners and operators that allow direct third-party posting and provide or enable computer access by multiple users also fall under the immunity provision.[33]

The **immunity** afforded by the CDA is not absolute and may be forfeited if the site owner invites the posting of illegal materials or makes actionable postings itself. In addition, if the owner or operator of the website is an author of the defamatory statement posted online, then the immunity provision does not apply. In *Whitney Information Network, Inc. v. Xcentric Venture, LLC*, 199 Fed. Appx. 738 (11th Cir. 2006), operators of a consumer advocacy website failed to establish that they were entitled to immunity from suit under the Communications Decency Act (CDA) since the website owners were the authors of some of the objectionable statements on their website, not merely publishers of third-party statements.

Immunity
Any exemption from a duty, liability, or service of process; especially an exemption granted to a public official or governmental unit. A defense to tort liability.

Section 230 of the Communications Decency Act has become one of the most important statutes impacting online speech, as well as one of the most criticized. Section 230 has been described both as the savior of free speech in the digital age and as an ill-conceived shield for scoundrels.

An empirical study published in 2010 in the *Loyola of Los Angeles Law Review* analyzed how plaintiffs and defendants have fared under Section 230. The study found that while Section 230 has largely protected intermediaries from liability for third-party speech, more than a third of the claims at issue in the cases survived a Section 230 defense.[34] Even in cases where the court dismissed the claims, intermediaries bore liability in the form of litigation costs, and it took courts, on average, nearly a year to issue decisions addressing an intermediary's defense under Section 230.

(c) Protection for "good samaritan" blocking and screening of offensive material

(1) Treatment of publisher or speaker

No provider or user of an interactive computer service shall be treated as the publisher or speaker of any information provided by another information content provider.

(2) Civil liability

No provider or user of an interactive computer service shall be held liable on account of—

(A) any action voluntarily taken in good faith to restrict access to or availability of material that the provider or user considers to be obscene, lewd, lascivious, filthy, excessively violent, harassing, or otherwise objectionable, whether or not such material is constitutionally protected; or

(B) any action taken to enable or make available to information content providers or others the technical means to restrict access to material described in paragraph (1).

FIGURE 9.2 Text of § 230 of the Communications Decency Act (CDA), Codified in 47 U.S.C. § 230(c)

Johnson v. Arden, 614 F.3d 785 (8th Cir. 2010) (Case 9.1) illustrates how courts apply Section 230 of the CDA in that an ISP host, and not an information content provider, is entitled to immunity under the CDA.

Privileges

Along with the immunity provision in Section 230 of the CDA, defendants in a defamation action may also assert a privilege defense. The law recognizes that certain communications, though possibly defamatory, are shielded from litigation to prevent

CASE 9.1

The Case of the Defamed Cat Breeders

Johnson v. Arden, *614 F.3d 785 (8th Cir. 2010)*

Susan and Robert Johnson filed a state civil suit making multiple claims against several defendants as a result of allegedly defamatory statements posted on an internet discussion board. The defendants removed the case to federal court. The original complaint included six defendants; however, the Johnsons located and served only InMotion Hosting, Inc. ("InMotion"), Melanie Lowry, and Heineman.

The district court dismissed the claims against InMotion with prejudice, finding that the Communications Decency Act (CDA) of 1996, 47 U.S.C. § 230(c)(1) and (e)(3) protects InMotion. On appeal, the Johnsons argue that the district court erred in dismissing the claims against InMotion, Heineman. For the reasons stated below, we disagree and affirm.

I. Background

The Johnsons reside in Unionville, Missouri, where they own and operate the exotic cat breeding business known as the Cozy Kitten Cattery. The Cozy Kitten Cattery is a Missouri limited liability company formed in 2007. Its principal office and place of business is located in Missouri, and the Johnsons are its sole members. Around December 2004, the Johnsons obtained a registered federal trademark and service mark for "Cozy Kitten Cattery." The Johnsons operate their cat breeding business under that trademark and licensed the use of that trademark and service mark to Cozy Kitten Cattery, LLC. The Johnsons advertise their business on the internet and have a website with the web address www.CozyKittens.com.

Someone posted several allegedly defamatory statements about the Cozy Kitten Cattery on the interactive website www.ComplaintsBoard.com. In response, the Johnsons and Cozy Kittens

Cattery filed suit against Elizabeth Arden d/b/a www.ComplaintsBoard.com, Michelle Reitenger, www.ComplaintsBoard.com, InMotion, Lowry, and Heineman in Putnam County, Missouri. Counts I, II and III allege that all six defendants conspired to use www.ComplaintsBoard.com to post false statements about the Johnsons, including statements that the Johnsons kill cats, the Johnsons "rip off" cat breeders, the Johnsons steal kittens, the Johnsons' cats and kittens are infected, and the Johnsons are con artists. The Johnsons assert that they requested all defendants to remove the statements but that the statements were not removed for more than 48 hours. The Johnsons assert that they suffered lost sales of kittens and cats, lost revenue and lost goodwill and will continue to suffer damages because of the statements posted on the interactive website.

InMotion Hosting, Inc.

InMotion is a California corporation and maintains its principal place of business there. InMotion, as an internet service provider (ISP), only hosted the www.ComplaintsBoard.com website. InMotion does not operate www.ComplaintsBoard.com or create any of its content. InMotion does not monitor or control the content of its customer's websites, including www.ComplaintsBoard.com.

The website www.ComplaintsBoard.com is published worldwide on the internet. The website is interactive, permitting and encouraging individuals to post complaints about businesses and business owners. Individuals seeking to post complaints on the website are required to register with the website and provide identifying information, such as their name and email address.

Procedural History

The defendants removed the case to federal court based on diversity of citizenship. Heineman filed a motion to dismiss contending that she was not properly served and that the district court had improper venue and lacked personal jurisdiction under Federal Rule of Civil Procedure 12(b)(2). The district court granted Heineman's motion for lack of personal jurisdiction. The Johnsons then filed a motion for an order of default against InMotion, which had not yet filed any pleadings in the district court. The district court denied the motion.

InMotion then filed its motion to dismiss under Rule 12(b), contending that it was not properly served, the district court did not have venue, the complaint failed to state a claim for relief, it had insufficient contacts with Missouri to be sued there, and Missouri was an inconvenient forum. InMotion did not raise the CDA as a defense. The district court raised the CDA sua sponte in its order granting InMotion's motion to dismiss.

The district court entered an order dismissing the claims against InMotion with prejudice and dismissing the claims against Lowry and Heineman without prejudice.

II. Discussion

On appeal, the Johnsons argue that the district court erred in . . . dismissing the claims against InMotion, after finding that InMotion was immune from suit under the CDA.

A. Communications Decency Act

The Johnsons first argue that the district court erroneously dismissed their claims after concluding InMotion is immune under the CDA. The Johnsons contend that 47 U.S.C. § 230(c)(1) and (e)(3) merely provide that a provider of internet services shall not be treated as the publisher or speaker of information on the internet provided by another party but does not immunize a provider from suit. The Johnsons assert that Missouri law provides for joint liability where a wrong is done by concert of action and common intent and purpose. According to the Johnsons, the CDA would only bar actions against website operators deemed to be the "publisher or speaker" of defamatory material.

InMotion responds that the district court correctly found that InMotion was immune from suit under the CDA. Additionally, InMotion asserts that it maintained no control and had no influence over the content that the Johnsons alleged was posted on www.ComplaintsBoard.com by unrelated third parties. Because of this, InMotion maintains, it could not have "acted in concert" or "intentionally inflicted emotional distress" in a manner that caused any damage to the Johnsons.

(continued)

(continued)

This case presents an issue of first impression for this court, as we have not previously interpreted § 230(c). "Statutory interpretation is a question of law that we review de novo." *Minn. Supply Co. v. Raymond Corp.*, 472 F.3d 524, 537 (8th Cir.2006). The CDA states that "[n]o provider or user of an interactive computer service shall be treated as the publisher or speaker of any information provided by another information content provider," 47 U.S.C. § 230(c)(1), and expressly preempts any state law to the contrary, id. § 230(e)(3). The CDA defines an "information content provider" as "any person or entity that is responsible, in whole or in part, for the creation or development of information provided through the internet or any other interactive computer service." Id. at § 230(f)(3).

Read together, these provisions bar plaintiffs from holding ISPs legally responsible for information that third parties created and developed. "Congress thus established a general rule that providers of interactive computer services are liable only for speech that is properly attributable to them." *Nemet Chevrolet, Ltd. v. Consumeraffairs.com, Inc.*, 591 F.3d 250, 254 (4th Cir.2009).

"The majority of federal circuits have interpreted the CDA to establish broad 'federal immunity to any cause of action that would make service providers liable for information originating with a third-party user of the service' " [citations omitted].

It is undisputed that InMotion did not originate the material that the Johnsons deem damaging. InMotion is not a "publisher or speaker" as § 230(c)(1) uses those terms, therefore, the district court held that InMotion cannot be liable under any state-law theory to the persons harmed by the allegedly defamatory material. Five circuit courts agree [citations omitted].

District courts in this circuit have reached the same conclusion. See, e.g., *PatentWizard, Inc. v. Kinko's, Inc.*, 163 F.supp.2d 1069,1072 (D.S.D.2001) (holding that "§ 230 of the Communication[s] Decency Act errs on the side of robust communication and prevents the plaintiffs from moving forward with their claims" that a company that allowed users to access the internet via its computers could be held liable for the actions of one of those users).

The Johnsons cite *Chicago Lawyers' Committee for Civil Rights Under Law, Inc. v. Craigslist, Inc.*, 519 F.3d 666 (7th Cir.2008), for support. *Craigslist* held that "§ 230(c) as a whole cannot be understood as a general prohibition of civil liability for web-site operators and other online content hosts. . . ." Id. at 669. However, while the Seventh Circuit construes § 230(c)(1) to permit liability for ISPs, it limited that liability to ISPs that intentionally designed their systems to facilitate illegal acts, such as stealing music. Specifically, Craigslist held that an ISP could not be held liable for allowing third parties to place ads in violation of the Fair Housing Act on its website if the ISP did not induce the third party to place discriminatory ads.

The record contains no evidence that InMotion designed its website to be a portal for defamatory material or do anything to induce defamatory postings. We conclude that the CDA provides ISPs like InMotion with federal immunity against state tort defamation actions that would make service providers liable for information originating with third-party users of the service such as the other defendants in this case.

Therefore we decline the Johnsons' invitation to construe § 230(c)(1) as permitting liability against InMotion for material originating with a third party.

Because InMotion was merely an ISP host and not an information content provider, the Johnsons' claims against InMotion fail as a matter of law under § 230(c)(1), and the district court properly dismissed the claims.

Case Questions

1. Why did the plaintiff cat breeders sue InMotion?
2. What does the immunity provision under § 230 of the Communications Decency Act provide?
3. Why did the court hold that InMotion was immune under the CDA?
4. Under what circumstances would the immunity provision under Section 230 of the Communications Decency Act not apply to a website owner or operator?
5. Should § 230 of the Communications Decency Act by repealed or amended? What are the arguments both in support and opposition to this immunity provision?

a chilling effect on speech. There are two forms of privilege: absolute privilege and qualified (also called "conditional" or "common interest") privilege. An absolute privilege differs from a qualified privilege in that it provides immunity regardless of the purpose or motive of the defendant or the reasonableness of the defendant's conduct. **Absolute privilege** is a privilege that immunizes an actor from suit, no matter how wrongful the action might be, and even though it is done with an improper motive. An absolute privilege occurs when public policy requires that a speaker be immune from suit. A **qualified privilege** is a privilege that immunizes a person from suit only when the privilege is properly exercised in the performance of a legal or moral duty.

Absolute Privilege
A privilege that immunizes an actor from suit, no matter how wrongful the action might be, and even though it is done with an improper motive.

Qualified Privilege
Privilege in tort cases that immunizes a person from suit only when the privilege is properly exercised in the performance of a legal or moral duty.

ABSOLUTE PRIVILEGE Under the old English common law, absolute privilege was recognized as a means to protect speech and debate in Parliament. Absolute privilege generally applies to statements made by judges and lawmakers in legislative or judicial proceedings. An absolute privilege wholly protects an entitled individual from or is a complete bar to a claim of defamation. Absolute immunity precludes liability regardless of the defendant's state of mind or intent. Even if the statements are defamatory, the defendant will not be liable because an absolute privilege provides complete immunity from suit in a defamation action. Absolute privileges completely immunize statements made in judicial, legislative, or administrative proceedings from defamation liability. For example, a member of Congress has absolute immunity in a defamation case for statements made by the member of Congress during floor debates broadcast over the Internet on C-Span. Absolute privilege applies to those situations where the importance of the unrestricted exchange of information is so great that even defamatory statements made with actual malice are privileged. A statute may also provide immunity from a defamation action and is identical to an absolute privilege.

For the absolute privilege to apply, the defamatory statement must be made to further a purpose falling within the public interest underlying the privilege. Statements made in a judicial proceeding, such as affidavits, witness testimony, and statements made by lawyers during a trial, are absolutely privileged and are not actionable for defamation. Even if the statements made in the judicial proceeding (such as a trial) are subsequently published on the Internet, absolute privilege still applies. In *Norman v. Borison*, 192 Md. App. 405, 994 A.2d 1019 (Md. Ct. App. 2010), an attorney who posted complaints in a class-action lawsuit on the Internet could claim absolute privilege. The court held that posting the complaints on the Internet was protected since the federal court judge handling the class action litigation had expressly permitted the use of the Internet to communicate with class action litigants.

Immunity, however, does not apply to all acts related to legal proceedings. *Yoder v. Workman*, 224 F. Supp. 2d 1077 (S.D. W.Va. 2002) (Case 9.2) demonstrates a situation where the court rejected a claim for judicial immunity involving alleged defamatory statements made by a West Virginia Supreme Court Justice in a press release posted on the court website because the judge was not acting in an official capacity. The federal court judge ruled that only official acts of the state supreme court justice related to legal proceedings are entitled to immunity.

QUALIFIED PRIVILEGE The recognition of a qualified privilege grew out of the public interest in encouraging full and fair statements by individuals who have a legal or moral duty to communicate about persons in whom both the sender and receiver have an interest. A qualified privilege is a privilege that immunizes a person from suit only when the privilege is properly exercised in the performance of a legal or moral duty.

CASE 9.2

The Case of the Defamation Action Against the State Supreme Court Justice

Yoder v. Workman, *224 F. Supp. 2d 1077 (S.D. W.Va. 2002)*

I. Factual and Procedural Background

Defendant now moves to dismiss the amended complaint for failure to state a claim, pursuant to Rule 12(b)(6). Fed.R.Civ.P. 12(b)(6). She argues the allegedly defamatory statement of reasons for judicial recusal 1) does not reference Yoder, 2) is subject to absolute judicial immunity and absolute or qualified privilege, and 3) does not contain a provably false statement of fact.

II. Discussion

A. Motion to Dismiss

Our Court of Appeals has often stated the settled standard governing the disposition of a motion to dismiss pursuant to Rule 12(b)(6), Federal Rules of Civil Procedure:

B. Reference to Yoder

The essential elements for a successful common law defamation action by a private individual are (1) defamatory statements, (2) a nonprivileged communication to a third party, (3) falsity, (4) reference to the plaintiff, (5) at least negligence on the part of the publisher, and (6) resulting injury [citations omitted]. Workman's first objection is that her press release did not refer to Yoder and thus cannot be defamatory of him.

The allegedly defamatory statements in the press release say:

> Mr. Chafin and his stable of lawyers have engaged in a vitriolic campaign of judge-shopping. This campaign of spurious and unethical legal actions and false allegations against me has been designed to stalk, harass and defame me as a member of the Judiciary because the legal rulings in which I participated with the other Justices of the Supreme Court did not suit them.

The comments [to Restatement (Second) of Torts § 564A (1977)] explain: "When the group or class defamed is sufficiently small, the words may reasonably be understood to have personal reference and application to any member of it so that he is defamed as an individual." For [these] reasons, Yoder was identifiable as a member of the small group or stable of lawyers potentially defamed by Workman's statement.

C. Judicial Immunity

"When acting in his judicial capacity a judge is immune from civil liability for any and all official acts" [citations omitted]." Absolute judicial immunity applies (1) to all judicial acts unless (2) those acts fall clearly outside the judge's subject matter jurisdiction" [citations omitted]. The test for whether a judge's act is a judicial one is also two-fold. The first factor is whether the act is one normally performed by a judge. The issue is the nature of the act, not the identity of the actor. The second factor is whether the parties dealt with the judge in his judicial capacity and looks to the expectation of the parties.

The issue here is whether a judge's publishing a press release on the court's website to explain and elaborate her recusal notice is an act normally performed by a judge. The obvious answer is no. Courts speak through their orders. They do not issue press releases or other "public relations" materials to explain, justify or further inform the public about their decisions.

Judicial codes of conduct prohibit judges from making "any public or nonpublic comment about any pending or impending proceeding which might reasonably be expected to affect its outcome or impair its fairness." Code of Judicial Conduct Canon 3(B)(9). In this case the public comment accompanied a recusal notice, so the justice herself was no longer involved. Nevertheless, the case continued pending before the court and public comment by a justice about the parties and lawyers involved was inappropriate at best. A press release about the recusal order was not a judicial act and, as such, absolute judicial immunity does not apply to shield its author.

Workman also contends the press release, if not absolutely privileged, was subject to a qualified privilege. As she reports, it is well-settled that a "qualified privilege exists when a person publishes a subject in good faith about a subject in which he has an interest or duty and limits the publication of the statement to those persons who have a legitimate interest in the subject matter." Workman's press release was published on the state Supreme Court's website, however, and not limited to those with an interest in the matter, but made available to the general world-wide public via the Internet. Accordingly, no qualified privilege is available to her publication.

D. Statement of Fact or Rhetorical Hyperbole

Finally, Workman contends that the press release statements are rhetorical hyperbole and constitutionally-protected opinion, rather than provably false statements of fact. To repeat, the statements complained of are:

Mr. Chafin and his stable of lawyers have engaged in a vitriolic campaign of judge-shopping. This campaign of spurious and unethical legal actions and false allegations against me has been designed to stalk, harass and defame me as a member of the Judiciary because the legal rulings in which I participated with the other Justices of the Supreme Court did not suit them.

With regard to opinion, the Supreme Court has said, "Under the First Amendment there is no such thing as a false idea. However pernicious an opinion may seem, we depend for its correction not on the conscience of judges and juries but on the competition of other ideas." *Gertz v. Robert Welch, Inc.*, 418 U.S. 323, 339–40, 94 S.Ct. 2997, 41 L.Ed.2d 789 (1974). The Court later clarified that this statement was intended to reiterate Justice Holmes' classic "marketplace of ideas" concept and not create a wholesale defamation exception for anything that might be labeled "opinion." *Milkovich v. Lorain Journal Co.*, 497 U.S. 1, 18, 110 S.Ct. 2695, 111 L.Ed.2d 1 (1990). This Bresler-Letter Carriers-Falwell line of cases instead provides protection for statements that cannot "reasonably [be] interpreted as stating actual facts" about an individual. As noted above, the allegedly defamatory statements made in the press release can reasonably be interpreted as stating facts about Yoder.

For these reasons, the allegedly defamatory statements are neither rhetorical hyperbole nor constitutionally-protected "opinion," but could be determined by a reasonable factfinder to imply an assertion that Yoder performed spurious and unethical legal actions, made false allegations, and stalked, harassed and defamed the Defendant.

III. Conclusion

Accordingly, the Court DENIES Defendant's motion to dismiss Plaintiff's' complaint for failure to state a claim upon which relief can be granted.

Case Questions

1. In what way did the press release posted on the court website identity the plaintiff?
2. Why was the judge not entitled to judicial immunity?
3. Why did the court determine that the statements were opinion?
4. What damages could the plaintiff potentially recover in the defamation case?

For example, qualified privilege has been extended to members of a faculty tenure committee, physicians of a health insurance plan, and members of the governing body of a tenants association. Qualified privilege has also been applied to statements made by employers to employees relative to performance.

Unlike absolute privileges, a qualified privilege can be asserted as a defense if the plaintiff can demonstrate malice. Malice includes both common-law malice and actual malice. Common-law malice involves spite or ill will. Actual malice, which is governed by the *New York Times* standard, involves a situation where the defendant knew of or acts with reckless disregard as to falsity of statement.

Police officers have a qualified privilege to disseminate information in the course of a criminal investigation unless they acted with malice For example, in *Flowers v. City of Minneapolis*, 558 F.3d 794 (8th Cir. 2009), an allegedly defamatory e-mail sent by a police officer about an African-American resident was conditionally privileged, since it was made with a proper purpose of investigating possible gang activity in the resident's neighborhood.

Opinion

If a statement is opinion rather than a fact, the plaintiff will not recover in a defamation action. While defamation law recognizes that an individual's right to protect his or her reputation is a basic part of our society, another staple of our society is the right of individuals to speak and write freely. Statements that merely express an opinion—no matter how offensive, vituperative, or unreasonable—are not actionable. The determination as to whether a statement is fact or opinion is based on what the average person hearing or reading the communication would take it to mean. Loose, figurative, or hyperbolic language is not sufficient to maintain an action for defamation. Statements that are merely offensive but not false and disparaging are not defamatory.

Opinions are commonly expressed in e-mail messages, online discussion boards, blogs, and websites. In *Purcell v. Ewing*, 560 F. Supp. 2d 337 (M.D. Pa. 2008), a federal court in Pennsylvania held that a statement in an online message board that, in a photograph, the plaintiff looked like "someone accused of child molestation" and that he was a "pervert to look out for" were non-actionable statements of opinion. The statements purported to arise from nothing more than the poster's personal perception of a particular photograph, and no reader could reasonably believe that the posting derived from any implied defamatory facts. If the statement includes verifiable facts as opposed to protected opinions or satire or parody, then the defendant may be held liable in a defamation suit. In *Super Future Equities, Inc. v. Wells Fargo Bank Minnesota*, N.A., 553 F. Supp. 2d 680 (N.D. Tex. 2008), the court held that a disclaimer on a website that read: "This is my private information and opinion" did not transform the statements into opinion. The court in *Super Future Equities, Inc. v. Wells Fargo Bank Minnesota* stated that the test is whether the publication could be reasonably understood as describing actual facts and not whether some actual readers were misled.

Truth

Because falsity is an essential element in a defamation case, truth is a perfect defense to a defamation action.[35] Stated another way, truth is a complete or absolute defense in a defamation case. The defense of truth can be successfully asserted even if the publication is not technically true in all respects. Thus, a publication that is "substantially true" is not defamatory. The law recognizes that a statement may be substantially truthful if it contains minor inaccuracies.[36] The test of substantial truth is whether the libel as published would have a different effect on the mind of the reader from which the pleaded truth would have produced.[37] If the plaintiff cannot prevail on a defamation claim, the plaintiff may still be able to recovery in a tort claim for invasion of privacy involving public disclosure of private facts discussed in further detail in Chapter 8.

Consent

In a defamation action, consent of the person injured is a complete defense. Stated another way, a plaintiff will not recover on a defamation claim when the plaintiff has consented, authorized, procured, or invited the statement. The defense of consent has been incorporated into a three-part analysis. The publication of a defamatory statement is privileged if (1) there was either express or implied consent to the publication; (2) the statements were relevant to the purpose for which consent was given; and (3) the publication of those statements was limited to those with a legitimate interest in their content.[38]

Mistake

As a general rule, mistake is not a defense to defamation. The standard is not what the defendant intended, but what a reasonable person may have understood. Mistake, however, may be relevant to the amount of damages awarded by a jury. Also, if the defendant makes a mistake in good faith, this might be relevant to determining whether or not malice has been established. Similarly, publishing an apology or a retraction is not a defense in a defamation action, but it may help mitigate or reduce the damages. Removing the defamatory statement from a website or publishing a retraction may help appease some individuals and companies who have been harmed and avoid litigation and conflicts.

Anti-SLAPP Laws

Defendants in defamation cases may also rely on anti-SLAPP laws as a defense. In an effort to curb plaintiffs from using the legal system to silence opposition and chill free speech, twenty-six states have enacted **anti-SLAPP (strategic lawsuit against public participation) statutes** or anti-SLAPP laws.[39] A **strategic lawsuit against public participation (SLAPP)** is a suit brought by a developer, corporate executive, or elected official to stifle those who protest against some type of high-dollar initiative or who take an adverse position on a public-interest issue (often involving the environment).[40] Anti-SLAPP laws are designed to bar meritless lawsuits filed with the intent to chill the exercise of First Amendment right on a matter of public interest. The purpose is to toss out meritless suits that are meant solely to silence speech.

Anti-SLAPP laws are also applicable with Internet speech. Many companies sue individuals who post anonymous messages on Internet financial message boards or in online chat rooms. While some of these lawsuits may have merit, others are merely retaliatory attempts by the companies to silence their anonymous critics on the boards and intimidate other Internet users to keep their criticisms to themselves. A **CyberSLAPP** is a SLAPP against anonymous Internet posters.[41]

In California, which has a broad anti-SLAPP law, once an anti-SLAPP motion is filed, all discovery is stayed. Therefore, the plaintiff's attempts to discover the true identity of a person must wait until after the court determines if the plaintiff has established enough evidence that there is a probability that the plaintiff will prevail on the claim. Anti-SLAPP laws allow for early procedural review and a mandatory award of attorney's fees for the defendant using the anti-SLAPP statute as a defense if the judge rules in the defendant's favor.

Anti-SLAPP Law
Law designed to bar meritless lawsuits filed with the intent to chill the exercise of First Amendment rights on a matter of public interest. *See also* SLAPP (strategic lawsuit against public participation).

SLAPP
A strategic lawsuit against public participation—a suit brought by a developer, corporate executive, or elected official to stifle those who protest against some type of high-dollar initiative or who take an adverse position on a public-interest issue (often involving the environment).—Also termed SLAPP suit. *See also* SLAPP law.

A Strategic Lawsuit Against Public Participation (SLAPP) is a suit brought by a developer, corporate executive, or elected official to stifle those who protest against some type of high-dollar initiative or who take an adverse position on a public-interest issue (often involving the environment).

A"CyberSLAPP" is a SLAPP against anonymous Internet posters.

California's Anti-SLAPP (Strategic Lawsuit Against Public Participation) statute, codified in Cal. Code Civ. Proc. § 425.16, reads:

(a) The Legislature finds and declares that there has been a disturbing increase in lawsuits brought primarily to chill the valid exercise of the constitutional rights of freedom of speech and petition for the redress of grievances. The Legislature finds and declares that it is in the public interest to encourage continued participation in matters of public significance, and that this participation should not be chilled through abuse of the judicial process. To this end, this section shall be construed broadly.

(b) (1) A cause of action against a person arising from any act of that person in furtherance of the person's right of petition or free speech under the United States Constitution or the California Constitution in connection with a public issue shall be subject to a special motion to strike, unless the court determines that the plaintiff has established that there is a probability that the plaintiff will prevail on the claim.

(2) In making its determination, the court shall consider the pleadings, and supporting and opposing affidavits stating the facts upon which the liability or defense is based.

(3) If the court determines that the plaintiff has established a probability that he or she will prevail on the claim, neither that determination nor the fact of that determination shall be admissible in evidence at any later stage of the case, or in any subsequent action, and no burden of proof or degree of proof otherwise applicable shall be affected by that determination in any later stage of the case or in any subsequent proceeding.

FIGURE 9.3 Text of California's Anti-SLAPP Statute

The Electronic Frontier Foundation (EFF), founded in 1990, is a non-profit civil liberties group that defends freedom in technology law, policy, standards, and treaties. The EFF regularly brings and defends lawsuits in pursuit of its goals and objectives, including the rights of anonymous bloggers. The EFF engages in extensive litigation, policy work, media work, public education, and activism. Many of the most significant technology law cases have involved the EFF, including *MGM Studios, Inc. v. Grokster, Ltd.* Craig Newmark, founder of Craigslist, is one of the supporters of the Electronic Frontier Foundation. For more information about the EFF, visit www.eff.org.

FIGURE 9.4 The Electronic Frontier Foundation (EFF)

CRIMINAL DEFAMATION

Criminal Libel Malicious libel that is designed to expose a person to hatred, contempt, or ridicule and that may subject the author to criminal sanctions.

Criminal Defamation *See* criminal libel.

Another important consideration with online speech is the possibility of a criminal prosecution for libel. **Criminal libel** is sometimes called **criminal defamation**. At least nineteen states criminalize general libel. Three other states criminalize specific types of libel.[42] The general libel statutes fall into two categories: those that focus on causing a "breach of the peace" and those that focus on publishing a statement or object tending to impeach the honesty, integrity, virtue, or reputation or expose the natural defects of someone and thereby to expose that person to public hatred, contempt, or ridicule.

Criminal libel prosecutions have been relatively rare since the U.S. Supreme Court established new constitutional standards for state criminal libel laws in 1964 in *Garrison v. Louisiana*, 379 U.S. 64 (1964). According to one study, the rise of the Internet, however, in the mid-1990s coincided with a modest increase in the number of threatened and actual prosecutions for speech.[43] According to the study, approximately one-third of the recent criminal libel cases involved Internet speech.

As with other legal actions involved Internet speech, criminal libel laws are subject to the First Amendment. In 2002, the Utah Supreme Court struck down Utah's criminal libel statute as overbroad and unconstitutional in violation of the First Amendment. The case, *In re I.M.L.*, 61 P.3d 1038 (Utah 2002), involved a high school student, who was charged with criminal libel for creating an Internet web site on which he displayed disparaging comments about his teachers, classmates, and principal. The Utah Supreme Court opinion ruled that "[f]reedom of speech is not only the hallmark of a free people, but is, indeed, an essential attribute of the sovereignty of citizenship [internal citation omitted]. Free speech must be balanced, however, against the values protected by the law of defamation, invasion of privacy, and abuse of personal identity."[44] Although most state criminal libel laws have been repealed by state legislatures or judicially struck down, criminal libel in the age of the Internet could rise again and become a tool in the hands of government officials seeking to punish unpopular or minority speech. Not all criminal-libel statutes are per se unconstitutional, and a criminal defamation statute that clearly states the elements of the crime of defamation may be held constitutional.[45] Although there have been few Internet criminal defamation cases, the prospect of criminal prosecution for online defamation remains a possibility.

BUSINESS DISPARAGEMENT

Business disparagement, also called business defamation, commercial disparagement, product disparagement, injurious falsehood, or trade libel, is another potential cause of action relating to online speech. Business disparagement is the common-law tort of belittling someone's business, goods, or services with a remark that is false or misleading but not necessarily defamatory.[46] To succeed in a business disparagement case, the plaintiff must prove that (1) the defendant made the disparaging remark; (2) the defendant either intended to injure the business, knew the statement was false, or recklessly disregarded whether it was true; and (3) the statement resulted in special damages to the plaintiff.[47]

Business Disparagement Common-law tort of belittling someone's business, goods, or services with a remark that is false or misleading but not necessarily defamatory. Also called business defamation, commercial disparagement, product disparagement, injurious falsehood, or trade libel.

The comments in Restatement (Second) of Torts § 623A explain the difference between the torts of business disparagement and defamation. While both business disparagement and defamation involve imposing liability for injuries stemming from publication to third parties of a false statement affecting the plaintiff, the two torts protect different interests and have entirely different origins. The action for defamation is to protect the personal reputation of the injured party and arose from the old actions for libel and slander. The purpose of injurious falsehood is to protect economic interests of the injured party against pecuniary loss resulting from the publication. Damages available in an action for injurious falsehood or business disparagement include loss of prospective or actual customers or sales, and expenses necessary to counteract the disparagement.

In 2009, the Nevada Supreme Court examined a business disparagement case involving e-mail messages in *Clark County School Dist. v. Virtual Educ. Software, Inc.*, 213 P.3d 496 (Nev. 2009). Virtual Education Software, Inc. (VESI), a Nevada corporation that markets and sells computer-based instruction for educators and business professionals, brought a business defamation claim against Clark County School District stemming from a series of letters and e-mail messages. The trial court awarded a total of $340,622 in damages to the software provider, but the Nevada Supreme Court reversed that decision and held that the school district was not liable for the e-mail messages since there was no evidence of malice in the communication. Although there was substantial evidence for the jury to conclude that the information contained in the e-mail communications was false and disparaging, the company failed to prove that the school district maliciously intended to cause pecuniary loss, or that the school district acted with malice because it knew the statements were false or acted in reckless disregard of their falsity.

The malice requirement is a high threshold for plaintiffs to meet. Courts will only impose liability for business disparagement stemming from online communications in the most egregious cases.

Summary

The First Amendment to the U.S. Constitution states that Congress shall make no law abridging the freedom of speech or the press. The First Amendment applies to state action and state actors at the federal and state levels. Courts may find that legislation violates the U.S. Constitution based on either vagueness or overbreadth doctrines. The First Amendment applies to expressive conduct as well as actual speech, including computer source code. Some types of speech, such as obscenity, fighting words, child pornography, and defamation, are not protected under the First Amendment. Courts are generally opposed to prior restraints, governmental restrictions on speech before publication. In jurisdictions without a reporter's shield law, including the federal courts, reporters, including online journalists and bloggers, may be held in contempt for refusing to comply with a court order for disclosure of a confidential sources. Those who communicate defamatory statements in the online environment may be liable for defamation. Defamation is the act of harming the reputation of another by making a false statement to a third person. A statement is defamatory when it tends to injure a person's reputation and consequently exposes the person to public hatred, contempt, ridicule, or financial injury, or where it impeaches any person's honesty, integrity, virtue, or reputation. In *New York Times Co. v. Sullivan*, the U.S. Supreme Court imposed the constitutional requirement that a public figure plaintiff must prove "actual malice" to prevail on a defamation claim. Private plaintiffs only need to prove that the defendant acted negligently. The potential defenses in a defamation case include immunity under § 230 (Section 230) of the Communications Decency Act (CDA), privileges, opinion, truth, consent, and anti-SLAPP (strategic lawsuit against public participation) legislation. Because of the anonymous nature of the Internet, finding the true identity of a person transmits a defamatory statement may be a challenge. Defamation suits are difficult to win, and even if the plaintiff wins, defendants may not have the assets to satisfy a judgment. Although criminal defamation cases are rare and many criminal libel laws have been declared unconstitutional, the possibility of criminal prosecution for online defamation exists. Business disparagement is the common-law tort of belittling someone's business, goods, or services with a remark that is false or misleading but not necessarily defamatory. The purpose of business disparagement is to protect economic interests of the injured party against pecuniary loss resulting from the publication.

Key Terms

absolute privilege *171*
actual malice *164*
anti-SLAPP statutes *175*
business disparagement *177*
criminal defamation *176*
criminal libel *176*
cyber-SLAPP *175*
defamation *163*
defamation per quod *163*
defamatory per se *163*
defamatory *163*
First Amendment *159*
immunity *167*
libel *163*
qualified privilege *171*
prior restraint *162*
slander *163*
Strategic Lawsuit against Public Participation SLAPP *175*
Speech Clause *159*

Review Questions

1. Why are courts generally opposed to prior restraints?
2. What types of speech are not protected under the First Amendment?
3. What are the elements in a defamation action?
4. How can a person be considered a "public figure" in a defamation action?
5. What is the actual malice requirement in a defamation action?
6. What protection does Section 230 of the Communications Decency Act provide?
7. What are the potential defenses in an online defamation action?
8. Compare and contrast business disparagement with defamation.

Discussion Questions

1. The U.S. Department of Justice sought a court order in 2011 to obtain personal information from the Twitter accounts of three people linked to the WikiLeaks probe, including WikiLeaks founder Julian Assange. The U.S. Justice Department opened a criminal probe of WikiLeaks shortly after the disclosure of diplomatic cables and classified documents. Should the government be entitled to obtain screen names, mailing addresses, telephone numbers, credit card and bank account information, and Internet protocol addresses in the WikiLeaks probe? To what extent does the First Amendment protect Assange and others who played a role in leaking classified documents? If you were a juror in a criminal prosecution of Assange, could you find him guilty for disclosing classified documents and diplomatic cables?
2. Video blogger Josh Wolf spent more than seven months in jail for refusing to comply with a subpoena seeking his testimony and video footage about a violent protest that he had covered. When should a reporter or blogger be held in contempt for failing to comply with a subpoena? Would you support a federal reporter's shield law? Why or why not?
3. Some people argue that the modern law of defamation is in need of substantial reform. One South Carolina Supreme Court Justice observed: "I am firmly convinced that the present status of our defamation jurisprudence is so convoluted, so hopelessly and irretrievably confused, that nothing short of a fresh start can bring any sanity, and predictability, to this very important area of the law." See *Holtzscheiter v. Thomson Newspapers, Inc.*, 506 S.E.2d 497, 514 (S.C. 1998). What is your reaction to this statement? What reforms, if any, would you support in the law of defamation as it relates to online speech?

Exercises

1. You are the owner of XYZ Software LLC (a fictitious software company) that has recently released "Build-A-Budget" which is a new personal finance software with a mobile application. You run a search on Google for the new software and find an online magazine, www.techscoopblog.com (a fictitious online magazine) with an article that includes a review of the software with false and defamatory comments. The article claims that downloading the "Build-A-Budget" software from the company's website will result in malware and computer viruses to anyone who downloads the software. The statements in the article are false and disparaging. Draft a letter to the owner and operator of the online magazine, www.techscoopblog.com, demanding that the website remove the defamatory article and publish a retraction or else you will seek legal action in a court of law.
2. *Hypothetical:* Jane runs a blog where she discusses random entertainment and fashion. Jane posts a blog entry about Acme Handbags where Jane wrote "My Acme Handbag ripped after two weeks of normal wear and tear and is a cheap Gucci knock-off. This is the worst handbag that I have ever bought. I don't know why anyone would ever buy this piece of trash. I think I may have even gotten a rash on my arm from using the bag. They are ugly, poorly made, and potentially hazardous to your health!" The owner of Acme Handbags brings a civil action against Jane for defamation and business disparagement. What potential defenses could Jane assert? What is Jane's strongest defense? Which of the defenses discussed in this chapter would not apply?
3. A tenant at an apartment in Chicago, Illinois, composed the following Tweet on Twitter, a free social networking site: "@JessB123 You should just come anyway. Who said sleeping in a moldy apartment was bad for you? Horizon realty thinks it's ok." The apartment owner sued the tenant under a theory of libel per se, claiming that the alleged defamatory statement damaged its business reputation as a Chicago landlord. The tenant files a motion to dismiss claiming that the statement was made in a social context where the average reader would understand that the statement was the tenant's opinion and not an objectively verifiable fact. How should the court decide the case? See *Horizon Group Management, L.L.C. v. Bonnen*, 2009L008675 (Circ. Ct. Cook County, Ill., filed Jul. 20, 2009), available at http://www.citmedialaw.org/threats/horizon-group-v-bonnen/.
4. Visit the website for the Electronic Frontier Foundation (www.eff.com) and go to the tab for "Take Action" and find out how you can help support the cause of the EFF. Then engage in advocacy for one of the causes of the EFF (or another nonprofit advocacy group related to online speech).
5. Visit the website for the Citizen Media Law Project's online forums at http://www.citmedialaw.org/forum. Select one of the forums and then write an initial post in that topic and respond to at least two other persons. Then capture a screenshot of your responses.

Related Internet Sites

http://www.internetdefamationlawblog.com/
Internet and Defamation Law Blog

http://www.medialaw.org/
Media Law Resource Center

http://mlrcblogsuits.blogspot.com/
Media Law Resource Center Suits

http://www.eff.org
Electronic Frontier Foundation

http://www.defamationlawblog.com/
California Defamation Law Blog

http://lawprofessors.typepad.com/firstamendment/
First Amendment Law Professor Blog

http://injury.findlaw.com/defamation-libel-slander/
FindLaw Overview of Defamation, Libel, and Slander

http://www.firstamendmentcenter.org/speech/internet/index.aspx
First Amendment Center Article on Internship Speech

http://blog.ericgoldman.org/
Technology and Marketing Law Blog

http://www.netchoice.org/
NetChoice, an e-commerce trade group whose members include AOL, eBay, NewsCorp, and Yahoo!

http://www.casp.net/
California Anti-SLAPP Project

http://www.cyberslapp.org/
CyberSLAPP.org, a joint project of Public Citizen, EFF, the American Civil Liberties Union, the Center for Democracy and Technology, and the Electronic Privacy Information Center

http://www.citmedialaw.org/
Citizen Medial Law Project

End Notes

1. *Jones v. Dirty World Entertainment Recordings*, LLC, 766 F. Supp. 2d 828 (E.D. Ky. 2011).
2. Anthony Ciolli, *Chilling Effects: The Communications Decency Act and the Online Marketplace of Ideas*, 63 U. MIAMI L. REV. 137, 217 (2008).
3. U.S. Const. amend. I.
4. 16A Am. Jur. 2d Constitutional Law § 424.
5. 16A Am. Jur. 2d Constitutional Law § 425.
6. See *Federer v. Gephardt*, 363 F.3d 754, 759 (8th Cir. 2004).
7. *Farese v. Scherer*, 342 F.3d 1223, 1233 (11th Cir. 2003).
8. Leslie Cooper Mahaffey, *"There Is Something Unique . . . about the Government Funding of the Arts for First Amendment Purposes": An Institutional Approach to Granting Government Entities Free Speech Rights*, 60 DUKE L.J. 1239 (2011).
9. *Fox Television Stations, Inc. v. F.C.C.*, 613 F.3d 317, 327 (2nd Cir. 2010).
10. *4805 Convoy, Inc. v. City of San Diego*, 183 F.3d 1108, 1112 (9th Cir. 1999).
11. Matthew R. Millikin, Note, *www.misappropriation.com: Protecting Trade Secrets After Mass Dissemination on the Internet*, 78 WASH. U. L.Q. 931, 948 (2000).
12. 16A Am. Jur. 2d Constitutional Law § 518.
13. 16A Am. Jur. 2d Constitutional Law § 501.
14. 16A Am. Jur. 2d Constitutional Law § 540.
15. First Amendment Protection Afforded to Web Site Operators, 30 A.L.R.6th 299.
16. *In re Grand Jury Subpoena*, 201 F. App'x 430 (9th Cir. 2006).
17. Anthony L. Fargo, *Analyzing Federal Shield Law Proposals: What Congress Can Learn from the States*, 11 COMM. L. & POL'Y 35, 46–9 (2006).
18. Michael Kahn, *The Origination and Early Development of Free Speech in the United States*, 76-OCT FLA. B.J. 71.
19. Black's Law Dictionary (9th ed. 2009).
20. *Pope v. Motel 6*, 114 P.3d 277, 282 (Nev. 2005).
21. *New England Tractor–Trailer Training of Conn., Inc. v. Globe Newspaper Co.*, 395 Mass. 471, 474 (1985).
22. See *Milum v. Banks*, 642 S.E.2d 892, 898 (Ga. 2007).
23. *Gertz v. Robert Welch, Inc.*, 418 U.S. 323, 351 (1974).
24. Id.
25. Frank J. Cavico, *Defamation in the Private Sector: The Libelous and Slanderous Employer*, 24 U. DAYTON L. REV. 405, 447 (1999).
26. 50 Am. Jur. 2d Libel and Slander § 362.
27. Right of Corporation, Absent Specific Statutory Subpoena Power, to Disclosure of Identity of Anonymous or Pseudonymous Internet User, 120 A.L.R.5th 195.
28. See *Mobilisa, Inc. v. Doe*, 170 P.3d 712 (Ariz. Ct. App. Div. 1 2007).
29. Liability of Internet Service Provider for Internet or E-mail Defamation, 84 A.L.R.5th 169.
30. Jeffrey Segal, Michael H. Sacopulos, and Domingo H. Rivera, *Legal Remedies for Online Defamation of Physicians*, 30 J. Legal Med. 349, 372 (2009).
31. Alyssa J. Long, *Internet and Social Media*, 73 TEX. B.J. 202 (2010).
32. Validity, Construction, and Application of Immunity Provisions of Communications Decency Act, 47 U.S.C.A. § 230., 52 A.L.R. Fed. 2d 37.
33. *Fair Housing Council of San Fernando Valley v. Roommates.com*, LLC, 521 F.3d 1157 (9th Cir. 2008).

34. David Ardia, *Free Speech Savior or Shield for Scoundrels: An Empirical Study of Intermediary Immunity under Section 230 of the Communications Decency Act*, 43 LOY. L.A. L. REV. 373 (2010).

35. *Lucas v. Cranshaw*, 659 S.E.2d 612, 615 (Ga. Ct. App. 2009).

36. *Currier v. W. Newspapers, Inc.*, 855 P.2d 1351, 1354 (Ariz. 1993).

37. Mitchell H. Rubinstein, *A Peek at New York Defamation Law*, 82-DEC NYSTBJ 58 (2010).

38. 50 Am. Jur. 2d Libel and Slander § 254.

39. London Wright-Pegs, *The Media SLAPP Back: An Analysis of California's Anti-SLAPP Statute and the Media Defendant*, 16 U.C.L.A. ENT. L. REV. 323, 338 (2009).

40. Black's Law Dictionary (9th ed. 2009).

41. Michael W. Taylor, *A Blogger, Google, and a "Skank": An Analysis of Whether Google has a Fiduciary Obligation to its Bloggers*, 113 W. VA. L. REV. 1001, 1020 (2011).

42. Susan W. Brenner and Megan Rehberg, *"Kiddie Crime"? The Utility of Criminal Law in Controlling Cyberbullying*, 8 FIRST AMEND. L. REV. 1, 48 (2009).

43. Edward L. Carter, *Outlaw Speech on the Internet: Examining the Link Between Unique Characteristics of Online Media and Criminal Libel Prosecutions*, 21 SANTA CLARA COMPUTER & HIGH TECH. L.J. 289, 298–99 (2005).

44. *In re I.M.L.*, 61 P.3d 1038, 1043 (Utah 2002).

45. 50 Am. Jur. 2d Libel and Slander § 502 (citing *Thomas v. City of Baxter Springs*, 369 F. Supp. 2d 1291 (D. Kan. 2005)).

46. 50 Am. Jur. 2d Libel and Slander § 524.

47. Black's Law Dictionary (9th ed. 2009).

CHAPTER

10 Constitutional and Statutory Privacy Protections

Relying on the government to protect your privacy is like asking a peeping tom to install your window blinds.

JOHN PERRY BARLOW[1]

LEARNING OBJECTIVES

After completing this chapter, you will be able to:

1. Explain the right of privacy afforded under the United States Constitution and state constitutions.
2. Explain and apply to specific applications the key federal laws that relate to online privacy, including the Privacy Act of 1974, the Freedom of Information Act (FOIA), Gramm-Leach-Bliley Act (GLBA), and the Health Insurance Portability and Accountability Act (HIPAA).

CONSTITUTIONAL RIGHT TO PRIVACY

Although the U.S. Constitution does not expressly include the term *privacy* anywhere in the document, the U.S. Supreme Court has implied a federal constitutional right to privacy.[2] The U.S. Supreme Court has recognized the right to privacy from the penumbras of the U.S. Constitution. In the 1965 case of *Griswold v. Connecticut*, 381 U.S. 479, 484 (1965), the Court found a right to privacy in the penumbras of the First, Third, Fourth, Fifth, and Ninth Amendments in finding privacy in a marital relationship. In *Griswold*, the Court struck down prohibitions on birth control for married couples and explicitly recognized the right to privacy for the first time based on various constitutional provisions. Courts have found that various guarantees in the Bill of Rights create zones of privacy. Since *Griswold*, the Court has relied upon the penumbral right to privacy to protect decisions relating to marriage, procreation, contraception, family relationships, and child rearing, and education.

Building upon the principles enunciated in *Griswold* in which the Court for the first time expressly held that the Constitution protected a right of privacy, the Court declared that warrantless wiretapping was unconstitutional in *Katz v. United States*, 389 U.S. 347 (1967). The Court reasoned that the recognition of a right of privacy does not require a physical intrusion upon an individual's property, but instead derives from an individual's "reasonable expectation of privacy." In 2003, in *Lawrence v. Texas*, 539 U.S. 558, 562 (2003), the Court further expanded the right to privacy by holding that privacy protects the conduct between consenting homosexual adults in the home.

While the U.S. Constitution does not expressly include the term *privacy*, ten states have explicit rights of privacy in their state constitutions. The ten states that have expressly adopted a right to privacy in their constitutions are Alaska, Arizona, California, Florida, Hawaii, Illinois, Louisiana, Montana, South Carolina, and Washington.[3] For example, Art. I, § 1 of the California Constitution provides that "[a]ll people are by nature free and independent and have inalienable rights. Among these are enjoying and defending life and liberty, acquiring, possessing, and protecting property, and pursuing and obtaining safety, happiness, and privacy." Unlike the federal Constitution, California also enforces this interest against private parties and not just state actors.

State constitutions have played a key role in expanding privacy rights in the online environment. In *State v. Reid*, 389 N.J. Super. 563, 914 A.2d 310 (App. Div. 2007), the New Jersey Supreme Court found that under the New Jersey state constitution, individuals have reasonable expectations of privacy in their Internet Protocol (IP) addresses, and law enforcement may not compel disclosure of the subscriber information linked to an IP address from an ISP without a grand jury subpoena.[4] Some legal scholars argue that the state right of privacy has become dynamic, and thus more responsive to the evolving needs of a changing society.[5] State courts have led the movement to recognize new rights by expanding the conception of self-determination. State constitutional law has become a vital source of protection for privacy rights, and both the U.S. Constitution and state constitutions must be considered to fully understand the right to privacy.[6]

Although courts have recognized privacy rights in a variety of situations, Congress and state legislatures provide additional statutory protection of privacy concerns in a number of circumstances. An examination of privacy rights in America requires an analysis of privacy-related statutes. Congress has enacted a patchwork of information privacy statutes. The key federal statutes that protect privacy rights, especially in the online environment, include the Privacy Act, Freedom of Information Act (FOIA), Gramm-Leach-Bliley Act (GLBA), Fair and Accurate Credit Transaction Act (FACTA), Fair Credit Reporting Act (FCRA), Health Insurance Portability and Accountability Act (HIPAA), Family Educational Rights and Privacy Act of 1974 (FERPA), Drivers' Privacy Protection Act (DPPA), Children's Online Privacy Protection Act (COPPA), Electronic Communications Privacy Act (ECPA), and the Video Privacy Protection Act.[7] In all, there are more than thirty federal laws, as well as innumerable state laws that affect the handling of personal information.

KEY FEDERAL PRIVACY STATUTES

While Congress has not enacted comprehensive privacy legislation that applies to all types of personal data, lawmakers have passed significant statutes that apply to particular types of information.

Privacy Act of 1974 (Privacy Act)

Adopted as part of the Watergate-era reform, Congress adopted the federal **Privacy Act of 1974 (Privacy Act)**, 5 U.S.C. § 552a, as the first national privacy protection statute.

Privacy Act
A federal law that regulates the collection, maintenance, use, and dissemination of information about individuals by federal agencies. Also called Privacy Act of 1974. 5 U.S.C. § 552a.

The Privacy Act recognized the need to balance an individual's interest in information privacy with the institutional practice of storing data in a computerized recordkeeping system. Theoretically, the Privacy Act regulates virtually all federal government handling of personal information.

The Privacy Act regulates the collection, maintenance, use, and dissemination of information about individuals by federal agencies. The Privacy Act gives agencies detailed instructions for managing their records and provides for various sorts of civil relief to individuals aggrieved by failures on the government's part to comply with the requirements.

One form of civil relief is that an individual can seek money damages when an agency intentionally or willfully fails to comply with the Privacy Act's requirements which results in an adverse effect on an individual. To state a claim for money damages for an adverse determination under the Privacy Act, a plaintiff must allege that (1) they have been aggrieved by an adverse determination; (2) the agency failed to maintain their records with the degree of relevancy necessary to assure fairness in the determination; (3) the agency's reliance on the irrelevant records was the proximate cause of the adverse determination; and (4) the agency acted intentionally or willfully in failing to maintain relevant records.[8]

Some courts have considered Privacy Act claims involving Internet-related content and e-mail messages. In *Oja v. U.S. Army Corps of Engineers*, 440 F.3d 1122 (9th Cir. 2006), a federal employee brought an action alleging that the United States Army Corps of Engineers (USACE) violated his rights under the Privacy Act when it disclosed his personal information by posting it on the public Internet website for the USACE. The federal appeals court determined that although the employer may have acted improperly in posting the employee's personal information on the website, the Privacy Act did not require the employer to disclose an improper posting to the employee and granted summary judgment in favor of the USACE, in that the claim was time-barred and the statute of limitations had run.

One part of the Privacy Act, U.S.C. § 552a(e)(7), also provides that agencies will not maintain records that describe how an individual exercises First Amendment right unless there is a valid law enforcement purpose.

In *Sieverding v. U.S. Dept. of Justice*, 693 F. Supp. 2d 93 (D. D.C. 2010), records allegedly describing First Amendment activities of an arrestee fell within the exception of valid law enforcement purposes under the Privacy Act's ban on keeping such records. The records included a request for assistance in a fugitive investigation that was pertinent to law enforcement activity and an e-mail from the United States Marshals Service (USMS) to the arrestee's congressional representative containing copies of arrest warrants and related documents. However in *Gerlich v. U.S. Dept. of Justice*, 659 F. Supp. 2d 1 (D. D.C. 2009), the court held that applicants for honors and summer law programs within the United States Department of Justice properly stated a claim for a Privacy Act violation by alleging that a United States Department of Justice official conducted Internet searches regarding political and ideological affiliations of applicants. Under the Privacy Act, 5 U.S.C. § 552a(a)(4), a "record" is any item, collection, or grouping of information about an individual that is maintained by an agency and that contains that person's name or the identifying information. In *Gerlich*, the records at issue were Internet printouts and the handwritten notes allegedly created by an agency official.

Although the Privacy Act extended the scope of privacy law, the Privacy Act fails to preserve important privacy principles in many areas of American life. The Privacy Act applies only to federal agencies and does not apply to private entities such as banks, insurance companies, and credit companies.[9]

The Freedom of Information Act

The federal **Freedom of Information Act (FOIA)**, codified in 5 U.S.C. § 552, is a federal law that gives citizens the right to access information from the federal government. It is often described as the law that keeps citizens in the know about their government. The FOIA is a federal statute that establishes guidelines for public disclosure of documents and materials created and held by federal agencies.[10] The basic purpose of the statute is to give the public access to official information so that the public will be better informed and the government will be more accountable for its actions. The FOIA reflects a general philosophy of full agency disclosure unless information falls under one of the exemptions in the statute. Disclosure, not secrecy, is the dominant objective of the FOIA.[11]

Freedom of Information Act (FOIA)
A federal law that establishes guidelines for public disclosure of documents and materials created and held by federal agencies. 5 U.S.C. § 552. *See also* Reverse-FOIA.

Enacted in 1966, the Freedom of Information Act (FOIA) provides that any person has a right, enforceable in court, to obtain access to federal agency records, except to the extent that such records (or portions of them) are protected from public disclosure by one of nine exemptions or by one of three special law enforcement record exclusions. A FOIA request can be made for any agency record. Each agency's website contains information about the type of records that agency maintains.

(b) This section does not apply to matters that are —

(1) (A) specifically authorized under criteria established by an Executive order to be kept secret in the interest of national defense or foreign policy and (B) are in fact properly classified pursuant to such Executive order;

(2) related solely to the internal personnel rules and practices of an agency;

(3) specifically exempted from disclosure by statute specifically exempted from disclosure by statute (other than section 552b of this title), if that statute—(A)(i) requires that the matters be withheld from the public in such a manner as to leave no discretion on the issue; or (ii) establishes particular criteria for withholding or refers to particular types of matters to be withheld; and (B) if enacted after the date of enactment of the OPEN FOIA Act of 2009, specifically cites to this paragraph.

(4) trade secrets and commercial or financial information obtained from a person and privileged or confidential;

(5) inter-agency or intra-agency memorandums or letters which would not be available by law to a party other than an agency in litigation with the agency;

(6) personnel and medical files and similar files the disclosure of which would constitute a clearly unwarranted invasion of personal privacy;

(7) records or information compiled for law enforcement purposes, but only to the extent that the production of such law enforcement records or information (A) could reasonably be expected to interfere with enforcement proceedings, (B) would deprive a person of a right to a fair trial or an impartial adjudication, (C) could reasonably be expected to constitute an unwarranted invasion of personal privacy, (D) could reasonably be expected to disclose the identity of a confidential source, including a State, local, or foreign agency or authority or any private institution which furnished information on a confidential basis, and, in the case of a record or information compiled by criminal law enforcement authority in the course of a criminal investigation or by an agency conducting a lawful national security intelligence investigation, information furnished by a confidential source, (E) would disclose techniques and procedures for law enforcement investigations or prosecutions, or would disclose guidelines for law enforcement investigations or prosecutions if such disclosure could reasonably be expected to risk circumvention of the law, or (F) could reasonably be expected to endanger the life or physical safety of any individual;

(8) contained in or related to examination, operating, or condition reports prepared by, on behalf of, or for the use of an agency responsible for the regulation or supervision of financial institutions; or

(9) geological and geophysical information and data, including maps, concerning wells.

FIGURE 10.1 FOIA Exemptions, Codified in 5 U.S.C. § 552(b)

Many states have enacted their own freedom of information acts. These statutes are also called open or public-records acts, or right to know acts. The dominant purpose of a state public-records law is to afford the public broad access to governmental records.[12] State freedom of information acts are remedial in nature, and any doubt is to be resolved in favor of the disclosure of the records. Exemptions are narrowly interpreted, and the burden is on the public agency opposing disclosure.

Reverse-FOIA suit
A lawsuit by the owner of a trade secret or other information exempt from disclosure under a Freedom of Information Act to prevent a governmental entity from making that information available to the public. *See also* Freedom of Information Act (FOIA).

A related concept to a FOIA request is a reverse FOIA suit. A **reverse FOIA suit** is a lawsuit by the owner of a trade secret or other information exempt from disclosure under the FOIA to prevent a governmental entity from making that information available to the public.[13] In a reverse-FOIA action, a person or entity seeks to prevent an agency from releasing information to a third-party in response to a FOIA request.

Because of the expanding use of computers in business and government and the change to computer-based information and data systems within the work place, Congress passed the Electronic Freedom of Information Act (E-FOIA) Amendments in 1996, Electronic Freedom of Information Act of 1996, Pub. L. No. 104–231, 110 Stat. 3048 (1996). The purpose of this amendment was to enhance government transparency and accountability and provide public access to electronic records held by the government including microfiche and computer disks.

E-FOIA
Freedom of Information Act (FOIA) request submitted electronically.

Prior to the passage of E-FOIA, courts allowed agencies to refuse requests for electronic data.[14] In the E-FOIA 1996 amendment, Congress expanded the definition of "records" to include electronic records. Under the **E-FOIA,** the agency is required to provide the information in the desired format if it is "readily reproducible" from the agency's records. The E-FOIA amendments attempted to create more government accountability to the public regarding its internal operations.

The U.S. Supreme Court unanimously held in *FCC v. AT&T Inc.,* 131 S. Ct. 1177 (2011) (Case 10.1) that a corporation does not have a right of "personal privacy" under the Freedom of Information Act (FOIA) disclosure exemption for law enforcement records. The FOIA request at issue related to an investigation by the Federal Communications Commission (FCC) Enforcement Bureau after a voluntary report by AT&T Inc. that the corporation might have overcharged the Government for services the corporation provided to an FCC-administered program to enhance access by schools and libraries to advanced telecommunications and information services. Justice John Roberts delivered the opinion of the unanimous court in March 2011. Justice Elena Kagan took no part in the decision.

CASE 10.1

The Case Finding No Personal Privacy Rights for Corporations under FOIA

FCC v. AT&T Inc., ***131 S. Ct. 1177 (2011)***

The Freedom of Information Act requires federal agencies to make records and documents publicly available upon request, unless they fall within one of several statutory exemptions. One of those exemptions covers law enforcement records, the disclosure of which "could reasonably be expected to constitute an unwarranted invasion of personal privacy." 5 U.S.C. § 552(b)(7)(C). The question presented is whether corporations have "personal privacy" for the purposes of this exemption.

The Freedom of Information Act request at issue in this case relates to an investigation of respondent AT&T Inc., conducted by the Federal Communications Commission. AT&T participated in an FCC-administered program—the E-Rate (or Education-Rate) program—that was created to enhance access for schools and libraries to advanced telecommunications and information services. In August 2004, AT&T voluntarily reported to the FCC that it might have overcharged the Government for services it provided as part of the program. The FCC's Enforcement Bureau launched an investigation. As part of that investigation, AT&T provided the Bureau various documents, including responses to interrogatories, invoices, emails with pricing and billing information, names and job descriptions of employees involved, and AT&T's assessment of whether those employees had violated the company's code of conduct.

The FCC petitioned this Court for review of the Third Circuit's decision and CompTel filed as a respondent supporting petitioners. We granted certiorari and now reverse.

Like the Court of Appeals below, AT&T relies on the argument that the word "personal" in Exemption 7(C) incorporates the statutory definition of the word "person." The Administrative Procedure Act defines "person" to include "an individual, partnership, corporation, association, or public or private organization other than an agency." 5 U.S.C. § 551(2). Because that definition applies here, the argument goes, "personal" must mean relating to those "person[s]": namely, corporations and other entities as well as individuals. This reading, we are told, is dictated by a "basic principle of grammar and usage."

We disagree. Adjectives typically reflect the meaning of corresponding nouns, but not always. Sometimes they acquire distinct meanings of their own.

Even in cases such as these there may well be a link between the noun and the adjective. What is significant is that, in ordinary usage, a noun and its adjective form may have meanings as disparate as any two unrelated words. The FCC's argument that "personal" does not, in fact, derive from the English word "person," but instead developed along its own etymological path, simply highlights the shortcomings of AT&T's proposed rule.

"Person" is a defined term in the statute; "personal" is not. When a statute does not define a term, we typically "give the phrase its ordinary meaning." "Personal" ordinarily refers to individuals. We do not usually speak of personal characteristics, personal effects, personal correspondence, personal influence, or personal tragedy as referring to corporations or other artificial entities. This is not to say that corporations do not have correspondence, influence, or tragedies of their own, only that we do not use the word "personal" to describe them.

Certainly, if the chief executive officer of a corporation approached the chief financial officer and said, "I have something personal to tell you," we would not assume the CEO was about to discuss company business. Responding to a request for information, an individual might say, "that's personal." A company spokesman, when asked for information about the company, would not. In fact, we often use the word "personal" to mean precisely the opposite of business-related: We speak of personal expenses and business expenses, personal life and work life, personal opinion and a company's view.

Dictionaries also suggest that "personal" does not ordinarily relate to artificial "persons" such as corporations.

AT&T dismisses these definitions, correctly noting that "personal"—at its most basic level—simply means "[o]f or pertaining to a particular person." Webster's New International Dictionary 1828 (2d ed.1954). The company acknowledges that "in non-legal usage, where a 'person' is a human being, it is entirely unsurprising that the word 'personal' is used to refer to human beings." But in a watered-down version of the "grammatical imperative" argument, AT&T contends that "person"—in common legal usage—is understood to include a corporation. "Personal" in the same context therefore can and should have the same scope, especially here in light of the statutory definition.

The construction of statutory language often turns on context. But here the context to which AT&T points does not dissuade us from the ordinary meaning of "personal." We have no doubt that "person," in a legal setting, often refers to artificial entities. The Dictionary Act makes that clear. 1 U.S.C. § 1 (defining "person" to include "corporations, companies, associations, firms, partnerships, societies, and joint stock companies, as well as individuals"). But AT&T's effort to ascribe a corresponding legal meaning to "personal" again elides the difference between "person" and "personal."

When it comes to the word "personal," there is little support for the notion that it denotes corporations, even in the legal context.

AT&T's argument treats the term "personal privacy" as simply the sum of its two words: the privacy of a person. Under that view, the defined meaning of the noun "person," or the asserted

(*Continued*)

(Continued)

specialized legal meaning, takes on greater significance. But two words together may assume a more particular meaning than those words in isolation. We understand a golden cup to be a cup made of or resembling gold. A golden boy, on the other hand, is one who is charming, lucky, and talented. A golden opportunity is one not to be missed. "Personal" in the phrase "personal privacy" conveys more than just "of a person." It suggests a type of privacy evocative of human concerns—not the sort usually associated with an entity like, say, AT&T.

Despite its contention that "[c]ommon legal usage" of the word "person" supports its reading of the term "personal privacy," AT&T does not cite a single instance in which this Court or any other (aside from the Court of Appeals below) has expressly referred to a corporation's "personal privacy." Nor does it identify any other statute that does so. On the contrary, treatises in print around the time that Congress drafted the exemptions at hand reflect the understanding that the specific concept of "personal privacy," at least as a matter of common law, did not apply to corporations.

AT&T contends that this Court has recognized "privacy" interests of corporations in the Fourth Amendment and double jeopardy contexts, and that the term should be similarly construed here. But this case does not call upon us to pass on the scope of a corporation's "privacy" interests as a matter of constitutional or common law. The discrete question before us is instead whether Congress used the term "personal privacy" to refer to the privacy of artificial persons in FOIA Exemption 7(C); the cases AT&T cites are too far afield to be of help here.

AT&T concludes that the FCC has simply failed to demonstrate that the phrase "personal privacy" "necessarily excludes the privacy of corporations." But construing statutory language is not merely an exercise in ascertaining "the outer limits of [a word's] definitional possibilities," AT&T has given us no sound reason in the statutory text or context to disregard the ordinary meaning of the phrase "personal privacy."

The meaning of "personal privacy" in Exemption 7(C) is further clarified by the rest of the statute. Congress enacted Exemption 7(C) against the backdrop of pre-existing FOIA exemptions, and the purpose and scope of Exemption 7(C) becomes even more apparent when viewed in this context.

The phrase "personal privacy" first appeared in the FOIA exemptions in Exemption 6, enacted in 1966, eight years before Congress enacted Exemption 7(C). See 80 Stat. 250, codified as amended at 5 U.S.C. § 552(b)(6). Exemption 6 covers "personnel and medical files and similar files the disclosure of which would constitute a clearly unwarranted invasion of personal privacy." § 552(b)(6). Not only did Congress choose the same term in drafting Exemption 7(C), it also used the term in a nearly identical manner.

Although the question whether Exemption 6 is limited to individuals has not come to us directly, we have regularly referred to that exemption as involving an "individual's right of privacy."

Shortly after Congress passed the 1974 amendments that enacted Exemption 7(C), the Attorney General issued a memorandum to executive departments and agencies explaining that "personal privacy" in that exemption "pertains to the privacy interests of individuals."

We reject the argument that because "person" is defined for purposes of FOIA to include a corporation, the phrase "personal privacy" in Exemption 7(C) reaches corporations as well. The protection in FOIA against disclosure of law enforcement information on the ground that it would constitute an unwarranted invasion of personal privacy does not extend to corporations. We trust that AT&T will not take it personally.

The judgment of the Court of Appeals is reversed.

Case Questions

1. What was the FOIA exemption at issue in *FCC v. AT&T Inc.*?
2. What arguments did AT&T give in support of its position?
3. Why did the U.S. Supreme Court hold that a corporation does not have a right of "personal privacy" under the Freedom of Information Act (FOIA) disclosure exemption for law enforcement records?
4. Should corporations be entitled to the same rights as natural persons for privacy purposes and under FOIA? Why or why not?

Gramm-Leach-Bliley Act

The Financial Modernization Act of 1999, also known as the **Gramm-Leach-Bliley Act (GLBA)**, 15 U.S.C. §§ 6801 to 6809, provides for the protection of consumer financial information held by banks, securities firms, insurance companies, and other financial institutions.[15] Specifically, the Safeguards Rule, implemented under the GLBA, requires financial institutions to have a security plan to protect the confidentiality and integrity of personal consumer information.

Gramm-Leach-Bliley Act (GLBA)
A federal law that provides for the protection of consumer financial information held by banks, securities firms, insurance companies, and other financial institutions. Also called the Financial Modernization Act of 1999. 15 U.S.C. §§ 6801–6809.

With passage of the GLBA, Congress established the policy that each financial institution has an affirmative and continuing obligation to respect the privacy of its customers and to protect the security and confidentiality of those customers' nonpublic personal information.[16] Appropriate enforcement agencies must establish appropriate standards for the financial institutions subject to their jurisdiction relating to administrative, technical, and physical safeguards (1) to insure the security and confidentiality of customer records and information; (2) to protect against any anticipated threats or hazards to the security or integrity of such records; and (3) to protect against unauthorized access to or use of such records or information that could result in substantial harm or inconvenience to any customer.

The information privacy provisions of the Gramm-Leach-Bliley Act (GLBA) mandates that financial institutions shall not disclose nonpublic personal information without first notifying clients of the financial institution's disclosure policies and affording clients the opportunity to bar any disclosure of such information by "opting out." The GLBA provides exceptions to its notification and opt-out procedures such as complying with discovery requests in judicial proceedings.

The Gramm-Leach-Bliley Act does not provide a private right of action, and therefore individuals cannot file lawsuits for GLBA violations.[17] Rather, the Federal Trade Commission (FTC) is the main federal agency responsible for enforcing the GLBA and educating the public.[18]

In February 2010, the Federal Trade Commission notified almost 100 organizations that personal information, including sensitive data about customers and/or employees, had been shared from the organizations' computer networks and is available on peer-to-peer (P2P) file-sharing networks to any users of those networks, who could use it to commit identity theft or fraud. The FTC enforces laws that require companies in various industries to take reasonable and appropriate security measures to protect sensitive personal information, including the Gramm-Leach-Bliley Act and Section 5 of the FTC Act. The FTC sent notices to both private and public entities,

(a) Privacy obligation policy
It is the policy of the Congress that each financial institution has an affirmative and continuing obligation to respect the privacy of its customers and to protect the security and confidentiality of those customers' nonpublic personal information.

(b) Financial institutions safeguards
In furtherance of the policy in subsection (a) of this section, each agency or authority described in section 6805(a) of this title shall establish appropriate standards for the financial institutions subject to their jurisdiction relating to administrative, technical, and physical safeguards—

(1) to insure the security and confidentiality of customer records and information;
(2) to protect against any anticipated threats or hazards to the security or integrity of such records; and
(3) to protect against unauthorized access to or use of such records or information which could result in substantial harm or inconvenience to any customer.

FIGURE 10.2 Legislative Purpose of the Gramm-Leach-Bliley Act, 15 U.S.C.A. § 6801

including schools and local governments, that failure to prevent information from being shared to a P2P network could be a violation of the GLBA. Failure to prevent personal information from being shared on networks, including P2P networks, could potentially lead to fines and penalties in an enforcement action brought by the FTC.[19]

Fair Credit Reporting Act and Fair and Accurate Credit Transaction Act

Fair and Accurate Credit Transaction Act (FACTA) A federal law that amended the **Fair Credit Reporting Act (FCRA)** by implementing new procedures and mechanisms to combat identity theft. 15 U.S.C. § 1681(b).

Fair Credit Reporting Act (FCRA) A federal law that established national credit reporting standards in an effort to ensure accuracy and confidentiality in connection with credit reports. 15 U.S.C. § 1681.

The **Fair and Accurate Credit Transaction Act of 2003 (FACTA)**, 15 U.S.C. § 1681(b), amended the **Fair Credit Reporting Act (FCRA)** which was set to expire. The Fair Credit Reporting Act of 1970 originally established national credit reporting standards in an effort to ensure "accuracy and confidentiality" in connection with credit reports. FACTA, sometimes also called the FACT Act, amended the FCRA by implementing new procedures and mechanisms to combat identity theft. FACTA was adopted out of a growing concern that information sharing over the Internet required stronger regulations in order to better protect consumers. The purpose of the FCRA is "to require that consumer reporting agencies adopt reasonable procedures for meeting the needs of commerce for consumer credit, personnel, insurance, and other information in a manner which is fair and equitable to the consumer." The FACTA rules apply to financial institutions and creditors.[20]

For credit card sales, FACTA also requires that businesses print no more than "the last 5 digits of the card number or the expiration date upon any receipt provided to the cardholder at the point of sale."[21] For willful violations of this provision, businesses are liable for actual damages sustained by the consumer of not less than $100 and not more than $1,000. FACTA claims are commonly brought as class actions due to the low level of damages authorized and the commonality of material facts between plaintiffs. An important feature of FACTA claims is that to succeed the plaintiff must prove that the defendant violated the statute "willfully."

Under the "Red Flag" rules adopted by the FTC under FACTA, financial institutions and creditors must develop and put into operation written identity theft prevention programs. Those programs must provide for the identification, detection, and response to patterns, practices, or specific activities known as "red flags" that could indicate identity theft. FACTA focuses on preventative measures necessary for financial institutions and creditors rather than reactionary measures taken by the consumer victims whose identities are stolen.[22]

Red Flag Rule A rule under the Fair and Accurate Credit Transaction Act that requires financial institutions and creditors to develop and put into operation written identity theft prevention programs.

The **Red Flag Rule** helps to prevent identity theft where the FCRA previously fell short by focusing on preventative mechanisms to prevent identity theft or mitigate the harm. FCRA only allowed a consumer to place a fraud alert in a credit report file after the consumer suspected that they had been the victim of identity theft. The Red Flag Rule promulgated under FTAC is an important regulatory mechanism with personal information.

With the rise in online financial transactions among consumers, the threat of identity theft looms. FCTA and the Red Flag Rule aim to prevent and minimize the harm associated with identity theft.

Health Insurance Portability and Accountability Act

Health Insurance Portability and Accountability Act (HIPAA) A federal law that protects the confidentiality of health information as it is transmitted through and collected by electronic portals.

In an attempt to protect the confidentiality of health information as it is transmitted through and collected by electronic portals, Congress adopted the **Health Insurance Portability and Accountability Act of 1996 (HIPAA)**. The correct acronym for the Health Insurance Portability and Accountability Act is "HIPAA" and not "HIPPA." The acronym for HIPAA is often misspelled as HIPPA. As the primary law that establishes the U.S. legal framework for health information privacy, HIPAA aimed to establish standards for privacy and security of "personal health information" (PHI) and address conflicting state privacy laws relating to health information. In 2009, Congress enacted the Health Information Technology for Economic and Clinical Health Act (HITECH) Act of 2009 amending HIPAA.[23] HITECH clarified and extended the scope and application of HIPAA to outside vendors who also have access to personal health information.

The U.S. Department of Health and Human Services (HHS) has also adopted important regulations under HIPAA with the Privacy Rule and the Security Rules. These rules define the rights of patients with regard to protected health information and the obligations of covered entities and business associates that possess personal health information. The HIPAA Security Rule, codified in 45 CFR Part 160 and Subparts A and C of Part 164, "establishes national standards to protect individuals' electronic personal health information that is created, received, used, or maintained by a covered entity" and "requires appropriate administrative, physical and technical safeguards to ensure the confidentiality, integrity, and security of electronic protected health information."

Although there are benefits in using Electronic Health Records (EHRs), such as increased cost savings and more efficient health care, potential risks with EHRs also exist, including privacy and security concerns.[25] Health care providers maintain records that include the private health information of their patients, along with other confidential personal and financial data, which are attractive targets for identity thieves and other cybercriminals. For example, in October 2010, approximately 280,000 Medicaid members, including members' health plan identification numbers and some health records, were put at risk when two insurance providers announced the loss of a storage device that contained personal health information.

Medical identity theft (MIT) is also a growing concern. Medical identity theft is generally defined as the theft of personally identifiable health information in order to gain access to health treatment or to fraudulently file for reimbursements for false medical treatment. In one case, a medical office worker stole the electronic records of over 1,000 patients, selling them to a relative who made nearly $3 million dollars by filing false medical claims.

HIPAA originally regulated protected health information (PHI) held by "covered entities," defined as health plans, health care clearinghouses, and health care providers who transmit health information electronically in certain information transactions. HIPAA originally excluded significant entities involved in electronic health information exchanges, such as personal health record (PHR) vendors. In reality, many health care providers utilize outside contractors to perform many functions such as computer systems work or billing. Those third-party entities can receive personal health information in the performance of their duties, and are addressed in the Privacy Rule under the category of "business associates."

HITECH clarified and extended the regulation of business associates by providing that they are subject to the same privacy regulations applied to covered entities. The purpose of HITECH is to put business associates under the same umbrella as covered entities in the protection of privacy and security of protected health information. Under the HHS regulation in 45 C.F.R. § 160.103, a "business associate" is "a person or entity that performs certain functions or activities that involve the use or disclosure of protected health information." Business associate activities include claims processing, data analysis, utilization review, and billing. Business associate services are limited to legal, actuarial, accounting, consulting, data aggregation, management, administrative, accreditation, or financial services.

In order to disclose PHI to business associates, a covered entity must have assurances that the use of the information will be limited to that for which it was transferred, that the entity has sufficient security to protect the information, and that it will cooperate with the covered entity to protect the information as required under the Privacy

Rule. Those assurances must be included in the agreement between the covered entity and the business associate.

Like the Gramm-Leach-Bliley Act, HIPAA does not have a private right of action to file a complaint in a court for damages. A person whose personal health information privacy has been violated must file a complaint with the U.S. Department of Human Services Office of Civil Rights (OCR). HHS will then investigate the alleged violation and possibly bring an action against the entity that has violated HIPAA.

A complaint under HIPAA must contain the following requirements: (1) be filed in writing, either on paper or electronically, by mail, fax, or e-mail; (2) name the covered entity involved and describe the acts or omissions you believe violated the requirements of the Privacy or Security Rule; and (3) be filed within 180 days of when you knew that the act or omission complained of occurred. OCR may extend the 180-day period if you can show "good cause." HHS recommends using the OCR Health Information Privacy Complaint Form (see Figure 10.3) for filing complaints. Under HIPAA an entity cannot retaliate against a person for filing a complaint.[27]

The HITECH Act increased civil monetary penalties for violations of HIPPA and also extended criminal liability for wrongful disclosure of PHI. The HITECH Act also authorized State Attorneys General to bring a civil action in federal district court against individuals who violate HIPAA and gave the Secretary of HHS the right to intervene in such actions. Under the HITECH Act, HHS can impose civil monetary penalties for each HIPAA violation ranging from at least $100 to a maximum of $50,000 for the lowest category violation. Under the highest category violation, HHS can impose a $50,000 penalty per violation. Additionally, the HITECH Act increased the maximum penalty that HHS can impose for all such violations of the same HIPAA provision in a calendar year from $25,000 to $1.5 million. Civil penalties now increase in tiers depending on whether the violation was committed unknowingly or due to reasonable cause or willful neglect.

In July 2010, Connecticut Attorney General Richard Blumenthal entered into an agreement with Health Net for failing to secure patient health and financial information for the first settlement of a HIPAA enforcement action brought by a state attorney general under the HITECH Act.[28] The case against Health Net involved the loss of a hard drive containing more than 500,000 individuals' records including clinical data and social security numbers. As part of the settlement agreement, Health Net agreed to a corrective action plan that required Health Net to implement several detailed measures to protect health information and other private data in compliance with HIPAA. Health Net also agreed to a $250,000 payment to the state of Connecticut representing statutory damages and may have to pay an additional $500,000 to the state of Connecticut if it is established that the lost disk drive was accessed and personal information was used illegally, thereby impacting plan members. It was noted in the settlement agreement that Health Net spent more than $7 million to investigate the circumstances surrounding the missing portable disk drive, to notify Health Net members, and to offer credit monitoring and identity theft insurance.[29]

Federal prosecutors have also successfully obtained convictions in criminal cases for HIPAA violations. In January 2010, Dr. Huping Zhou, a licensed cardiothoracic surgeon in China who worked at the UCLA School of Medicine as a researcher, was sentenced to four months in prison for improperly accessing medical records of high-profile celebrities. Zhou's incarceration became the first incarceration for a HIPAA violation for unauthorized access of medical records. Zhou received a notice of intent to dismiss him from UCLA Healthcare for job performance reasons unrelated to his illegal access of medical records. For the next three weeks, Zhou accessed the UCLA patient records system 323 times with most of the accesses involving well-known celebrities. Zhou pleaded guilty to four misdemeanor counts of violating the federal privacy provisions of HIPAA.[30]

Form Approved: OMB No. 0990-0269.
See OMB Statement on Reverse.

DEPARTMENT OF HEALTH AND HUMAN SERVICES
OFFICE FOR CIVIL RIGHTS (OCR)
HEALTH INFORMATION PRIVACY COMPLAINT

YOUR FIRST NAME	YOUR LAST NAME
HOME PHONE (Please include area code)	WORK PHONE (Please include area code)

STREET ADDRESS	CITY

STATE	ZIP	E-MAIL ADDRESS (If available)

Are you filing this complaint for someone else? ☐ Yes ☐ No

If Yes, whose health information privacy rights do you believe were violated?

FIRST NAME	LAST NAME

Who (or what agency or organization, e.g., provider, health plan) do you believe violated your (or someone else's) health information privacy rights or committed another violation of the Privacy Rule?
PERSON / AGENCY / ORGANIZATION

STREET ADDRESS	CITY

STATE	ZIP	PHONE (Please include area code)

When do you believe that the violation of health information privacy rights occurred?
LIST DATE(S)

Describe briefly what happened. How and why do you believe your (or someone else's) health information privacy rights were violated, or the privacy rule otherwise was violated? Please be as specific as possible. (Attach additional pages as needed)

Please sign and date this complaint. You do not need to sign if submitting this form by email because submission by email represents your signature.

SIGNATURE	DATE *(mm/dd/yyyy)*

Filing a complaint with OCR is voluntary. However, without the information requested above, OCR may be unable to proceed with your complaint. We collect this information under authority of the Privacy Rule issued pursuant to the Health Insurance Port ability and Accountability Act of 1996. We will use the information you provide to determine if we have jurisdiction and, if so, how we will process your complaint. Information submitted on this form is treated confidentially and is protected under the provisions of the Privacy Act of 1974. Names or other identifying information about individuals are disclosed when it is necessary for investigation of possible health information privacy violations, for internal systems operations, or for routine uses, which include disclosure of information outside the Department for purposes associated with health information privacy compliance and as permitted by law. It is illegal for a covered entity to intimidate, threaten, coerce, discriminate or retaliate against you for filing this complaint or for taking any other action to enforce your rights under the Privacy Rule. You are not required to use this form. You also may write a letter or submit a complaint electronically with the same information. To submit an electronic complaint, go to OCR's Web site at: **www.hhs.gov/ocr/privacy/hipaa/complaints/index.html**. To mail a complaint see reverse page for OCR Regional addresses.

HHS-700 (7/09) (FRONT) PSC Graphics (301) 443-1090 EF

FIGURE 10.3 U.S. Department of Health and Human Services Health Information Privacy Complaint Form

Medical providers and business associates covered under HIPAA and the HITECH Act must be vigilant in protecting personal health information and electronic health records (EHRs). The purposes of HIPAA and the HITECH Act are to ensure that sensitive medical, personal, and financial information is protected. If personal health information is improperly compromised, the U.S. Department of Health and Human Services, federal prosecutors, and State Attorneys General may bring enforcement actions for health information privacy violations.

Drivers Privacy Protection Act

Drivers Privacy Protection Act (DPPA) A federal law that restricts the disclosure of driver license information by state authorities. 18 U.S.C. § 2725.

The **Drivers Privacy Protection Act (DPPA)** restricts the disclosure of driver license information by state authorities.[31] The DPPA was a legislative response to the murder of actress Rebecca Schaeffer, star of the hit television series, *My Sister Sam*, where an assailant used publicly available driver license information to stalk and then murder the victim.[32] Schaeffer was murdered by a stalker who obtained her home address from a private investigator using the California motor vehicles database. Prior to the passage of the DPPA, states had made millions of dollars auctioning off their motor vehicle and driver's license records. Colorado earned approximately $4.4 million, Florida made $33 million, and New York made $17 million in a year.[33] The DPPA now restricts the sale of driver license information by state agencies to commercial entities, including online databases.

Family Educational Rights and Privacy Act

Like the Privacy Act, GLBA, and HIPPA, the Family Educational Rights and Privacy Act (FERPA) is federal law aimed at protecting privacy.[34] FERPA focuses on protecting the privacy of students' education records. FERPA applies to all schools that receive funds under an applicable program of the U.S. Department of Education, including both public and private schools. FERPA applies to preschools, K–12, and post-secondary schools. FERPA includes two important requirements: (1) parents/adult students have the right to access their own education records; and (2) in general (and with more than a dozen exceptions), schools cannot disclose education records or their contents to third parties without the written consent of the parent/adult student.[35] For example, one of the exceptions under FERPA regulations allows for disclosure of records without consent where there is an emergency related to the health or safety of a student or others. FERPA requires that schools and their agents must have written permission from a parent or adult student before releasing information from a student's record.

Civil litigants and criminal defendants along with the media and commercial entities are increasingly demanding access to student records through subpoena requests. FERPA establishes procedural requirements for complying with subpoenas of student records that schools make a "reasonable effort" to provide precompliance notice to the parent/adult student whose records have been subpoenaed. FERPA does not provide substantive protection of such records from subpoena. Civil litigants have successfully obtained student records in a number of cases. For example, music companies claiming illegal downloads of copyrighted music have successfully subpoenaed electronic student records from universities that are Internet service providers in order to find the identities of students. Some students have argued that online plagiarism detection software, such as Turnitin produced by iParadigms, violates student privacy protections under FERPA; however, courts have not yet addressed this issue, instead focusing on copyright issues.[36]

In *Gonzaga University v. Doe*, 536 U.S. 273 (2002), the U.S. Supreme Court held that FERPA does not create a private cause of action under 42 U.S.C. § 1983, so a student may not personally sue a school for damages if protected information is wrongly released.

Since FERPA does not have a private cause of action, enforcement of FERPA violations is limited. One example of a FERPA violation without an enforcement remedy involved a reporter who discovered records, including grades and standardized test scores, for 6000-plus students on a school's website. Some schools have also put webcams in their classrooms and allow unlimited public access. Some argue that Congress needs to amend FERPA by establishing a meaningful enforcement mechanism and other provisions for effective protection of student privacy. Under the current law involving the privacy of student records, only the Secretary of the U.S. Department of Education can sue schools to enforce FERPA violations.

Children's Online Privacy Protection Act

In response to a report from the Federal Trade Commission (FTC) that websites collected personal information directly from children with limited mechanisms for parental control over the collection and use of the information, Congress adopted the **Children's Online Privacy Protection Act of 1998 (COPPA)**, 15 U.S.C. §§ 6501–6506. Protecting the privacy of children in the online environment and maintaining the security of children's personal information collected online were among the objectives of the Act.

Children's Online Privacy Protection Act (COPPA)
Federal law passed in protecting the privacy of children in the online environment and maintaining the security of children's personal information collected online. 15 U.S.C. §§ 6501–6506.

The crux of COPPA's protections is the requirement that website operators obtain "verifiable parental consent" before collecting information from children. The Rule adopted by the FTC in 16 C.F.R. § 312.5 states that "[a]n operator is required to obtain verifiable parental consent before any collection, use, and/or disclosure of personal information from children."

The FTC has the exclusive authority to bring actions against websites for COPPA violations. Since COPPA was enacted, there have been several high-profile enforcement actions against websites for COPPA violations.

In 2003, the FTC levied civil penalties of $100,000 and $85,000 against Mrs. Fields Cookies and Hershey's Foods, respectively, for COPPA violations. In the enforcement action against Hershey, the FTC deemed the website's methods of obtaining parental consent insufficient. In September 2006, the FTC settled with UMG Recordings for a civil penalty of $400,000 for collecting personal information on children under the age of thirteen and for failing to maintain an adequate privacy policy.[37] UMG requested users' birthdays before allowing them to enter the website, but did not take any steps to secure parental consent when users indicated they were under the age of thirteen. In recent years, the FTC has targeted social networking sites for COPPA violations. For example, in 2006, the FTC brought an enforcement action against the social networking website Xanga for $1 million in civil penalties—the largest COPPA fine to date.

Like FERPA, some argue that COPPA is outdated and needs to be updated, since the Internet by its nature is a fluid, dynamic, and ever-changing medium. Age falsification by minors is one of the potential problems with the existing COPPA regulatory scheme. Privacy concerns on social networking sites such as Facebook, especially with regard to teenagers, will likely dominate privacy law debates for years to come.[38]

Electronic Communications Privacy Act

Electronic Communications Privacy Act (ECPA)
A federal law that regulates surveillance of electronic communications. 18 U.S.C. §§ 2701–2712.

In 1986, Congress enacted the **Electronic Communications Privacy Act (ECPA)** to prohibit unauthorized access to computer systems and gaining access through false pretenses or hacking.[39] The ECPA protects the privacy of peoples' wire, oral, and electronic communications from unlawful wiretapping, eavesdropping, and other forms of unauthorized access and disclosure by private businesses, law enforcement, and other government officials. The ECPA prohibits any person, including businesses and law enforcement, from unlawfully and intentionally intercepting the contents of telephone and other electronic communications or gaining unauthorized access to the contents of electronic communications in electronic storage. Live telephone communications, voice mail messages, e-mail messages, text messages, and instant messages are all forms of wire and electronic communications that are protected by the ECPA. Unless the interception or unauthorized access of a wire, oral, or electronic communication is covered by one of several statutory exceptions or defenses, violation of the ECPA is both a civil violation and a federal crime.

Unlike other federal privacy statutes, the ECPA creates a civil right of action against persons who gain unauthorized access to communications facilities and thereby access electronic communications stored incident to their transmission.[40] The ECPA also provides for criminal sanctions for violations of the statute. The ECPA contains two distinct titles: Title I contains prohibitions against the "interception" of electronic communications. Title II, the Stored Communications Act, limits the accessibility to electronically stored communications. Violators may face fines of up to $10,000 and imprisonment of up to five years for a Title I violation and fines of a minimum of $1000 per violation and up to ten years in prison for a Title II violation. Citizens may sue for civil damages, punitive damages if the violation is willful or intentional, attorneys' fees, and litigation costs. ECPA dramatically strengthened both the civil and criminal penalties private actors faced for violations of privacy and unauthorized disclosure of personal information.[41]

In the case of *In re DoubleClick Inc. Privacy Litigation*, 154 F. Supp. 2d 497 (S.D.N.Y. 2001), plaintiffs brought a class action lawsuit against DoubleClick alleging invasions of privacy through the use of cookies, alleging violations of Title II of the ECPA. DoubleClick is a company that specializes in collecting, compiling, and analyzing information about Internet users in order to place customized advertisements in the web pages they visit. The court held, however, that DoubleClick's cookies only collect information concerning users' activities on DoubleClick-affiliated websites and that that authorization was not needed as the communications at issue were outside the scope of Title II of the ECPA. The congressional intent of the ECPA was to protect communications held in interim storage by electronic communication service providers. Since DoubleClick's cookies remained on users' computers indefinitely, they were not in electronic storage under the ECPA and therefore not protected by the ECPA.

The ECPA has also been used as a defense by criminal defendants in criminal prosecutions. Suppression of evidence obtained in violation of the ECPA is available for wire or oral communications, but is not available for e-mail.

The ECPA has been the subject of lawsuits involving privacy in the workplace involving employers and employees. Both Title I and Title II of the ECPA include a consent exception applicable to the workplace. An employer can avoid liability under the ECPA by unilaterally imposing, as a term and condition of employment, a broad computer use policy reserving to the employer the right to intercept, monitor, and access emails and other files contained on a workplace computer. In *Bohach v. City of Reno*, 932 F. Supp. 1232, 1236 (D. Nev. 1996), the court held that an employer could, without violating ECPA Title II, retrieve pager text messages stored on its computer system because the employer "is the 'provider' of the 'electronic communications service' at issue here" and "service providers [may] do as they wish when it comes to accessing communications in electronic storage." If employees want to maintain privacy in their communications, they should use their own electronic device and not an electronic device provided by the employer.

In civil cases, the ECPA provides privacy protection for mobile communications such as the contents of text messages, voice-mail messages, and live mobile phone conversations. With the increased use of portable electronic devices and the potential for unauthorized access, ECPA is an important piece of federal legislation in protecting privacy rights in the online environment.

Video Privacy Protection Act

The **Video Privacy Protection Act of 1998 (VPPA)**, 18 U.S.C. § 2710, protects personal information in video rentals. Victims of unauthorized disclosure of their personally identifiable information may bring a civil cause of action and recover statutory damages of at least $2,500, punitive damages, and attorneys' fees. The VPPA provides exceptions for law enforcement agents who present a warrant, a grand jury subpoena, or a court order. The act was passed after Judge Robert Bork's video rentals were obtained by a Washington D.C. newspaper in an attempt to dig up embarrassing information while the U.S. Senate was debating his 1987 nomination to the Supreme Court.[42]

Video Privacy Protection Act (VPPA) Federal law that protects personal information in video rentals. 18 U.S.C. § 2710.

In five separate lawsuits filed in early in 2011 in the U.S. District Court for the Northern District of California, plaintiffs accused Netflix, the popular Internet video rental site, of violating the Video Privacy Protection Act.[43] People watching videos on Netflix take up more bandwidth on the Internet than users of any other website or service in North America, according to a 2011 study by broadband analytics firm Sandvine. At peak Internet hours, as much as 30 percent of online traffic is generated by Netflix subscribers who watch movies or television shows online.[44] Each of the five plaintiffs alleges that Netflix retains private customer information, such as credit card numbers and rental histories, even after subscribers cancel their membership, in violation of the Video Privacy Protection Act. According to an article from CNET News, Michael Sevy, a former Netflix subscriber from Michigan, accused Netflix of violating the VPPA by collecting, storing, and maintaining for an indefinite period of time, the video rental histories of every customer that has ever rented a DVD from Netflix.[45] Each of the plaintiffs in the five separate lawsuits against Netflix seeks class action status. Netflix is vehemently defending the lawsuits, and the litigation will likely continue in the courts for years to come and set an important precedent for the future scope and application of the Video Privacy Protection Act and privacy in video rentals.

Summary

Although the U.S. Constitution does not expressly include a right to privacy, U.S. Supreme Court has recognized a right to privacy based on an interpretation of the First, Third, Fourth, Fifth, and Ninth Amendments. Some state constitutions also provide for an express right to privacy. While Congress has not enacted comprehensive privacy legislation, various statutes provide some levels of privacy protection, including protection in the online environment. The key federal statutes in protecting privacy include the Privacy Act, Freedom of Information Act (FOIA), Gramm-Leach-Bliley Act (GLBA), Fair and Accurate Credit Transaction Act (FACTA), Fair Credit Reporting Act (FCRA), Health Insurance Portability and Accountability Act (HIPAA), Family Educational Rights and Privacy Act of 1974 (FERPA), Drivers' Privacy Protection Act (DPPA), Children's Online Privacy Protection Act (COPPA), Electronic Communications Privacy Act (ECPA), and the Video Privacy Protection Act. Some commentators argue that federal privacy legislation, which is a patchwork of different privacy laws, is outdated and needs to be amended or overhauled to better protect privacy with the increased use of the Internet and information technology.

Key Terms

Children's Online Privacy Protection Act (COPPA) *195*
Drivers Privacy Protection Act (DPPA) *194*
e-FOIA *186*
Electronic Communications Privacy Act (ECPA) *195*
Fair and Accurate Credit Transaction Act (FACTA) *190*
Fair Credit Reporting Act (FCRA) *190*
Freedom of Information Act (FOIA) *185*
Gramm-Leach-Bliley Act (GLBA) *189*
Health Insurance Portability and Accountability Act (HIPAA) *190*
privacy act *183*
red flag rule *190*
Reverse-FOIA Suit *186*
Video Privacy Protection Act (VPPA) *197*

Review Questions

1. What is the name of the 1965 U.S. Supreme Court case that first recognized a right to privacy?
2. Why are state constitutions important when it comes to privacy rights?
3. What does the Privacy Act of 1974 provide?
4. What are the purposes of the federal Freedom of Information Act (FOIA)?
5. Name three exemptions under FOIA.
6. What is the purpose of the Gramm-Leach-Bliley Act?
7. How is the Gramm-Leach-Bliley Act enforced?
8. How does the Red Flag Rule under FACTA help prevent identity theft?

Discussion Questions

1. Some state constitutions provide for an express right to privacy. Would you support a provision in your state's constitution for a right to privacy? Is an express right to privacy in either the U.S. Constitution or state constitutions redundant in light of U.S. Supreme Court decisions?
2. One of the exemptions under the federal Freedom of Information Act (FOIA) relates to classified matters or national defense. Who should decide whether information is classified? What procedures should be available to appeal a decision designating information as classified? Should photographs of prisoners at Guantanamo Bay be classified or made publicly available to the public? Should the government release photos of Osama Bin Laden's corpse? Why or why not?
3. Which is a more important public policy: protecting privacy rights or open government? When there is a conflict between privacy interests and open government, which should prevail?
4. Should Congress amend existing privacy laws by providing for a private right of action so that a person can personally sue a defendant for damages if private information is wrongly released?

Exercises

1. You are working as a manager for a telecommunications company and want to find out information held by the Federal Communications Commission (FCC) concerning licensing agreements for a competing telecommunications company. Research the requirements and procedure for a submitting an FOIA request with the Federal Communications Commission (FCC) and how to submit an e-FOIA request. Then write a memorandum to your supervisor where you explain the procedure for submitting the FOIA request with the FCC.
2. You are working for a financial institution that needs to comply with the Gramm-Leach-Bliley Act (GLBA). Specifically, the financial institution needs to monitor network and host activity to identify potential policy violations. Conduct research on three different companies that provide GLBA software. Then write a memorandum to your supervisor where you summarize the different GLBA software and make a recommendation for a particular type of GLBA software.
3. Select a federal agency and prepare and submit an actual Privacy Act request for yourself. Think of records or information that may be maintained by a federal agency that you would like to see and prepare an actual FOIA request to the appropriate agency.

4. Write a memorandum that discusses how the terrorist attacks on the United States on September 11, 2001, have impacted what information federal agencies post on their websites and whether the federal government has imposed greater restrictions on information that can be legally accessed through the Privacy Act and the FOIA.
5. *Hypothetical:* John is the parent of a twelve-year old daughter named Erin. Erin, along with some friends at her school, joins a new social networking site called XYZ.net (a fictitious website). Erin enters her personal information on the website during registration but lies about her age claiming she is age sixteen. The social networking site has also gained unauthorized access to the computer network at Erin's middle school to target more of Erin's classmates to join the site and to obtain personal information. XYZ.net then sells the personal information to third parties who use the personal information for Internet-based advertising. Discuss which federal statutes XYZ.net has violated, and discuss what legal actions John can pursue. Explain the potential consequences for XYZ.net.

Related Internet Sites

http://www.hhs.gov/ocr/privacy/
U.S. Department of Health and Human Services Health Information Privacy Resources

http://business.ftc.gov/privacy-and-security/gramm-leach-bliley-act
Federal Trade Commission (FTC) Gramm-Leach-Bliley Act Resources

http://www.justice.gov/oip/foia-guidance-resources.html
U.S. Department of Justice FOIA Guidance and Resources

http://www.foia.gov/
U.S. Department of Justice FOIA Resources

http://www.tncrimlaw.com/foia_indx.html
A Citizen's Guide On Using The Freedom of Information Act And The Privacy Act of 1974 To Request Government Records

End Notes

1. John Perry Barlow (EFF), *Decrypting the Puzzle Palace*, 35 COMMUNICATIONS OF THE ACM 25–31 (July 1992); Joseph Reagle, Internet Quotation Appendix, available at: http://cyber.law.harvard.edu/archived_content/people/reagle/inet-quotations-19990709.html/.
2. *Carey v. Population Servs. Int'l*, 431 U.S. 678, 685 (1977).
3. Patrick J. Alach, *Paparazzi and Privacy*, 28 LOY. L.A. ENT. L. Rev. 205, n. 34 (2008). See also National Conference of State Legislatures, Privacy Protections in State Constitutions, available at: http://www.ncsl.org/IssuesResearch/TelecommunicationsInformationTechnology/PrivacyProtectionsinStateConstitutions/tabid/13467/Default.aspx/.
4. *State v. Reid*, 389 N.J. Super. 563, 914 A.2d 310 (App. Div. 2007).
5. Paul M. Schwartz, *From Victorian Secrets to Cyberspace Shaming*, 76 U. CHI. L. REV. 1407, 1417–18 (2009).
6. Jeffrey M. Shaman, *The Right of Privacy in State Constitutional Law*, 37 RUTGERS L.J. 971, 1085 (2006).
7. Dana Beldiman, *An Information Society Approach to Privacy Legislation: How to Enhance Privacy While Maximizing Information Value*, 2 J. MARSHALL REV. INTELL. PROP. L. 71, 74–75 (2002).
8. *Chambers v. U.S. Dep't of Interior*, 568 F.3d 998, 1006 (D.C. Cir. 2009).
9. Bryan S. Schultz, *Electronic Money, Internet Commerce, and the Right to Financial Privacy: A Call for New Federal Guidelines*, 67 U. CIN. L. REV. 779, 791–792 (1999).
10. U.S. Department of Justice, What is FOIA?, available at: http://www.foia.gov/about.html/.
11. 37A Am. Jur. 2d Freedom of Information Acts § 1.
12. 37A Am. Jur. 2d Freedom of Information Acts § 2.
13. Black's Law Dictionary (9th ed. 2009).
14. Anderson Evan Thomas, *Remaining Covered by the "Near Blanket" of Deference: Berman v. Central Intelligence Agency and the CIA's Continual Use of Exemption 3 to Deny FOIA Requests Berman v. Central Intelligence Agency, 501 F.3d 1136 (9th Cir. 2007)*, 28 MISS. C. L. REV. 497, 505 (2009).
15. Gramm-Leach-Bliley Act, Pub. L. No. 106-102, 113 Stat. 1338, codified at 15 U.S.C. §§ 6801–6809.
16. Fed. Trade Commission, The Gramm-Leach Bliley Act, available at: http://www.ftc.gov/privacy/privacyinitiatives/glbact.html/.
17. See *Dunmire v. Morgan Stanley DW, Inc.*, 475 F.3d 956 (8th Cir. 2007) (recognizing no private action).
18. Validity, Construction, and Application of Information Privacy Provisions of Gramm-Leach-Bliley Act, 15 U.S.C.A. §§ 6801 to 6809, and Regulations Promulgated Thereunder, 5 A.L.R. Fed. 2d 497.

19. Press Release, Federal Trade Comm'n, Widespread Data Breaches Uncovered by FTC Probe (Feb. 22, 2010), available at: http://www.ftc.gov/opa/2010/02/p2palert.shtm/.
20. FTC Identity Theft Rules, 16 C.F.R. § 681.1.
21. 15 U.S.C. § 1681c(g)(1).
22. Fernando M. Pinguelo and Bradford W. Muller, *Virtual Crimes, Real Damages: A Primer on Cybercrimes in the United States and Efforts to Combat Cybercriminals*, 16 VA. J.L. & TECH. 116 (2011).
23. Health Information Technology for Economic and Clinical Health Act, Pub. L. No. 111-5, §13301, 123 Stat. 226, 246–47 (2009).
24. Health Information Technology for Economic and Clinical Health Act, Pub. L. No. 111-5, §13301, 123 Stat. 226, 246–47 (2009).
25. Janine Hiller, et al., *Privacy and Security in the Implementation of Health Information Technology (Electronic Health Records): U.S. And EE Compared*, 17 B.U. J. SCI. & TECH. L. 1 (2011).
26. HHS.gov, Health Information Privacy, available at: http://www.hhs.gov/ocr/privacy/hipaa/administrative/securityrule/.
27. U.S. Department of Health & Human Services, Health Information Privacy: How to File a Complaint, available at: http://www.hhs.gov/ocr/privacy/hipaa/complaints/index.htmlat.
28. Heather Delgado, *Recent Developments with HIPAA*, Aspatore, 2010 WL 4775236 at *4, Nov. 2010.
29. *Stipulated Judgment for State of Connecticut v. Health Net of the Northeast Inc., Health Net of Connecticut Inc., United Health Group, Inc. and Oxford Health Plans, LLC*, Civ. No. 3: 10CV57 (PCD), (U.S. Dist. Ct. of Ct. July 6, 2010).
30. Press Release, U.S. Attorney's Office, Central District of California, Ex-UCLA Healthcare Employee Pleads Guilty to Four Counts Of Illegally Peeking at Patient Records (Jan. 8, 2010), available at: http://www.justice.gov/usao/cac/pressroom/pr2010/004.html.
31. Drivers Privacy Protection Act of 1994, 18 U.S.C. § 2725.
32. 139 Cong. Rec. S15745-01, *515762 (1993) (statement of Sen. Boxer).
33. Flora J. Garcia, *Data Protection, Breach Notification, and the Interplay Between State and Federal Law: The Experiments Need More Time*, 17 FORDHAM INTELL. PROP. MEDIA & ENT. L.J. 693, 715 (2007).
34. Family Educational Rights and Privacy Act of 1974, 20 U.S.C. § 1232(g).
35. *The Law, Digitally Speaking*, CHRON. HIGHER EDUC., Apr. 4, 2008, at 14.
36. Lynn Daggett, *FERPA in the 21st Century: Failure to Effectively Regulate Policy for All Students*, 58 CATH. U.L. REV. 59, 93, 111–112 (2008)
37. Press Release, FTC, UMG Recordings, Inc. to Pay $400,000, Bonzi Software, Inc. to Pay $75,000 to Settle COPPA Civil Penalty Charges (Sept. 13, 2006), available at: http://www.ftc.gov/opa/2004/02/bonzi-umg.shtm/.
38. Lauren A. Matecki, *Update: COPPA Is Ineffective Legislation! Next Steps for Protecting Youth Privacy Rights in the Social Networking Era*, 5 NW J. L. & SOC. POL'Y 369 (2010).
39. Electronic Communications Privacy Act of 1986, Pub. L. No. 99-508, 100 Stat. 1848 (codified as amended at 18 U.S.C. §§ 2701–12.
40. 18 U.S.C. § 2518(10)(a).
41. Nancy J. King, *Direct Marketing, Mobile Phones, and Consumer Privacy: Ensuring Adequate Disclosure and Consent Mechanisms for Emerging Mobile Advertising Practices*, 60 FED. COMM. L.J. 229, 286 (2008).
42. Mary Margaret Penrose, *In the Name of Watergate: Returning FERPA to Its Original Design*, 14 N.Y.U. J. LEGIS. & PUB. POL'Y 75, note 170 (2011).
43. Greg Sandoval, *Privacy lawsuits rain down on Netflix*, CNET News, Mar. 21, 2011, available at: http://news.cnet.com/8301-31001_3-20045358-261.html/.
44. Cecilia Kang, *Netflix Video Viewing Devours Bandwidth*, Wash. Post, May 18, 2011, at A11.
45. Sandoval, *supra* note 43.

CHAPTER

11 Special Topics in Online Privacy

The biggest message we have heard recently is that people want easier control over their information. Simply put, many of you thought our controls were too complex.... We just missed the mark.

MARK ZUCKERBERG, *Founder and Chief Executive of Facebook*[1]

LEARNING OBJECTIVES

After completing this chapter, you will be able to:

1. Explain the legal and policy issues surrounding data privacy with social networking sites, search queries, online advertising, data mining, online privacy policies, and workplace policies.
2. Discuss legislative proposals in addressing online privacy concerns.
3. Discuss alternatives to regulating online privacy, including self-regulation and co-regulation.

CHAPTER OVERVIEW

The rapid growth of the Internet and digital information has created new challenges for information privacy. Companies such as Google save and store search queries and can often trace them back to individuals. Websites track how visitors use their sites and frequently share this information with others. Social networking sites, Internet search queries, online advertising, data mining, online privacy policies, and workplace policies are all important issues with online privacy. This chapter discusses the legal and policy issues surrounding these issues with online privacy.

SOCIAL NETWORKING SITES

Online **social networking sites**, such as Facebook, have become hugely popular. Facebook, the world's most popular social networking site, surpassed Google as the most visited website in the U.S.

Social Networking Site Web-based services that allow individuals to (1) construct a public or semi-public profile within a bounded system, (2) articulate a list of other users with whom they share a connection, and (3) view and traverse their list of connections and those made by others within the system.

in 2010, according to Internet tracker Experian Hitwise and the *Los Angeles Times*.[2] According to a 2007 study by the National School Boards Association, 96% of students with access to the Internet have visited a social networking site. Facebook boasts more than 500 million active users who upload more than 30 billion pieces of content to the site each month.[3]

Social networking sites are defined as "web-based services that allow individuals to (1) construct a public or semi-public profile within a bounded system, (2) articulate a list of other users with whom they share a connection, and (3) view and traverse their list of connections and those made by others within the system."[4]

Social networking offers a convenient means to stay connected but also comes with a trade-off in privacy. A host of privacy concerns surround social networking sites like Facebook and Twitter. Many attorneys use social networking sites to gather evidence used in legal and administrative proceedings.[5] Doing background searches of content posted on social networking sites is now routine for prospective employees and love interests.

Some accused criminal defendants have been caught posting the details of their crimes on social networking sites. Judges can also consider evidence from social networking sites during sentencing. For example, at sentencing for Jessica Binkerd, who was convicted of vehicular manslaughter without gross negligence and driving under the influence of alcohol causing injury, the judge disregarded the probation department's recommendation of less than a one-year jail sentence, choosing instead to impose a much harsher penalty of five years and four months in state prison. Binkerd posted pictures on MySpace wearing an "I heart Patr-n" T-shirt and drinking with friends after the fatal accident. The sentencing judge indicated the photos showed a lack of remorse that warranted a tougher sentence.[6]

Even the IRS and the U.S. Department of Justice have publicly acknowledged their use of social networking sites to investigate taxpayers and suspects. No privilege or confidentiality exists with communications transmitted via online social media.

Information that people post on social networking sites could be used against them when they least expect it. Once information has been posted on a social networking site, it is difficult to delete the information. For example, even after a Facebook user requests to delete his or her account, Facebook retains the account information for an undisclosed period of time, and may save information indefinitely.[7]

Despite privacy warnings available on most social networking sites, many users mistakenly think they have privacy in what they post. Based on one survey, only 30 percent of online social network users claimed to know that they have the option to control privacy features such as the visibility of their profiles.[8]

Courts have consistently held that individuals have no reasonable expectation of privacy under the Fourth Amendment when they disclose information to a third party. The U.S. Supreme Court held in *United States v. Miller*, 425 U.S. 435 (1976), that there is no reasonable expectation of privacy in information held by a third party under the Fourth Amendment. The case involved cancelled checks conveyed to the banks that the government later requested from the banks. The Court held that the Fourth Amendment does not prohibit the obtaining of information revealed to a third party, even if the information is revealed on the assumption that it will be used only for a limited purpose and that the confidence placed in the third party will not be betrayed.

The U.S. Supreme Court's decision in *Miller* is sweeping and applies to any type of private information conveyed to third parties, including information transmitted to a third party such as a social networking site. Once a person uploads photographs, videos, or other personal information to an online social networking site, that person relinquishes any reasonable expectation of constitutional privacy they have in that information. Individuals have a right to keep information private, but once they share it with others, privacy rights end.

In *Courtright v. Madigan*, No. 09-CV-208-JPG, 2009 WL 3713654, at *2 (S.D. Ill. Nov. 4, 2009) a federal court ruled that the plaintiff had no expectation of privacy that his MySpace.com account would remain private. Similarly, in *United States v. Perrine*, 518 F.3d 1196, 1199, 1204 (10th Cir. 2008), when law enforcement obtained records from Yahoo! linking a screen name to an IP address registered to the defendant, the Tenth Circuit held that the Fourth Amendment was not implicated because the defendant had no expectation of privacy in information he had voluntarily transmitted to a third-party Internet provider. Likewise, employees do not have a privacy interest in what they post to their profile on a social networking site. Federal courts have unanimously held that a person has no expectation of privacy in Internet subscriber information. It is well settled that a person has no reasonable expectation of privacy in information conveyed to third parties such as a social networking site. Once a person hits Send, privacy is gone.

The existing legal framework provides little protection for those whose privacy rights have been eroded with online social networking sites. Some litigation, however, is currently pending against online social networking sites for privacy violations. In 2011, the father of a Brooklyn teenager accused Facebook of using children's names and likenesses in ads without getting permission from their parents or guardians.[9] The father filed the action seeking Facebook's revenues under the New York Civil Rights Law, which prohibits companies from using a person's name or photograph for advertising purposes without consent. The parents of two California teens filed a similar lawsuit against Facebook in Los Angeles Superior Court. Common-law torts and state actions for invasion of privacy are likely the best options under the current law against online social networking sites for privacy breaches, but to date, no known cases have determined that a social networking site is liable for invasion of privacy under the common-law tort of invasion of privacy or a state action.

In the absence of privacy protection recognized by the courts under the Fourth Amendment or common-law torts, new federal legislation is needed to safeguard and regulate Internet privacy for online social networking sites and other websites that collect information about users. In 2011, Senators John Kerry and John McCain introduced the Commercial Privacy Bill of Rights Act of 2011 (S. 799, 112th Congress).[10] The Internet privacy bill, which has the support of the Obama administration, would impose new rules on companies that gather personal data, including offering people access to data about them, or the ability to block the information from being used or distributed. The bill would regulate Facebook, Google, and other websites that collect information about users. The measure aims to protect Internet users by forcing companies to explain how they collect information and what they do with it. The bill would also make it harder for websites to target individuals through personally identifiable information and create profiles about them. Online privacy, especially with social media, will be a hot topic of debate on Capitol Hill and in state legislatures in the coming years.

INTERNET SEARCH QUERIES

Internet search engines such as Google, which hold a vast amount of personal information, raise a host of online privacy issues. Princeton computer scientist Edward Felten called the privacy issues with search engines "perhaps the most difficult privacy [problem] in all of human history."[11]

A person's Internet search queries can contain very sensitive and private information. A search query is a word or string of words used to correlate with a list of matching websites. When AOL publicly released the search queries of some 650,000 search users, the logs included queries such as "can you adopt after a suicide attempt," "cocaine in urine," and "How to deal with mental abuse in a Christian marriage."[12] Even though the search logs identified users only by pseudonymous numbers, reporters showed by example that it was possible to take a list of searches and identify the searcher. People often search for their own names, addresses, and other personally identifying details. Even where the information cannot be linked to a particular person, information from search queries can still be used in ways that causes privacy concerns.

Search queries, whether obtained from the search engine or from other sources, can be highly incriminating evidence. For example, in *United States v. Schuster*, 467 F.3d 614, 617 (7th Cir. 2006), the judge considered the defendant's search on Google for "make device interfere wireless network" in determining damages caused to interfering with a network and upheld factual findings based in part on Google searches by the defendant.

In 2005, the U.S. Department of Justice (DOJ) issued subpoenas to Google, America Online, Yahoo!, and Microsoft to compel the release of randomly selected user search records.[13] The DOJ hoped that search engines could help them prove that the Child Online Protection Act (COPA) was more effective in protecting children from harmful exposure on the Internet. While AOL and Yahoo! complied with the subpoenas, Google refused to comply with the request. Google argued that even randomly selected search strings could be revealing if a user searched for his or her own name, social security number, or credit card number. Google also argued that its business was predicated on protecting its users' privacy. The court in *Gonzales v. Google, Inc.*, 234 F.R.D. 674 (N.D. Cal. 2006) (Case 11.1) held that Google was compelled only to generate a list of URLs but was not required to turn over actual user search queries. *Gonzales v. Google* is the leading case involving the privacy of Internet search queries.

CASE 11.1

The Google Search Query Case

Gonzales v. Google, Inc., *234 F.R.D. 674 (N.D. Cal. 2006).*

I. Introduction

This case raises three vital interests: (1) the national interest in a judicial system to reach informed decisions through the power of a subpoena to compel a third party to produce relevant information; (2) the third-party's interest in not being compelled by a subpoena to reveal confidential business information and devote resources to a distant litigation; and (3) the interest of individuals in freedom from general surveillance by the Government of their use of the Internet or other communications media.

United States Attorney General Alberto R. Gonzales has subpoenaed Google, Inc., ("Google") to compile and produce a massive amount of information from Google's search index, and to turn over a significant number of search queries entered by Google users. Google timely objected to the Government's request. For the reasons explained in this Order, the motion to compel, as modified, is GRANTED as to the sample of URLs from Google search index and DENIED as to the sample of users' search queries from Google's query log.

II. Procedural Background

In 1998, Congress enacted the Child Online Protection Act ("COPA"), which is now codified as 47 U.S.C. § 231. COPA prohibits the knowing making of a communication by means of the World Wide Web, "for commercial purposes that is available to any minor and that includes material that is harmful to minors," subject to certain affirmative defenses.

[T]he Government initiated a study designed to somehow test the effectiveness of blocking and filtering software. To provide it with data for its study, the Government served a subpoena on Google, America Online, Inc. ("AOL"), Yahoo! Inc. ("Yahoo"), and Microsoft, Inc. ("Microsoft"). The subpoena required that these companies produce a designated listing of the URLs which would be available to a user of their services. The subpoena also required the companies to produce the text of users' search queries. AOL, Yahoo, and Microsoft appear to be producing data pursuant to the Government's request. Google, however, objected.

Google is a Delaware corporation headquartered in Mountain View, CA, that, like AOL, Yahoo, and Microsoft, also provides search engine capabilities. Based on the Government's estimation, and uncontested by Google, Google's search engine is the most widely used search engine in the world, with a market share of about 45%. The search engine at Google yields URLs in response to a search query entered by a user. The search queries entered may be of varying lengths, and incorporate a number of terms and connectors. Upon receiving a search query, Google produces a responsive list of URLs from its search index in a particular order based on algorithms proprietary to Google.

[Following negotiations with Google, the Government restricted the scope of its request, and the Government now seeks only 50,000 URLs from Google's search index and 5,000 entries from Google's query log.]

Despite these modifications in the scope of the subpoena, Google maintained its objection to the Government's requests. Before the Court is a motion to compel Google to comply with the modified subpoena, namely, for a sample of 50,000 URLs from Google's search index and 5,000 search queries entered by Google's users from Google's query log.

III. Standards

Rule 45 of the Federal Rules of Civil Procedure governs discovery of nonparties by subpoena. Fed. R. Civ. P. 45 ("Rule 45").

Rule 26(b), in turn, permits the discovery of any non-privileged material "relevant to the claim or defense of any party," where "relevant information need not be admissible at trial if the discovery appears reasonably calculated to lead to the discovery of admissible evidence." Rule 26(b)(1).

In addition to the discovery standards under Rule 26 incorporated by Rule 45, Rule 45 itself provides that "on timely motion, the court by which a subpoena was issued shall quash or modify the subpoena if it . . . subjects a person to undue burden." Rule 45(3)(A). Thus, a court determining the propriety of a subpoena balances the relevance of the discovery sought, the requesting party's need, and the potential hardship to the party subject to the subpoena.

IV. Discussion

Google primarily argues that the information sought by the subpoena is not reasonably calculated to lead to evidence admissible in the underlying litigation, and that the production of information is unduly burdensome. The Court discusses each of these objections in turn, as well as the Court's own concerns about the potential interests of Google's users.

A. Relevance

Any information sought by means of a subpoena must be relevant to the claims and defenses in the underlying case.

Google's arguments challenging the relevance of the search queries to the Government's study center around its contention that a number of additional factors exist which may mitigate the correlation between a search query and the search result. In particular, Google cites to the presence of a safe search filter, customized searches, or advanced preferences all potentially activated at the user end and not reflected in the user's search string. Google also argues that the list of search queries does not distinguish between sources of the queries such as adults, minors, automatic queries generated by a program, known as "bot" queries, and artificial queries generated by individual users. Contrary to Google's belief, the broad standard of relevance under

(Continued)

(Continued)

Rule 26 does not require that the information sought necessarily be directed at the ultimate fact in issue, only that the information sought be reasonably calculated to lead to admissible evidence in the underlying litigation. Thus, the presence of these additional factors may impact the probative value of the Government's expert report in the Eastern District of Pennsylvania on the effectiveness of filtering software in preventing minors from accessing "harmful to minors" material on the Internet, but at this stage, the Court does not find the search queries to be entirely irrelevant to the creation of a test set on which to test the effectiveness of search filters in general.

B. Undue Burden

This Court is particularly concerned anytime enforcement of a subpoena imposes an economic burden on a non-party. Under Rule 45(3)(a), a court may modify or quash a subpoena even for relevant information if it finds that there is an undue burden on the non-party.

The Government only intends to run 1,000 to 5,000 of the search queries through the Google search engine. Given the volume and rate of the proposed study, the Court finds that the additional burden on Google's search engine caused by the Government's study as represented to the Court, is likely to be de minimis.

Google also argues that it will be unduly burdened by loss of user trust if forced to produce its users' queries to the Government. Google claims that its success is attributed in large part to the volume of its users and these users may be attracted to its search engine because of the privacy and anonymity of the service. According to Google, even a perception that Google is acquiescing to the Government's demands to release its query log would harm Google's business by deterring some searches by some users.

Google's own privacy statement indicates that Google users could not reasonably expect Google to guard the query log from disclosure to the Government. Google's privacy statement at www.google.com/privacypolicy.html states only that Google will protect "personal information" of users. "Personal information" is expressly defined for users at www.google.com/privacy faq.html as "information that you provide to us which personally identifies you, such as your name, email address or billing information, or other data which can be reasonably linked to such information by Google." Google's privacy policy does not represent to users that it keeps confidential any information other than "personal information." Neither Google's URLs nor the text of search strings with "personal information" redacted, are reasonably "personal information" under Google's stated privacy policy. Google's privacy policy indicates that it has not suggested to its users that non-"personal information" such as that sought by the Government is kept confidential.

However, even if an expectation by Google users that Google would prevent disclosure to the Government of its users' search queries is not entirely reasonable, the statistic cited by Dr. Stark that over a quarter of all Internet searches are for pornography indicates that at least some of Google's users expect some sort of privacy in their searches. The expectation of privacy by some Google users may not be reasonable, but may nonetheless have an appreciable impact on the way in which Google is perceived, and consequently the frequency with which users use Google. Such an expectation does not rise to the level of an absolute privilege, but does indicate that there is a potential burden as to Google's loss of goodwill if Google is forced to disclose search queries to the Government.

Faced with duplicative discovery, and with the Government not expressing a preference as to which source of the test set of URLs it prefers, this Court exercises its discretion pursuant to Rule 26(b)(2) and determines that the marginal burden of loss of trust by Google's users based on Google's disclosure of its users' search queries to the Government outweighs the duplicative disclosure's likely benefit to the Government's study. Accordingly, the Court grants the Government's motion to compel only as to the sample of 50,000 URLs from Google's search index.

C. Protective Order

As trade secret or confidential business information, Google's production of a list of URLs to the Government shall be protected by protective order.

D. Privacy

The Court raises, sua sponte [on its own without being raised by either party], its concerns about the privacy of Google's users apart from Google's business goodwill argument. Even though counsel for the Government assured the Court that the information received will only be used for the present litigation, it is conceivable that the Government may have an obligation to pursue information received for unrelated litigation purposes under certain circumstances regardless of the restrictiveness of a protective order. The Court expressed this concern at oral argument as to queries such as "bomb placement white house," but queries such as "communist berkeley parade route protest war" may also raise similar concerns. In the end, the Court need not express an opinion on this issue because the Government's motion is granted only as to the sample of URLs and not as to the log of search queries.

V. Conclusion

As expressed in this Order, the Court's concerns with certain aspects of the Government's subpoena have been mitigated by the reduced scope the Government's present requests. With these limitations . . . Google is ordered to confer with the Government to develop a protocol for the random selection and afterward immediate production of a listing of 50,000 URLs in Google's database.

To the extent the motion seeks an order compelling Google to disclose search queries of its users the motion is DENIED. The Court retains jurisdiction to enforce this Order.

Case Questions

1. Why did Google object to turning over the search queries to the Government?
2. What issue did the court raise on its own?
3. Why did the court grant the subpoena requests to turn over the URLs but deny the request for the search queries?
4. Do you think the Government could use the search queries for other purposes? Why or why not? Was this an important concern by the court?

Because Silicon Valley in California is home to many Internet and technology companies, many Internet-related cases are decided in the U.S. District Court for the Northern District of California. Judge James Ware, Chief Judge of the U.S. District Court for the Northern District of California whose chambers are located in San Jose, has presided over several high-profile Internet cases. Ware presided over the Facebook Privacy Litigation case, *In re Facebook Privacy Litigation*, No. C10-02398 (N.D. Cal. May 12, 2011), the domain name case involving "sex.com," *Kremen v. Cohen*, No. C 98-20718, 2000 WL 1811403 (N.D. Cal. Nov. 27, 2000), and the Google search query case, *Gonzales v. Google*, Inc., 234 F.R.D. 674 (N.D. Cal. 2006).

Born in Birmingham, Alabama, Ware received a B.A. in 1969 from California Lutheran University and a J.D. from Stanford Law School in 1972. Ware was a U.S. Army Reserve Second Lieutenant in 1972 and also served in the U.S. Army as a Military Police Officer in 1973. From 1972 until 1988, Ware worked as an attorney in private practice in Palo Alto, California. From 1988-1990, Ware served as a judge for the Santa Clara County Superior Court. Ware was nominated as a U.S. District Court Judge in 1990 by President George H. W. Bush and confirmed by the Senate later that year. President Bill Clinton nominated Ware to the United States Court of Appeals for the Ninth Circuit but Ware withdrew his nomination after a scandal that resulted in a public reprimand. Ware admitted to lying about his brother being killed in 1963 by a racist's bullet in Alabama. He became Chief Judge of the Northern District of California on January 1, 2011, when Judge Vaughn Walker retired.

FIGURE 11.1 Judge James Ware[14,15]

ONLINE ADVERTISING

Online advertising has grown tremendously in recent years. Online advertising eclipsed radio advertising in 2007, and by 2011, online advertising is projected to surpass television revenues.[16] Internet advertising has grown in part because of its targeted approach to consumers. That targeted approach also raises privacy-related concerns. A variety of federal and state laws govern online advertising and marketing, including the Controlling the Assault of Non-Solicited Pornography and Marketing Act of 2003 (CAN-SPAM Act) and the Federal Trade Commission Act (FTC Act).

Can-Spam Act

Spam
Unsolicited commercial e-mail.

One of the most popular, and often hated, forms of Internet advertising is unsolicited commercial e-mail commonly referred to as "spam." **Spam** is typically understood to refer broadly to unsolicited e-mail messages (or "junk" e-mail), typically commercial in nature.[17]

In 2003, Congress adopted the Controlling the Assault of Non-Solicited Pornography and Marketing Act of 2003 (CAN-SPAM Act), Pub. L. No. 108-187, 117 Stat. 2699 in an effort to combat spam.[18] For the text of the CAN-SPAM Act, see Appendix C.

Controlling the Assault of Non-Solicited Pornography and Marketing Act (CAN-SPAM Act)
A federal law establishing civil and criminal liability for unsolicited commercial e-mail. 15 U.S.C. §§ 7701–7713.

The **CAN-SPAM Act**, 15 U.S.C. § 7706(g)(3)(A), provides for statutory damages of up to $100 per violating message and $1,000,000 in aggregate along with reasonable costs, including reasonable attorneys' fees. The Act also allows for treble damages, or three times the amount otherwise available, for aggregated or willful violations. The CAN-SPAM Act also provides for criminal penalties.[19] An individual who is found guilty of fraud or other intentionally deceptive violations of the Act could be sentenced to up to five years in prison. The criminal provisions of CAN-SPAM are for the most egregious violations and prohibit sexually explicit e-mail that fails to include a label designating it as sexually explicit. Chapter 7 discusses the criminal aspects of spam in greater detail.

The FTC often brings enforcement actions against companies that violate the CAN-SPAM Act. For example, in an action filed by the FTC in 2007, a federal judge ordered Sili Neutraceuticals, LLC and Brian McDaid to pay more than $2.5 million for making false advertising claims and sending illegal e-mail messages in violation of the FTC Act and the CAN-SPAM Act.[20] Soli Neutraceuticals violated the CAN-SPAM Act by sending commercial e-mail messages for weight-loss and anti-aging products that have misleading subject headings, that fail to provide clear and conspicuous notice of the opportunity to decline to receive further spam from the sender, and/or a functioning return e-mail address, and the senders' valid physical postal address.

Congress conferred standing only on a narrow group of possible plaintiffs for violations of the CAN-SPAM Act: the Federal Trade Commission, certain state and federal agencies, state attorneys general, and "Internet access service" (IAS) providers adversely affected by violations of the CAN-SPAM Act. **Standing** is a party's right to make a legal claim or seek judicial enforcement of a duty or right.[21]

Standing
A party's right to make a legal claim or seek judicial enforcement of a duty or right.

The CAN-SPAM Act also preempts most state anti-spam statutes and also removed private rights of action granted in state anti-spam statutes. In the CAN-SPAM Act of 2003, Congress did not grant standing for private parties who wished to bring an action against spammers.

In *Gordon v. Virtumundo, Inc.*, 575 F.3d 1040 (9th Cir. 2009), the Ninth Circuit analyzed standing under the CAN-SPAM Act for "Internet access service" (IAS) providers and held that CAN-SPAM's private standing requirements should be narrowly construed. Under the narrow definition in *Gordon*, IAS providers entitled to bring a private action under the CAN-SPAM include Internet Service Providers (ISPs) such as Comcast, and Verizon DSL but excludes professional litigants and other small-time private plaintiffs like blog owners or personal website operators.

The court also held that eligible private plaintiffs must demonstrate actual harm of a specific type and causation. Before *Gordon*, a cottage industry of professional plaintiffs dedicated to profiting from statutory damages codified in the CAN-SPAM Act developed. Plaintiff James S. Gordon was described as an "anti-spam enthusiast" and "professional plaintiff," whose sole source of income was monetary settlements from his litigation campaign. His technique was to configure several Internet domains and e-mail inboxes under his control to not only passively accept spam but also to actively seek it. Once spam messages began arriving, Gordon would sue the senders or relaying providers. The Ninth Circuit chilled the potential anti-spam litigation industry with its decision in *Gordon*. Private individuals can still submit complaints with the FTC, their Internet Service Provider, and the state attorney general for alleged CAN-SPAM Act violations, but the Ninth Circuit's landmark decision in *Gordon* limits the ability of private plaintiffs to bring a private action under the CAN-SPAM Act.[22]

Companies that utilize e-mail and the Internet for marketing purposes should ensure that they comply with the requirements in the CAN-SPAM Act and the FTC Act (See Figure 11.2: The CAN-SPAM Act: A Compliance Guide for Business).

The Federal Trade Commission provides a compliance guide for the CAN-SPAM Act. Listed below are the CAN-SPAM Act's main requirements:

(1) **Don't use false or misleading header information**. Your "From," "To," "Reply-To," and routing information – including the originating domain name and email address – must be accurate and identify the person or business who initiated the message.
(2) **Don't use deceptive subject lines.** The subject line must accurately reflect the content of the message.
(3) **Identify the message as an ad.** The law gives you a lot of leeway in how to do this, but you must disclose clearly and conspicuously that your message is an advertisement.
(4) **Tell recipients where you're located.** Your message must include your valid physical postal address. This can be your current street address, a post office box you've registered with the U.S. Postal Service, or a private mailbox you've registered with a commercial mail receiving agency established under Postal Service regulations.
(5) **Tell recipients how to opt out of receiving future email from you.** Your message must include a clear and conspicuous explanation of how the recipient can opt out of getting email from you in the future. Craft the notice in a way that's easy for an ordinary person to recognize, read, and understand. Creative use of type size, color, and location can improve clarity. Give a return email address or another easy Internet-based way to allow people to communicate their choice to you. You may create a menu to allow a recipient to opt out of certain types of messages, but you must include the option to stop all commercial messages from you. Make sure your spam filter doesn't block these opt-out requests.
(6) **Honor opt-out requests promptly.** Any opt-out mechanism you offer must be able to process opt-out requests for at least 30 days after you send your message. You must honor a recipient's opt-out request within 10 business days. You can't charge a fee, require the recipient to give you any personally identifying information beyond an email address, or make the recipient take any step other than sending a reply email or visiting a single page on an Internet website as a condition for honoring an opt-out request. Once people have told you they don't want to receive more messages from you, you can't sell or transfer their email addresses, even in the form of a mailing list. The only exception is that you may transfer the addresses to a company you've hired to help you comply with the CAN-SPAM Act.
(7) **Monitor what others are doing on your behalf.** The law makes clear that even if you hire another company to handle your email marketing, you can't contract away your legal responsibility to comply with the law. Both the company whose product is promoted in the message and the company that actually sends the message may be held legally responsible.

FIGURE 11.2 The CAN-SPAM Act: A Compliance Guide for Business[23]

Federal Trade Commission Act

Federal Trade Commission Act (FTC Act or FTCA)
A federal law that prohibits unfair or deceptive acts or practices in the marketplace, including Internet advertising. 15 U.S.C. §§ 41–58.

Section 5 of the **Federal Trade Commission Act (FTC Act or FCTA)**, codified in 15 U.S.C. §§ 41–58, prohibits unfair or deceptive acts or practices in the marketplace, including Internet advertising. Adware and phishing are potential unfair and deceptive business practices under the FTC Act.

Under the Federal Trade Commission Act, advertising must be truthful and non-deceptive, advertisers must have evidence to back up their claims, and advertisements cannot be unfair. According to the FTC's Deception Policy Statement, an ad is deceptive if it contains a material statement that is likely to mislead consumers acting reasonably under the circumstances.

Under the FTC's Unfairness Policy Statement, an ad or business practice is unfair if it causes or is likely to cause substantial consumer injury which a consumer could not reasonably avoid and it is not outweighed by the benefit to consumers. The remedies that the FTC or the courts have imposed include (1) cease and desist orders; (2) civil penalties, consumer redress, and other monetary remedies; and (3) corrective advertising, disclosures and other informational remedies.[24]

Adware
Advertising software programs; software application that displays advertising banners while the program is running.

The Federal Trade Commission (FTC) actively pursues companies that install advertising software programs (adware) on consumers' computers in violation of the violation of the FTC Act. **Adware** is generally defined as any software application that displays advertising banners while the program is running.[25]

In 2006, Zango, Inc., formerly known as 180solutions, Inc., one of the world's largest distributors of adware, paid $3 million to settle FTC charges that they used unfair and deceptive methods to download adware and obstruct consumers from removing it. The FTC charged that Zango's failure to disclose that downloading the free content and software would result in installation of the adware was deceptive, and that its failure to provide consumers with a reasonable and effective means to identify, locate, and remove the adware from their computers was unfair, in violation of the FTC Act.[26]

Phishing
The sending of a fraudulent electronic communication that appears to be a genuine message from a legitimate entity or business for the purpose of inducing the recipient to disclose sensitive personal information.

The FTC also has jurisdiction to bring anti-phishing suits under its legislative mandate to regulate false and deceptive advertising. **Phishing** is the sending of a fraudulent electronic communication that appears to be a genuine message from a legitimate entity or business for the purpose of inducing the recipient to disclose sensitive personal information. Chapter 7 discusses the criminal aspects of phishing in greater detail.

In addition, the FTC regulates online buzz marketing and endorsements, including online customer testimonials and celebrity endorsements.[27] "Buzz marketing" is a technique that attempts to generate conversations among and with current and potential customers. The growth of online advertising has also led to more online buzz marketing.[28] In 2009, the FTC updated the FTC Guides Concerning Use of Endorsements and Testimonials in Advertising (also called the FTC Guides on Endorsements) to reflect the FTC's recognition of more buzz and stealth marketing, particularly on the Internet. Although the FTC Guides on Endorsements are not themselves statutory or regulatory authority, they outline and provide guidance on the FTC's position on endorsements. In a new example in the FTC Guides on Endorsements, the FTC clarified its position that the greater the degree of coordination between the consumer and the advertiser, the more likely the consumer's blog about a product could be considered an endorsement subject to regulation. The updated FTC Guides on Endorsements require that an advertiser who uses consumer endorsements must possess and rely upon adequate substantiation to support efficacy claims made through endorsements, just as the advertiser would be required to do if it had made the representation directly.

A number of states have also adopted legislation similar to the FTC Act to prohibit unfair and deceptive trade practices in advertising. For example, the California False

Advertising Law and the Unfair Competition Law prohibit unfair, deceptive, untrue, or misleading advertising. In *Colgan v. Leatherman Tool Group, Inc.*, 38 Cal. Rptr. 3d 36, 50 (Cal. Ct. App. 2006), the California Court of Appeals held that a tool company violated the California False Advertising and Unfair Competition Laws by representing on its tools, website, and advertising that the tools were "Made in U.S.A." when parts of the products were manufactured outside the United States.

Companies that engage in online advertising should ensure that they comply with federal and state laws governing unfair and deceptive trade practices. The "Federal Trade Commission Advertising FAQ's: A Guide for Small Business" provides helpful information on compliance for Internet advertising.

Miscellaneous Federal and State Claims

Besides the CAN-SPAM Act and FTC Act, plaintiffs may bring actions for unlawful online advertising practices under other federal and state laws, such as the Computer Fraud and Abuse Act and various state laws.

In a privacy class action lawsuit against Facebook consolidated in the U.S. District Court for the Northern District of California, *In re Facebook Privacy Litigation*, No. C10-02398 (N.D. Cal. May 12, 2011), plaintiffs alleged violations of the Electronic Communications Privacy Act, the Stored Communications Act, California's anti-hacking law, and numerous state law claims. The facts boil down to Facebook's transmission to third-party advertisers of the user ID or "username" of Facebook users who clicked on advertisements between February 2010 and May 21, 2010. The transmission of this information formed the basis of putative class action claims for violations. In May 2011, the judge granted Facebook's motion to dismiss the complaint but granted leave for the plaintiffs to amend the complaint on certain counts. In the ruling, U.S. District Court Judge James Ware expressed skepticism about the overall merits of the case.[29]

Plaintiffs have also filed click fraud cases under various federal and state laws. **Click fraud** is defined as purposeful clicks on advertisements by someone other than a potential customer.[30] Click fraud generally encompasses any click made in bad faith. In 2006, Google settled a $90 million lawsuit after advertisers argued that it had not given them adequate compensation for fraudulent online ad clicks.[31] In June 2009, Microsoft filed a click fraud action against three Canadian residents in the U.S. District Court for the Western District of Washington. Microsoft became the first company to file a click fraud suit, creating a new scenario where the company, not a consumer, is the "victim." Microsoft alleged violations of the federal Computer Fraud and Abuse Act, the Washington Computer Spyware Act, and a variety of other state actions. Microsoft realized false clicks were being logged under the guise of multiple IP addresses for specific searches targeting automobile insurance and World of Warcraft, an online role-playing game.[32] The Microsoft click fraud case will set an important precedent for other click fraud cases.

Click Fraud
Purposeful clicks on advertisements by someone other than a potential customer. Click fraud generally encompasses any click made in bad faith.

Plaintiffs may also bring actions under state laws for privacy violations with online advertising, but to date, few plaintiffs have prevailed. In *Stayart v. Google Inc.*,— F.Supp.2d—, 2011 WL 855316 (E.D.Wis. March 8, 2011), the plaintiff brought an action against Google alleging that Google used her name for purposes of advertising in violation of Wisconsin law. The court dismissed the complaint and held that the user failed to allege facts sufficient to plausibly infer that Google used her name for advertising or trade purposes, as required to state a claim for unreasonable invasion of privacy under Wisconsin law.

While Facebook has often been the target of privacy concerns, Facebook has made some efforts to protect the privacy of its users. In *Facebook, Inc. v. Fisher*, No. C 09-05842 JF, 2009 WL 5095269 (N.D. Cal. Dec. 21, 2009) (Case 11.2), Facebook brought an action against defendants based on an ongoing phishing and spamming campaign against Facebook and its users claiming violations of the Controlling the Assault of Non-Solicited Pornography and Marketing Act (CAN-SPAM), the Computer Fraud and Abuse Act (CFAA), and other laws. The court granted Facebook's request for a temporary restraining order (TRO) to prevent the defendants from engaging in phishing and spamming activities against Facebook and Facebook users.

CASE 11.2

The Facebook Phishing and Spamming Case

Facebook, Inc. v. Fisher, *No. C 09-05842 JF, 2009 WL 5095269 (N.D. Cal. Dec. 21, 2009)*

Plaintiff Facebook, Inc. ("Facebook") alleges that Defendants Jeremi Fisher, Philip Porembski, and Ryan Shimeall, individually and through various affiliated corporate entities (collectively, "Defendants"), have engaged in an ongoing phishing and spamming campaign against Facebook and its users in violation of (1) the Controlling the Assault of Non-Solicited Pornography and Marketing Act ("CAN-SPAM"), 15 U.S.C. § 7701 et seq. ; (2) the Computer Fraud and Abuse Act ("CFAA"), 18 U.S.C. § 1030 et seq., (3) Cal. Penal Code § 502; and (4) Cal. Bus. & Prof.Code § 22948. Facebook also asserts a claim for breach of contract. Pursuant to Fed.R.Civ.P. 65(b), Facebook seeks a temporary restraining order ("TRO") enjoining Defendants from engaging in the alleged phishing and spamming activities against Facebook and its users. For the reasons set forth below, the motion will be granted.

I. Background

Facebook is a well-known social networking website with over 175 million users. Facebook users must register with the website and agree to Facebook's Terms of Use. Upon registration, users are given a unique username and password to access their own user profiles as well as the profiles of their "friends." Users may send messages to each other through the Facebook website, either by e-mail or by postings on a user's "wall." To preserve the integrity of its website, Facebook maintains strict policies against spam or any other form of unsolicited advertising. The Terms of Use prohibit any activity that would impair the operation of the website, including the use of data-mining "bots, robots, spiders, or scrapers" to gain access to users' login information, posting of unsolicited advertising or circulation of such advertising via e-mail, providing false personal information or falsely stating or otherwise misrepresenting oneself, or any use of another person's account without Facebook's prior authorization.

Facebook alleges that Defendants are registered Facebook users who are bound by the Terms of Use. Since November 2008, Defendants allegedly have engaged in a phishing and spamming scheme that has compromised the accounts of a substantial number of Facebook users. Defendants' activity allegedly has escalated substantially. The alleged scheme generally operates as follows: Defendants send emails to multiple Facebook users. The emails appear to be legitimate messages and ask the recipients to click on a link to another website. That website is a phishing site designed to trick users into divulging their Facebook login information. Once users divulge the information, Defendants then use it to send spam to the friends of the users, and as the cycle repeats the number of compromised Facebook accounts increases rapidly. Facebook also alleges that certain spam messages redirect users to websites that pay Defendants for each user visit. While Facebook has been reasonably successful in combating this scheme, the expanding scope of the operation has made it increasingly difficult to neutralize Defendants' activities.

II. Discussion

The standard for issuing a TRO is the same as that for issuing a preliminary injunction. In the Ninth Circuit, a party seeking a preliminary injunction must show either (1) a likelihood of success on the merits and the possibility of irreparable injury, or (2) that serious questions are raised and the balance of the hardships tips in the movant's favor. *Roe v. Anderson*, 134 F.3d 1400, 1401-02 (9th Cir.1998); *Apple Computer, Inc. v. Formula Int'l, Inc.*, 725 F.2d 521, 523 (9th Cir.1984). These formulations represent two points on a sliding scale in which the required degree of irreparable harm increases as the probability of success decreases.

In the instant case, Facebook engaged in substantial investigative activity before filing suit and has presented sufficient evidence in support of the instant motion to demonstrate a likelihood of success on the merits with respect to the claims asserted in the operative complaint. In addition, there is a clear possibility of irreparable injury with respect both to Facebook's reputation and to the personal privacy of Facebook users. See *Stuhlbarg Intern. Sales Co., Inc. v. John D. Brush and Co., Inc.*, 240 F.3d 832, 841 (9th Cir.2001) ("Evidence of threatened loss of prospective customers or goodwill certainly supports a finding of the possibility of irreparable harm."); see also *MySpace, Inc. v. Wallace*, 498 F.Supp.2d 1293, 1305 (C.D.Cal.2007) (activities similar to the scheme alleged in the instant case caused irreparable harm). Finally, the balance of hardships clearly favors Facebook because it has expended significant time and resources to combat Defendants' activities, which as noted above are expanding at a considerable rate. See id. ("The balance of hardships tips sharply in favor of Plaintiff here. Plaintiff has already expended substantial time and money in combating Defendant's unsolicited messages and postings, and has dealt with over 800 resulting user complaints.") Likewise, Defendants will suffer little or no hardship if enjoined from their allegedly illegal scheme. Accordingly, Facebook is entitled to temporary injunctive relief.

Order

Good cause therefor appearing, IT IS HEREBY ORDERED that:

1. Defendants Jeremi Fisher, Philip Porembski, Ryan Simeall, and Choko Systems LLC, Harm, Inc., PP Web Services LLC, and iMedia Online Services LLC, and all of their officers, agents, servants, employees and attorneys and persons in active concert or participation with them who receive actual notice of this Order are hereby enjoined from:
   a. Initiating or procuring transmission of unsolicited commercial electronic messages on or through Facebook's computers, Facebook's website, Facebook's networks, or to Facebook users;
   b. Accessing or attempting to access Facebook's website, networks, data, information, user information, profiles, computers, and/or computer systems;
   c. Soliciting, requesting, or taking any action to induce Facebook users to provide identifying information or representing that such solicitation, request, or action is being done with Facebook's authorization or approval;
   d. Retaining any copies, electronic or otherwise, of any Facebook information, including login information and/or passwords, obtained through illegitimate and/or unlawful actions;
   e. Engaging in any activity that alters, damages, deletes, destroys, disrupts, diminishes the quality of, interferes with the performance of, or impairs the functionality of Facebook's computers, computer system computer network, data, website, or services;
   f. Engaging in any unlawful activities alleged in the operative complaint;
   g. Entering or accessing the physical premises or facilities of Facebook or its counsel; and
   h. Engaging in any activity that violates, and/or encourages, induces or facilitates violations of the Terms of Use attached as Exhibit A to this 4 Order.
2. This Order shall take effect immediately and shall remain in effect pending a hearing in this Court on Facebook's motion for a preliminary injunction.

Case Questions

1. Why was Facebook seeking injunctive relief against the defendants in *Facebook, Inc. v. Fisher?*
2. Why was Facebook entitled to a temporary restraining order?
3. Why do you think Facebook sought an injunction rather money damages?

DATA MINING

Data Mining
A series of techniques used to extract intelligence from vast stores of digital information.

Another privacy concern with the expansion of the Internet involves data mining. Significant legal and policy issues surround data mining. **Data mining** is defined in many different ways but generally involves a series of techniques used to extract intelligence from vast stores of digital information.[33] Database mining can also be defined as encompassing a wide spectrum of data-based activities ranging from "subject-based" searches for information on specified individuals to "pattern-based" searches for unusual or predetermined patterns of activities or relationships.

The government has increasingly used data mining for a variety of purposes. The government today increasingly relies on personal data obtained from both third parties and also directly from individuals to administer programs such as Social Security and Medicare. For example, a 2004 report by the General Accounting Office ("GAO") found that forty-two federal departments—including every cabinet-level agency that responded to the survey—engaged in, or were planning to engage in, 122 pattern-based data mining efforts involving personal information. Law enforcement personnel also use data mining to investigate potential acts of terrorism and Medicare fraud.

Besides the government, websites and network advertisers sometimes sell personal information that they have collected to data brokers. Data brokers are entities that collect and sell commercial data, including personally identifiable information, to others, including governments. Increasingly, data brokers extract and analyze personal information from online sources along with public records and other publicly available information. ChoicePoint, Acxiom, and LexisNexis are three of the leading commercial data brokers.

Privacy policy experts have raised concerns about data mining, especially pattern-based data mining used by the government.[34] The constitutional presumption of innocence and the Fourth Amendment principle that the government must have individual suspicion before it can conduct a search are at issue with pattern-based database mining. Data mining also creates the danger of false positives where an innocent person is placed on a government watch list, investigated, or detained.[35]

Under the current law, data mining is largely unregulated. The U.S. Supreme Court decision in *United States v. Miller*, 425 U.S. 435 (1976), that no reasonable expectation of privacy exists in information held by third parties under the Fourth Amendment also applies to data mining.[36]

A few state legislatures have passed laws to prohibit or limit the use of data mining for marketing purposes. For example, Maine, New Hampshire, and Vermont have adopted data mining legislation.[37] Data mining legislation also raises questions about commercial free speech under the First Amendment. In 2011, the U.S. Supreme Court held in *IMS Health, Inc. v. Sorrell*, 131 S. Ct. 2653 (2011), that Vermont's Prescription Confidentiality Law, which prohibited certain data mining of health information, is subject to heightened judicial scrutiny under the First Amendment. The court held that the Vermont law violated the First Amendment since the law restricted free speech based on the content of the speech and based on the identity of the speaker. Other states have also proposed data mining legislation but the Supreme Court's ruling in the Vermont data mining law raises constitutional questions under the First Amendment.

Some argue that Congress needs to pass legislation and create clear legal standards for data mining, especially with health data and government data mining. Strong opposition to data mining legislation also exists, particularly among data mining companies and pharmaceutical companies. In 2009, Senators Herb Kohl of Wisconsin and Dick Durbin of Illinois introduced an amendment to the Senate health care bill that would effectively ban pharmaceutical data mining, the drug company practice of buying prescription records to target sales pitches to doctors.[38] The amendment, however, failed to receive the necessary votes and the measure stalled. Congress, state legislatures, and courts will continue to examine privacy issues with online data mining in the coming years.

ONLINE PRIVACY POLICIES

Online privacy policies are also an important consideration when it comes to online privacy. A common industry practice is the adoption of an online privacy policy. One study found that 94% of Fortune 100 companies have posted an online privacy.[39] An online privacy policy generally outlines for consumers and visitors the data practices of a particular company or organization. Typically, the policy is available via a link from a company's home page labeled "Privacy" or something similar.[40] Courts sometimes call an online privacy a "browse-wrap agreement" between the site and the user, on which acceptance is based on use of the site. Chapter 6 provides more discussion on the enforceability of browse-wrap agreements.

Google's privacy policy is typical of the topics commonly found in online privacy policies. Google's policy addresses four of the basic information privacy principle: notice, consent, security, and access. Specifically, Google's privacy policy has provisions for the kind of information collected, the intended use of information gathered, the availability of opt-out procedures, the data security measures in place, and how the consumer might access the information that is collected. Companies often modify their privacy policies. For example, Google's Privacy Policy states "Please note that this Privacy Policy may change from time to time."[41]

Facebook's privacy policy has been the subject of significant debate and controversy. Like Google's Privacy Policy, Facebook's privacy policy allows Facebook to change its privacy policy unilaterally. In 2006, Facebook attempted to implement a new feature called "Newsfeeds," which displayed a list of a member's every action to all one's "Friends" on Facebook. This outraged members, the largest group being Students Against Facebook Newsfeeds. Facebook partially retreated from its original plan and allowed users more control and also the ability to exclude certain items from appearing on other Friends' Newsfeeds.[42]

In April of 2010, Facebook again unilaterally modified its terms of use agreement and privacy policy. The new policy "required users to opt out if they wished to keep information private, making most of the information public by default." The "opt out" provision required a member to sift through approximately 150 options and determine to whom the information would be made available, making what privacy controls were available "effectively unusable for many people." Facebook also had plans for an "instant personalization" feature that allowed outside partner sites (such as pandora.com and yelp.com) to gain access to personal data of members. After outrage from users, privacy advocates, and government officials, Facebook announced a change to this policy.[43] Facebook simplified controls on how a user can limit categories of information but still kept the default that content is publicly available. Mark Zuckerberg, founder and chief executive of Facebook, wrote in an editorial appearing in the *Washington Post* stating "[t]he biggest message we have heard recently is that people want easier control over their information. Simply put, many of you thought our controls were too complex. . . . We just missed the mark."[44]

The enforceability of an online privacy policy sometimes arises in the context of a breach of contract action between a user and the company that maintains the online privacy policy. In *Young v. Facebook, Inc.*, No. 5:10-cv-03579-JF/PVT, 2010 WL 4269304 (N.D.Cal. Oct. 25, 2010), plaintiff Karen Beth Young filed a complaint in the Superior Court of California against Facebook, alleging various claims, including breach of contract, after Facebook permanently disabled Young's Facebook account. Facebook claimed that Young violated the Facebook Statement of Rights and Responsibilities for behavior identified as harassing or threatening to other people on Facebook, including sending friend requests to people she did not know, regularly contacting strangers, and soliciting others for dating or business purposes. Facebook notified Young that her account would not be reactivated for any reason, and that she would not be provided further information about her violation or an opportunity to appeal. Young then filed a complaint in California state court, but the court dismissed the breach of contract claim because Young only generally alleged that Facebook violated its Statement of Rights and Responsibilities, its advertised Facebook Principles, and its Privacy Policy, but Young failed to identify with any particularity how Facebook breached any obligation owed to her. The Court in *Young v. Facebook* also held that the Facebook Principles do not create legal obligations or grant a user the right to enforce those principles in court. The court cited *Green v. America Online*, 318 F.3d 465, 472 (3rd Cir. 2003), which held that Green "failed to state a claim for breach of contract because . . . by their terms, the Member Agreement and Community Guidelines were not intended to confer any rights on Green and AOL did not promise to protect Green from the acts of other subscribers." Because courts have often found that privacy policies do not confer any legal rights or obligations, users will face challenges in a breach of contract action alleging violations of online privacy policies.

Besides possible litigation, online privacy policies can also be subject to regulatory enforcement by the Federal Trade Commission (FTC). Section 5 of the Federal Trade Commission Act, codified in 15 U.S.C. § 45, prohibits unfair acts or practices in or affecting commerce. Under the Act, the FTC has authority to "enforce the promises in privacy statements, including promises about the security of consumers' personal information." The FTC uses this authority to hold companies liable for breaches of privacy in violation of their online privacy policies.

For example, in 2006 the FTC entered into a settlement agreement with Guidance Software Inc. after the software company failed to take reasonable security measures to protect sensitive customer data, contradicting security promises made on its website.[45] According to the FTC, Guidance's data-security failure allowed hackers to access sensitive credit card information for thousands of consumers. The settlement required Guidance Software to implement a comprehensive information-security program and obtain audits by an independent third-party security professional every other year for ten years. According to the FTC complaint, Guidance failed to implement simple, inexpensive, and readily available security measures to protect consumers' data. Despite claims about data security made on Guidance's website, the company created unnecessary risks to credit card information by permanently storing it in clear readable text.

The FTC also brought an enforcement action against online pharmacies in 2000 that made false statements in their privacy and security policies. Operators of a group of online pharmacies agreed to settle FTC charges that their promotional claims were false and violated federal laws. The complaint alleged that the operators promoted themselves as having medical and pharmaceutical facilities they didn't actually have and making privacy and confidentiality assurances they didn't keep. The settlements required that the defendants post a privacy policy that discloses the types of personal identifying information they are collecting, either actively or passively, through such technologies as computer cookies; the uses that will be made of the data; the means by which a consumer may access and review his or her personal information; and, a means by which a consumer may modify or delete personal information on file. The defendants were also required to establish and maintain reasonable procedures to protect the confidentiality, security, and integrity of personal information collected from consumers. The settlements also contain record-keeping provisions to allow the FTC to monitor compliance with the order.[46]

The Center for Digital Democracy (CDD) is a nonprofit consumer-advocacy group focused on digital media and protecting privacy. Founded in 2001, CDD has been at the forefront of research, public education, and advocacy on protecting consumers in the digital age. CDD's public education programs focus on informing consumers, policy makers, and the press about contemporary digital marketing issues, including its impact on public health, children and youth, and financial services. CDD often files complaints with the FCC and lobbies members of Congress to help secure privacy rights with digital media. For more information about the CDD, visit www.democraticmedia.org.

FIGURE 11.3 The Center for Digital Democracy: Privacy Advocacy Group

Users, privacy advocates, and government officials continue to criticize Facebook's privacy policy, and members of Congress have considered legislation such as the Commercial Privacy Bill of Rights Act of 2011 (S. 799). The FTC is investigating Facebook's privacy controls, which the company changed in April and May of 2010; Rep. Joe Barton, Republican of Texas and Rep. Edward Markey, Democrat of Massachusetts, have also probed Facebook about privacy practices, particularly on user information shared with third-party apps and websites.

Facebook, which didn't even lobby the federal government prior to 2009, has increased its lobbying efforts in the wake of growing pressure from lawmakers and regulators about its privacy policies. According the *Wall Street Journal*, Facebook spent $351,000 on federal lobbying in 2010.[47] This is still a fraction of the amount spent by other technology companies. By comparison, Google Inc. spent $5.2 million, and Microsoft Corp. spent $6.9 million in federal lobbying in 2010.[48] In the first quarter of 2011, Facebook reported its highest single quarter yet on federal lobbying expenditures in spending $230,000—an increase of more than 455 percent from the roughly $41,400 it spent during the same period the previous year.[49] Facebook also has a new Washington office and has hired outside lobbying firms and more staffers. Congress will continue to scrutinize Facebook's privacy policy in the coming years.

As a best practice, companies should adopt an online privacy policy and regularly review the policy. Any changes in the privacy policy should be clearly communicated to users and customers. Companies should also make sure that they enforce the promises they make in privacy statements, including promises about the security of consumers' personal information. Otherwise, the FTC might bring an enforcement action.

WORKPLACE PRIVACY

Historically, workplace privacy disputes involved searches of lockers and desk drawers. In the digital age, computers, phones, and other electronic devices are the subjects of workplace privacy disputes. Generally speaking, employees have a reduced expectation of privacy in the workplace.

For public employees, courts apply the reasonable expectation of privacy test to determine whether a government search of a private workplace violates an employee's Fourth Amendment rights.[50]

Private employees are limited in their protection to the laws of the particular state in which they work. Many states have adopted constitutional provisions mandating a right to privacy for all employees, and some state constitutions have been interpreted to protect the private employee's right to privacy in the workplace.[51]

The 1987 U.S. Supreme Court decision in *O'Connor v. Ortega*, 480 U.S. 709 (1987), established the judicial framework for analyzing the scope of employee privacy protections in the electronic workplace for public employees under the Fourth Amendment. Under *O'Connor*, whether an expectation of privacy in the workplace will be deemed reasonable and therefore enforceable under the Fourth Amendment will depend on a case-by-case analysis of the actual office practices and procedures and may be further reduced by legitimate employer regulation.

There are limits to an employer's ability to monitor and control employees. For public employers, surveillance must be conducted in a way that does not interfere with the employee's reasonable expectation of privacy.

Courts have found no reasonable expectation of privacy in an employee's workplace computer when the employer notifies employees of the policy. For example, in *United States v. Ziegler*, 474 F.3d 1184 (9th Cir. 2007), the Ninth Circuit held that no objectively reasonable expectation of privacy existed where the employee's workplace computer was routinely monitored and the employer's privacy policy provided sufficient notice of such monitoring). Similarly, in *Biby v. Bd. of Regents, of the Univ. of Neb.*, 419 F.3d 845, 850–51 (8th Cir. 2005), the Eighth Circuit held than an employment policy saying the employer could search the employee' computer was enough to find no reasonable expectation of privacy.

On the other hand, if the employer does not have a policy in place or does not provide notice to employees, then courts may find a reasonable expectation of privacy in the workplace. In *Leventhal v. Knapek*, 266 F.3d 64, 74 (2nd Cir. 2001), the Second Circuit held that because the employer did not practice routine searches of workplace computers and did not have a general privacy policy, the employee had a reasonable expectation of privacy in contents of their work computer. In *United States v. Slanina*, 283 F.3d 670, 677 (5th Cir. 2002), the court held that "given the absence of a city policy placing [the employee] on notice that his computer usage would be monitored and the lack of any indication that other employees had routine access to his computer, we hold that [the employee's] expectation of privacy was reasonable."

Companies and managers should adopt a company privacy policy and provide sufficient notice to employees of the policy to mitigate potential litigation brought by employees.

In 2010, the U.S. Supreme Court considered whether a government employer's search of an employee's text messages on an employer-owned pager violated the employee's Fourth Amendment right to protection against unreasonable searches. In *City of Ontario v. Quon*, 130 S. Ct. 2619, 2629 (2010), a city police officer brought an action under 42 U.S.C. § 1983 action against the city, police department, and police chief alleging that the police department's review of the officer's text messages violated the Fourth Amendment. The court held that the city's review of officer's text messages was reasonable, and thus did not violate Fourth Amendment.

In *Quon*, the U.S. Supreme Court also cautioned that courts "must proceed with care when considering the whole concept of privacy expectations in communications made on electronic equipment. . . . The judiciary risks error by elaborating too fully on the Fourth Amendment implications of emerging technology before its role in society has become clear." The Court observed that with dynamic changes in new technology and what society accepts as proper behavior with that new technology, the judiciary should take caution and proceed with care.

The U.S. Supreme Court's holding in *Quon* was largely confined to the facts of the case and left open questions related to the reasonableness of employees' expectations of privacy, employer monitoring, employee notice requirements, search procedures, and the applicability of Fourth Amendment protections in the private workplace.[52] Many questions involving employee privacy in the workplace remain unquestioned, and courts will continue to analyze and clarify these questions with new technological achievements on a case-by-case basis.

SELF-REGULATION AND REFORMS

While some groups and policy-makers favor government regulation to set strict limits in addressing online privacy, other groups argue that self-regulation offers a better approach. **Self-regulation** is a regulatory system in which business representatives define and enforce standards for their sector with little or no government involvement. Self-regulation has so far prevailed over government regulation when it comes to the protection of online privacy.[53]

Self-regulation
The process by which an identifiable group of people or industry governs or directs their own activities by their own rules.

Proponents of self-regulation maintain that the market, either alone or in combination with industry self-regulation, can do a better job in protecting personal information than government mandated statutes and regulations. Supporters of self-regulation contend that Internet businesses already have a market incentive to protect user privacy to avoid losing customers. For example, if users do not like the privacy controls with a particular online social networking site, users can go to a competing online social networking site that better protects privacy. Government regulation is slow with the ever-changing nature of the Internet, while self-regulation can better predict and respond to new changes in technology. Supporters of self-regulation also contend that industry will be more likely to accept and comply with rules designed and imposed by their peers.

The Federal Trade Commission (FTC) established voluntary guidelines for appropriate online data practices with the "Fair Information Practice Principles." The Fair Information Practice Principles (see Appendix D) encouraged commercial websites to follow the core principles of notice/awareness, choice/consent, access/participation, integrity/security, and enforcement/redress. For example, the section on notice/awareness in the Fair Information Practice Principles states, "The most fundamental principle is notice. Consumers should be given notice of an entity's information practices before any personal information is collected from them. Without notice, a consumer cannot make an informed decision as to whether and to what extent to disclose personal information."[54] The main problem with the Fair Information Practice Principles is that few companies have implemented the guidelines.

The Direct Marketing Association (DMA)'s online privacy principles and information practice guidance is another example of industry self-regulation. The DMA guidelines call for marketers operating websites to post an easy-to-find notice to consumers of the marketer's information collection practices, and to provide consumers with an opportunity to prohibit disclosure of their information. The DMA guidelines, however, fail to include basic protections, such as access to the individual's information and the assurance that the information is secure and accurate. The DMA guidelines also do not have an enforcement mechanism.[55]

Co-regulation
Government and industry share responsibility in setting goals, developing rules, and enforcing standards. Also called collaborative governance or contractual regulation. *See also* negotiated rulemaking.

Co-regulation is an alternative to government regulation and self-regulation. Co-regulation combines the strengths of the government regulation and self-regulation. With co-regulation, government and industry share responsibility in setting goals, developing rules, and enforcing standards. Co-regulation is sometimes called collaborative governance or contractual regulation. Some administrative agencies use **negotiated rulemaking** ("reg-neg") which is rulemaking through the use of a negotiated rulemaking committee. A "negotiated rulemaking committee" is an advisory committee established to consider and discuss issues for the purpose of reaching a consensus in the development of a proposed rule. For example, the Environmental Protection Agency (EPA) used negotiated rulemaking for complex regulations needed to implement the Clean Water Act's Phase II Stormwater program.[56]

Negotiated Rulemaking (neg-reg)
Rulemaking through the use of a negotiated rulemaking committee. A negotiated rulemaking committee is an advisory committee established to consider and discuss issues for the purpose of reaching a consensus in the development of a proposed rule.

Laissez-faire is French for "let people do as they choose." With laissez-faire, government abstains from interfering in economic or commercial affairs. In a 2000 report to Congress on online access and security, the FTC noted "significant consumer privacy concerns" arising from "the prevalence, ease, and relatively low cost" of collecting and transferring personal data.

Under the current structure with online privacy, Congress has taken a laissez-faire approach and favored industry self-regulation as the best means of protecting the personal privacy of online users without burdening industry with government interference. **Laissez-faire** is French for "let people do as they choose."[57] With laissez-faire, government abstains from interfering in economic or commercial affairs. In a 2000 report to Congress on online access and security, the FTC noted "significant consumer privacy concerns" arising from "the prevalence, ease, and relatively low cost" of collecting and transferring personal data.[58] The FTC conceded that industry self-regulation was inadequate to address online privacy. The FTC dramatically reversed its prior favorable position on self-regulation and called for federal privacy legislation to balance commerce and privacy interests on the Internet.[59]

Many scholars and privacy advocates agree with the FTC that self-regulation has been a failure and that new reforms are needed. One challenge with self-regulation is the difficulty of monitoring whether companies comply with standards established by the industry. Other criticisms of self-regulation include the lack of enforcement and no system of redress for breaches of industry set guidelines. Without enforcement and accountability, companies have no incentive to comply. The existing patchwork of U.S. privacy law fails to ensure across-the-board conformity with the standard measure of privacy protection in the Fair Information Practice Principles. Some argue for the passage of omnibus U.S. legislation protecting "informational self-determination" that would mandate specific procedures for giving individuals greater control over information about them.[60] The adequacy of U.S. information privacy law, especially with online privacy, is an ongoing topic of heated debate.

Summary

The rapid growth of the Internet has created new challenges and issues with privacy interests in digital information. While social networking sites such as Facebook and Twitter are very popular, these sites raise concerns about privacy. Privacy in Internet search queries is also a growing concern. A variety of federal and state laws govern online advertising. The CAN-SPAM Act that prohibits certain types of spam, and the FTC Act prohibits false and deceptive trade practices such as phishing and certain adware. Data mining creates additional privacy concerns, especially with health information and government data mining. Some courts have held that online privacy policies do not confer any legal rights or obligations, but the FTC may bring an enforcement action against a company that violates the terms of its own online privacy policy. Workplace privacy policies are also a hot issue when it comes to online privacy. For public employees, courts apply the reasonable expectation of privacy test to determine whether a government search of a private workplace violates an employee's Fourth Amendment rights. Under the current regulatory scheme, Congress has generally favored self-regulation over government regulation with online privacy but some groups have called for more government regulation of online privacy or co-regulation to better protect privacy interests in the online environment.

Key Terms

adware *210*
CAN-SPAM Act *208*
click fraud *211*
co-regulation *219*
data mining *214*
Federal Trade Commission Act (FTC Act) *210*
laissez-faire *220*
negotiated rulemaking *219*
phishing *210*
self-regulation *219*
social networking site *201*
spam *208*
standing *208*

Review Questions

1. Describe the privacy legal issues associated with online social networking sites?
2. What is the purpose of the Commercial Privacy Bill of Rights Act of 2011?
3. What did the court decide in *Gonzales v. Google, Inc.*, 234 F.R.D. 674 (N.D. Cal. 2006), about privacy with Internet search engines?
4. What are the potential consequences for spam and phishing?
5. Describe the role of the Federal Trade Commission with online advertising?
6. What is data mining? Describe the privacy issues associated with data mining?
7. To what extent can an employer monitor an employee's text messages on an employer-owned phone or pager?
8. What are the main parts of a typical online privacy policy?
9. What are the arguments in favor and against self-regulation with online privacy?

Discussion Questions

1. Which is a better method for protecting personal privacy on the Internet: government regulation or industry self-regulation? Discuss the advantages and disadvantages of both methods?
2. Courts currently recognize several privileges such as the attorney-client privilege and the physician-patient privilege. Would you support legislation that recognized a privilege in Internet search queries to prevent discoverability and admissibility in legal proceedings? Would you support any exceptions such as a legitimate law enforcement purpose with a warrant?
3. In the CAN-SPAM Act of 2003, Congress did not grant standing for private parties who wished to bring an action against companies that send spam or bulk unsolicited e-mail. Congress also preempted some state anti-spam laws that created a private right of action for private parties. Should private parties be able to bring a private right of action against spammers? Why or why not?

Exercises

1. *Business Plan Assignment:* You and a business partner want to start up a new social networking site designed specifically for health care and medical professionals. This will be a personal and professional networking site geared toward physicians and nurses. Physicians can exchange clinical experiences, review cases, and share clinical knowledge. Write a business plan for the new social networking site. The business plan should include an executive summary, a description of the business, a plan for how you will market and manage your business, financial projections. In the business plan, you should also discuss legal and privacy issues with health information and how the site will be compliant with the Health Insurance Portability and Accountability Act (HIPAA). Visit the website for the U.S. Small Business Administration at www.business.gov for business plan templates, video tutorials, and step-by-step guides for writing a business plan.
2. Run a search on the Library of Congress THOMAS website at http://thomas.loc.gov to find the text and bill status for the Commercial Privacy Bill of Rights Act of 2011 (S. 799) introduced by Senators Kerry and McCain during in the 112th Congress. What are the key provisions in the bill? What is the current status of the bill? Conduct a search to find any similar bills pending in the U.S. House of Representatives and identify the bill number and sponsor(s). Discuss whether you support or oppose the Commercial Privacy Bill of Rights Act of 2011.
3. Find the online privacy policies for eBay and the Federal Trade Commission (FTC). Discuss both the similarities and differences in the two privacy policies.
4. While online privacy law in the United States is more of a piecemeal approach with a preference for industry self-regulation, the European Union has adopted a more comprehensive approach under Directive 95/46/EC also called the "Data Protection" directive. Conduct online research of the EU "Data Protection" directive and then write a memorandum on whether or not you would support a similar approach in the United States. You might start your research with the European Commission website at www.europa.eu and run a search for "Data Protection."

5. *Hypothetical:* John is a police officer for Columbia City and uses his own personal handheld electronic device on the job to send text messages using his employer's wireless network. Some of the text messages are work-related, and other text messages are personal in nature. Columbia City obtains transcripts of John's text messages sent while on the job and terminates John for improper conduct. John then sues the city under 42 U.S.C. § 1983, alleging that the police department's review of the officer's text messages violates the Fourth Amendment. Using the same facts as the U.S. Supreme Court case in *City of Ontario v. Quon* except that now the employee is using an employee-owned portable electronic device that uses the employer's wireless network, discuss whether John would prevail in the action against the city and what remedies (damages and/or injunctive relief) he would recover.

Related Internet Sites

http://business.ftc.gov/privacy-and-security
Federal Trade Commission Privacy and Security Website

http://thomas.loc.gov/
THOMAS—Legislative Information from the Library of Congress, including pending legislation

http://www.democraticmedia.org/
Center for Digital Democracy

http://www.uspirg.org/
U.S. PIRG, the federation of state Public Interest Research Groups (PIRGs)

End Notes

1. Mark Zuckerberg, *From Facebook, Answering Privacy Concerns with New Settings*, Washington Post, May 24, 2010, available at: http://www.washingtonpost.com/wp-dyn/content/article/2010/05/23/AR2010052303828.html.
2. Jessica Guynn, *Google Aims to Rekindle Old Fire*, L.A. TIMES, Jan. 22, 2011, at A1.
3. Facebook, Statistics, available at: http://www.facebook.com/press/info.php?statistics.
4. Danah M. Boyd and Nicole B. Ellison, *Social Network Sites: Definition, History, and Scholarship*, 13 J. COMPUTER-MEDIATED COMM. 2 (2007).
5. Brian Kane, *A Casual Tweet to Formal Reprimand: The Precarious Presence of Social Media in Legal Circles*, 54-APR ADVOCATE (Idaho) 18 (2011).
6. Christina R. Weatherford, *Judicial Sentencing Discretion Post-Booker: Are Judges Getting a Distorted View Through the Lens of Social Networking Sites?*, 27 GA. St. U. L. REV. 673 (2011).
7. Privacy: Deactivating, Deleting, and Memorializing Accounts, Facebook, available at: http://www.facebook.com/help/?page=842.
8. *Weatherford*, 27 Ga. St. U. L. REV. at 692–93.
9. Reuters, *Brooklyn Father Sues Facebook for Using Son's Name in Ads*, May 4, 2011, available at: http://newsandinsight.thomsonreuters.com/Legal/News/2011/05_May/Brooklyn_father_sues_Facebook_for_using_son_s_name_in_ads/.
10. Cecilia Kang, *Kerry, McCain Offer Bill to Protect Web Users' Privacy Rights*, WASH. POST, Apr. 12, 2011.
11. Omer Tene, *What Google Knows: Privacy and Internet Search Engines*, 2008 UTAH L. REV. 1433, 1435 (2008), citing Economist Special Briefing, *Inside the Googleplex*, Economist, Aug. 30, 2007, at 56–8, available at: http://www.economist.com/business/displaystory.cfm?story_id=9719610/.
12. James Grimmelmann, *The Structure of Search Engine Law*, 93 IOWA L. REV. 1, 18 (2007).
13. Andrew William Bagley, *Don't Be Evil: The Fourth Amendment in the Age of Google, National Security, and Digital Papers and Effects*, 21 Alb. L.J. SCI. & TECH. 153, 165 (2011).
14. U.S. District Court for the Northern District of California, Chief Judge James Ware, available at: http:// www.cand.uscourts.gov/jw/.
15. Harriet Chiang, *Federal Judge in San Jose Publicly Reprimanded for Lying*, SAN FRANCISCO CHRONICLE, Aug. 19, 1998, at A17.
16. An Examination of the Google Doubleclick Merger and the Online Advertising Industry: Hearing Before the Subcomm. on Antitrust, Competition Policy and Consumer Rights of the S. Comm. on the Judiciary, 110th Cong. 5 (2007) (referring to comments made by Bradford L. Smith, Senior Vice President, General Counsel, and Corporate Secretary of Microsoft, Inc., and David Drummond, Senior Vice President of Corporate Development and Chief Legal Officer of Google, Inc.).
17. *United States v. Kelley*, 482 F.3d 1047, 1055 (9th Cir.2007) (Thomas, J., dissenting).

18. Fernando M. Pinguelo and Bradford W. Muller, *Virtual Crimes, Real Damages: A Primer on Cybercrimes in the United States and Efforts to Combat Cybercriminals*, 16 VA. J.L. & TECH. 116 (2011).
19. 15 U.S.C. § 7706(a), (b), (f), (g).
20. Press Release, Federal Trade Commission, Judge Agrees with FTC, Orders Spammers to Pay More Than $2.5 Million and Stop Selling Bogus Weight-Loss and Anti-Aging Products (Feb. 4, 2008), available at: http://www.ftc.gov/opa/2008/02/sili.shtm/.
21. Black's Law Dictionary (9th ed. 2009).
22. Susuk Lim, *Death of the Spam Wrangler: CAN-SPAM Private Plaintiffs Required to Show Actual Harm*, 6 Wash. J. L. TECH. & ARTS 155 (2010).
23. Federal Trade Commission, The CAN-SPAM Act: A Compliance Guide for Business, available at: http://business.ftc.gov/documents/bus61-can-spam-act-compliance-guide-business/.
24. Federal Trade Commission, Advertising FAQ's: A Guide for Small Business, available at: http://business.ftc.gov/documents/bus35-advertising-faqs-guide-small-business/.
25. Laura L. Edwards, Comment, *Oh, What a Tangled World Wide Web We Weave: An Analysis of Washington's Computer Spyware Act in a National Context*, 31 SEATTLE U. L. REV. 645, note 77 (2008) (citing SearchCIO-Midmarket.com Definitions, http://searchcio-midmarket.techtarget.com/sDefinition/0,,sid183_gci521293,00.html).
26. Press Release, Federal Trade Commission, Zango, Inc. Settles FTC Charges (Nov. 3, 2006), available at: http://www.ftc.gov/opa/2006/11/zango.shtm.
27. 16 C.F.R. § 255.5.
28. Robert Sprague and Mary Ellen Wells, *Regulating Online Buzz Marketing: Untangling a Web of Deceit*, 47 AM. BUS. L.J. 415, 430–432 (2010).
29. Eric Goldman, *Technology & Marketing Law Blog, Facebook Scores Initial Win Against Privacy Plaintiffs Over Data Leakage Claims—In re Facebook Privacy Litigation* (May 13, 2011), available at: http://blog.ericgoldman.org/archives/2011/05/facebook_scores.htm/.
30. Amy Tracy, *Technology Law—Great Google-Y Moogley: The Effect and Enforcement of Click Fraud and Online Advertising*, 32 U. Ark. LITTLE ROCK L. REV. 347, 358 (2010).
31. Susanna Hamner, *Pay-Per-Click Web Advertisers Combat Costly Fraud*, N.Y. TIMES, MAY 13, 2009, at B3.
32. Brian S. Kabateck and Artin Gholian, *The Computer Fraud and Abuse Act May Become the Best Tool for Fighting Internet Advertising Click Fraud*, 33APR L.A. LAW. 22 (2010).
33. Fred H. Cate, *Government Data Mining: The Need for a Legal Framework*, 43 HARV. C.R.-C.L. L. REV. 435, 438 (2008).
34. Ira S. Rubinstein and Ronald D. Lee, *Data Mining and Internet Profiling: Emerging Regulatory and Technological Approaches*, 75 U. CHI. L. REV. 261, 263 (2008).
35. Dennis D. Hirsch, *The Law and Policy of Online Privacy: Regulation, Self-Regulation, or Co-Regulation?*, 34 SEATTLE U. L. REV. 439, 450 (2011).
36. *United States v. Miller*, 425 U.S. at 443.
37. 22 Me. Rev. Stat. § 1711-E(2)-(2.A); N.H. Rev. Stat. Ann. § 318:47-f; 18 Vt. Stat. Ann. § 4631(d).
38. Matthew Perrone, *2 Senators Move to Block Mining Rx Data*, ORLANDO SENTINEL, Dec. 11, 2009, at B5.
39. Suhong Li and Chen Zhang, *An Analysis of Online Privacy Policies of Fortune 100 Companies, in Online Consumer Protection: Theories of Human Relativism* 269, 277 (Kuanchin Chen & Adam Fadlalla eds., 2009).
40. Robert Todd Graham Collins, *The Privacy Implications of Deep Packet Inspection Technology: Why the Next Wave in Online Advertising Shouldn't Rock the Self-Regulatory Boat*, 44 Ga. L. Rev. 545, 564 (2010).
41. Google Privacy Center: Privacy Policy, available at: http://www.google.com/intl/en/privacy/privacy-policy.html.
42. Mary Graw Leary, *Reasonable Expectations of Privacy for Youth in a Digital Age*, 80 MISS. L.J. 1035, 1050–51 (2011).
43. Id.
44. Mark Zuckerberg, *From Facebook, Answering Privacy Concerns with New Settings*, WASHINGTON POST, May 24, 2010, available at: http://www.washingtonpost.com/wp-dyn/ content/article/2010/05/23/AR2010052303828.html.
45. Federal Trade Commission, Guidance Software Inc. Settles FTC Charges (Nov. 16, 2006), available at: http:// www.ftc.gov/opa/2006/11/guidance.shtm/.
46. Federal Trade Commission, Online Pharmacies Settle FTC Charges (July 12, 2000), available at: http://www.ftc.gov/opa/2000/07/iog.shtm/.
47. Elizabeth Williamson, Amy Schatz, and Geoffrey A Fowler, *Facebook Seeking Friends in Beltway*, WALL ST. J., Apr. 20, 2011, at A1.
48. Evan Mackinder, *Pace of Federal Lobbying Slows in First Quarter*, State News Service, Apr. 21, 2011.
49. The Center for Digital Democracy, About CDD, available at: http://www.democraticmedia.org/about-cdd/.
50. *O'Connor v. Ortega*, 480 U.S. 709, 719 (1987).
51. Brandon Sipherd and Christopher Volpe, *Evaluating the Legality of Employer Surveillance under the Family and Medical Leave Act: Have Employers Crossed the Line?*, 27 HOFSTRA LAB. & EMP. L.J. 467, 492 (2010).
52. Allan S. Bloom, *The Impact of Supreme Court Employment Law Cases*, 2011 Edition, Aspatore, 2011 WL 971875 (2011).
53. Dennis D. Hirsch, *The Law and Policy of Online Privacy: Regulation, Self-Regulation, or Co-Regulation*, 34 SEATTLE U. L. REV. 439, 457–58 (2011).

54. Federal Trade Commission, Fair Information Practice Principles, available at: http://www.ftc.gov/reports/privacy3/fairinfo.shtm/.
55. Jonathan P. Cody, *Protecting Privacy over the Internet: Has the Time Come to Abandon Self-Regulation?*, 48 Cath. U. L. Rev. 1183, 1219 (1999).
56. Erin Ryan, *Negotiating Federalism*, 52 B.C. L. Rev. 1, 55 (2011) (citing EPA Office of Water, Overview of the Storm Water Program 8 (1996), available at: http://www.epa.gov/npdes/pubs/owm0195.pdf).
57. Black's Law Dictionary (9th ed. 2009).
58. Federal Trade Commission, Final Report of the FTC Advisory Committee on Online Access and Security (May 2000), available at: http://www.ftc.gov/acoas/papers/finalreport.htm/.
59. Marsha Cope Huie et al., *The Right to Privacy in Personal Data: The E.U. Prods the U.S. and Controversy Continues*, 9 Tulsa J. Comp. & Int'l L. 391, 396 (2002).
60. Kenneth A. Bamberger and Deirdre K. Mulligan, *Privacy on the Books and on the Ground*, 63 Stan. L. Rev. 247, 255 (2011).

APPENDIX A

Digital Millennium Copyright Act (DMCA), 17 U.S.C. § 512 Safe Harbor Provision

(a) Transitory digital network communications.—A service provider shall not be liable for monetary relief, or, except as provided in subsection (j), for injunctive or other equitable relief, for infringement of copyright by reason of the provider's transmitting, routing, or providing connections for, material through a system or network controlled or operated by or for the service provider, or by reason of the intermediate and transient storage of that material in the course of such transmitting, routing, or providing connections, if—

(1) the transmission of the material was initiated by or at the direction of a person other than the service provider;

(2) the transmission, routing, provision of connections, or storage is carried out through an automatic technical process without selection of the material by the service provider;

(3) the service provider does not select the recipients of the material except as an automatic response to the request of another person;

(4) no copy of the material made by the service provider in the course of such intermediate or transient storage is maintained on the system or network in a manner ordinarily accessible to anyone other than anticipated recipients, and no such copy is maintained on the system or network in a manner ordinarily accessible to such anticipated recipients for a longer period than is reasonably necessary for the transmission, routing, or provision of connections; and

(5) the material is transmitted through the system or network without modification of its content.

(b) System caching.—

(1) Limitation on liability.—A service provider shall not be liable for monetary relief, or, except as provided in subsection (j), for injunctive or other equitable relief, for infringement of copyright by reason of the intermediate and temporary storage of material on a system or network controlled or operated by or for the service provider in a case in which—

(A) the material is made available online by a person other than the service provider;

(B) the material is transmitted from the person described in subparagraph (A) through the system or network to a person other than the person described in subparagraph (A) at the direction of that other person; and

(C) the storage is carried out through an automatic technical process for the purpose of making the material available to users of the system or network who, after the material is transmitted as described in subparagraph (B), request access to the material from the person described in subparagraph (A), if the conditions set forth in paragraph (2) are met.

(2) Conditions.—The conditions referred to in paragraph (1) are that—

(A) the material described in paragraph (1) is transmitted to the subsequent users described in paragraph (1)(C) without modification to its content from the manner in which the material was transmitted from the person described in paragraph (1)(A);

(B) the service provider described in paragraph (1) complies with rules concerning the refreshing, reloading, or other updating of the material when specified by the person making the material available online in accordance with a generally accepted industry standard data communications protocol for the system or network through which that person makes the material available, except that this subparagraph applies only if those rules are not used by the person described in paragraph (1)(A) to prevent or unreasonably impair the intermediate storage to which this subsection applies;

(C) the service provider does not interfere with the ability of technology associated with the material to return to the person described in paragraph (1)(A) the information that would have been available to that person if the material had been obtained by the subsequent users described in paragraph (1)(C) directly from that person, except that this subparagraph applies only if that technology—

- **(i)** does not significantly interfere with the performance of the provider's system or network or with the intermediate storage of the material;
- **(ii)** is consistent with generally accepted industry standard communications protocols; and
- **(iii)** does not extract information from the provider's system or network other than the information that would have been available to the person described in paragraph (1)(A) if the subsequent users had gained access to the material directly from that person;

(D) if the person described in paragraph (1)(A) has in effect a condition that a person must meet prior to having access to the material, such as a condition based on payment of a fee or provision of a password or other information, the service provider permits access to the stored material in significant part only to users of its system or network that have met those conditions and only in accordance with those conditions; and

(E) if the person described in paragraph (1)(A) makes that material available online without the authorization of the copyright owner of the material, the service provider responds expeditiously to remove, or disable access to, the material that is claimed to be infringing upon notification of claimed infringement as described in subsection (c)(3), except that this subparagraph applies only if—

- **(i)** the material has previously been removed from the originating site or access to it has been disabled, or a court has ordered that the material be removed from the originating site or that access to the material on the originating site be disabled; and
- **(ii)** the party giving the notification includes in the notification a statement confirming that the material has been removed from the originating site or access to it has been disabled or that a court has ordered that the material be removed from the originating site or that access to the material on the originating site be disabled.

(c) Information residing on systems or networks at direction of users.—

(1) In general.—A service provider shall not be liable for monetary relief, or, except as provided in subsection (j), for injunctive or other equitable relief, for infringement of copyright by reason of the storage at the direction of a user of material that resides on a system or network controlled or operated by or for the service provider, if the service provider—

(A)
- **(i)** does not have actual knowledge that the material or an activity using the material on the system or network is infringing;
- **(ii)** in the absence of such actual knowledge, is not aware of facts or circumstances from which infringing activity is apparent; or
- **(iii)** upon obtaining such knowledge or awareness, acts expeditiously to remove, or disable access to, the material;

(B) does not receive a financial benefit directly attributable to the infringing activity, in a case in which the service provider has the right and ability to control such activity; and

(C) upon notification of claimed infringement as described in paragraph (3), responds expeditiously to remove, or disable access to, the material that is claimed to be infringing or to be the subject of infringing activity.

(2) Designated agent.—The limitations on liability established in this subsection apply to a service provider only if the service provider has designated an agent to receive notifications of claimed infringement described in paragraph (3), by making available through its service, including on its website in a location accessible to the public, and by providing to the Copyright Office, substantially the following information:

(A) the name, address, phone number, and electronic mail address of the agent.

(B) other contact information which the Register of Copyrights may deem appropriate.

The Register of Copyrights shall maintain a current directory of agents available to the public for inspection, including through the Internet, and may require payment of a fee by service providers to cover the costs of maintaining the directory.

(3) Elements of notification.—

(A) To be effective under this subsection, a notification of claimed infringement must be a written communication provided to the designated agent of a service provider that includes substantially the following:

(i) A physical or electronic signature of a person authorized to act on behalf of the owner of an exclusive right that is allegedly infringed.

(ii) Identification of the copyrighted work claimed to have been infringed, or, if multiple copyrighted works at a single online site are covered by a single notification, a representative list of such works at that site.

(iii) Identification of the material that is claimed to be infringing or to be the subject of infringing activity and that is to be removed or access to which is to be disabled, and information reasonably sufficient to permit the service provider to locate the material.

(iv) Information reasonably sufficient to permit the service provider to contact the complaining party, such as an address, telephone number, and, if available, an electronic mail address at which the complaining party may be contacted.

(v) A statement that the complaining party has a good faith belief that use of the material in the manner complained of is not authorized by the copyright owner, its agent, or the law.

(vi) A statement that the information in the notification is accurate, and under penalty of perjury, that the complaining party is authorized to act on behalf of the owner of an exclusive right that is allegedly infringed.

(B) **(i)** Subject to clause (ii), a notification from a copyright owner or from a person authorized to act on behalf of the copyright owner that fails to comply substantially with the provisions of subparagraph (A) shall not be considered under paragraph (1)(A) in determining whether a service provider has actual knowledge or is aware of facts or circumstances from which infringing activity is apparent.

(ii) In a case in which the notification that is provided to the service provider's designated agent fails to comply substantially with all the provisions of subparagraph (A) but substantially complies with clauses (ii), (iii), and (iv) of subparagraph (A), clause (i) of this subparagraph applies only if the service provider promptly attempts to contact the person making the notification or takes other reasonable steps to assist in the receipt of notification that substantially complies with all the provisions of subparagraph (A).

(d) Information location tools.—A service provider shall not be liable for monetary relief, or, except as provided in subsection (j), for injunctive or other equitable relief, for infringement of copyright by reason of the provider referring or linking users to an online location containing infringing material or infringing activity, by using information location tools, including a directory, index, reference, pointer, or hypertext link, if the service provider—

(1) (A) does not have actual knowledge that the material or activity is infringing;

(B) in the absence of such actual knowledge, is not aware of facts or circumstances from which infringing activity is apparent; or

(C) upon obtaining such knowledge or awareness, acts expeditiously to remove, or disable access to, the material;

(2) does not receive a financial benefit directly attributable to the infringing activity, in a case in which the service provider has the right and ability to control such activity; and

(3) upon notification of claimed infringement as described in subsection (c)(3), responds expeditiously to remove, or disable access to, the material that is claimed to be infringing or to be the subject of infringing activity, except that, for purposes of this paragraph, the information described in subsection (c)(3)(A)(iii) shall be identification of the reference or link, to material or activity claimed to be infringing, that is to be removed or access to which is to be disabled, and information reasonably sufficient to permit the service provider to locate that reference or link.

(e) Limitation on liability of nonprofit educational institutions.—

(1) When a public or other nonprofit institution of higher education is a service provider, and when a faculty member or graduate student who is an employee of such institution is performing a teaching or research function, for the purposes of subsections (a) and (b) such faculty member or graduate student shall be considered to be a person other than the institution, and for the purposes of subsections (c) and (d) such faculty member's or graduate student's knowledge or awareness of his or her infringing activities shall not be attributed to the institution, if—

(A) such faculty member's or graduate student's infringing activities do not involve the provision of online access to instructional materials that are or were required or recommended, within the preceding 3-year period, for a course taught at the institution by such faculty member or graduate student;

(B) the institution has not, within the preceding 3-year period, received more than two notifications described in subsection (c)(3) of claimed infringement by such faculty member or graduate student, and such notifications of claimed infringement were not actionable under subsection (f); and

(C) the institution provides to all users of its system or network informational materials that accurately describe, and promote compliance with, the laws of the United States relating to copyright.

(2) For the purposes of this subsection, the limitations on injunctive relief contained in subsections (j)(2) and (j)(3), but not those in (j)(1), shall apply.

(f) Misrepresentations.—Any person who knowingly materially misrepresents under this section—

(1) that material or activity is infringing, or

(2) that material or activity was removed or disabled by mistake or misidentification, shall be liable for any damages, including costs and attorneys, fees, incurred by the alleged infringer, by any copyright owner or copyright owner's authorized licensee, or by a service provider, who is injured by such misrepresentation, as the result of the service provider relying upon such misrepresentation in removing or disabling access to the material or activity claimed to be infringing, or in replacing the removed material or ceasing to disable access to it

(g) Replacement of removed or disabled material and limitation on other liability.—

(1) No liability for taking down generally.—Subject to paragraph (2), a service provider shall not be liable to any person for any claim based on the service provider's good faith disabling of access to, or removal of, material or activity claimed to be infringing or based on facts or circumstances from which infringing activity is apparent, regardless of whether the material or activity is ultimately determined to be infringing.

(2) Exception.—Paragraph (1) shall not apply with respect to material residing at the direction of a subscriber of the service provider on a system or network controlled or operated by or for the service provider that is removed, or to which access is disabled by the service provider, pursuant to a notice provided under subsection (c)(1)(C), unless the service provider—

(A) takes reasonable steps promptly to notify the subscriber that it has removed or disabled access to the material;

(B) upon receipt of a counter notification described in paragraph (3), promptly provides the person who provided the notification under subsection (c)(1)(C) with a copy of the counter notification, and informs that person that it will replace the removed material or cease disabling access to it in 10 business days; and

(C) replaces the removed material and ceases disabling access to it not less than 10, nor more than 14, business days following receipt of the counter notice, unless its designated agent first receives notice from the person who submitted the notification under subsection (c)(1)(C) that such person has filed an action seeking a court order to restrain the subscriber from engaging in infringing activity relating to the material on the service provider's system or network.

(3) Contents of counter notification.—To be effective under this subsection, a counter notification must be a written communication provided to the service provider's designated agent that includes substantially the following:

(A) A physical or electronic signature of the subscriber.

(B) Identification of the material that has been removed or to which access has been disabled and the location at which the material appeared before it was removed or access to it was disabled.

(C) A statement under penalty of perjury that the subscriber has a good faith belief that the material was removed or disabled as a result of mistake or misidentification of the material to be removed or disabled.

(D) The subscriber's name, address, and telephone number, and a statement that the subscriber consents to the jurisdiction of Federal District Court for the judicial district in which the address is located, or if the subscriber's address is outside of the United States, for any judicial district in which the service provider may be found, and that the subscriber will accept service of process from the person who provided notification under subsection (c)(1)(C) or an agent of such person.

(4) **Limitation on other liability.**—A service provider's compliance with paragraph (2) shall not subject the service provider to liability for copyright infringement with respect to the material identified in the notice provided under subsection (c)(1)(C).

(h) **Subpoena to identify infringer.**—

(1) **Request.**—A copyright owner or a person authorized to act on the owner's behalf may request the clerk of any United States district court to issue a subpoena to a service provider for identification of an alleged infringer in accordance with this subsection.

(2) **Contents of request.**—The request may be made by filing with the clerk—

(A) a copy of a notification described in subsection (c)(3)(A);

(B) a proposed subpoena; and

(C) a sworn declaration to the effect that the purpose for which the subpoena is sought is to obtain the identity of an alleged infringer and that such information will only be used for the purpose of protecting rights under this title.

(3) **Contents of subpoena.**—The subpoena shall authorize and order the service provider receiving the notification and the subpoena to expeditiously disclose to the copyright owner or person authorized by the copyright owner information sufficient to identify the alleged infringer of the material described in the notification to the extent such information is available to the service provider.

(4) **Basis for granting subpoena.**—If the notification filed satisfies the provisions of subsection (c)(3)(A), the proposed subpoena is in proper form, and the accompanying declaration is properly executed, the clerk shall expeditiously issue and sign the proposed subpoena and return it to the requester for delivery to the service provider.

(5) **Actions of service provider receiving subpoena.**—Upon receipt of the issued subpoena, either accompanying or subsequent to the receipt of a notification described in subsection (c)(3)(A), the service provider shall expeditiously disclose to the copyright owner or person authorized by the copyright owner the information required by the subpoena, notwithstanding any other provision of law and regardless of whether the service provider responds to the notification.

(6) **Rules applicable to subpoena.**—Unless otherwise provided by this section or by applicable rules of the court, the procedure for issuance and delivery of the subpoena, and the remedies for noncompliance with the subpoena, shall be governed to the greatest extent practicable by those provisions of the Federal Rules of Civil Procedure governing the issuance, service, and enforcement of a subpoena duces tecum.

(i) **Conditions for eligibility.**—

(1) **Accommodation of technology.**—The limitations on liability established by this section shall apply to a service provider only if the service provider—

(A) has adopted and reasonably implemented, and informs subscribers and account holders of the service provider's system or network of, a policy that provides for the termination in appropriate circumstances of subscribers and account holders of the service provider's system or network who are repeat infringers; and

(B) accommodates and does not interfere with standard technical measures.

(2) Definition.—As used in this subsection, the term "standard technical measures" means technical measures that are used by copyright owners to identify or protect copyrighted works and—

(A) have been developed pursuant to a broad consensus of copyright owners and service providers in an open, fair, voluntary, multi-industry standards process;

(B) are available to any person on reasonable and nondiscriminatory terms; and

(C) do not impose substantial costs on service providers or substantial burdens on their systems or networks.

(j) Injunctions.—The following rules shall apply in the case of any application for an injunction under section 502 against a service provider that is not subject to monetary remedies under this section:

(1) Scope of relief.—(A) With respect to conduct other than that which qualifies for the limitation on remedies set forth in subsection (a), the court may grant injunctive relief with respect to a service provider only in one or more of the following forms:

(i) An order restraining the service provider from providing access to infringing material or activity residing at a particular online site on the provider's system or network.

(ii) An order restraining the service provider from providing access to a subscriber or account holder of the service provider's system or network who is engaging in infringing activity and is identified in the order, by terminating the accounts of the subscriber or account holder that are specified in the order.

(iii) Such other injunctive relief as the court may consider necessary to prevent or restrain infringement of copyrighted material specified in the order of the court at a particular online location, if such relief is the least burdensome to the service provider among the forms of relief comparably effective for that purpose.

(B) If the service provider qualifies for the limitation on remedies described in subsection (a), the court may only grant injunctive relief in one or both of the following forms:

(i) An order restraining the service provider from providing access to a subscriber or account holder of the service provider's system or network who is using the provider's service to engage in infringing activity and is identified in the order, by terminating the accounts of the subscriber or account holder that are specified in the order.

(ii) An order restraining the service provider from providing access, by taking reasonable steps specified in the order to block access, to a specific, identified, online location outside the United States.

(2) Considerations.—The court, in considering the relevant criteria for injunctive relief under applicable law, shall consider—

(A) whether such an injunction, either alone or in combination with other such injunctions issued against the same service provider under this subsection, would significantly burden either the provider or the operation of the provider's system or network;

(B) the magnitude of the harm likely to be suffered by the copyright owner in the digital network environment if steps are not taken to prevent or restrain the infringement;
(C) whether implementation of such an injunction would be technically feasible and effective, and would not interfere with access to noninfringing material at other online locations; and
(D) whether other less burdensome and comparably effective means of preventing or restraining access to the infringing material are available.

(3) Notice and ex parte orders.—Injunctive relief under this subsection shall be available only after notice to the service provider and an opportunity for the service provider to appear are provided, except for orders ensuring the preservation of evidence or other orders having no material adverse effect on the operation of the service provider's communications network.

(k) Definitions.—

(1) Service provider.—

(A) As used in subsection (a), the term "service provider" means an entity offering the transmission, routing, or providing of connections for digital online communications, between or among points specified by a user, of material of the user's choosing, without modification to the content of the material as sent or received.
(B) As used in this section, other than subsection (a), the term "service provider" means a provider of online services or network access, or the operator of facilities therefor, and includes an entity described in subparagraph (A).

(2) Monetary relief.—As used in this section, the term "monetary relief" means damages, costs, attorneys, fees, and any other form of monetary payment.

(l) Other defenses not affected.—The failure of a service provider's conduct to qualify for limitation of liability under this section shall not bear adversely upon the consideration of a defense by the service provider that the service provider's conduct is not infringing under this title or any other defense.

(m) Protection of privacy.—Nothing in this section shall be construed to condition the applicability of subsections (a) through (d) on—

(1) a service provider monitoring its service or affirmatively seeking facts indicating infringing activity, except to the extent consistent with a standard technical measure complying with the provisions of subsection (i); or
(2) a service provider gaining access to, removing, or disabling access to material in cases in which such conduct is prohibited by law.

(n) Construction.—Subsections (a), (b), (c), and (d) describe separate and distinct functions for purposes of applying this section. Whether a service provider qualifies for the limitation on liability in any one of those subsections shall be based solely on the criteria in that subsection, and shall not affect a determination of whether that service provider qualifies for the limitations on liability under any other such subsection.

APPENDIX B

Trademark Dilution Revision Act of 2006, Pub. L. No. 109-312, 120 Stat 1730

PL 109–312 (HR 683)
October 6, 2006

SECTION 1. SHORT TITLE

15 U.S.C. § 1051 NOTE

(a) SHORT TITLE.—This Act may be cited as the "Trademark Dilution Revision Act of 2006".
(b) REFERENCES.—Any reference in this Act to the Trademark Act of 1946 shall be a reference to the Act entitled "An Act to provide for the registration and protection of trademarks used in commerce, to carry out the provisions of certain international conventions, and for other purposes", approved July 5, 1946 (15 U.S.C. 1051 et seq.).

<< 15 U.S.C. § 1125 >>

SEC. 2. DILUTION BY BLURRING; DILUTION BY TARNISHMENT

Section 43 of the Trademark Act of 1946 (15 U.S.C. 1125) is amended—
(1) by striking subsection (c) and inserting the following:

(c) DILUTION BY BLURRING; DILUTION BY TARNISHMENT.—

(1) INJUNCTIVE RELIEF.—Subject to the principles of equity, the owner of a famous mark that is distinctive, inherently or through acquired distinctiveness, shall be entitled to an injunction against another person who, at any time after the owner's mark has become famous, commences use of a mark or trade name in commerce that is likely to cause dilution by blurring or dilution by tarnishment of the famous mark, regardless of the presence or absence of actual or likely confusion, of competition, or of actual economic injury.

(2) DEFINITIONS.— **(A)** For purposes of paragraph (1), a mark is famous if it is widely recognized by the general consuming public of the United States as a designation of source of the goods or services of the mark's owner. In determining whether a mark possesses the requisite degree of recognition, the court may consider all relevant factors, including the following:

- **(i)** The duration, extent, and geographic reach of advertising and publicity of the mark, whether advertised or publicized by the owner or third parties.
- **(ii)** The amount, volume, and geographic extent of sales of goods or services offered under the mark.
- **(iii)** The extent of actual recognition of the mark.
- **(iv)** Whether the mark was registered under the Act of March 3, 1881, or the Act of February 20, 1905, or on the principal register.

(B) For purposes of paragraph (1), 'dilution by blurring' is association arising from the similarity between a mark or trade name and a famous mark that impairs the distinctiveness of the famous mark. In determining whether a mark or trade name is likely to cause dilution by blurring, the court may consider all relevant factors, including the following:

- **(i)** The degree of similarity between the mark or trade name and the famous mark.
- **(ii)** The degree of inherent or acquired distinctiveness of the famous mark.
- **(iii)** The extent to which the owner of the famous mark is engaging in substantially exclusive use of the mark.

- **(iv)** The degree of recognition of the famous mark.
- **(v)** Whether the user of the mark or trade name intended to create an association with the famous mark.
- **(vi)** Any actual association between the mark or trade name and the famous mark.

(C) For purposes of paragraph (1), 'dilution by tarnishment' is association arising from the similarity between a mark or trade name and a famous mark that harms the reputation of the famous mark.

(3) EXCLUSIONS.—The following shall not be actionable as dilution by blurring or dilution by tarnishment under this subsection:

(A) Any fair use, including a nominative or descriptive fair use, or facilitation of such fair use, of a famous mark by another person other than as a designation of source for the person's own goods or services, including use in connection with—

- **(i)** advertising or promotion that permits consumers to compare goods or services; or
- **(ii)** identifying and parodying, criticizing, or commenting upon the famous mark owner or the goods or services of the famous mark owner.

(A) All forms of news reporting and news commentary.

(B) Any noncommercial use of a mark.

(4) BURDEN OF PROOF.—In a civil action for trade dress dilution under this Act for trade dress not registered on the principal register, the person who asserts trade dress protection has the burden of proving that—

(A) the claimed trade dress, taken as a whole, is not functional and is famous; and

(B) if the claimed trade dress includes any mark or marks registered on the principal register, the unregistered matter, taken as a whole, is famous separate and apart from any fame of such registered marks.

(5) ADDITIONAL REMEDIES.—In an action brought under this subsection, the owner of the famous mark shall be entitled to injunctive relief as set forth in section 34. The owner of the famous mark shall also be entitled to the remedies set forth in sections 35(a) and 36, subject to the discretion of the court and the principles of equity if—

(A) the mark or trade name that is likely to cause dilution by blurring or dilution by tarnishment was first used in commerce by the person against whom the injunction is sought after the date of enactment of the Trademark Dilution Revision Act of 2006; and

(B) in a claim arising under this subsection—

- **(i)** by reason of dilution by blurring, the person against whom the injunction is sought willfully intended to trade on the recognition of the famous mark; or
- **(ii)** by reason of dilution by tarnishment, the person against whom the injunction is sought willfully intended to harm the reputation of the famous mark.

(6) OWNERSHIP OF VALID REGISTRATION A COMPLETE BAR TO ACTION.—The ownership by a person of a valid registration under the Act of March 3, 1881, or the Act of February 20, 1905, or on the principal register under this Act shall be a complete bar to an action against that person, with respect to that mark, that—

(A) **(i)** is brought by another person under the common law or a statute of a State; and

(ii) seeks to prevent dilution by blurring or dilution by tarnishment; or

(B) asserts any claim of actual or likely damage or harm to the distinctiveness or reputation of a mark, label, or form of advertisement.

(7) SAVINGS CLAUSE.—Nothing in this subsection shall be construed to impair, modify, or supersede the applicability of the patent laws of the United States."; and

<< 15 U.S.C. § 1125 >>

(2) in subsection (d)(1)(B)(i)(IX), by striking "(c)(1) of section 43" and inserting "(c)".

SEC. 3. CONFORMING AMENDMENTS

<< 15 US.C. § 1052 >>

(a) MARKS REGISTRABLE ON THE PRINCIPAL REGISTER.— Section 2(f) of the Trademark Act of 1946 (15 U.S.C. 1052(f)) is amended—

(1) by striking the last two sentences; and

(2) by adding at the end the following: "A mark which would be likely to cause dilution by blurring or dilution by tarnishment under section 43(c), may be refused registration only pursuant to a proceeding brought under section 13. A registration for a mark which would be likely to cause dilution by blurring or dilution by tarnishment under section 43(c), may be canceled pursuant to a proceeding brought under either section 14 or section 24.".

<< 15 U.S.C. § 1063 >>

(b) OPPOSITION.—Section 13(a) of the Trademark Act of 1946 (15 U.S.C. 1063(a)) is amended in the first sentence by striking "as a result of dilution" and inserting "the registration of any mark which would be likely to cause dilution by blurring or dilution by tarnishment".

<< 15 U.S.C. § 1064 >>

(c) CANCELLATION.—Section 14 of the Trademark Act of 1946 (15 U.S.C. 1064) is amended, in the matter preceding paragraph "(1) by striking", including as a result of dilution under section 43(c), "and inserting", including as a result of a likelihood of dilution by blurring or dilution by tarnishment under section "43(c),"

<< 15 U.S.C. § 1092 >>

(d) MARKS FOR THE SUPPLEMENTAL REGISTER.—The second sentence of section 24 of the Trademark Act of 1946 (15 U.S.C. 1092) is amended to read as follows: "Whenever any person believes that such person is or will be damaged by the registration of a mark on the supplemental register—

(1) for which the effective filing date is after the date on which such person's mark became famous and which would be likely to cause dilution by blurring or dilution by tarnishment under section 43(c); or

(2) on grounds other than dilution by blurring or dilution by tarnishment, such person may at any time, upon payment of the prescribed fee and the filing of a petition stating the ground therefor, apply to the Director to cancel such registration.

<< 15 U.S.C. § 1127 >>

(e) DEFINITIONS.—Section 45 of the Trademark Act of 1946 (15 U.S.C. 1127) is amended by striking the definition relating to the term "dilution".

APPENDIX C

The Controlling the Assault of Non–Solicited Pornography and Marketing Act of 2003 (CAN-SPAM Act), Pub. L. No. 108-187, 117 Stat. 2699

PL 108-187 (S 877)

December 16, 2003

An Act To regulate interstate commerce by imposing limitations and penalties on the transmission of unsolicited commercial electronic mail via the Internet.

Be it enacted by the Senate and House of Representatives of the United States of America in Congress assembled,

<< 15 U.S.C. § 7701 NOTE >>

SECTION 1. SHORT TITLE

This Act may be cited as the "Controlling the Assault of Non–Solicited Pornography and Marketing Act of 2003", or the "CAN–SPAM Act of 2003".

<< 15 U.S.C. § 7701 >>

SEC. 2. CONGRESSIONAL FINDINGS AND POLICY

(a) FINDINGS.—The Congress finds the following:

- **(1)** Electronic mail has become an extremely important and popular means of communication, relied on by millions of Americans on a daily basis for personal and commercial purposes. Its low cost and global reach make it extremely convenient and efficient, and offer unique opportunities for the development and growth of frictionless commerce.
- **(2)** The convenience and efficiency of electronic mail are threatened by the extremely rapid growth in the volume of unsolicited commercial electronic mail. Unsolicited commercial electronic mail is currently estimated to account for over half of all electronic mail traffic, up from an estimated 7 percent in 2001, and the volume continues to rise. Most of these messages are fraudulent or deceptive in one or more respects.
- **(3)** The receipt of unsolicited commercial electronic mail may result in costs to recipients who cannot refuse to accept such mail and who incur costs for the storage of such mail, or for the time spent accessing, reviewing, and discarding such mail, or for both.
- **(4)** The receipt of a large number of unwanted messages also decreases the convenience of electronic mail and creates a risk that wanted electronic mail messages, both commercial and noncommercial, will be lost, overlooked, or discarded amidst the larger volume of unwanted messages, thus reducing the reliability and usefulness of electronic mail to the recipient.
- **(5)** Some commercial electronic mail contains material that many recipients may consider vulgar or pornographic in nature.
- **(6)** The growth in unsolicited commercial electronic mail imposes significant monetary costs on providers of Internet access services, businesses, and educational and nonprofit institutions that carry and receive such mail, as there is a finite volume of mail that such providers, businesses, and institutions can handle without further investment in infrastructure.
- **(7)** Many senders of unsolicited commercial electronic mail purposefully disguise the source of such mail.

(8) Many senders of unsolicited commercial electronic mail purposefully include misleading information in the messages' subject lines in order to induce the recipients to view the messages.

(9) While some senders of commercial electronic mail messages provide simple and reliable ways for recipients to reject (or "opt-out" of) receipt of commercial electronic mail from such senders in the future, other senders provide no such "opt-out" mechanism, or refuse to honor the requests of recipients not to receive electronic mail from such senders in the future, or both.

(10) Many senders of bulk unsolicited commercial electronic mail use computer programs to gather large numbers of electronic mail addresses on an automated basis from Internet websites or online services where users must post their addresses in order to make full use of the website or service.

(11) Many States have enacted legislation intended to regulate or reduce unsolicited commercial electronic mail, but these statutes impose different standards and requirements. As a result, they do not appear to have been successful in addressing the problems associated with unsolicited commercial electronic mail, in part because, since an electronic mail address does not specify a geographic location, it can be extremely difficult for law-abiding businesses to know with which of these disparate statutes they are required to comply.

(12) The problems associated with the rapid growth and abuse of unsolicited commercial electronic mail cannot be solved by Federal legislation alone. The development and adoption of technological approaches and the pursuit of cooperative efforts with other countries will be necessary as well.

(b) CONGRESSIONAL DETERMINATION OF PUBLIC POLICY.—On the basis of the findings in subsection (a), the Congress determines that—

(1) there is a substantial government interest in regulation of commercial electronic mail on a nationwide basis;

(2) senders of commercial electronic mail should not mislead recipients as to the source or content of such mail; and

(3) recipients of commercial electronic mail have a right to decline to receive additional commercial electronic mail from the same source.

<< 15 USC § 7702 >>

SEC. 3. DEFINITIONS

In this Act:

(1) AFFIRMATIVE CONSENT.—The term "affirmative consent", when used with respect to a commercial electronic mail message, means that—

(A) the recipient expressly consented to receive the message, either in response to a clear and conspicuous request for such consent or at the recipient's own initiative; and

(B) if the message is from a party other than the party to which the recipient communicated such consent, the recipient was given clear and conspicuous notice at the time the consent was communicated that the recipient's electronic mail address could be transferred to such other party for the purpose of initiating commercial electronic mail messages.

(2) Commercial electronic mail message—

(A) IN GENERAL.—The term "commercial electronic mail message" means any electronic mail message the primary purpose of which is the commercial advertisement or promotion of a commercial product or service (including content on an Internet website operated for a commercial purpose).

- **(B)** TRANSACTIONAL OR RELATIONSHIP MESSAGES.—The term "commercial electronic mail message" does not include a transactional or relationship message.
- **(C)** REGULATIONS REGARDING PRIMARY PURPOSE.—Not later than 12 months after the date of the enactment of this Act, the Commission shall issue regulations pursuant to section 13 defining the relevant criteria to facilitate the determination of the primary purpose of an electronic mail message.
- **(D)** REFERENCE TO COMPANY OR WEBSITE.—The inclusion of a reference to a commercial entity or a link to the website of a commercial entity in an electronic mail message does not, by itself, cause such message to be treated as a commercial electronic mail message for purposes of this Act if the contents or circumstances of the message indicate a primary purpose other than commercial advertisement or promotion of a commercial product or service.

(3) COMMISSION.—The term "Commission" means the Federal Trade Commission.

(4) DOMAIN NAME.—The term "domain name" means any alphanumeric designation which is registered with or assigned by any domain name registrar, domain name registry, or other domain name registration authority as part of an electronic address on the Internet.

(5) ELECTRONIC MAIL ADDRESS.—The term "electronic mail address" means a destination, commonly expressed as a string of characters, consisting of a unique user name or mailbox (commonly referred to as the "local part") and a reference to an Internet domain (commonly referred to as the "domain part"), whether or not displayed, to which an electronic mail message can be sent or delivered.

(6) ELECTRONIC MAIL MESSAGE.—The term "electronic mail message" means a message sent to a unique electronic mail address.

(7) FTC ACT.—The term "FTC Act" means the Federal Trade Commission Act (15 U.S.C. 41 et seq.).

(8) HEADER INFORMATION.—The term "header information" means the source, destination, and routing information attached to an electronic mail message, including the originating domain name and originating electronic mail address, and any other information that appears in the line identifying, or purporting to identify, a person initiating the message.

(9) INITIATE.—The term "initiate", when used with respect to a commercial electronic mail message, means to originate or transmit such message or to procure the origination or transmission of such message, but shall not include actions that constitute routine conveyance of such message. For purposes of this paragraph, more than one person may be considered to have initiated a message.

(10) INTERNET.—The term "Internet" has the meaning given that term in the Internet Tax Freedom Act (47 U.S.C. 151 nt).

(11) INTERNET ACCESS SERVICE.—The term "Internet access service" has the meaning given that term in section 231(e)(4) of the Communications Act of 1934 (47 U.S.C. 231(e)(4)).

(12) PROCURE.—The term "procure", when used with respect to the initiation of a commercial electronic mail message, means intentionally to pay or provide other consideration to, or induce, another person to initiate such a message on one's behalf.

(13) PROTECTED COMPUTER.—The term "protected computer" has the meaning given that term in section 1030(e)(2)(B) of title 18, United States Code.

(14) RECIPIENT.—The term "recipient", when used with respect to a commercial electronic mail message, means an authorized user of the electronic mail address to which the message was sent or delivered. If a recipient of a commercial electronic mail message has one or more electronic mail addresses in addition to the address to which the message was sent or delivered, the recipient shall be treated as a separate recipient with respect to each such address. If an electronic mail address is reassigned to a new user, the new user shall not be treated as a recipient of any commercial electronic mail message sent or delivered to that address before it was reassigned.

(15) ROUTINE CONVEYANCE.—The term "routine conveyance" means the transmission, routing, relaying, handling, or storing, through an automatic technical process, of an electronic mail message for which another person has identified the recipients or provided the recipient addresses.

(16) SENDER.—

(A) IN GENERAL.—Except as provided in subparagraph (B), the term "sender", when used with respect to a commercial electronic mail message, means a person who initiates such a message and whose product, service, or Internet website is advertised or promoted by the message.

(B) SEPARATE LINES OF BUSINESS OR DIVISIONS.—If an entity operates through separate lines of business or divisions and holds itself out to the recipient throughout the message as that particular line of business or division rather than as the entity of which such line of business or division is a part, then the line of business or the division shall be treated as the sender of such message for purposes of this Act.

(17) Transactional or relationship message—

(A) IN GENERAL.—The term "transactional or relationship message" means an electronic mail message the primary purpose of which is—

(i) to facilitate, complete, or confirm a commercial transaction that the recipient has previously agreed to enter into with the sender;

(ii) to provide warranty information, product recall information, or safety or security information with respect to a commercial product or service used or purchased by the recipient;

(iii) to provide—

(I) notification concerning a change in the terms or features of;

(II) notification of a change in the recipient's standing or status with respect to; or

(III) at regular periodic intervals, account balance information or other type of account statement with respect to, a subscription, membership, account, loan, or comparable ongoing commercial relationship involving the ongoing purchase or use by the recipient of products or services offered by the sender;

(iv) to provide information directly related to an employment relationship or related benefit plan in which the recipient is currently involved, participating, or enrolled; or

(v) to deliver goods or services, including product updates or upgrades, that the recipient is entitled to receive under the terms of a transaction that the recipient has previously agreed to enter into with the sender.

(B) MODIFICATION OF DEFINITION.—The Commission by regulation pursuant to section 13 may modify the definition in subparagraph (A) to expand or contract the categories of messages that are treated as transactional or relationship messages for purposes of this Act to the extent that such modification is necessary to accommodate changes in electronic mail technology or practices and accomplish the purposes of this Act.

<< 15 U.S.C. § 7703 >>

SEC. 4. PROHIBITION AGAINST PREDATORY AND ABUSIVE COMMERCIAL E-MAIL

(a) OFFENSE.—

(1) IN GENERAL.—Chapter 47 of title 18, United States Code, is amended by adding at the end the following new section:

<< 18 U.S.C. § 1037 >>

"§ 1037. Fraud and related activity in connection with electronic mail

(a) IN GENERAL.—Whoever, in or affecting interstate or foreign commerce, knowingly—

(1) accesses a protected computer without authorization, and intentionally initiates the transmission of multiple commercial electronic mail messages from or through such computer,

(2) uses a protected computer to relay or retransmit multiple commercial electronic mail messages, with the intent to deceive or mislead recipients, or any Internet access service, as to the origin of such messages,

(3) materially falsifies header information in multiple commercial electronic mail messages and intentionally initiates the transmission of such messages,

(4) registers, using information that materially falsifies the identity of the actual registrant, for five or more electronic mail accounts or online user accounts or two or more domain names, and intentionally initiates the transmission of multiple commercial electronic mail messages from any combination of such accounts or domain names, or

(5) falsely represents oneself to be the registrant or the legitimate successor in interest to the registrant of 5 or more Internet Protocol addresses, and intentionally initiates the transmission of multiple commercial electronic mail messages from such addresses, or conspires to do so, shall be punished as provided in subsection (b).

(b) PENALTIES.—The punishment for an offense under subsection (a) is—

(1) a fine under this title, imprisonment for not more than 5 years, or both, if—

(A) the offense is committed in furtherance of any felony under the laws of the United States or of any State; or

(B) the defendant has previously been convicted under this section or section 1030, or under the law of any State for conduct involving the transmission of multiple commercial electronic mail messages or unauthorized access to a computer system;

(2) a fine under this title, imprisonment for not more than 3 years, or both, if—

(A) the offense is an offense under subsection (a)(1);

(B) the offense is an offense under subsection (a)(4) and involved 20 or more falsified electronic mail or online user account registrations, or 10 or more falsified domain name registrations;

(C) the volume of electronic mail messages transmitted in furtherance of the offense exceeded 2,500 during any 24-hour period, 25,000 during any 30-day period, or 250,000 during any 1-year period;

(D) the offense caused loss to one or more persons aggregating $5,000 or more in value during any 1-year period;

(E) as a result of the offense any individual committing the offense obtained anything of value aggregating $5,000 or more during any 1-year period; or

(F) the offense was undertaken by the defendant in concert with three or more other persons with respect to whom the defendant occupied a position of organizer or leader; and

(3) a fine under this title or imprisonment for not more than 1 year, or both, in any other case.

(c) FORFEITURE.—

(1) IN GENERAL.—The court, in imposing sentence on a person who is convicted of an offense under this section, shall order that the defendant forfeit to the United States—

(A) any property, real or personal, constituting or traceable to gross proceeds obtained from such offense; and

(B) any equipment, software, or other technology used or intended to be used to commit or to facilitate the commission of such offense.

(2) PROCEDURES.—The procedures set forth in section 413 of the Controlled Substances Act (21 U.S.C. 853), other than subsection (d) of that section, and in Rule 32.2 of the Federal Rules of Criminal Procedure, shall apply to all stages of a criminal forfeiture proceeding under this section.

(d) DEFINITIONS.—In this section:

(1) LOSS.—The term 'loss' has the meaning given that term in section 1030(e) of this title.

(2) MATERIALLY.—For purposes of paragraphs (3) and (4) of subsection (a), header information or registration information is materially falsified if it is altered or concealed in a manner that would impair the ability of a recipient of the message, an Internet access service processing the message on behalf of a recipient, a person alleging a violation of this section, or a law enforcement agency to identify, locate, or respond to a person who initiated the electronic mail message or to investigate the alleged violation.

(3) MULTIPLE.—The term 'multiple' means more than 100 electronic mail messages during a 24-hour period, more than 1,000 electronic mail messages during a 30-day period, or more than 10,000 electronic mail messages during a 1-year period.

(4) OTHER TERMS.—Any other term has the meaning given that term by section 3 of the CAN-SPAM Act of 2003."

APPENDIX D

Federal Trade Commission Fair Information Practice Principles

Federal Trade Commission
Fair Information Practice Principles

A. FAIR INFORMATION PRACTICE PRINCIPLES GENERALLY

Over the past quarter century, government agencies in the United States, Canada, and Europe have studied the manner in which entities collect and use personal information—their "information practices"—and the safeguards required to assure those practices are fair and provide adequate privacy protection.(27) The result has been a series of reports, guidelines, and model codes that represent widely-accepted principles concerning fair information practices.(28) Common to all of these documents [hereinafter referred to as "fair information practice codes"] are five core principles of privacy protection: (1) Notice/Awareness; (2) Choice/Consent; (3) Access/Participation; (4) Integrity/Security; and (5) Enforcement/Redress.

1. Notice/Awareness

The most fundamental principle is notice. Consumers should be given notice of an entity's information practices before any personal information is collected from them. Without notice, a consumer cannot make an informed decision as to whether and to what extent to disclose personal information.(29) Moreover, three of the other principles discussed below—choice/consent, access/participation, and enforcement/redress—are only meaningful when a consumer has notice of an entity's policies, and his or her rights with respect thereto.(30)

While the scope and content of notice will depend on the entity's substantive information practices, notice of some or all of the following have been recognized as essential to ensuring that consumers are properly informed before divulging personal information:

—identification of the entity collecting the data;(31)
—identification of the uses to which the data will be put;(32)
—identification of any potential recipients of the data;(33)
—the nature of the data collected and the means by which it is collected if not obvious (passively, by means of electronic monitoring, or actively, by asking the consumer to provide the information);(34)
—whether the provision of the requested data is voluntary or required, and the consequences of a refusal to provide the requested information;(35) and
—the steps taken by the data collector to ensure the confidentiality, integrity and quality of the data.(36)

Some information practice codes state that the notice should also identify any available consumer rights, including: any choice respecting the use of the data;(37) whether the consumer has been given a right of access to the data;(38) the ability of the consumer to contest inaccuracies;(39) the availability of redress for violations of the practice code;(40) and how such rights can be exercised.(41)

In the Internet context, notice can be accomplished easily by the posting of an information practice disclosure describing an entity's information practices on a company's site on the Web. To be effective, such a disclosure should be clear and conspicuous, posted in a prominent location, and readily accessible from both the site's home page and any Web page where information is collected from the consumer. It should also be unavoidable and understandable so that it gives consumers meaningful and effective notice of what will happen to the personal information they are asked to divulge.

2. Choice/Consent

The second widely-accepted core principle of fair information practice is consumer choice or consent.(42) At its simplest, choice means giving consumers options as to how any personal information collected from them may be used. Specifically, choice relates to secondary uses of information—i.e., uses beyond those necessary to complete the contemplated transaction. Such secondary uses can be internal, such as placing the consumer on the collecting company's mailing list in order to market additional products or promotions, or external, such as the transfer of information to third parties.

Traditionally, two types of choice/consent regimes have been considered: opt-in or opt-out. Opt-in regimes require affirmative steps by the consumer to allow the collection and/or use of information; opt-out regimes require affirmative steps to prevent the collection and/or use of such information. The distinction lies in the default rule when no affirmative steps are taken by the consumer.(43) Choice can also involve more than a binary yes/no option. Entities can, and do, allow consumers to tailor the nature of the information they reveal and the uses to which it will be put.(44) Thus, for example, consumers can be provided separate choices as to whether they wish to be on a company's general internal mailing list or a marketing list sold to third parties. In order to be effective, any choice regime should provide a simple and easily-accessible way for consumers to exercise their choice.

In the online environment, choice easily can be exercised by simply clicking a box on the computer screen that indicates a user's decision with respect to the use and/or dissemination of the information being collected. The online environment also presents new possibilities to move beyond the opt-in/opt-out paradigm. For example, consumers could be required to specify their preferences regarding information use before entering a Web site, thus effectively eliminating any need for default rules.(45)

3. Access/Participation

Access is the third core principle. It refers to an individual's ability both to access data about him or herself—i.e., to view the data in an entity's files — and to contest that data's accuracy and completeness.(46) Both are essential to ensuring that data are accurate and complete. To be meaningful, access must encompass timely and inexpensive access to data, a simple means for contesting inaccurate or incomplete data, a mechanism by which the data collector can verify the information, and the means by which corrections and/or consumer objections can be added to the data file and sent to all data recipients.(47)

4. Integrity/Security

The fourth widely accepted principle is that data be accurate and secure. To assure data integrity, collectors must take reasonable steps, such as using only reputable sources of data and cross-referencing data against multiple sources, providing consumer access to data, and destroying untimely data or converting it to anonymous form.(48)

Security involves both managerial and technical measures to protect against loss and the unauthorized access, destruction, use, or disclosure of the data.(49) Managerial measures include internal organizational measures that limit access to data and ensure that those individuals with access do not utilize the data for unauthorized purposes. Technical security measures to prevent unauthorized access include encryption in the transmission and storage of data; limits on access through use of passwords; and the storage of data on secure servers or computers that are inaccessible by modem.(50)

5. Enforcement/Redress

It is generally agreed that the core principles of privacy protection can only be effective if there is a mechanism in place to enforce them.(51) Absent an enforcement and redress mechanism, a fair information practice code is merely suggestive rather than prescriptive, and does not ensure compliance with core fair information practice principles. Among the alternative enforcement approaches are industry self-regulation; legislation that would create private remedies for consumers; and/or regulatory schemes enforceable through civil and criminal sanctions.(52)

A. SELF-REGULATION(53) To be effective, self-regulatory regimes should include both mechanisms to ensure compliance (enforcement) and appropriate means of recourse by injured parties (redress).(54) Mechanisms to ensure compliance include making acceptance of and compliance with a code of fair information practices a condition of membership in an industry association;(55) external audits to verify compliance; and certification of entities that have adopted and comply with the code at issue.(56) A self-regulatory regime with many of these principles has recently been adopted by the individual reference services industry.(57)

Appropriate means of individual redress include, at a minimum, institutional mechanisms to ensure that consumers have a simple and effective way to have their concerns addressed.(58) Thus, a self-regulatory system should provide a means to investigate complaints from individual consumers and ensure that consumers are aware of how to access such a system.(59)

If the self-regulatory code has been breached, consumers should have a remedy for the violation. Such a remedy can include both the righting of the wrong (e.g., correction of any misinformation, cessation of unfair practices) and compensation for any harm suffered by the consumer.(60) Monetary sanctions would serve both to compensate the victim of unfair practices and as an incentive for industry compliance. Industry codes can provide for alternative dispute resolution mechanisms to provide appropriate compensation.

B. PRIVATE REMEDIES A statutory scheme could create private rights of action for consumers harmed by an entity's unfair information practices. Several of the major information practice codes, including the seminal 1973 HEW Report, call for implementing legislation.(61) The creation of private remedies would help create strong incentives for entities to adopt and implement fair information practices and ensure compensation for individuals harmed by misuse of their personal information. Important questions would need to be addressed in such legislation, e.g., the definition of unfair information practices; the availability of compensatory, liquidated and/or punitive damages;(62) and the elements of any such cause of action.

C. GOVERNMENT ENFORCEMENT Finally, government enforcement of fair information practices, by means of civil or criminal penalties, is a third means of enforcement. Fair information practice codes have called for some government enforcement, leaving open the question of the scope and extent of such powers.(63) Whether enforcement is civil or criminal likely will depend on the nature of the data at issue and the violation committed.(64)

B. APPLICATION OF FAIR INFORMATION PRACTICE PRINCIPLES TO INFORMATION COLLECTED FROM CHILDREN

The fair information practice codes discussed above do not address personal information collected from children. They are, however, applicable to parents, in light of the special status that children generally have been accorded under the law. This status as a special, vulnerable group is premised on the belief that children lack the analytical abilities and judgment of adults.(65) It is evidenced by an array of federal and state laws that protect children, including those that ban sales of tobacco and alcohol to minors, prohibit child pornography, require parental consent for medical procedures, and make contracts with children voidable. In the specific arenas of marketing and privacy rights, moreover, several federal statutes and regulations recognize both the need for heightened protections for children and the special role that parents play in implementing these protections.(66)

1. Parental Notice/Awareness and Parental Choice/Consent

It is parents who should receive the notice and have the means to control the collection and use of personal information from their children. The Commission staff set forth this principle in a July 15, 1997 letter to the Center for Media Education.(67) In addition, the letter identifies certain practices that appear to violate the Federal Trade Commission Act:

- **(a)** It is a deceptive practice to represent that a site is collecting personal identifying information from a child for a particular purpose (e.g. to earn points to redeem a premium), when the information will also be used for another purpose that parents would find material, in the absence of a clear and prominent disclosure to that effect; and
- **(b)** It is likely to be an unfair practice to collect personal identifying information, such as a name, e-mail address, home address, or phone number, from children and to sell or otherwise disclose such identifying information to third parties, or to post it publicly online, without providing parents with adequate notice and an opportunity to control the collection and use of the information through prior parental consent.

This letter applies the Commission's Section 5 authority for the first time to the principles of notice and choice in the online collection of information from children. The principles set out in the staff opinion letter form an appropriate basis for public policy in this area.

To assure that notice and choice are effective, a Web site should provide adequate notice to a parent that the site wishes to collect personal identifying information from the child,(68) and give the parent an opportunity to control the collection and use of that information. Further, according to the staff opinion letter, in cases where the information may be released to third parties or the general public, the site should obtain the parent's actual or verifiable consent(69) to its collection.(70)

The content of the notice should include at a minimum, the elements described above,(71) but, in addition, should take into account the fact that online activities may be unique and unfamiliar to parents. Thus, a notice should be sufficiently detailed to tell parents clearly the type(s) of information the Web site collects from children and the steps parents can take to control the collection and use of their child's personal information. Where a Web site offers children interactive activities such as chat, message boards, free e-mail services, posting of home pages and key pal programs, it should explain to parents the nature of these activities and that children's participation enables others to communicate directly with them. Such notice empowers parents to monitor their children's interactions and to help protect their children from the risks of inappropriate online interactions.

2. Access/Participation and Integrity/Security

Since parents may not be fully aware of what personal information a site has collected from their child, the access/participation principle is a particularly important one with respect to information collected from children. To provide informed consent to the retention and/or use of information collected from their children, parents need to be given access to the information collected from their children, particularly if any of the information is collected prior to providing notice to the parent. The principle of integrity, which addresses the accuracy of the data, is also important for children's information. Parents have an interest in assuring that whatever information Web sites collect from children or have otherwise obtained about their children is accurate. This is particularly important in contexts that involve decisions that impact on the child or family, such as educational or health decisions. In addition, since children's information is considered to be a more sensitive type of information, sites should take the same steps identified above to assure that children's data is secure from unauthorized uses or disclosures.

GLOSSARY

absolute privilege A privilege that immunizes an actor from suit, no matter how wrongful the action might be, and even though it is done with an improper motive.

actual malice Knowledge (by the person who utters or publishes a defamatory statement) that a statement is false, or reckless disregard about whether the statement is true.

actus reus Latin for "guilty act." The wrongful deed that comprises the physical components of a crime and that generally must be coupled with mens rea to establish criminal liability; a forbidden act.

adware Advertising software programs; software application that displays advertising banners while the program is running.

Anticybersquatting Consumer Protection Act (ACPA) A 1999 federal law authorizing a trademark owner to obtain a federal-court order transferring ownership of a domain name from a cybersquatter to the trademark owner. Also called Trademark Cyberpiracy Prevention Act. 15 U.S.C. § 1125.

anti-SLAPP Law Law designed to bar meritless lawsuits filed with the intent to chill the exercise of First Amendment rights on a matter of public interest. *See also* **SLAPP** (strategic lawsuit against public participation).

arbitration Method of dispute resolution involving one or more neutral third parties who are usually agreed to by the disputing parties and whose decision is binding.

Berne Convention An international copyright treaty providing that works created by citizens of one signatory nation will be fully protected in other signatory nations, without the need for local formalities. Also called the Berne Convention for the Protection of Literary and Artistic Property.

Board of Patent Appeals and Interferences (BPAI) The quasi-judicial body in the U.S. Patent and Trademark Office that hears (1) appeals from patent applicants whose claims have been rejected by a patent examiner, and (2) interference contests between two or more applicants trying to patent the same invention. The U.S. Court of Appeals for the Federal Circuit hears appeals from this tribunal.

browsewrap agreement Terms and conditions of use posted on a website typically as a hyperlink at the bottom of the screen. Unlike a clickwrap agreement, a browsewrap agreement allows the user to view the terms of the agreement, but does not require the user to take any affirmative action before the website performs its end of the contract. *See* **Clickwrap Agreement**.

business disparagement Common-law tort of belittling someone's business, goods, or services with a remark that is false or misleading but not necessarily defamatory. Also called business defamation, commercial disparagement, product disparagement, injurious falsehood, or trade libel.

Business Method Patent A U.S. patent that describes and claims a series of process steps that, as a whole, constitutes a method of doing business. Also called cyberpatent.

Children's Online Privacy Protection Act (COPPA) Federal law passed in protecting the privacy of children in the online environment and maintaining the security of children's personal information collected online. 15 **U.S.C. §§ 6501–6506**.

choice of law The question of which jurisdiction's law should apply in a given case.

choice-of-law provision A contractual provision by which the parties designate the jurisdiction whose law will govern any disputes that may arise between the parties. Also called choice-of-law clause.

click fraud Purposeful clicks on advertisements by someone other than a potential customer. Click fraud generally encompasses any click made in bad faith.

clickwrap agreement An electronic version of a shrinkwrap license in which a computer user agrees to the terms of an electronically displayed agreement by pointing the cursor to a particular location on the screen and then clicking. Usually requires express acceptance only once but may include a clause providing for a user's ongoing-acceptance of any changes to the agreement's terms, whether or not the user is notified of the changes. Also called point-and-click agreement. *See also* Browsewrap Agreement.

Commerce Clause U.S. Const. art. I, § 8, cl. 3, which gives Congress the exclusive power to regulate commerce among the states, with foreign nations, and with Indian tribes.

common law The body of law derived from judicial decisions, rather than from statutes or constitutions. Also called caselaw.

Communications Decency Act (CDA) A federal law aimed at combating child pornography. In *Reno v. American Civil Liberties Union*, 521 U.S. 844 (1997), the U.S. Supreme Court struck down those portions of the act as unconstitutional, but provisions banning transmission of obscene speech to minors, remain in effect. 47 U.S.C. § 223.

computer crime Any violations of criminal law that involve a knowledge of computer technology for their perpetration, investigation, or prosecution. Also called cybercrime. Computer Fraud and Abuse Act (CFAA) A federal law establishing civil liability for gaining unauthorized access to a computer and causing damage to that computer. Also called Computer Fraud and Abuse Act or FCFAA. 18 U.S.C. § 1030.

Controlling the Assault of Non-Solicited Pornography and Marketing Act (CAN-SPAM Act) A federal law establishing civil and criminal liability for unsolicited commercial e-mail. 15 U.S.C. §§ 7701–7713.

copyright The right to copy a property right in an original work of authorship fixed in any tangible medium of expression, giving the holder the exclusive right to reproduce, adapt, distribute, perform, and display the work. Copyright includes literary, musical, dramatic, choreographic, pictorial, graphic, sculptural, and architectural works; motion pictures and other audiovisual works; and sound recordings.

Copyright Act of 1976 A major revision of U.S. copyright law, extending the term of protection to the life of the author plus 50 years, measured from the date of creation; greatly expanding the types of works that qualify for protection; dropping the requirement that the work be published before it can be protected; making fair use a statutory defense to a claim in infringement; and preempting state common-law copyright. Also called 1976 Copyright Act. 17 U.S.C. §§ 101 et seq.

copyright infringement The act of violating any of a copyright owner's exclusive rights granted by the Copyright Act.

Copyright Term Extension Act (CTEA) Act passed by Congress in 1998 that extended the duration of copyright protection by 20 years for works copyrighted after January 1, 1923. 17 U.S.C. §§ 302–304.

co-regulation Government and industry share responsibility in setting goals, developing rules, and enforcing standards. Also called collaborative governance or contractual regulation. *See also* **negotiated rulemaking**.

criminal defamation *See* **criminal libel**.

criminal libel Malicious libel that is designed to expose a person to hatred, contempt, or ridicule and that may subject the author to criminal sanctions.

cyberbullying Bullying by use of any electronic device through means including, but not limited to, e-mail, instant messaging, text messages, blogs, mobile phones, pagers, online games, and websites.

cybercrime *See* **computer crime**.

cyberlaw The field of law dealing with the Internet, encompassing cases, statutes, regulations, and disputes that affect people and businesses interacting through computers. Cyberlaw addresses issues of online speech and business that arise because of the nature of the medium, including intellectual property rights, free speech, privacy, e-commerce, and safety, as well as questions of jurisdiction.

cyberpatent A type of utility patent granted on an invention that combines business methods and software programs for Internet applications. Also called Internet patent.

cyber-SLAPP A strategic lawsuit against public participation (SLAPP) against anonymous Internet posters. *See also* **SLAPP**.

cyberstalking Stalking involving the use of the Internet, e-mail, or other electronic communications devices to stalk another person.

cyberterrorism Using computer technology to engage in terrorist activity.

cybertort A cause of action that exists due to harmful Internet contact. Any tort action that involves the Internet or use of a computer.

data mining A series of techniques used to extract intelligence from vast stores of digital information.

defamation The act of harming the reputation of another by making a false statement to a third person. A false written or oral statement that damages another's reputation.

defamation per quod Defamation that either (1) is not apparent but is proved by extrinsic evidence showing its injurious meaning or (2) is apparent but is not a statement that is actionable per se.

defamatory Tending to harm a person's reputation, usually by subjecting the person to public contempt, disgrace, or ridicule, or by adversely affecting the person's business.

defamatory per se A statement that is defamatory in and of itself and is not capable of an innocent meaning.

design patent A patent granted for a new, original, and ornamental design for an article of manufacture; a patent that protects a product's appearance or nonfunctional aspects. Design patents have a term of only 14 years from the date the patent is granted.

derivative work A work that is based on a preexisting work. Only the holder of the copyright on the original form can produce or permit someone else to produce a derivative work.

Digital Millennium Copyright Act (DMCA) A 1998 federal law harmonizing United States copyright protection with international law, limiting copyright liability for Internet service providers, and expanding software owners' ability to copy programs. Extends copyright protection to computer programs, movies, and other audiovisual works worldwide; attempts to regulate cyberspace; forbids devices whose purpose is to evade digital antipiracy tools; and bars the production or distribution of falsified copyright-management information. 17 U.S.C. §§ 1301–1332.

digital signature A secure, digital code attached to an electronically transmitted message that uniquely identifies and authenticates the sender. Consists of a "hashed" number combined with a number assigned to a document (a private-encryption key).

dilution Unauthorized acts that tend to blur the distinctiveness of a famous mark or to tarnish it.

domain name The words and characters that website owners designate for their registered Internet addresses.

Dormant Commerce Clause The constitutional principle that the Commerce Clause prevents state regulation of interstate commercial activity even when Congress has not acted under its Commerce Clause power to regulate that activity. Also called negative commerce clause.

Drivers Privacy Protection Act (DPPA) A federal law that restricts the disclosure of driver license information by state authorities. 18 U.S.C. § 2725.

Due Process Clause The constitutional provision that prohibits the government from unfairly or arbitrarily depriving a person of life, liberty, or property. There are two Due Process Clauses in the U.S. Constitution, one in the Fifth Amendment applying to the federal government, and one in the Fourteenth Amendment applying to the states (although the Fifth Amendment's Due Process Clause also applies to the states under the incorporation doctrine).

e-commerce The practice of buying and selling goods and services through online consumer services on the Internet.

economic tort A tort that impairs some aspect of an economic interest or business relationship and causes economic loss rather than property damage or bodily harm. Business torts include tortious interference with contractual relations, intentional interference with prospective economic advantage, unfair business practices, misappropriation of trade secrets, and product disparagement.

e-FOIA Freedom of Information Act (FOIA) request submitted electronically.

Electronic Communications Privacy Act (ECPA) A federal law that regulates surveillance of electronic communications. 18 U.S.C. §§ 2701–2712.

electronic signature An electronic symbol, sound, or process that is either attached to or logically associated with a document (such as a contract or other record) and executed or adopted by a person with the intent to sign the document. Types of electronic signatures include a typed name at the end of an e-mail, a digital image of a handwritten signature, and the click of an "I accept" button on an e-commerce site.

Electronic Signatures in Global and National Commerce Act (E-SIGN Act) A federal law that establishes the legal equivalency of electronic contracts, electronic signatures, and other electronic records with their paper counterparts. 15 U.S.C. §§ 7001–7031.

end user license agreement (EULA) A clipwrap agreement or a browsewrap agreement.

E-SIGN Act *See* **Electronic Signatures in Global and National Commerce Act (E-SIGN Act).**

exclusionary rule A rule that excludes or suppresses evidence obtained in violation of an accused person's constitutional rights.

Extradition The official surrender of an alleged criminal by one state or nation to another having jurisdiction over the crime charged; the return of a fugitive from justice, regardless of consent, by the authorities where the fugitive is found.

Fair and Accurate Credit Transaction Act (FACTA) A federal law that amended the **Fair Credit Reporting Act (FCRA)** by implementing new procedures and mechanisms to combat identity theft. 15 U.S.C. § 1681(b).

Fair Credit Reporting Act (FCRA) A federal law that established national credit reporting standards in an effort to ensure accuracy and confidentiality in connection with credit reports. 15 U.S.C. § 1681.

fair use A reasonable and limited use of a copyrighted work without the author's permission, such as quoting from a book in a book review or using parts of it in a parody. Fair use is a defense to an infringement claim, depending on the following statutory factors: (1) the purpose and character of the use, (2) the nature of the copyrighted work, (3) the amount of the work used, and (4) the economic impact of the use. 17 U.S.C. § 107.

false light In an invasion-of-privacy action, a plaintiff's allegation that the defendant attributed to the plaintiff views that he or she does not hold and placed the plaintiff before the public in a highly offensive and untrue manner.

Federal Trade Commission Act (FTC Act or FTCA) A federal law that prohibits unfair or deceptive acts or practices in the marketplace, including Internet advertising. 15 U.S.C. §§ 41–58.

Federal Wiretap Act (Title III) A federal law that prohibits any person from intercepting or attempting to intercept any wire, oral, or electronic communication. 18 U.S.C. § 2511.

First Amendment The constitutional amendment, ratified with the Bill of Rights in 1791, guaranteeing the freedoms of speech, religion, press, assembly, and petition.

first sale doctrine The rule that the purchaser of a physical copy of a copyrighted work, such as a book or CD, may give or sell that copy to someone else without infringing the copyright owner's exclusive distribution rights.

forum selection clause A contractual provision in which the parties establish the place (such as the country, state, or type of court) for specified litigation between them. Also called "choice-of-exclusive-forum clause."

Fourth Amendment The constitutional amendment, ratified with the Bill of Rights in 1791, prohibiting unreasonable searches and seizures and the issuance of warrants without probable cause.

Freedom of Information Act (FOIA) A federal law that establishes guidelines for public disclosure of documents and materials created and held by federal agencies. 5 U.S.C. § 552. *See also* Reverse-FOIA.

fruit-of-the-poisonous-tree doctrine The rule that evidence derived from an illegal search, arrest, or interrogation is inadmissible because the evidence (the "fruit") was tainted by the illegality (the "poisonous tree").

Full Faith and Credit Clause Clause in Article VI § 1 of the U.S. Constitution, which requires states to give effect to the acts, public records, and judicial decisions of other states.

Gramm-Leach-Bliley Act (GLBA) A federal law that provides for the protection of consumer financial information held by banks, securities firms, insurance companies, and other financial institutions. Also called the Financial Modernization Act of 1999. 15 U.S.C. §§ 6801–6809.

Health Information Technology for Economic and Clinical Health Act (HITECH Act) A federal law amending HIPAA that clarified and extended the scope and application of HIPAA to outside vendors who also have access to personal health information.

Health Insurance Portability and Accountability Act (HIPAA) A federal law that protects the confidentiality of health information as it is transmitted through and collected by electronic portals.

ICANN (Internet Corporation for Assigned Names and Numbers) Nonprofit corporation that oversees domain names.

identity theft The unlawful taking and use of another person's identifying information for fraudulent purposes.

immunity Any exemption from a duty, liability, or service of process; especially an exemption granted to a public official or governmental unit. A defense to tort liability.

income tax A tax on an individual's or entity's net income. The federal income tax in the Internal Revenue Code is the federal government's primary source of revenue, and most states also have income taxes.

in rem jurisdiction A court's power to adjudicate the rights to a given piece of property, including the power to seize and hold it.

integration clause A contractual provision stating that the contract represents the parties' complete and final agreement and supersedes all informal understandings and oral agreements relating to the subject matter of the contract. Also called merger clause or entire-agreement clause.

intellectual property A category of intangible rights protecting commercially valuable products of the human intellect that comprises primarily copyright, trademark, patent, and trade secret rights.

intentional infliction of emotional distress (IIED) The tort of intentionally or recklessly causing another person severe emotional distress through one's extreme or outrageous acts.

interference An administrative proceeding in the USPTO to determine who is entitled to the patent when two or more applicants claim the same invention, or when an application interferes with an existing patent. This proceeding occurs when the same invention is claimed (1) in two pending applications, or (2) in one pending application and a patent issued within a year of the pending application's filing date.

internet patent *See* **cyberpatent**.

Internal Revenue Code (IRC) Title 26 of the U.S. Code, containing all current federal tax laws.

Internal Revenue Service (IRS) A unit in the U.S. Department of the Treasury responsible for enforcing and administering the internal-revenue laws and other tax laws except those relating to alcohol, tobacco, firearms, and explosives.

Internet Tax Freedom Act (ITFA) A federal law that mainly prevents states from imposing a sales tax on Internet connection fees. Despite its name, ITFA does not prevent state and local governments from imposing sales tax collection requirements on companies selling over the Internet.

invasion of privacy An unjustified exploitation of one's personality or intrusion into one's personal activities, actionable under tort law and sometimes under constitutional law.

jurisdiction A court's power to decide a case or issue a decree.

laches An unreasonable delay in asserting one's rights that causes prejudice or harm to another; a common defense asserted in intellectual property infringement actions.

laissez-faire French for "let (people) do (as they choose)." Governmental abstention from interfering in economic or commercial affairs.

Lanham Act The federal statute, found in Title 15 United States Code, that governs the law of trademarks. Also called the United States Trademark Act.

libel A defamatory statement expressed in a fixed medium, especially writing but also a picture, sign, or electronic broadcast. *See also* **defamation**.

likelihood-of-confusion test A test for trademark infringement, based on the probability that a substantial number of ordinarily prudent buyers will be misled or confused about the source of a product.

long-arm statute Statute that provides for jurisdiction over a nonresident defendant who has had some contact with the jurisdiction in which the petition is filed.

Madrid Protocol An international agreement that provides for an international trademark registration system.

Markman hearing In patent cases, a hearing at which the court receives evidence and arguments concerning the construction to be given to terms in a patent claim at issue.

Based on *Markman v. Westview Instruments, Inc.*, 52 F.3d 967, 984–85 (Fed. Cir. 1995).

mens rea Latin for "guilty mind." The state of mind that the prosecution, to secure a conviction, must prove that a defendant had when committing a crime; criminal intent or recklessness.

merger clause *See* **integration** Clause.

method patent A patent having method or process claims that define a series of actions leading to a tangible physical result. Also called process patent.

negligence The failure to exercise the standard of care that a reasonably prudent person would have exercised in a similar situation; any conduct that falls below the legal standard established to protect others against unreasonable risk of harm, except for conduct that is intentionally, wantonly, or willfully disregardful of others' rights.

negligent infliction of emotional distress The tort of causing another severe emotional distress through one's negligent conduct.

negotiated rulemaking (neg-reg) Rulemaking through the use of a negotiated rule-making committee. A negotiated rulemaking committee is an advisory committee established to consider and discuss issues for the purpose of reaching a consensus in the development of a proposed rule.

Official Gazette for Trademarks (OG) The weekly publication of the USPTO of trademarks for purposes of opposition that contains bibliographic information and a representative drawing for each mark published, along with a list of cancelled and renewed registrations.

Paris Convention An international agreement providing that foreign trademark and patent owners may obtain in a member country the same protection for their trademarks and patents as can citizens of the member country. Also called the Paris Convention for the Protection of Industrial Property.

patent The right to exclude others from making, using, marketing, selling, offering for sale, or importing an invention for a specified period (20 years from the date of filing), granted by the federal government to the inventor if the device or process is novel, useful, and nonobvious.

patent agent A specializedlegal professional—not necessarily a licensed lawyer—who prepares and prosecutes patent applications before the Patent and Trademark Office. Patent agents must be licensed by the Patent and Trademark Office.

patent prosecution The process of applying for a patent through the U.S. Patent and Trademark Office and negotiating with the patent examiner.

personal jurisdiction A court's power to bring a person into its adjudicative process; jurisdiction over a defendant's personal rights, rather than merely over property interests. Also called "in personam jurisdiction" or "jurisdiction over the person."

phishing The sending of a fraudulent electronic communication that appears to be a genuine message from a legitimate entity or business for the purpose of inducing the recipient to disclose sensitive personal information.

Principal Register Publication maintained by the USPTO, that lists distinctive marks approved for federal trademark registration.

prior art In patent cases, knowledge that is publicly known, used by others, or available on the date of invention to a person of ordinary skill in an art, including what would be obvious from that knowledge.

prior restraint A governmental restriction on speech or publication before its actual expression.

Privacy Act A federal law that regulates the collection, maintenance, use, and dissemination of information about individuals by federal agencies. Also called Privacy Act of 1974. 5 U.S.C. § 552a.

Privileges and Immunities Clause The constitutional provision in U.S. Const. art. IV, § 2, cl. 1 prohibiting a state from favoring its own citizens by discriminating against other states' citizens who come within its borders.

PROTECT Act The Prosecutorial Remedies and Other Tools to End the Exploitation of Children Today Act of 2003 (PROTECT Act) is a federal law that establishes stronger laws to combat child pornography and exploitation by revising and strengthening the prohibition on computer-generated child pornographic images, prohibiting any obscene materials that depict children, and providing tougher penalties compared to existing law. 18 U.S.C. § 2252A.

public domain Works that are not protected by intellectual-property rights and are therefore available for anyone to use without liability for infringement. When copyright, trademark, patent, or trade-secret rights are lost or expire, the intellectual property they had protected becomes part of the public domain.

qualified privilege Privilege in tort cases that immunizes a person from suit only when the privilege is properly exercised in the performance of a legal or moral duty.

red flag rule A rule under the Fair and Accurate Credit Transaction Act that requires financial institutions and creditors to develop and put into operation written identity theft prevention programs.

Restatement One of several influential treatises published by the American Law Institute describing the law in a given area and guiding its development such as the Restatement (Second) of Contracts and the Restatement (Second) of Torts.

reverse-FOIA suit A lawsuit by the owner of a trade secret or other information exempt from disclosure under a Freedom of Information Act to prevent a governmental entity from making that information available to the public. *See also* **Freedom of Information Act (FOIA)**.

right of publicity The right to control the use of one's own name, picture, or likeness and to prevent another from using it for commercial benefit without one's consent.

SAFE WEB Act The Undertaking Spam, Spyware, and Fraud with Enforcers Beyond Borders Act of 2006 (SAFE WEB Act) is a federal law that strengthens the ability of the Federal Trade Commission (FTC) to enforce the CAN-SPAM Act outside of U.S. borders.

Sales and Use Tax Agreement (SSUTA) A set of universal rules aimed to simplify and modernize sales and use tax collection and administration in the United States.

sales tax A tax imposed on the sale of goods and services, usually measured as a percentage of their price.

self-regulation The process by which an identifiable group of people or industry governs or directs their own activities by their own rules.

service mark A word, logo, phrase, or device used to indicate the source, quality, and ownership of a service.

service of process The formal delivery of a writ, summons, or other legal process. Also called "service."

severability clause Provision that keeps the remaining provisions of a contract or statute in force if any portion of that contract or statute is judicially declared void, unenforceable, or unconstitutional.

sexting The practice of sending or posting sexually suggestive text messages and images, including nude or semi-nude photographs, via cellular telephones or over the Internet.

slander A defamatory assertion expressed in a transitory form, especially speech.

SLAPP A strategic lawsuit against public participation—a suit brought by a developer, corporate executive, or elected official to stifle those who protest against some type of high-dollar initiative or who take an adverse position on a public-interest issue (often involving the environment). Also termed SLAPP suit. *See also* **SLAPP** law.

social networking site Web-based services that allow individuals to (1) construct a public or semi-public profile within a bounded system, (2) articulate a list of other users with whom they share a connection, and (3) view and traverse their list of connections and those made by others within the system.

spam Unsolicited commercial e-mail.

Speech Clause The First Amendment provision that "Congress shall make no law . . . abridging the freedom of **speech."**

standing A party's right to make a legal claim or seek judicial enforcement of a duty or right.

Statute of Frauds A statute (based on the English Statute of Frauds) designed to prevent fraud and perjury by requiring certain contracts to be in writing and signed by the party to be charged.

Streamlined Sales Tax Project (SSTP) A multi-state initiative to make sales tax laws, rules, and systems more uniform across states and, thus, make it easier for vendors to collect states' sales taxes.

strict liability Liability that does not depend on actual negligence or intent to harm, but that is based on the breach of an absolute duty to make something safe.

subject matter jurisdiction Jurisdiction over the nature of the case and the type of relief sought; the extent to which a court can rule on the conduct of persons or the status of things.

substantial nexus test Test set forth in *Quill v. North Dakota*, 504 U.S. 298 (1992) that retailers are exempt from collecting sales taxes in states where they have no "nexus" or physical presence, such as a store, office, or warehouse.

tax gap The extent to which taxpayers fail to file their federal tax returns and to pay the correct tax on time that stems from underreporting, underpayment, and nonfiling.

Telecommuter Tax Fairness Act A legislative proposal that would eliminate the punitive tax on telecommuters by prohibiting states from taxing the wages that nonresidents earn in their home states.

terms of use agreement (TOA) A clipwrap agreement or a browsewrap agreement.

tort A civil wrong, other than breach of contract, for which a remedy may be obtained, usually in the form of damages; a breach of a duty that the law imposes on persons who stand in a particular relation to one another.

tortfeasor One who commits a **tort**; a wrongdoer.

trademark a word, logo, phrase, or device used to indicate the source, quality, and ownership of a product or service.

Trademark Dilution Revision Act (TDRA) Law passed by Congress in 2006 to overturn the holding of the U.S. Supreme Court in *Mosley v. V Secret Catalogue, Inc.*, 537 U.S. 418 (2003), which required plaintiffs to establish proof of "actual dilution." Now, a plaintiff needs to only establish a "likelihood of dilution." The TDRA identifies a number of statutory factors to consider when determining whether plaintiff's mark is famous.

Trademark Electronic Application System (TEAS) The USPTO's system for electronic filing of trademark documents, including applications for trademarks.

Trademark Electronic Search System (TESS) The USPTO's online search engine allows visitors to search the USPTO's database of registered trademarks and prior pending applications.

Trademark Trial and Appeal Board (TTAB) An administrative board within the USPTO that hears and decides adversary proceedings between two parties, namely, oppositions (party opposes a mark after publication in the Official Gazette) and cancellations (party seeks to cancel an existing registration). The TTAB also handles interference and concurrent use proceedings, as well as appeals of final refusals issued by USPTO examining attorneys within the course of the prosecution of applications.

trade name A name used to identify a company or business.

transformative use Use of copyrighted material in a manner, or for a purpose, that differs from the original use in such a way that the expression, meaning, or message is essentially new.

Treasury Regulations Regulations promulgated by the U.S. Treasury Department to explain or interpret a section of the Internal Revenue Code.

unclean hands A defense often raised in infringement actions; an assertion that the plaintiff's own wrongful conduct precludes recovery and relief.

Uniform Commercial Code (UCC) A uniform law that governs commercial transactions, including sales of goods, secured transactions, and negotiable instruments. The UCC has been adopted in some form by every state and the District of Columbia.

Uniform Computer Information Transactions Act (UCITA) A model law that regulates software licensing and computer-information transactions. UCITA applies to contracts for the licensing or purchase of software, contracts for software development, and contracts for access to databases through the Internet.

Uniform Domain Name Dispute Resolution Policy (UDRP) The dispute resolution policy adopted by ICANN.

Uniform Electronic Transactions Act (UETA) A 1999 model law designed to support electronic commerce by providing means for legally recognizing and retaining electronic records, establishing how parties can bind themselves in an electronic transaction, and providing for the use of electronic records by governmental agencies.

United Nations Convention on Contracts for the International Sale of Goods (CISG) An international treaty that establishes uniform rules to govern international commercial contracts in order to remove "legal barriers in . . . and promote the development of international trade." In 1986, the United States became a party to the CISG, which went into force in 1988. U.S. courts are required to apply the treaty, where appropriate, to settle international contract disputes rather than using the previously applicable Uniform Commercial Code (UCC) rules of the various states.

United States Patent and Trademark office (USPTO or PTO) Federal agency within the U.S. Department of Commerce charged with registering trademarks and granting patents.

United States Tax Court A federal court that hears appeals by taxpayers from adverse IRS decisions about tax deficiencies.

Unlawful Internet Gambling Act (UIGEA) A federal law outlawing unlawful Internet gambling and by providing a safe harbor for certain types of transactions. 31 U.S.C. § 5362.

U.S. Court of Appeals for the Federal Circuit An intermediate-level appellate court with jurisdiction to hear appeals in patent cases and some administrative agencies. Among the purposes of its creation were ending forum-shopping in patent suits, settling differences in patent-law doctrines among the circuits, and allowing a single forum to develop the expertise needed to rule on complex technological questions that arise in patent suits. Also called Federal Circuit or CAFC.

use tax A tax imposed on the use of certain goods that are bought outside the taxing authority's jurisdiction. Designed to discourage the purchase of products that are not subject to the sales tax.

utility patent A patent granted for one of the following types of inventions: a process, a machine, a manufacture, or a composition of matter (such as a new chemical). Utility patents are the most commonly issued patents.

venue The proper or a possible place for a lawsuit to proceed, usually because the place has some connection either with the events that gave rise to the lawsuit or with the plaintiff or defendant. The county or other territory over which a trial court has jurisdiction.

Video Privacy Protection Act (VPPA) Federal law that protects personal information in video rentals. 18 U.S.C. § 2710.

wire fraud An act of fraud using electronic communications, as by making false representations on the telephone to obtain money. The federal Wire Fraud Act provides that any artifice to defraud by means of wire or other electronic communications (such as radio or television) in foreign or interstate commerce is a crime. 18 U.S.C. § 1343.

INDEX

Q

R

S

T